Contents

Acknowledgements

Permissions

We are grateful to the following for permission to reproduce copyright material:

ALVA for material within the ALVA Case Study, reproduced with permission; Asperion Guest House for their slogan/ethos, reproduced with permission of Asperion Guest House www.asperion.co.uk; British Airways for details about Business Class Travel within the British Airways Case Study, reproduced with permission; English Heritage for data, the table 'Number of visits, members and educational visits 2005-2008', text from http://www.english-heritage.org.uk/server/show/ nav.8340, and the English Heritage logo, copyright © English Heritage 2010; First Great Western for 'Your concerns – our commitments' First Great Western complaints handling policy http://www.firstgreatwestern.co.uk/Documents/Custom/FGW_Complaints.pdf, reproduced with permission; Hoseasons Holidays Limited for a screenshot from ww.hoseasons.co.uk, by kind permission of Hoseasons Holidays; Helicon Publishing/RM Education Plc for data from the *Hutchinson World Weather Guide* copyright © RM, 2009. All rights reserved; Institute of Customer Service for their Customer Service Definition, granted by permission of the Institute of Customer Service www.instituteofcustomerservice.com; Key Publishing Ltd for details about Air Malta, from *Airliner World*. October 2009 copyright © Key Publishing Ltd; Merlin Entertainments Group for the Thorpe Park slogan and details within the Merlin Case Study reproduced with permission of Merlin Entertainments Group; National Express for details within the National Express Case Study and the 'London to Glasgow, Aberdeen & Inverness' National Express timetable, http://dundeebuses.info, reproduced with permission; National Rail for material in the Railcards Case Study, from National Rail Timetable, reproduced with permission; National Trust for details in the National Trust Case Study and material from the National Trust core purpose and company logo copyright © National Trust; Network Rail for Figure 9.2 'Date and time symbols, Catering symbols and station symbols' from National Rail; and Figure 9.3 'National Rail Timetable for London and West Midlands to NorthWest England and Scotland', www.networkrail.co.uk, reproduced by permission of Network Rail; News Wales for text from www.newswales.co.uk, reproduced with permission of News Wales; Oxford University Press for a definition from *New Oxford Dictionary of English* edited by Pearsall, J., copyright © Oxford University Press 1998; Office for National Statistics for data from 'Top five inbound markets' from *International Passenger Survey*, 2008; 'Internet Access Households and Individuals' *Statistical Bulletin, August 2009, United Kingdom*, 'UK residents' visits abroad by purpose' from Travel Trends 2008, and National Statistics Classifications © Crown copyright 2009. Crown Copyright material is reproduced with permission of the controller of the HMSO; Ryanair for details within the Ryanair Case Study, reproduced with permission from Ryanair, Europes' biggest Lowfair Airline; Saga Holidays for details about Saga Cruises within the Saga case study, reproduced with permission from Saga Group Ltd; Superbreak Mini-Holidays Ltd for details with the Superbreak Case Study, reproduced with permission; Thomas Cook UK Limited for their 'Customer Service Commitment' charter, August 2009, http://www.thomascookairlines. co.uk/customer_service_commitment.asp reproduced with permission; Surfers Against Sewage for details in the Surfers Against Sewage case study, reproduced with permission www.sas.org.uk; Tourism Concern for material in the Tourism Concern Case Study, reproduced with permission; TUI Travel plc for material within the Thomson Holidays Case Study reproduced with permission of TUI Group 2009; Virgin Atlantic Airways Ltd for their slogan 'To grow a profitable airline where people love to fly and people love to work' and material from the 'Dress and Grooming Guide' from the *Virgin Uniform Manual*, copyright © Virgin Atlantic Airways Ltd; VisitBritain and TEAM The Consultancy for Tourism Destinations for Figure 1.1 'Purpose of trip UK Tourism 2006 (domestic and inbound)' and 'Purpose of trip UK outbound tourism 2006' from *UK State of Tourism - Final Report 2008*. Team Tourism Consultancy for Visit Britain; and Table 1.2 Key tourism facts (2008), copyright © VisitBritain; and VisitEngland for details within National Quality Assessment Scheme Case Study, details from VisitEngland research and VisitEngland award logo's, copyright © VisitEngland.

Every effort has been made to contact copyright holders of material reproduced in this book. Any omissions will be rectified in subsequent printings if notice is given to the publishers.

Photo credits

The author and publisher would like to thank the following individuals and organisations for permission to reproduce photographs:

Unit 1 p.**1** Charles Bowman/Robert Harding; p. **3** Photos.com; p. **5** Pearson Education Ltd; p. **11** Image Courtesy of Virgin Limobike (ceri@virginlimobike.com); p. **20** Courtesy of Center Parcs; p. **22** Charles Bowman/Robert Harding; p. **24** Lance Bellers/Shutterstock; p. **35** Yuri Arcurs/Shutterstock

Unit 2 p. **37** shutterstock/iofoto; p. **39** Pearson Education Ltd. Studio 8. Clark Wiseman; p. **49** Carlo Seller/Shutterstock; p. **59** Yuri Arcurs/Shutterstock; p. **59** Art Directors & Trip/Alamy; p. **60** Courtesy of Virgin Atlantic; p. **63** BAA Aviation Photo Library/Inpress/Steve Bates; p. **71** Shutterstock/Elena Elisseeva; p. **73** Yuri Arcurs/Shutterstock

Unit 3 p. **75** Yuvis Studio/ Shutterstock Images; p. **77** Shutterstock/Yuri Arcurs; p. **82** Digital Vision; p. **84** Digital Vision; p. **87** Nikonaft/ Shutterstock Images; p. **89** Eric Isselee/Shutterstock Images; p. **93** Yuvis Studio/Shutterstock Images; p. **95** Robyn Beck/AFP/Getty Images; p. **105** Flashon Studio. Shutterstock

Unit 4 p. **107** Lucy P/Alamy; p. **109** Pearson Education Ltd. Studio 8. Clark Wiseman; p. **119** Olga Besnard/ Shutterstock Images; p. **127** Steve Gill/Alamy; p. **131** Lucy P/Alamy; p. **138** Digital Vision; p. **143** Yuri Arcurs. Shutterstock

Unit 5 p. **145** Malamus/Shutterstock Images; p. **147** Pearson Education Ltd. Jules Selmes; p. **159** Olive Drew/National Geographic/Getty Images; p. **166** oblong1. Shutterstock; p. **169** Photodisc. Photolink; p. **170** Alexander Gitlits/Shutterstock; p. **171** Ilene MacDonald/Alamy; p. **181** Shutterstock/123stocks

Unit 6 p. **183** Gail Johnson/Shutterstock Images; p. **185** Shutterstock/Supri Suharjoto; p. **186** John Foxx Collection/Imagestate; p. **186** Karl Weatherly/Photodisc; p. **186** John Foxx Collection/Imagestate p. **198** Jon Arnold Images Ltd/Alamy; p. **204** Angie Sharp/Alamy; p. **209** Yuri Arcurs. Shutterstock

Unit 7 p. **211** Rainprei. Shutterstock; p. **213** © 2009 Photos.com, a division of Getty Images; p. **218** Rainprei. Shutterstock; p. **224** Neal and Molly Jansen/Alamy; p. **226** Malcolm Fife. Photodisc; p. **228** David R Frazier Photolibrary Inc/Alamy; p. **233** Dusan Zidar. Shutterstock

Unit 8 p. **235** Shutterstock/iofoto; p. **237** Pearson Education Ltd. Rob Judges; p. **239** Steffen Foerster Photography/ Shutterstock Images; p. **240** Caroline Von Tuempling/Iconical/Getty Images; p. **241** John Foxx Collection/Imagestate; p. **242** Victor Shova/Shutterstock Images; p. **247** Jim Reed/Robert Harding World Imagery/Digital Vision; p. **253** Shutterstock/szefei

Unit 9 p. **255** Colinpics/Alamy; p. **257** Pearson Education Ltd. Studio 8. Clark Wiseman; p. **260** Photo courtesy of Virgin Trains; p. **265** Courtesy of National Express; p. **274** Colinpics/Alamy; p. **279** Dmitrijs Bindemanis/ Shutterstock Images; p. **283** BAA Aviation Photo Library/Inpress/Steve Bates; p. **285** Shutterstock/lancelee

Unit 10 p. **287** Pascal Crapet/Stone/Getty Images; p. **289** Pearson Education Ltd. Studio 8. Clark Wiseman; p. **309** Ryan McVay/Photodisc; p. **310** Pascal Crapet/Stone/Getty Images; p. **317** Pearson Education Ltd. David Sanderson

Unit 11 p. **319** Tony Watson / Alamy; p. **321** Pearson Education Ltd. Studio 8. Clark Wiseman; p. **325** Peter Macdiarmid/Getty Images; p. **329** Jeff Greenberg/Alamy; p. **334** Zsolt Nyulaszi/Shutterstock Images; p. **337** Shutterstock/Kurhan

Unit 12 p. **339** Cephas Picture Library/Alamy; p. **341** Pearson Education Ltd. Jules Selmes; p. **344** David R Frazier Photolibrary Inc/Alamy; p. **346** Jasper Juinen/Getty Images; p. **348** Masterfile; p. **353** Yuri Arcurs/Shutterstock Images; p. **356** Corbis; p. **359** Yuri Arcurs. Shutterstock

Unit 13 p. **361** Dmitrijs Bindemanis/ Shutterstock Images; p. **363** Pearson Education Ltd. Jules Selmes; p. **366** Image Courtesy of Chris Foster at MOSI; p. **374** Alexander Gordeyev/ Shutterstock Images; p. **374** Robert Freid/Alamy; p. **379** Shutterstock/Flashon Studio

About your BTEC Level 2 First Travel and Tourism

Choosing to study for a BTEC Level 2 First Travel and Tourism qualification is a great decision to make for lots of reasons. Studying Travel and Tourism will allow you to broaden your knowledge of the sector as well as deepening your skills.

Your BTEC Level 2 First Travel and Tourism is a **vocational** or **work-related** qualification. This doesn't mean that it will give you all the skills you need to do a job, but it does mean that you'll have the opportunity to gain specific knowledge, understanding and skills that are relevant to your chosen subject or area of work.

What will you be doing?

The qualification is structured into **mandatory units** (ones you must do) and **optional units** (ones you can choose to do). This book contains all 3 mandatory and 10 optional units, giving you a broad choice whichever qualification you are working towards.

- BTEC Level 2 First **Certificate** in Travel and Tourism: 2 mandatory units and optional units that provide a combined total of 15 credits

- BTEC Level 2 First **Extended Certificate** in Travel and Tourism: 3 mandatory units and optional units that provide a combined total of 30 credits

- BTEC Level 2 First **Diploma** in Travel and Tourism: 3 mandatory units and optional units that provide a combined total of 60 credits

Unit number	Credit value	Unit name	Cert	Ex. Cert	Diploma
1	5	The UK travel and tourism sector	M	M	M
2	5	Understanding customer Service in travel and tourism	O	M	M
3	5	Understanding the nature and effects of world travel	M	M	M
4	5	The development of the UK travel and tourism sector	O	O	O
5	5	Developing customer service Skills in travel and tourism	O	O	O
6	5	UK tourism destinations	O	O	O
7	5	European holiday destination		O	O
8	5	Worldwide holiday destinations		O	O
9	5	Holiday planning		O	O
10	10	Exploring marketing in travel and tourism			O
11	5	Preparing for employment in travel and tourism			O
12	5	Developing employability skills for travel and tourism			O
13	5	Organising a travel and tourism study visit			O

How to use this book

This book is designed to help you through your BTEC Level 2 First Travel and Tourism course. This book contains many features that will help you use your skills and knowledge in work-related situations and assist you in getting the most from your course.

Introduction

These introductions give you a snapshot of what to expect from each unit – and what you should be aiming for by the time you finish it!

Assessment and grading criteria

This table explains what you must do in order to achieve each of the assessment criteria for each unit. For each assessment criterion, shown by the grade button **P1**, there is an assessment activity.

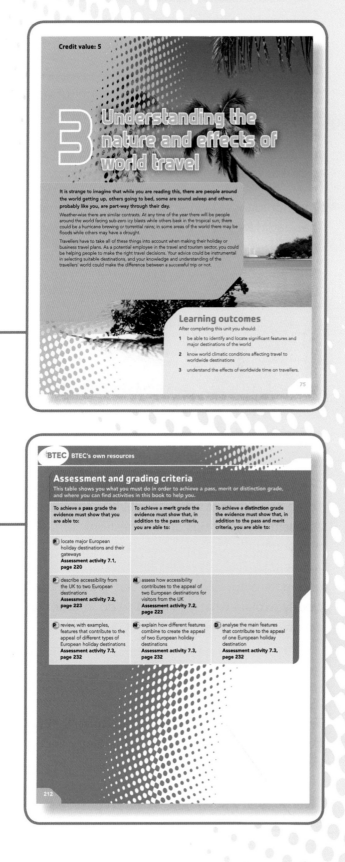

Credit value: 5

3 Understanding the nature and effects of world travel

It is strange to imagine that while you are reading this, there are people around the world getting up, others going to bed, some are sound asleep and others, probably like you, are part-way through their day.

Weather-wise there are similar contrasts. At any time of the year there will be people around the world facing sub-zero icy blasts while others bask in the tropical sun; there could be a hurricane brewing or torrential rains; in some areas of the world there may be floods while others may have a drought.

Travellers have to take all of these things into account when making their holiday or business travel plans. As a potential employee in the travel and tourism sector, you could be helping people to make the right travel decisions. Your advice could be instrumental in selecting suitable destinations, and your knowledge and understanding of the travellers' world could make the difference between a successful trip or not.

Learning outcomes

After completing this unit you should:

1 be able to identify and locate significant features and major destinations of the world

2 know world climatic conditions affecting travel to worldwide destinations

3 understand the effects of worldwide time on travellers.

75

BTEC BTEC's own resources

Assessment and grading criteria

This table shows you what you must do in order to achieve a pass, merit or distinction grade, and where you can find activities in this book to help you.

To achieve a pass grade the evidence must show that you are able to:	To achieve a merit grade the evidence must show that, in addition to the pass criteria, you are able to:	To achieve a distinction grade the evidence must show that, in addition to the pass and merit criteria, you are able to:
P1 locate major European holiday destinations and their gateways **Assessment activity 7.1, page 220**		
P2 describe accessibility from the UK to two European destinations **Assessment activity 7.2, page 223**	**M1** assess how accessibility contributes to the appeal of two European destinations for visitors from the UK **Assessment activity 7.2, page 223**	
P3 review, with examples, features that contribute to the appeal of different types of European holiday destinations **Assessment activity 7.3, page 232**	**M2** explain how different features combine to create the appeal of two European holiday destinations **Assessment activity 7.3, page 232**	**D1** analyse the main features that contribute to the appeal of one European holiday destination **Assessment activity 7.3, page 232**

212

Assessment

Your tutor will set **assignments** throughout your course for you to complete. These may take the form of a role play, map work, written reports, projects and presentations. The important thing is that you evidence your skills and knowledge to date.

Stuck for ideas? Daunted by your first assignment? These students have all been through it before…

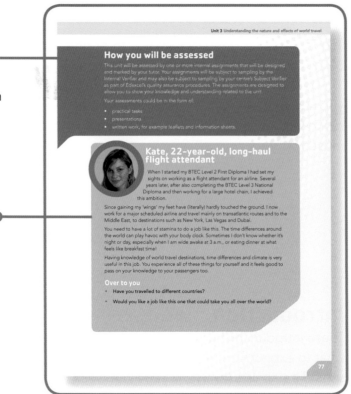

How you will be assessed

This unit will be assessed by one or more internal assignments that will be designed and marked by your tutor. Your assignments will be subject to sampling by the Internal Verifier and may also be subject to sampling by your centre's Subject Verifier as part of Edexcel's quality assurance procedures. The assignments are designed to allow you to show your knowledge and understanding related to the unit.

Your assessments could be in the form of:

- practical tasks
- presentations
- written work, for example leaflets and information sheets.

Kate, 22-year-old, long-haul flight attendant

When I started my BTEC Level 2 First Diploma I had set my sights on working as a flight attendant for an airline. Several years later, after also completing the BTEC Level 3 National Diploma and then working for a large hotel chain, I achieved this ambition.

Since gaining my 'wings' my feet have (literally) hardly touched the ground. I now work for a major scheduled airline and travel mainly on transatlantic routes and to the Middle East, to destinations such as New York, Las Vegas and Dubai.

You need to have a lot of stamina to do a job like this. The time differences around the world can play havoc with your body clock. Sometimes I don't know whether it's night or day, especially when I am wide awake at 3 a.m., or eating dinner at what feels like breakfast time!

Having knowledge of world travel destinations, time differences and climate is very useful in this job. You experience all of these things for yourself and it feels good to pass on your knowledge to your passengers too.

Over to you

- Have you travelled to different countries?
- Would you like a job like this one that could take you all over the world?

Activities

There are different types of activities for you to do: **assessment activities** are suggestions for tasks that you might do as part of your assignment and will help you develop your knowledge, skills and understanding, Each of these has **grading tips** that clearly explain what you need to do in order to achieve a pass, merit or distinction grade.

BTEC Assessment activity 4.5

For your tour operator presentation discuss how organisations are responding to the challenges created by the issues that you have looked at. You should bring together all of the knowledge that you gained by completing 4 and 5, then select and discuss how organisations are responding to the challenges created by the issues.

This question will enable you to achieve ⓓ.

Grading tips ⓓ

- Think about the economic, political, environmental and social issues that you have learned about. Impacts on the various organisations should be fully analysed and discussed and you should explain how organisations are responding to the challenges they are facing.
- Can you think of recent examples where a single issue has had a massive impact on a number of organisations operating within the sector?

- You should choose issues which have happened within the last two years.
- Support your discussions with data, statistics, articles and interviews with travel specialists.
- ⓓ Your discussion could be in a written or a verbal format.

Activity: Selling opportunities

Think of as many other situations as you can in the travel and tourism sector when there are opportunities to sell.

There are also suggestions for activities that will give you a broader grasp of the industry and deepen your skills.

Personal, learning and thinking skills (PLTS)

Throughout your BTEC Level 2 First Travel and Tourism course, there are lots of opportunities to develop your personal, learning and thinking skills. Look out for these as you progress.

PLTS

Completing assessment tasks to time can help to develop your skills as a **self-manager**.

Functional skills

It's important that you have good English, maths and ICT skills – you never know when you'll need them, and employers will be looking for evidence that you've got these skills too.

Functional skills

Writing an information booklet will help you develop your **English** skills by communicating information and ideas effectively.

Key terms

Technical words and phrases are easy to spot, and definitions are included. The terms and definitions are also in the glossary at the back of the book.

Key terms

regeneration – the improvement or development of derelict land for residential or commercial purposes.

WorkSpace

Case studies provide snapshots of real workplace issues, and show how the skills and knowledge you develop during your course can help you in your career.

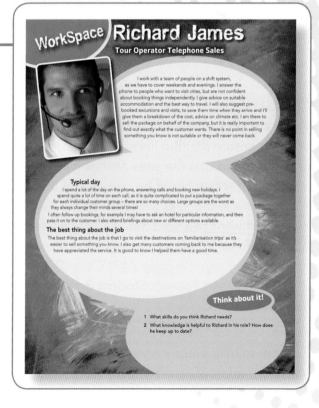

WorkSpace **Richard James**
Tour Operator Telephone Sales

I work with a team of people on a shift system, as we have to cover weekends and evenings. I answer the phone to people who want to visit cities, but are not confident about booking things independently. I give advice on suitable accommodation and the best way to travel. I will also suggest pre-booked excursions and visits, to save them time when they arrive and I'll give them a breakdown of the cost, advice on climate etc. I am there to sell the package on behalf of the company, but it is really important to find out exactly what the customer wants. There is no point in selling something you know is not suitable or they will never come back.

Typical day
I spend a lot of the day on the phone, answering calls and booking new holidays. I spend quite a lot of time on each call, as it is quite complicated to put a package together for each individual customer group – there are so many choices. Large groups are the worst as they always change their minds several times!
I often follow up bookings, for example I may have to ask a hotel for particular information, and then pass it on to the customer. I also attend briefings about new or different options available.

The best thing about the job
The best thing about the job is that I go to visit the destinations on 'familiarisation trips' as it's easier to sell something you know. I also get many customers coming back to me because they have appreciated the service. It is good to know I helped them have a good time.

Think about it!

1 What skills do you think Richard needs?
2 What knowledge is helpful to Richard in his role? How does he keep up to date?

Just checking

When you see this sort of activity, take stock! These quick activities and questions are there to check your knowledge. You can use them to see how much progress you've made.

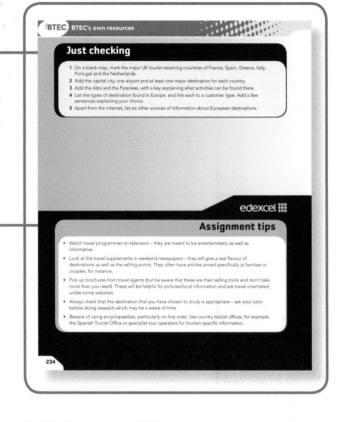

Edexcel's assignment tips

At the end of each chapter, you'll find hints and tips to help you get the best mark you can, such as the best websites to go to, checklists to help you remember processes and really useful facts and figures.

Don't miss out on these resources to help you!

Have you read your BTEC Level 2 First Study Skills Guide? It's full of advice on study skills, putting your assignments together and making the most of being a BTEC Travel and Tourism student.

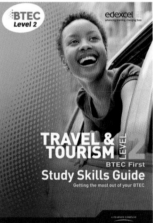

Hotlinks

There are links to relevant websites in this book. In order to ensure that the links are up to date, that the links work, and that the sites are not inadvertently linked to sites that could be considered offensive, we have made the links available on the Pearson website at www.pearsonschoolsandfecolleges. co.uk/hotlinks. When you access the site, search for either the express code 7494V, title BTEC Level 2 First Travel and Tourism Student Book or ISBN 9781846907494.

Your book is just part of the exciting resources from Edexcel to help you succeed in your BTEC course. Visit www.edexcel.com/BTEC or www.pearsonfe. co.uk/BTEC 2010 for more details.

1 The UK travel and tourism sector

Travel and tourism is now one of the largest sectors in the world in terms of generating jobs and income. It is a dynamic and vibrant sector which makes a major contribution to the UK economy.

Travel and tourism has become an important part of how we live today and most people travel regularly for work and leisure. The UK also attracts many visitors from overseas, who arrive to visit friends and relatives, for business and pleasure.

This unit explores the main types of tourism, the motivating factors for travel, and the contribution that travel and tourism has on the UK economy. You will learn about the wide range of organisations that operate within the sector, their roles and inter-relationships.

This unit has links to *Unit 4: Development of the UK travel and tourism sector*, where you will explore further the development of travel agents, transport providers, and some of the economic issues surrounding the sector. There are also links to *Unit 11: Preparing for employment in travel and tourism*, where you will explore the range of different jobs in the sector.

Learning outcomes

After completing this unit you should:

1 understand the concept of the travel and tourism sector

2 know the roles and interrelationships of organisations within the UK travel and tourism sector.

Assessment and grading criteria

This table shows you what you must do in order to achieve a pass, merit or distinction grade, and where you can find activities in this book to help you.

To achieve a **pass** grade the evidence must show that you are able to:	To achieve a **merit** grade the evidence must show that, in addition to the pass criteria, you are able to:	To achieve a **distinction** grade the evidence must show that, in addition to the pass and merit criteria, you are able to:
P1 review the main types of tourism and the reasons why people travel **Assessment activity 1.1, page 9**	**M1** explain how the different types of tourism contribute to the UK economy **Assessment activity 1.1, page 9**	**D1** evaluate the positive aspects of interrelationships on UK travel and tourism organisations **Assessment activity 1.2, page 34**
P2 assess the contribution of tourism to the UK economy **Assessment activity 1.1, page 9**		
P3 outline the roles of the different types of organisation in the UK travel and tourism sector (IE1) **Assessment activity 1.2, page 34**	**M2** analyse the interrelationships between organisations in the travel and tourism sector **Assessment activity 1.2, page 34**	
P4 describe the different types of inter-relationship between travel and tourism organisations **Assessment activity 1.2, page 34**		

Shabaz, 15-year-old learner

This unit has really opened my eyes to the size and scale of the UK travel and tourism sector and the impact it has on the UK economy. I thought tourism was just about taking holidays and visiting attractions but this unit has helped me to see there is much more to the sector than that.

I really enjoyed carrying out research with other students in my class to identify the reasons people were travelling to my town. We designed a questionnaire and asked lots of visitors outside our local train station why they were travelling in the area. The research helped me to realise that people travel for lots of different reasons and that they all spend money with many different businesses as they go.

I also enjoyed working as part of a group to find out about what different travel and tourism organisations actually do. I had no idea there were so many different types of organisation in the travel and tourism sector, from hotels and travel agencies to tourist boards and car hire companies.

I liked creating a presentation about my chosen organisations to show what they do and how they work with others to offer a better service to their customers.

Over to you

- What areas of this unit might you find the most challenging?

- Which section of the unit are you most looking forward to?

- What preparation can you do in readiness for the unit assessment(s)?

1. Understand the concept of the travel and tourism sector

Set off

Travel or tourism?

On your own, make a note of any trips you, or people you know, have taken. Who went? Where did you/they go? What was the reason for the trip? You might find it helpful to record your information in a table, such as the one below.

Where was the journey to?	Who was travelling?	What was the reason for the journey?	How long were you away from home?
Manchester	Me and my cousin	To visit my friend Jack	Two days

In groups, compare your lists. Were the reasons for travelling the same or different? In each case, would you think of the person travelling as a tourist? What do you think are the differences between travel and tourism?

1.1 Main types of tourism

What is travel and tourism?

Travel is about getting from one place to another, often making a journey using a method of transport such as a train, plane or car. However, not all travel can be classed as tourism.

Tourism is often understood as the activities of people travelling to, and staying in, places outside their usual environment for leisure, business and/or other purposes and for not more than a year at a time. It may involve an overnight stay, but this is not always the case. Those travelling, but not staying away from home overnight, are sometimes classed as day visitors or day tourists.

There are three main types of tourism:

Domestic tourism – taking holidays and trips in your own country

Outbound tourism – travelling to a different country for a visit or holiday

Inbound tourism – visitors from overseas coming into the country

Here are some examples of tourism: if a family from Birmingham in the Midlands were to take a short break to the seaside resort of Blackpool, they would be classed as domestic tourists. A group of American travellers visiting the UK for a three-week tour of the country would be classed as inbound tourists and a couple from Newcastle who take a one week package holiday to Greece would be classed as outbound tourists.

Activity: Tourism types

Working in pairs, think about the holidays, trips and visits taken by yourself, your friends and family. Label each activity as: leisure, business or VFR tourism; domestic, inbound or outbound tourism and any other category that may describe each activity. Record your information in a table, such as the one below.

Where was the visit to?	Who was travelling?	What was the reason for the journey?	How long were you away from home?	Tourism type(s)?

1.2 Reasons why people travel

People travel for lots of different reasons but mainly for leisure, business and to visit friends and relatives (VFR), either in the UK or abroad.

Leisure travel

Leisure travellers may be on holiday, or taking a trip of particular cultural or personal interest. When travelling for leisure reasons, tourists are taking trips and making journeys in their own leisure time; that is when they are not working.

Travelling for leisure may be within the UK (domestic tourism) or abroad (outbound tourism). Popular destinations for leisure travellers could include coastal resorts, rural and countryside areas, or towns and cities. Leisure travel may include visits to tourist attractions, bars, restaurants, events and evening entertainment.

Business travel

Business travellers will often attend meetings, conferences, exhibitions and events. When travelling for business reasons, travellers are attending locations and venues for work purposes and it is often the employer who pays for the travel and accommodation. Business travel can be within the UK or overseas and often involves visits to large cities and commercial areas that have the facilities to hold large conferences and events.

Visiting friends and relatives

Another very common reason for making a journey is to go and visit your friends and relatives, known as VFR. People may travel within the UK or abroad to visit their friends and relatives, particularly if they have emigrated to another country or have moved away for work or study.

The charts on page 6 show the different reasons why people travel within the UK and why they leave the UK to go abroad.

What different reasons might people have for travelling to London?

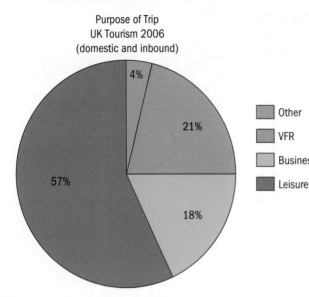

Figure 1.1 Purpose of trip 2006
(*Source: VisitBritain*)

Purpose of Trip
UK Tourism 2006
(domestic and inbound)

4%
21%
18%
57%

Other
VFR
Business
Leisure

Purpose of Trip
UK Outbound Tourism
2006

5%
17%
65%
13%

Other
VFR
Business
Leisure

Did you know?

- In 2007, 49,000 overseas visitors came to the UK to study, with Manchester having the largest student population in the whole of Europe. *Source: Visit Britain.*

- Although a few individuals have already paid huge amounts to travel into space, 'Space Tourism' may soon be a reality for many. Virgin Galactic is on course to become the world's first commercial space line with tickets on sale for $200,000.

- The term 'MICE' is often used to refer to business tourism which involves travel for Meetings, Incentives, Conferences and Exhibitions. Incentive travel is often used as a reward for good business performance, such as meeting a particular target.

Case study: Business class travel with British Airways

British Airways meet the needs of their outbound, or inbound, business travellers by providing a range of services and facilities in their Club World cabins and airport lounges.

Club World

The business class cabin and seat provide a range of options, including:

- touch button privacy screen to enclose the traveller in their own private personal space

- a generously sized desk, in-seat phone and personal laptop power socket

- personal locker for storing shoes, newspapers or laptop when dining or sleeping

- luxury wash bag containing in-flight skincare products, toothbrush, toothpaste, eye mask, earplugs and comfortable flight socks

- personal flat-screen TV with noise cancelling headphones.

On arrival at selected destinations, business travellers can prepare for the working day with a power-shower while their suit is being pressed. Free wireless internet access is also available in lounges for catching up on urgent emails.

1 Business class services are often much more expensive than those in standard or economy class. Why would businesses pay for these extra services and features?

2 Think about your local travel and tourism organisations. What do they provide for business travellers?

Other reasons

There are also a variety of other different reasons why people may choose to travel. The table on page 7 highlights some of these other reasons.

Table 1.1: Why people choose to travel

Tourism type	Reason for travel	Example
Agro tourism	Short for 'agriculture' where visitors are interested in farms and the countryside.	A family from Sheffield who travel out of the city to visit a farm – *domestic tourism*.
Dark tourism	Visiting sites associates with war, death and tragic events.	A group of schoolchildren who visit concentration or death camps in Germany and eastern Europe – *outbound tourism*.
Faith tourism	Religious travel for pilgrimage and travel to sacred sites of religious importance, such as Jerusalem and Mecca.	A group from a Roman Catholic church in Liverpool going to Lourdes – *outbound tourism*.
Health tourism	Travelling to have operations, or receive dental treatment, which may be cheaper and faster than in the UK.	An individual who travels to Poland to have a knee operation more quickly than waiting in the UK – *outbound tourism*.
Pink tourism	Attractions and events aimed at the Lesbian Gay Bisexual Transsexual (LGBT) community, for example Pride and Mardi Gras festivals.	A group of friends who travel from Berlin to Manchester for the Pride Festival – *inbound tourism*.
Sports tourism	Travelling to play in, or watch, sporting events and competitions such as the Olympics and the Football World Cup.	A group of football supporters from Barcelona travelling to Manchester for a Champions League match – *inbound tourism*.
Education tourism	Visiting a place of educational interest or studying a particular educational subject.	A group of college students who travel by train to London to visit the National Science Museum – *domestic tourism*.

1.3 Economic contribution of tourism

Whatever the reason for travel, or the type of tourism, the travel and tourism sector makes a major contribution, both directly and indirectly, to the UK **economy** in terms of **Gross Domestic Product (GDP)** and employment.

The economic value of tourism

Tourism is the fifth largest industry in the UK and is worth over £85 billion to the economy (which is around 3.7% of GDP). Tourism also benefits those who are not directly linked to the tourism industry, for example a business traveller to the UK may also spend money in shops, bars and restaurants and buy gifts to take home. Indirectly, UK tourism is worth much more to the UK, around £114 billion.

Activity: The local value of tourism

In small groups, carry out some research into the value of tourism to your local region. Your Regional Tourist Board or Regional Development Agency should have some useful figures to help you.

Key terms

Economy – is the wealth and resources of a country or region, especially in terms of production and consumption of goods and services.

Gross Domestic Product (GDP) – this can be thought of as the value of a country's economy. It measures the value of all goods and services over a specific time period (usually one year). Domestic and inbound tourism contribute to the UK's GDP but not all outbound tourism does as some of the money spent by outbound tourists will be in another country. The UK currently has the sixth biggest GDP in the world.

Did you know?

Visit Britain, the UK's national tourism agency, has the most recent data on UK tourism spending and visitor numbers. To obtain a secure link to this website, see the Hotlinks section on p.x.

Tourism employment

Tourism makes a big contribution to employment in the UK. This can be direct, indirect or induced employment and can be referred to as **tourism-related employment**.

Direct employment

Tourism contributes to the direct employment of around 1.4 million people (around 4.3% of the UK workforce) in a variety of different jobs. Direct jobs are those created by travel and tourism organisations themselves and can include jobs in hotels, in visitor attractions and with transport providers.

Indirect employment

These are jobs that are created to supply the goods and services purchased by travel and tourism organisations to meet the needs of visitors. Indirect tourism employment is responsible for creating around 2.65 million jobs. The jobs can include suppliers to hotels, visitor attractions and transport providers.

Induced employment

These are jobs that are created to provide services and facilities to those people directly employed in the travel and tourism sector. These jobs can include shop assistants, taxi drivers and construction workers.

Case study: Tourism economic multiplier

Paul and Sarah have recently opened a new indoor holiday village in western Scotland. They need to employ a number of people to help run the camp. These include:

- administrators
- managers
- bar staff
- shop assistants
- cleaners
- maintenance staff
- children's entertainers
- lifeguards.

These new jobs are *direct* employment in the tourism industry. The holiday camp also uses a variety of local suppliers, which include the local farm shop for food and milk supplies, the local laundry service to clean towels and bed linen and a local hardware supplier for equipment and cleaning chemicals. These suppliers need to take on additional casual employees to cope with the extra demand from the holiday camp. These *indirect* jobs are as a result of the new holiday camp.

The staff directly and indirectly employed in the local area because of the new holiday camp need their own accommodation, transport and food supplies and this in turn creates more of a demand from other local businesses such as estate agents, pubs and shops. This may mean that even more new staff are needed to be employed to cope with the extra demand. These would be *induced* jobs.

Think about visitors to your own local area. What jobs do they create – both directly and indirectly? Make a list and compare with a partner.

UK tourist numbers

The UK is a very popular tourist destination for overseas visitors, the sixth most popular in the world, attracting millions of tourists from around the world, particularly the USA, the Republic of Ireland, France and Germany. The top five inbound markets for the UK in 2008 are shown in Table 1.3.

Table 1.2: Key tourism facts (2008)

Key tourism facts (2008)	Number of tourists	Tourism spend
Inbound tourism to the UK		
Overseas visitor numbers	31.9 million	£16.3 billion
UK domestic tourism		
Holidays of one night or more	52.0 million	£11.4 billion
Overnight business trips	18.2 million	£4.5 billion
Overnight trips visiting friends and relatives (VFR)	44.1 million	£4.8 billion

Source: VisitBritain

Table 1.3: Top five inbound markets for the UK (2008)

Country	Visits (000)
France	3 636
Irish Republic	3 069
USA	2 959
Germany	2 905
Spain	1 977

Country	Spend (£m)
USA	2 228
Germany	1 130
France	1 054
Irish Republic	965
Spain	816

Source: UKinbound

BTEC Assessment activity 1.1

You have gained a work experience placement in the tourism department at the local council. Your supervisor has asked you to put together an information booklet, illustrated with statistics provided within charts and graphs, that will be sent to new travel and tourism businesses in the area.

1 You have been asked to review and write about:

- the three main types of tourism
- the reasons why people travel including leisure, business, visiting friends and relatives, and other reasons such as sport or education.

Question 1 will enable you to achieve **P1**.

2 Assess the economic contribution of tourism to the UK economy.

Question 2 will enable you to achieve **P2**.

3 Explain how the different types of tourism contribute to the UK economy.

Question 3 will enable you to achieve **M1**.

Grading tips

- **P1** Remember to review the three different types of tourism. Have you linked the different types of tourism to the reasons why people travel and given examples?
- **P2** have you described in your own words the term Gross Domestic Product (GDP)?
- **M1** remember to explain how tourism provides money and employment in the UK. Give specific examples for each type.

Remember

Tourism contributes to the UK economy both directly and indirectly. Direct contribution refers to spending and jobs specifically in the travel and tourism sector. Indirect contribution is made in industries which support travel and tourism activities, such as retail and manufacturing.

Functional skills

Writing an information booklet will help you develop your **English** skills by communicating information and ideas effectively.

PLTS

Completing assessment tasks to time can help to develop your skills as a **self-manager**.

2. Roles and interrelationships of organisations within the UK travel and tourism sector

There are many different organisations working across the whole of the UK travel and tourism sector. They can generally be categorised into the following elements shown in Figure 1.2.

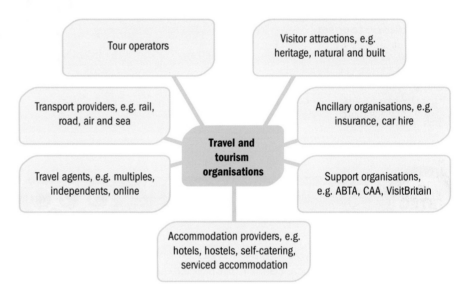

Figure 1.2: Organisations working across travel and tourism

2.1 Travel and tourism sectors

The travel and tourism sector can be broken down into three main sectors – the private, public and voluntary sectors.

Private sector

The private, or commercial sector, is made up of many travel and tourism organisations of different sizes, from very large international companies to small- and medium-sized independent businesses. Private sector organisations are owned and controlled by private individuals, or shareholders in the case of **limited companies**.

The main aim of private sector organisations is to make a profit. They achieve this by selling a range of products and services to tourists, from theme park tickets, to hotel rooms, to food, drink and souvenirs.

Private sector organisations in the travel and tourism sector can include accommodation providers, transport companies, tour operators and travel agents, and some visitor attractions. Many well-known tourism brands are part of the private sector including Thomas Cook, Virgin Atlantic Airways, Holiday Inn and the Merlin Entertainments Group.

Key term

Limited companies – there are two types of limited company: a private limited company (Ltd.) or a public limited company (PLC). Ownership of a limited company is divided into equal parts known as shares. Shareholders have bought one or more shares in the company. A public limited company is still a private sector organisation but can sell its shares on the Stock Market to any member of the public, while a private limited company cannot.

Case study: Merlin Entertainments Group

In May 2007, the Merlin Entertainments Group aquired the Tussauds Group forming the leading European visitor attractions group – and second largest in the world to Disney. Today, the group comprises 59 attractions in 13 countries across three continents welcoming over 35 million visitors a year. Merlin owns and runs some of the UK's best known visitor attractions including:

- Madame Tussauds
- LEGOLAND, Windsor
- Merlin Entertainments London Eye
- Alton Towers Resort
- Chessington World of Adventures
- Thorpe Park
- Warwick Castle
- SEA LIFE Centres and London Aquarium
- The Dungeons
- LEGOLAND Discovery Centre

1 What do you think the benefits are to tourists that all these attractions are owned by the same private organisation?
2 Can you think of any disadvantages of these attractions being owned by the same organisation?

Case study: Virgin Group

Richard Branson's Virgin Group is one of the most recognisable private sector brands with an impressive portfolio of companies in many different industries. Virgin Atlantic Airways, Virgin Holidays, Virgin Festivals, Virgin Trains, Virgin Limited Edition Hotels, Virgin Balloon Flights, Virgin Galactic and Virgin Limobikes are just a few of the companies that the group contributes to the UK travel and tourism sector.

1 Which of these different Virgin companies deal mainly with domestic, inbound or outbound tourists?
2 What is the impact of these Virgin Group companies on the UK economy?

Virgin Limobikes – a passenger motorbike and the quick way to get from A to B when in central London

Public sector

The public, or non-commercial sector, also includes a variety of different travel and tourism organisations. Public sector organisations are funded, and sometimes owned, by central and local government. The main aim of public sector organisations is often to provide a service, rather than make a profit.

Public sector organisations in the travel and tourism sector can include a range of support organisations, such as National Tourist Boards, funded by central government, and Regional Tourist Boards and Tourist Information Centres, usually funded by local and county councils.

Some visitor attractions, such as museums, parks and gardens are also in the public sector.

Case study: English Heritage

English Heritage is the Government's statutory adviser on the historic environment. Officially known as the Historic Buildings and Monuments Commission for England, English Heritage is sponsored by the Department for Culture, Media and Sport (DCMS).

Their powers and responsibilities are set out in the National Heritage Act (1983) and they report to Parliament through the Secretary of State for Culture, Media and Sport.

English Heritage is funded in part by the Government and in part from revenue (or any form of income) from over 400 of their historic properties, from membership and from other services. In 2008/09 English Heritage's public funding was worth £132.7 million, and income from other sources was £48.1 million.

English Heritage works in partnership with the central government departments, local authorities, voluntary bodies and the private sector.

Their stated aims are to:

- conserve and enhance the historic environment

- broaden public access to the heritage

- increase people's understanding of the past.

Table 1.4: English Heritage 2005-08

	2005/06	2006/07	2007/08
Number of visitors to staffed properties	5.0m	5.3m	5.3m
Number of members	595 000	630 000	665 000
Number of free educational visits	485 000	481 000	450 000

Source: English Heritage 2009

1 English Heritage is the public body with responsibility for protecting and promoting the historic environment in England, but which organisations have a similar responsibility in Scotland, Wales and Northern Ireland?

2 What do you think are the advantages of English Heritage being a public sector organisation?

Did you know?

The Department for Culture, Media and Sport (DCMS) is the department responsible for supporting the tourism industry at national level. They are responsible for government policy on the arts, sport, tourism, libraries, museums and galleries. DCMS are also the Department responsible for the 2012 Olympic Games and Paralympic Games. To obtain a secure link to this website, see the Hotlinks section on p.x.

Voluntary sector

The voluntary sector, sometimes known as the third or charitable sector, includes organisations that are not part of government (public sector), and do not exist to make a profit (private sector). They are independent organisations that aim to provide a particular service, or to promote a particular cause or viewpoint. Voluntary sector organisations are often funded through memberships, donations, grants and the sale of goods and services at events or through gift shops and cafes. Members of voluntary organisations often volunteer themselves to keep organisations open and meet the needs of tourists and visitors.

Examples of voluntary organisations within the travel and tourism sector include the National Trust, the Youth Hostel Association and Tourism Concern. Many local recreational clubs and historic railway trusts are voluntary organisations too.

Case study: Tourism Concern

Tourism Concern is an independent voluntary organisation and UK charity, set up to fight exploitation in the tourism industry and to campaign for ethical and fair trade tourism. They have a membership of almost 900 individuals and organisations and they work with partners in over 20 destination countries to ensure that tourism always benefits local people.

Tourism concern has five main principles:

- Independence – being a non-industry based organisation
- Listening – to communities and organisations requesting help

- Shared values and vision – working together with other organisations towards common goal
- Inclusivity – everyone has the right to take part in the decision-making
- Ethical practices – green policies and fair trade products.

Tourism Concern is funded through donations from individuals and trusts. Many people volunteer their time to help Tourism Concern meet its objectives.

1 What is the main role of Tourism Concern?
2 What else could Tourism Concern do to help raise funds for its work around the world?

Activity: Sector differences

Create a table which identifies the key differences between the private, public and voluntary sectors. Include role, aims, funding and examples from the travel and tourism sector.

2.2 Roles of organisations

As we have seen, different organisations have a range of different roles, aims and objectives. The different roles of travel and tourism organisations can include:

- **Supplying products and services:** The role of many private, public and voluntary sector organisations is to provide a range of goods and services to meet the needs of tourists and travellers. This could include saleable products and services such as hotel rooms, souvenirs, travel, holiday packages or free (complimentary) services, such as tourist information and advice.

- **Making a profit:** The primary role of most private sector organisations is to make a profit from the sale of their goods and services to tourists, for example Alton Towers, Virgin Trains, Thomas Cook, and Hilton Hotels all provide a range of different products and services for sale to tourists and travellers.

- **Regulation:** Many public sector organisations are set up in order to regulate the quality of a service provided to tourists and travellers, for example the Civil Aviation Authority (CAA), which regulates air travel in the UK, or the Office of Rail Regulation (ORR), which ensures that UK rail travel is safe and well maintained.

- **Promotion:** A major role of many public travel and tourism organisations is to promote a particular destination as an attractive location for tourists to visit. Tourist information centres and Regional Tourist Boards promote the different features of their local area to attract a range of different tourist and traveller types. The role of VisitBritain is primarily to promote the UK as a major tourism destination overseas. They produce publicity material and organise events that are designed to attract inbound tourists to the UK.

- **Supporting members:** The role of some organisations is to support the interests of their members. One of the key roles of ABTA - The Travel Foundation is to represent the interests of its members; it supports over 5000 travel agents and more than 900 tour operators and represents their voice when dealing with government and Europe.

As well as private, public and voluntary, the range of organisations in the travel and tourism sector can also be categorised as domestic, outbound and inbound organisations. In the next section we will explore the main roles of organisations in each of these categories.

2.3 Interrelationships between organisations

You have already explored a range of domestic, outbound and inbound tourism organisations from both the public and private sectors.

Working together

Often travel and tourism organisations will work together in order to:

- provide a better service to their customers

- receive greater protection for smaller, independent organisations

- influence government policy on important issues affecting the sector

- arrange discount packages and deals that will appeal to their customers

- raise awareness and promote the sector.

Many transport companies, for example, have partnerships with visitor attractions to offer travellers discounts and incentives to plan a visit. Most travel agents and tour operators are members of trade associations to provide their customers with peace of mind and booking protection. Many accommodation providers work closely with Enjoy England and the Automobile Association (AA), joining their quality accommodation accreditation schemes. Being involved in the star grading system often gives tourists confidence to choose those organisations.

Common ownership

Inter-relationships also exist where different brands or companies are owned and controlled by the same organisation. The major tour operators, for example, own their own hotels, airlines and travel agencies. This provides various benefits including:

- the ability to control the quality of all the different products in the package
- offering value for money holiday packages in a price competitive market
- giving the customer a seamless holiday experience.

Activity: All for one

In small groups, select one of the following organisations and research the different companies and brands that it owns and controls.

- Merlin Entertainments Group
- TUI AG
- Thomas Cook Group
- easyGroup
- Virgin Group.

Prepare a short presentation to the rest of your class on your findings.

What do you think are the advantages of one organisation controlling many different companies?

2.4 Domestic organisations

Domestic organisations are those which meet the needs of tourists travelling around the UK, such as tour operators, accommodation and transport providers, visitor attractions and other support and **ancillary organisations**.

Domestic tour operators

Domestic **tour operators** are organisations which arrange holidays and short-breaks in the UK for residents of the UK. They provide a range of accommodation, transport and entertainment options, including a variety of discount package deals which can combine a hotel stay, transport to a destination and evening entertainment.

Some domestic tour operators provide a range of themed packages such as theatre and attraction breaks, sports breaks, Christmas and New Year breaks and luxury spa weekends. Domestic tour operators may sell their products through a travel agent or direct to customers via the internet or telephone.

Key terms

Ancillary organisations – organisations that support travel and tourism. They offer tourists and travellers additional products and services that complement their main, or primary, product for example customers buying a package holiday may also require additional products and services, such as travel insurance and car hire, which are offered from ancillary organisations.

Tour operator – an organisation that puts together different components of a holiday which could include accommodation, transport, excursions and transfers. Tour operators have contracts with hoteliers, airlines and ground transport providers, and package these components together to sell to the customer either directly or through a travel agent. Tour operators produce brochures to distribute their holiday and short-break packages.

Case study: Superbreak

Based in York, Superbreak are the leading provider of UK short-breaks. Founded in 1983, they initially promoted just over 100 hotels. Today they specialise in the booking of thousands of 2- to 5-star hotels across the country as well as providing a range of themed short-break packages.

Superbreak sell directly to customers though their website and through a telephone call centre available seven days a week. They also sell their products through travel agencies and produce a range of brochures to highlight their various packages, which include theatre, attraction breaks, sporting events, spa breaks and even murder mystery breaks. To obtain a secure link to the Superbreak website, see the Hotlinks section on p.x.

1 Carry out some research at the website for Superbreak and make a list of all the different products and services offered by this domestic tour operator.

2 Do Superbreak work with any other travel and tourism organisations? Make a list of any you can find.

Transport providers

Transport providers allow tourists to move around the country either by road, rail or air. Domestic transport providers include bus and coach companies, railways and airlines (offering domestic flights). Each type of transport has a variety of different advantages and disadvantages depending on the needs of the traveller.

Road

Road passenger transport providers include bus and coach companies, operating locally and on a national level across the UK. There are generally two types of coach provider: scheduled and charter or hire companies. Scheduled providers run to a published timetable regardless of the number of passengers. Scheduled coach companies, such as National Express and Megabus, are familiar sights on the country's roads and motorways, moving tourists and travellers on to their next destinations.

Charter and hire coach companies range from small independent providers to national companies such as Shearings Holidays and National Holidays. There are many such companies in the UK which provide transport for a specific purpose, such as a touring holiday around Scotland or Wales. Charter providers often sell their holidays and short-breaks directly to customers and also through travel agents.

Rail

Rail travel has been increasing in popularity in recent years. There are 29 train operating companies (TOCs) providing passenger trains in the UK. The role of the train operating companies is to provide a safe and reliable transport system to the general public. Train operating companies are generally privately owned and aim to make a profit through the sale of tickets and on-board services.

A variety of railcards are available to provide discounts to certain groups, such as students, families and senior citizens. The Oyster Card system makes tube travel on London's underground network much cheaper for travellers.

Activity: All on-board

In pairs, carry out some internet research into a large train operating company such as Virgin Trains or First Group. To obtain a secure link to these websites, see the Hotlinks section on p.x.

- Make a list of the products and services that are available to passengers
- Describe the main roles of the train operating company.

Now prepare a short presentation on your findings for the rest of your group.

Air

Domestic air travel in the UK has also been increasing in recent years. An increase in low-cost scheduled (budget) airlines, the number of daily flights available and the expansion of regional airports have made it much easier for travellers to choose air travel to move around the UK.

Full-service scheduled airlines

Schedule airlines are privately owned companies that operate to a timetable. They will fly at the set time regardless of the number of passengers. The timetable often changes between a summer and winter schedule. Popular scheduled airlines offering UK domestic flights include British Airways and British Midland (BMI).

Low-cost scheduled airlines

Low-cost scheduled airlines are also known as 'budget' or 'no-frills' carriers. They operate to a scheduled timetable, but often with reduced services and strict terms and conditions. They usually charge for all additional extras such as food and drink, checked-in baggage and seat allocation.

Budget airlines include Ryanair, easyJet, Flybe and Jet2.com.

Did you know?

In April 2009, the Department for Transport predicted that the number of domestic air passengers is set to double from 50 million to 101 million per year by 2030.

Activity: Internal flights

Imagine you are working at the Tourist Information Centre in Edinburgh. A business tourist would like to get to London tomorrow and requests information on domestic flights to London Gatwick airport. She has one piece of hand-luggage and one piece of hold-luggage to be checked-in.

Using the internet, answer the following questions:

1 Which airlines operate a service from Edinburgh to London?
2 Are these carriers full-service or low-cost scheduled airlines?
3 How much is the cheapest single basic fare leaving tomorrow?
4 What is included in the fare price?

Accommodation

There are a variety of different accommodation options for tourists in the UK depending on their needs and budgets.

Hotels

Hotels vary enormously in terms of size, facilities, services and, of course, price. Many hotels are awarded from 1 to 5 stars as part of a classification scheme, which lets tourists know about the range and quality of a hotel's facilities and services. Hotels generally have at least six bedrooms and may be independently run or part of a large chain. Popular hotel chains include Holiday Inn, Marriott, Radisson and Hilton.

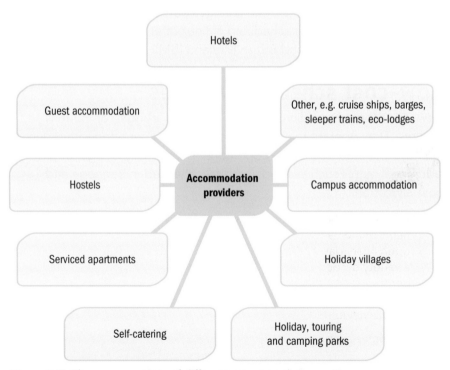

Figure 1.3: There are a variety of different accommodation options

Case study: National Quality Assessment Scheme

The National Quality Assessment Schemes are a broad range of schemes covering several different types of accommodation including hotels, guest accommodation, self-catering, caravan and camping parks, hostels, campus' etc.

The hotels scheme in particular requires hotels to provide a range of facilities, services and quality relative to their star rating. The Common Standards for Hotels and Guest Accommodation were agreed by the National Tourist Boards of England (VisitEngland, formerly VisitBritain), Scotland (VisitScotland) and Wales (VisitWales formerly Wales Tourist Board), the AA and the RAC (they no longer carry out inspections of accommodation).

The criteria for the gaining of a star rating is the same for all organisations carrying out assessments,

but each organisation has its own extra marketing awards for recognising different aspects of quality, for example the AA has rosettes for excellent food in hotels and restaurants and VisitEngland have Gold and Silver Awards for overall excellence in hotels and guest accommodation. Participation in the scheme is voluntary and participants pay a yearly membership fee. To obtain a secure link to The Quality Assessment website, see the Hotlinks section on p.x.

What do you think are the benefits for hotels in participating in a quality assessment scheme?

So called 'budget hotels' have become increasing popular in the UK, offering a more basic range of facilities and services at cheaper rates. Budget hotels are often located in city centres or by major roads and motorways and include brands such as Travelodge and Premier Inn.

Guest accommodation

Similar to hotels but often family run, guest accommodation includes guest houses, bed and breakfasts (B&Bs) and other smaller providers of serviced tourist accommodation, such as farmhouses and inns.

Hostels

Hostels, or youth hostels, generally provide a basic level accommodation and shared living and social spaces such as kitchens, lounges and bathrooms. Many provide dormitory style bedrooms, often sleeping four, six, eight, or even more people in each room, although many hostels now also offer private rooms and ensuite rooms (those with their own bathroom).

Did you know?

The UK Youth Hostel Association (YHA) operate a network of more than 200 youth hostels, bunkhouses and camping barns across England and Wales. The first youth hostel was started 100 years ago and since then the idea has spread right around the world. Anyone can stay with YHA, not just young people, although membership is usually required.

Case study: Ambleside Youth Hostel

Located on the shores of Lake Windermere in the heart of the Lake District, Ambleside Youth Hostel is open every day of the year and has 237 bed spaces in a variety of room combinations, from double rooms to dormitories with 10 beds. The hostel has a variety of facilities and services to meet the needs of different guests including:

- games room
- library
- conference facilities
- garden
- laundry and drying room
- kitchen and dining room
- TV lounge
- classroom
- shop
- cycle and luggage stores.

1 Which types of guest do you think will stay at the Ambleside Youth Hostel?

2 What is the advantage of having different rooming options?

19

Key term

Concierge – a concierge is a member of staff in a hotel or apartment complex who assists guests with storage of their luggage, booking of tours and tickets, for a theatre show for example, and providing general information and advice about the local area. The concierge is often located in the reception area.

Serviced apartments

Similar to self-catering properties, serviced apartments provide private kitchen and bathroom facilities but have a range of other hotel-like services such as housekeeping and a **concierge** service. Many serviced apartments are found in large city centres.

Self-catering

Self-catering properties are those with their own kitchen and bathroom facilities, such as cottages and apartments. Most take bookings by the week, often from Saturday to Saturday, but shorter breaks are also often available. Many accept pets and self-catering properties are often particularly popular in countryside and seaside areas.

Holiday village

A holiday village includes a range of purpose-built accommodation, such as chalets and lodges, with a range of facilities and services on site such as restaurants, bars, swimming pools, leisure facilities, outdoor activities and live entertainment. The activities may be included in the overall cost of the holiday or sold as additional extras.

Bookings are often made for a week or short-break and themed breaks are also often available. Many holiday villages are located at the seaside or in forest parks, such as Center Parcs, Haven, Butlins and Pontins.

Holiday, touring and camping sites

Holiday parks can offer a range of different services to domestic tourists, such as holiday homes and caravans for hire, pitches for visitors to bring their own touring caravans or areas for camping and pitching tents.

Many parks have central facilities for visitors including shops, a swimming pool and clubs. Many also offer evening entertainment for the whole family.

Campus accommodation

Many universities and colleges allow tourists to book their student accommodation outside of term time. Often with basic facilities, this can be a great option for groups looking for a good-value place to stay.

Visitor attractions

It is estimated that the UK has over 8000 visitor attractions. These range from theme parks and aquariums, to castles and stately homes. Attractions can be either natural or built (man-made). Some are classed as 'heritage attractions'. Visitor attractions can have one or many different roles.

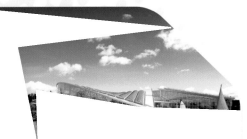

Center Parcs provide a range of lodge-style accommodation in their forest villages. What other facilities do they offer?

Table 1.5: Roles of visitor attractions

Education	The role of museums and visitor centres is to inform and educate visitors about the past, present and future. London has a fantastic selection of over 240 museums which have an educational role, including: • Science Museum • Transport Museum • Imperial War Museum • Design Museum • Bank of England Museum • Theatre Museum • Natural History Museum • London Fire Brigade Museum • Victoria and Albert Museum • Pumphouse Educational Museum • London Bridge Museum
Preservation and protection	Many heritage and conservation attractions are set up in order to preserve and protect destinations, buildings and sites of historic, social or cultural importance. Yorkshire has a variety of visitor attractions that preserve and protect areas of important historical value including: **Fountains Abbey in Ripon:** England's largest monastic ruin, founded in 1132. It is owned by the National Trust and is a designated World Heritage Site. **Saltaire:** A complete purpose-built and well-preserved industrial village built in 1876, named after its founder Sir Titus Salt. Saltaire includes a gallery, and shops, and is a World Heritage Site. **Standedge:** The UK's highest, longest and deepest canal tunnel, on the Huddersfield Narrow Canal. Now fully restored with Heritage Lottery funding, the attraction includes a visitor centre, exhibition and heritage trail. To obtain a secure link to these websites, see the Hotlinks section on p.x.
Entertainment	Some attractions are simply designed for fun and to entertain the visitor, for example theme parks such as Alton Towers, Blackpool Pleasure Beach, Thorpe Park, Drayton Manor and Chessington World of Adventures.

Natural attractions

Natural attractions have not been built by man and are a natural feature of the environment. They include:

- mountains
- caves
- forests.
- beaches
- rivers and lakes

Some destinations might be considered to be a natural attraction such as a national park or area of outstanding natural beauty (AONB).

Activity: What attracts you?

Individually, make a list of any visitor attractions you have visited over the last year. Remember to consider both natural and built attractions.

1 What attracted you to the visitor attraction?

2 What do you think is the main role of each attraction you visited?

3 Now work with a partner and compare your lists. Do you both agree on your findings? Discuss any differences you have found.

Why do people enjoy visiting Stonehenge?

Built attractions

Some built attractions charge an admission fee, while others are free. Built visitor attractions include:

- country parks
- gardens
- leisure/theme parks
- steam/heritage railways
- wildlife attractions/zoos
- places of worship.

- farms
- historic houses/castles
- museums/art galleries
- visitor/heritage centres
- workplaces

Built attractions are man-made; some are purpose-built to attract tourists, while others were originally built for a different purpose, but now also attract visitors.

Key term

World Heritage Site – UNESCO (United Nations Educational, Scientific and Cultural Organisation) designates sites of natural and cultural importance. There are over 890 World Heritage Sites, including 27 in the UK. Examples include Hadrian's Wall, Durham Castle, Tower of London, Kew Gardens, Giant's Causeway and the City of Bath.

Table 1.6: Built attractions

Built especially to attract tourists	Built for another main purpose
Leisure/theme parks	Farms
Country parks	Historic houses/castles
Museums/art galleries	Places of worship
Zoos	Steam/heritage railways

Case study: Stonehenge

Stonehenge is an ancient monument site over 5000 years old. The site is owned and managed by English Heritage and is part of a larger UNESCO **World Heritage Site** (WHS). Stonehenge is a built attraction (originally for another purpose) attracting over 887,000 visitors each year. Access inside the stone circle was stopped in 1978 because of vandalism and erosion due to increasing visitor numbers

Size and ownership

- The Stonehenge WHS covers 6500 acres. Ownership and management of the Stonehenge WHS is shared between English Heritage, the National Trust, the Ministry of Defence, the Royal Society for the Protection of Birds (RSPB), farmers and householders in Amesbury, Larkhill and the Woodford Valley.

- A large part of the landscape surrounding Stonehenge is owned by the National Trust.

Table 1.7: Visitor numbers to Stonehenge (excluding the Solstice and including free education visits and stone circle access)

1961	1971	1980
337 000	550 000	618 000

1990	2000	2008
687 000	790 000	887 000

Source: English Heritage & Stonehenge Complete

1 Do you think that tourists should still be allowed access inside the stone circle?

2 Stonehenge is a built attraction but what was it originally constructed for?

Case study: Association of Leading Visitor Attractions (ALVA)

The Association of Leading Visitor Attractions (ALVA) is made up of 42 members representing the UK's biggest and best known attractions. They are responsible for managing more than 1500 tourist sites that welcome over 100 million domestic and overseas visitors each year.

To be a member of ALVA, the attractions must host over a million visitors per year at their singly or centrally managed sites and be run in line with ALVA's mission statement and quality standards.

ALVA's role

ALVA seeks to represent the views of its members to the government, the travel and tourism sector, the media and the public. It also aims to promote co-operation and high standards of visitor management among its members.

The Association has five main objectives:

1 To stress continually to national and local government the importance of ensuring that tourism interests are fully considered in infrastructure decisions.

2 To encourage and influence national and local government in their funding support for the maintenance, upkeep and further development of visitor attractions, and the fabric of their building and estates.

3 To advise government during its consideration of fiscal and taxation issues which affect member attractions and the tourism industry in general.

4 To demonstrate to both central and local government the cost-effectiveness of the marketing and promotion of tourism, and the importance of adequate public funding of these activities.

5 To exchange information and ideas between members so that presentation, service, customer care, good practice and value for money are maintained at the highest standards.

ALVA members are categorised into five main groups:

- Museums and galleries
- Heritage
- Cathedrals
- Leisure, amusement and theme parks
- Gardens, zoos and conservation sites.

Within these categories some members are public bodies, others are in the private sector. Some charge for admission, while others do not and some operate all year round while others operate seasonally.

Current members include many of the UK's most famous museums, galleries and heritage sites, for example the British Museum, Tate Modern, the National Gallery, Natural History Museum, London Science Museum and the Tower of London.

To obtain a secure link to the ALVA website, see the Hotlinks section on p.x.

1 Identify two reasons why a visitor attraction may join ALVA.

2 Why might a leading visitor attraction choose not to join ALVA?

Activity: Leading attractions

Consider the list of visitor attractions in Table 1.5 on page 21.

1 Which have been built specifically to attract tourists and which were originally built for another main purpose?

2 Which of the attractions are free and which have paid admission?

Heritage attractions

Heritage attractions are those which conserve, protect and celebrate historical and past traditions, events and ways of living and working. Heritage visitor attractions (HVAs) can include castles, stately homes and their gardens, heritage visitor centres, as well as heritage coasts and trails.

Case study: Ironbridge Gorge

Ironbridge Gorge is a UNESCO World Heritage Site. It includes a collection of ten museums which celebrate the 'birth' of the industrial revolution and includes as visitor attractions furnaces, factories and workshops. The heritage site also includes the world's first cast iron bridge built in 1779.

As well as the museums, the site also includes a research library, a Tourist Information Centre, two youth hostels, archaeological sites, historic woodlands, housing, two chapels and two Quaker burial grounds.

1 What are the different roles of Ironbridge Gorge site?

2 Which travel and tourism sector is Ironbridge Gorge part of?

Ironbridge Gorge

Supporting organisations

The UK travel and tourism sector is supported and developed by a range of different local, regional and national organisations.

VisitBritain

VisitBritain is the UK's national tourism agency, promoting the UK to the rest of the world and encouraging domestic tourism in England. Formed in 2003 and funded by the Department for Culture, Media and Sport (DCMS), it works in partnership with thousands of different organisations across the UK.

As well as marketing and promotion, VisitBritain also advises the government on tourism matters, collates statistics and publishes a variety of market intelligence reports.

Enjoy England

Enjoy England is the official tourism board for England and is part of VisitBritain. Enjoy England aim to increase the value of English tourism through marketing and promotional campaigns, such as through TV campaigns and the Enjoy England website. Enjoy England offer information and advice to tourists through their website, carry out research on the UK tourism sector and coordinate the Quality Assurance Schemes for accommodation providers, visitor attractions and spas. To obtain a secure link to this website, see the Hotlinks section on p.x.

Activity: England rocks!

Enjoy England have a series of campaigns to promote all that's best about the country. Using the internet, find out what each of the campaigns listed below are promoting:

- England Rocks
- Taste England
- Rural Escapes.

To obtain a secure link to the Enjoy England website, see the Hotlinks section on p.x

Visit Wales

Visit Wales is the Welsh Assembly government's tourism team, within the Department for Heritage. Visit Wales is responsible for the promotion and development of tourism in Wales.

VisitScotland

VisitScotland is Scotland's national tourist board whose role is to provide a bookings and information service for visitors to Scotland. VisitScotland manages the national website where information and details of accommodation availability are offered to over five million users each year. To obtain a secure link to this website, see the Hotlinks section on p.x.

Northern Ireland Tourist Board

The Northern Ireland Tourist Board (NITB) is part of the Department of Enterprise, Trade and Investment Northern Ireland. It is the body responsible for the development, promotion and marketing of Northern Ireland as a tourist destination. It also advises the Department on tourism development policy.

Regional Tourism Boards

There is a network of Regional Tourist Boards (RTBs) whose role is to develop and promote tourism in their local area. RTBs are often funded through local and county councils, Regional Development Agencies (RDAs) and private tourism businesses.

Ancillary organisations

Ancillary organisations are additional businesses which support travel and tourism. They include restaurants, shops, travel insurance companies, car hire firms, and currency exchange bureaux.

Car hire

Car hire companies provide a range of different size vehicles, from small economy cars to large multi-person carriers. Tourists can hire vehicles for a few weeks or days and some companies even provide an hourly rental service.

Did you know?

England has nine RDAs. Their role is to develop the regional economy and encourage business development. RDAs have had a responsibility for tourism in their regions since 2003. For more information, and to obtain a secure link to the RDA website, see the Hotlinks section on p.x.

Many national hire companies have branches across the country and offer one-way rentals, so you can collect your vehicle from the airport, but drop it off in a different destination.

Examples of national car hire firms include Hertz, Avis, Enterprise and easyCar.com.

Insurance

Domestic insurance companies offer travellers various insurance packages which give them financial protection against accidents and injury, loss or theft of cash, documents and belongings, cancellations of accommodation bookings and journeys. Many transport providers and domestic tour operators are now offering customers additional insurance options at the time of booking. One example is National Express, who offer their customers an optional insurance policy to cover them against personal accident, loss of, or damage to, personal baggage and personal liability, from £1 per journey.

Case study: The Trainline.com and Columbus Direct

The Trainline.com provides a rail ticket booking service for passengers. They work in partnership with Columbus Direct to offer travellers optional insurance for their journey which covers:

- lost or stolen luggage or belongings
- journey cancellation due to accidental injury or illness
- personal accident or assault
- costs resulting from missing or delayed trains.

The cost of insurance cover can be added to the price of a single rail ticket.

What are the advantages of the Trainline.com and Columbus Direct working together in this way?

2.5 Outbound organisations

Outbound travel and tourism organisations provide products and services for outbound tourists.

Tour operators

Like domestic tour operators, outbound operators also arrange holidays and provide a range of discount package deals which can combine accommodation, transport to the destination and ground transport, such as a transfer from the airport to the hotel. Other services, such as excursions, meals and car hire may also be part of the package.

Tour operators are often known as travel wholesalers; they have contracts with accommodation and transport providers and are able to buy large quantities of hotel rooms and flights at a discount. This allows an operator to combine the different elements and sell the packge via travel agencies or direct to the customer, often at a cheaper price than if each component were to be sold separately.

The two largest tour operators in the UK are Thomson Holidays and the Thomas Cook Group.

Case study: Thomson Holidays

Thomson Holidays, a division of TUI UK and Ireland, is part of TUI Travel PLC, a leading international travel group, which operates in 180 countries worldwide. It serves more than 30 million customers and employs more than 50,000 people.

Thomson Holidays are the UK's leading leisure travel retailer and have over 650 retail stores, the Thomson Direct call centre and a website where customers can book and pay for holidays online. Thomson Holidays sell around 5 million holidays and flights a year.

Thomson Holiday's sister company is Thomson Airways, brought together by the merger of Thomsonfly and First Choice Airways. Thomson Airways fly to over 80 worldwide destinations from 23 UK airports. The main Thomson brand also includes several specialist holidays brands including Crystal Holidays, Thomson Ski and Snowboarding and Thomson Lakes and Mountains.

Source: TUI Group 2009

To obtain a secure link to the Thomson and TUI Group websites, see the Hotlinks section on p.x.

1 Using the internet, make a list of all the different UK travel companies and brands that are part of TUI Travel PLC.

2 What are the advantages of the common ownership of all these different companies and brands for the tourist?

Travel agents

Travel agents give advice and sell and administer the bookings for a number of different tour operators. There are an estimated 7 000 travel agency shops in the UK. Some of these agencies have **multiple** branches, while others are **independent** shops. Some larger branches provide a wider range of services, such as foreign currency exchange and arranging airport parking and car hire.

Some online travel agencies operate only on the internet and have no physical outlet on the high street. Examples of online agencies include Expedia, ebookers, Travelocity and Opodo.

Key terms

Multiples – travel agencies which have a large chain of branches, often found on the high street in most large towns and cities, for example Thomas Cook and Thomson Holidays. Due to their size, they can often provide a range of different products and services at discounted rates.

Independents – small, private businesses that have one or a small number of travel agencies, often found in small towns. They are able to offer specialist advice and have a large number of repeat customers.

Transport providers

The UK has a variety of ferry, rail and airline organisations providing transport services to other countries.

Ferries

Despite competition from the Channel Tunnel and budget airlines, there are still many scheduled ferry routes operating out of the UK. Daytime and overnight ferry services run from the Southeast of England to France, Belgium, Spain and the Channel Islands. Services run from Newcastle and Hull to Holland and from the Northwest and Wales to Ireland and the Isle of Man.

Main passenger ferry operators include P&O Ferries, Stena Line, Norfolk Line and Irish Ferries.

There are various different types of ferry, operating at different speeds. Some carry passengers only, although many also carry vehicles. Fast ferries, or catamarans, are water-jet powered and operate at much higher speeds than traditional multi-purpose ferries, providing shorter journey times.

Today's passenger ferries vary enormously in terms of on-board facilities and services. Many larger ferries are similar to small cruise ships, which can include a range of cabin accommodation, shops, restaurants and bars, cinemas, nightclubs, piano lounges and children's play areas.

As well as scheduled passenger services, there are various cruise services operating out of the UK. A cruise is a longer ferry journey to a specific destination and often includes calling at multiple ports, as, for example, on a Mediterranean or Caribbean cruise. Many cruises involve an initial flight to join the cruise ship before travelling on, although it is possible to cruise directly from the UK to Europe, the Mediterranean and across the Atlantic to America and Canada.

Case study: Ulysses

Ulysses is the largest car ferry in the world. Owned by Irish Ferries, Ulysses was built in Finland at a total cost of €100 million. It stands 12 decks high, at a height of 167 ft (51 m) from keel to mast. With almost three miles of parking space for 1342 cars, or 240 articulated trucks, per sailing no other passenger car ferry in the world can match its vehicle-carrying capacity.

Ulysses operates two return sailings between Dublin Port and Holyhead each day with a sailing time of just over three hours. Ulysses can carry up to 2000 passengers and crew on board per sailing.

Ulysses provides passengers with a variety of facilities and services, including shops, restaurants, bars, lounges, cinemas, entertainment centres, a promenade deck and even a walking tour, as well as a range of one and two bed ensuite cabins.

1 What is the role of Irish Ferries?
2 Which travel and tourism sector is Irish Ferries part of?
3 Using the Irish Ferries website, find out which other organisations Irish Ferries work with.

To obtain a secure link to the Irish Ferries website, see the Hotlinks section on p.x.

Outbound rail

The Channel Tunnel opened in 1994 and provides outbound tourists with a direct rail link to continental Europe. The tunnel carries high-speed Eurostar passenger trains and vehicle transport through Eurotunnel.

Eurostar

Eurostar provides direct passenger rail services to France and Belgium from London St. Pancras International. Eurostar runs up to 17 daily services to Paris and ten daily services to Brussels, with journey times from London–Paris around 2 hours 15 minutes, London–Brussels 1 hour 51 minutes and London–Lille 1 hour 20 minutes.

Eurostar launched services from Ebbsfleet International in 2007, located just off the M25 and close to Bluewater Shopping Centre. There are also direct services from London to the gates of Disneyland Resort Paris.

Eurostar offers passengers a range of leisure and business class services and facilities including internet access, a bar and meals service and the use of station lounges.

Activity: All aboard

The St. Jean family wishes to travel directly to Brussels on the Eurostar from St. Pancras International. They are arriving at the station by taxi and would like a flexible ticket in case there is heavy traffic.

1 Research the available train times for the Jean family's journey.
2 Calculate the costs for Standard and Leisure Select tickets for two adults and two children, aged 9 and 14.
3 What are the different services and facilities available with the different types of ticket?

Functional skills

Calculating costs will help you to improve your functional skills in mathematics.

Eurotunnel

Eurotunnel allows tourists to take their car, bikes and caravans across to continental Europe on-board the train. Passengers drive their vehicle directly into air-conditioned carriages and stay with their vehicles throughout the journey. Information screens keep travellers up-to-date with their journey.

Outbound airlines

As with domestic airlines, there are a wide range of organisations providing the outbound UK tourist with transport across the world. While low-cost scheduled airlines generally fly to a variety of **short-haul**, European destinations, other full-service airlines operate **long-haul** flights from the larger airports of London Heathrow, London Gatwick, Manchester and Birmingham International.

Full-service scheduled airlines include British Airways and Virgin Atlantic.

Charter airlines

Unlike scheduled airlines, a chartered flight has been contracted specifically to transport tourists to specific holiday destinations. Tour operators will buy seats on the flight to include in their package holiday deals. Many large tour operators have their own charter airlines in order to offer competitive package deals.

A charter flight often leaves very early in the morning, or late at night, as the fees charged by the airport are often much cheaper at this quieter time. Thomas Cook and Monarch Airlines operate both scheduled and charter flights.

Supporting organisations

There are various supporting organisations that provide a regulation and promotion role for outbound travel and tourism sector businesses.

ABTA – The Travel Association

Formed in 1950 by 22 travel companies, ABTA - The Travel Association, represents over 5000 travel agencies and more than 900 tour operations, throughout the UK. ABTA has both a commercial and regulatory role. It promotes the interests of its members who have to operate to a Code of Conduct produced by the organisation. ABTA members are **bonded** to protect traveller's money in the event of failure of a tour operator or travel agent.

ABTA's main aims are to maintain high standards of trading practice for the benefit of its members, the travel industry and the consumers that they serve. ABTA amalgamated with the Federation of Tour Operators (FTO) in July 2008.

Key terms

Short-haul – an imprecise term meaning flights shorter than three to four hours.

Long-haul – an imprecise term meaning flights longer than three to four hours.

Key term

Bonded – all tour operators and travel organisers must protect their customers by being bonded. This means if they go out of business before you travel, you should get your money back, or, if you are already abroad, you will be able to complete your holiday and return home without further payment.

Civil Aviation Authority

The Civil Aviation Authority (CAA) is the UK's aviation regulator. Its specific responsibilities include air safety, consumer protection, environmental research and airspace regulation.

The CAA also manages the UK's **Air Travel Organisers' Licensing (ATOL) scheme**, licenses UK airlines and manages consumer issues. The CAA also advises the government on aviation issues, represents consumer interests, conducts economic and scientific research and produces statistical data.

Activity: Consumer protection

As a group, discuss the protection that both ABTA membership and the ATOL scheme give to tourists.

1 What benefits do these organisations give to tour operators and travel agents?

2 Do you think holidaymakers are fully aware about both these protection schemes?

Key term

Air Travel Organisers' Licensing (ATOL) scheme – a financial protection scheme managed by the Civil Aviation Authority. All holiday companies in the UK selling flights and holiday packages that include a flight are required by law to hold a licence called an Air Travel Organiser's Licence (ATOL). ATOL protects travellers from losing their money or being stranded abroad by providing a fund to protect customers should a firm fail.

Ancillary organisations

As with domestic organisations, there are a variety of ancillary organisations which support outbound travel and tourism organisations, including car hire and insurance companies.

Examples of organisations providing travel insurance to outbound travellers can be found at Insure and Go, Columbus Direct, Direct-Travel and Atlas Direct. To obtain a secure link to these websites, see the Hotlinks section on p.x.

Other ancillary organisations can also offer outbound UK tourists other services, such as airport parking, access to airport lounges, tours and excursions and tickets for theatre shows and attractions.

2.6 Inbound organisations

Inbound travel and tourism organisations provide products and services for overseas visitors to the UK. They include tour operators, coach operators and guiding services, as well as support organisations, such as VisitBritain, which promote the UK overseas to inbound tourists.

Tour operators and guiding services

Some UK tour operators can organise travel services for groups of inbound tourists. After tourists have arrived by plane, these organisations can organise transfers, accommodation, tours, itineraries, events and entertainment options for them.

Many itineraries are created for specialist interests such as religion, education, music, literature, the monarchy and heritage. Tour operators offering inbound tourist services include Kuoni, Miki Travel and Gullivers Travel Associates.

Coach operators

A UK coach operator may well be one of the first UK travel and tourism organisations used by a group of inbound tourists arriving in the UK. Coach operators can provide a range of transport options for inbound tourists ranging from simple airport-to-accommodation transfers, to full tours of the UK using vehicles ranging from small seven-seat people carriers up to executive double-deck luxury coaches with around 80 seats. Many coaches now come equipped with a variety of services and facilities to provide comfort and convenience on longer journeys, including toilets, video/DVD players, refrigerators, tea and coffee facilities, reclining seats and air-conditioning.

There are hundreds of UK coach operators which provide services to UK inbound tourists. These operators may also be members of a supporting organisation such as the Guild of British Coach Operators or the Coach Tourism Council. To obtain a secure link to these websites, see the Hotlinks section on p.x.

Supporting organisations

UKinbound

UKinbound is a trade association founded in 1977 which represents the interests of the UK's inbound tourism businesses. Originally known as BITOA (British Incoming Tour Operators Association), UKinbound now have around 250 members, including guiding and tour organisers, accommodation providers, destination marketing companies, visitor attractions and other organisations that provide cultural, sporting and leisure activities for inbound tourists.

VisitBritain

VisitBritain promotes the UK to the rest of the world, encouraging inbound tourists to choose the UK as their next destination. VisitBritain has a network of overseas offices which help to publicise the features and attractions of the UK to overseas travellers. They also provide an advice and information service for those planning their visit to the UK and organise a series of events to help promote the UK abroad.

VisitBritain has won many awards for their work in promoting the UK as a tourist destination, including:

* World Travel Awards: World's Leading Tourism Authority Website: VisitBritain.com

* Group Travel Awards: Best On-Line Information

* The Times Online: Best Tourist Board Twitter Site

As well as developing the 'Britain brand', VisitBritain aim to:

* inspire travellers from overseas to visit and explore the UK

* deliver a global network to support tourism promotion overseas

* champion tourism and engage industry and Government in support of its growth

* maximise the tourism legacy benefits of the 2012 Olympic and Paralympic Games.

Meet England

Meet England is the official body responsible for promoting England as a meetings and events destination for business tourists. They provide advice and information on destinations, venues and travel arrangements for those organising conferences, exhibitions and events in the country.

Regional Tourism Boards

The network of Regional Tourist Boards (RTBs) helps to reinforce the work of VisitBritain and Meet England, by encouraging inbound tourists to visit a particular region of the UK. South West Tourism, for example, is the official Regional Tourist Board which works to encourage the development of tourism in Bath, Bristol, Bournemouth/Poole, Cornwall and the Isles of Scilly, Devon, Dorset, Somerset, Gloucestershire and Wiltshire.

Ancillary organisations

As with domestic and outbound tourism, there are a variety of ancillary organisations which support inbound travel and tourism organisations, including car hire companies such as Enterprise, easyCar and National. To obtain a secure link to these websites, see the Hotlinks section on p.x.

Assessment activity 1.2

P3 P4 M2 D1

In this assignment you will demonstrate your knowledge and understanding of the role of organisations within the UK travel and tourism sector and the types of inter-relationships between different travel and tourism organisations, why they exist and the benefits of these relationships.

You should create a presentation which covers the following information:

1 Outline the roles of the different types of organisation in the UK travel and tourism sector. **P3**

2 Describe the different types of inter-relationship between travel and tourism organisations. **P4**

3 Analyse the inter-relationships between organisations in the travel and tourism sector. **M2**

4 Evaluate the positive aspects of inter-relationships on UK travel and tourism organisations. **D1**

You should keep a record of your research notes and submit a copy of your presentation with your final assignment submission. Your tutor will complete an observation record of your performance.

Grading tips

- **P3** Have you given examples of each type of domestic, outbound and inbound organisation? Have you provided examples from both the public and private sector throughout your presentation?

- **M2** Have you explained how and why organisations in the travel and tourism sector inter-relate? Make sure you cover both types of inter-relationships (working together and common ownership) and cover all categories of organisation (domestic, outbound and inbound).

- **P4** You must give at least two examples of each type of inter-relationships. You should

give enough examples to include domestic, outbound and inbound organisations.

- **P4** and **M2** You should support your evidence with printouts of the details of the packages and any other relevant information.

- **D1** You should give an evaluation of at least two positive aspects of inter-relationships of organisations, covering working together and common ownership. Where possible you should support your in-depth evaluation with additional information such as articles, data and statistics.

PLTS

Exploring the roles of different types of organisations in the travel and tourism sector will help to develop your skills as an **independent enquirer**.

Functional skills

This actually gives you the opportunity to develop your **ICT** and **English** skills by searching for, and recording, different information sources regarding the roles of different types of organisations in the travel and tourism sector.

Ben Townsend

Tourist Information Assistant

I work in a busy Tourist Information Centre (TIC) dealing with a wide range of enquiries from members of the public. We help domestic tourists visiting the city just for the day or for a short-break as well as many visitors from overseas, who are travelling around the country and visiting the city as part of their tour.

We also get enquiries from business travellers and those visiting the local university for a conference or event. The best thing about my job is that no two days are ever the same. We get asked a lot of similar questions but you can never know what someone will ask when they call, email or visit the centre.

My main duties include:

- answering enquiries from visitors to the city either in person, over the telephone, by letter or by email
- booking accommodation
- selling a range of products and keeping the shelves fully stocked
- finding out train and bus times for visitors and booking tickets
- representing the city at trade shows and tourism events
- making attractive displays to promote local events and attractions.

Typical day

A typical day for me involves arriving at the TIC 30 minutes before we open to make sure the office is ready to welcome visitors. I open the post, make sure the shelves are fully stocked with leaflets and brochures and that all posters are displayed clearly.

I spend most of the morning dealing face to face with enquiries from visitors to the TIC. I also answer any telephone enquiries and deal with email requests in quieter periods.

The afternoon is often spent ordering leaflets and brochures and making sure the retail items for sale are fully stocked and displayed clearly.

Think about it!

1 Staff working in the TIC deal with a variety of domestic and inbound tourists and their enquiries. In small groups, make a list of the organisations that your local tourist office works with. Are they in the public or private sector?

2 Consider why your local TIC has relationships with other organisations in the travel and tourism sector. Explain the positive aspects of having these inter-relationships.

Just checking

1 Name the three main types of tourism.
2 Complete the table (below) to give an example for each reason that people travel.

Reasons why people travel	Example
Leisure	
Business	
VFR	

3 Define the term Gross Domestic Product (GDP).
4 Why is outbound tourism spending not included in a country's GDP value?
5 Around how many jobs in the UK are directly linked to tourism?
6 Describe the difference between the public and private sector.
7 Identify four different types of accommodation provider.
8 Name the two largest UK tour operators.
9 Describe the role of the Civil Aviation Authority (CAA).
10 Describe the role of VisitBritain
11 Identify two travel and tourism organisations that work together. Explain why they do this.
12 Identify one benefit of a tour operator joining and working together with the Federation of Tour Operators (FTO).

Assignment tips

- Remember to write your assignments in your own words. When you use other sources of information, make sure you clearly acknowledge where the information is from.

- Make sure you include examples of travel and tourism organisations from different sectors.

- Remember not to put too much information on your presentation slides.

- Practice your presentation with a friend and make a note of what you need to develop.

- Try not to read from your presentation slides. You may find it helpful to create prompt cards to remind you of key points.

- Use a variety of different information sources when completing your assignment, not just the internet.

- Keep copies of all your research, so you can provide evidence with your assignments.

2 Understanding customer service in travel and tourism

Travel and tourism is about people, all of whom have customer service needs and expectations. They may be travelling on business, or on holiday, or for other personal reasons. You, and the organisation you work for, provide the dreams and experiences for your customers. That's a really exciting and satisfying role to play in people's lives.

To meet the needs and desires of their customers, organisations have to make sure the products and services their customers receive give full satisfaction and even exceed expectations. There are many competitors in the travel and tourism sector, often providing very similar products at similar prices. It is the service the customer receives that will make them decide whether to buy from your organisation and, importantly, come back again for further business.

In this unit you will explore how different types of organisations approach customer service and you will investigate the systems and processes that are available to support the delivery of customer service.

Learning outcomes

After completing this unit you should:

1 understand different approaches to customer service in travel and tourism organisations

2 understand the needs and expectations of different types of customer in the travel and tourism sector.

Assessment and grading criteria

This table shows you what you must do in order to achieve a pass, merit or distinction grade, and where you can find activities in this book to help you.

To achieve a **pass** grade the evidence must show that you are able to:	To achieve a **merit** grade the evidence must show that, in addition to the pass criteria, you are able to:	To achieve a **distinction** grade the evidence must show that, in addition to the pass and merit criteria, you are able to:
P1 explain how different types of organisation approach customer service (IE1, IE2) **Assessment activities 2.1, 2.3, pages 52 and 57**	**M1** compare how two travel and tourism organisations approach and measure customer service **Assessment activity 2.3, page 57**	**D1** analyse how approaches to customer service link to the success of meeting and exceeding customer needs and expectations **Assessment activity 2.6, page 72**
P2 describe the methods used to measure and monitor customer service **Assessment activities 2.2, 2.3, pages 56 and 57**		
P3 review the needs of different types of customer and how they are recognised **Assessment activities 2.4, 2.6, pages 68 and 70**	**M2** analyse how organisations meet and exceed customer needs and expectations of customers through the recognition of their needs **Assessment activity 2.6, page 72**	
P4 explain how travel and tourism organisations meet and exceed customer expectations **Assessment activities 2.5, 2.6, pages 70 and 72**		

Selena, 17–year-old learner

This unit really helped me understand what customer service is all about. I realised it doesn't just happen; organisations have to truly understand their customers – who they are and what they need – and decide how they want to operate. Then they have to put processes and resources into place to make it happen. Their staff have to be willing and able to deliver excellent service to their customers.

I enjoyed learning from some real examples of how customer service is delivered. It was great to use examples I have personally experienced and compare them with others in my class.

The activities and case studies gave me plenty of opportunities to think about the subject. I found it really useful to work on some practical examples, sometimes on my own and sometimes in small groups. This prepared me for the assessment activities. Having completed this unit, I felt much more confident about moving on to the next unit to develop my customer service skills.

Over to you

- What skills and experience do you think you can use in this unit?

- Which parts of this unit do you think will be the most interesting and useful for you?

- Which parts of this unit do you think will be most challenging for you?

1. Different approaches to customer service in travel and tourism organisations

Set off

What is customer service?

1 In a small group, list as many words and phrases as you can think of to describe *good* customer service.

2 Then list as many words and phrases as you can think of to describe *bad* customer service.

What is customer service?

In this section you will look at different types and sizes of organisation, their policies, processes and resources, and how these will affect the **customer** service they provide. First you need to ask a very important question: *What is customer service?*

Every day you experience customer service. It may be when you buy something in a shop, travel on a bus, or go to a swimming pool or a music festival. Most of the time you may not even notice the service you have been given. Sometimes you will notice the service given because it is really bad or especially good.

Key term

Customer – somebody who receives customer service from a service deliverer. A customer may be a person, but may be an organisation. An internal customer comes from another part of the same organisation as the provider.

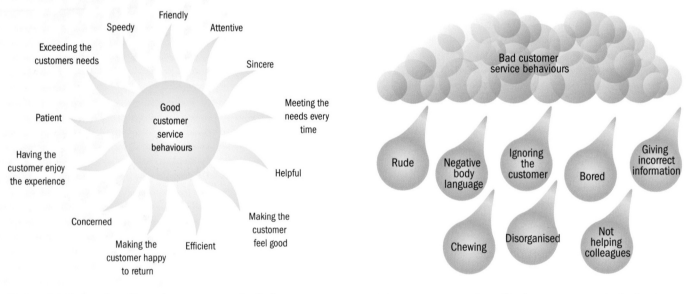

Figure 2.1: Examples of good customer service behaviours

Figure 2.2: Examples of bad customer service behaviours

The Institute of Customer Service defines customer service as 'the sum total of what an organisation does to meet customer expectations and produce customer satisfaction'.

Customer service is only possible if everyone in an organisation, (whether or not they have direct contact with the customer), aims to give customer satisfaction. A cruise line cannot give excellent service unless:

- the reservations staff are accurate when taking the bookings
- the ship's engineers are good at maintaining and operating the engines
- the captain and his crew sail the ship well
- the stores staff order sufficient food, drink and other supplies
- the cooks prepare excellent meals
- the operations staff make proper arrangements for the ship and its passengers when calling in at ports.

Activity: Meeting customer expectations

In pairs, or on your own, think about the customer service definition offered by the Institute of Customer Service. Is it sufficient to just 'meet' customer expectations? Justify your answer.

Three components of customer service

The three components of customer service are:

- **The product or service** – this is the item you are buying. It may be accommodation at a hotel, a flight, or a visit to a castle. Does it give you what you expected?

- **The process** – this is the process and procedures you had to use to buy and use the product. It might be how you were able to select and purchase your product, for example, by visiting a travel agent or using the internet. It might also be how you could use the product, for example could you check-in for your flight by using the internet, by using a self-service kiosk at the airport, or by going to a check-in desk?

- **The personal behaviour** – this is the human behaviour of the people you had dealings with when buying or using the product.

Did you know?

A survey asked people why they had stopped using products. Some respondents said it was because the product didn't meet their needs anymore, while others said it was because they didn't like the processes and procedures they had to use to buy and use the product. However, 70% of respondents said it was because of the behaviour of the person with whom they were dealing.

Activity: What is your customer service story?

Work in small groups on this activity. Think about examples of good and bad customer service experiences you have had and then select one. Share your experiences with your group.

Discuss whether it is an example of:

- good or bad product
- good or bad process and procedures
- good or bad personal behaviour
- or a combination of some or all of the components.

Customer service is important because:

- You want customers to be so pleased with you that they keep buying your products and services.
- You have to keep your customers away from your competitors.
- It can cost five times as much to win a new customer as it does to keep an existing one.
- Customers tell others of their good, or bad, customer experiences. Unfortunately, they are more likely to tell others of their bad experiences.
- Your organisation needs to compete on value rather than just price, i.e. customers are prepared to pay more for your product or service.
- Your organisation needs to be secure and be able to develop, and so do you.
- You want the buzz you get out of providing excellent customer service!

1.1 Organisations

The travel and tourism sector ranges from giant organisations with integrated businesses to small independent companies, and from those which supply the main goods and services to those which supply the support services. These include:

- transport operators, for example air, sea, rail and road
- accommodation, for example hotels, villas, campsites and holiday centres.
- attractions, for example theme parks, heritage sites and activity centres.
- secondary services, for example insurance, airport representatives, tourist offices and passport offices.

Did you know?

- Small-sized enterprises are organisations with a staff headcount of fewer than 50 people and annual turnover or (alternatively) annual balance sheet not exceeding €10m.
- Medium-sized enterprises are organisations with a staff headcount between 50 and 249 people and annual turnover not exceeding €50m or (alternatively) annual balance sheet not exceeding €43m.

Source: European Commission Definition (2005)

Size of the organisation

The size of the organisation, i.e. small, medium or large, may also have an impact upon the way it provides customer service.

Small organisations may have a **niche market** and know many of their clients as regular customers, which helps give a more personal style of customer service. Large organisations may depend more upon systems to help provide customer service but, with the right approach and staff who have a real desire to provide excellent care to their customers, they can still provide a personal style of service.

Types of organisation

Independent organisations are those organisations with just one, or a few, bases for example an independent travel agency might have up to five shops, but they are usually located in a small region of the country. They may know their clients well and offer a very personalised service.

Integrated organisations are those organisations, for example, tour operators, which integrate services vertically and horizontally. This gives them control over each level of the product they market. It also leads to an underlying consistency in the style and level of customer service across that integrated group. Integrating services vertically and horizontally will be examined further in *Unit 4: Development of the UK travel and tourism sector.*

The *private sector* is the commercial part of industry that exists to make a profit for its owners or shareholders. Private organisations make up the bulk of the organisations in the travel and tourism sector.

The *public sector* is non-commercial, which means it does not aim to make a profit, but rather to provide a service or to educate. Central, regional, or local government form the public sector and sometimes own and run attractions such as parks, museums, and tourist offices.

The *voluntary sector* is non-commercial and includes such organisations as the National Trust, English Heritage, and the Youth Hostel Association. These organisations rely upon donations and entrance fees and are often staffed by volunteers.

The same customer service principles apply whether the organisation is independent, integrated, privately or publicly owned, a public service or a voluntary organisation and whether the service is provided face to face, through the telephone or via a website.

1.2 Policies

Every organisation decides what its policies will be. These will be the guiding principles for everything which the organisation does. They will help decide on such things as what to sell, to whom, where and how, as well as how the organisation will interact with its customers, staff and general public.

Key term

Niche market – narrowly defined group of customers; a small but profitable section of the market.

Key term

Mission statement – a concise statement about an organisation's purpose. Mission statements vary, but usually contain information about products, services, beliefs and values.

Mission statements

Mission statements describe an organisation's purpose and values. They answer the question 'Why do we exist?' Mission statements have a major influence upon the strategy in an organisation, including the levels and styles of customer service, for example an airline with the mission statement of being a computer-led business with little face to face staff contact with passengers, may decide on a policy of only accepting website bookings and having self-service check-in at airports.

This would require a different customer service approach to, for example an airline with the mission of being the friendliest airline with staff available at every point of the passengers' travels. The first airline would invest in technology and procedures which would enable passengers to do things for themselves; the latter airline would invest in selecting and training customer caring staff, with procedures to support them. This does not mean one is better than the other, it just identifies that there is more than one way to meet customers' needs.

Case study: A selection of travel and tourism mission statements

Asperion Guest House, Surrey

'We aim to create a high-quality guest experience that is ethical, sustainable and rewarding.'

Virgin Atlantic

'To grow a profitable airline where people love to fly and people love to work.'

Merlin Entertainments Group

'The delivery to our visitors of high-quality, memorable visitor experiences.'

What similarities and differences do you notice in these mission statements?

What did you notice about the different mission statements? Asperion Guest House and Merlin Entertainments Group both value 'high-quality'. Asperion Guest House has ethical values and, together with Merlin Entertainments Group, wants their customers to have 'experiences'. Virgin Atlantic identifies profit as a mission, but also wants customers and staff loving the airline.

All the mission statements tell you something about why they exist (their purpose) and their values (what is important to them). This will affect their strategies (plans, policies and approach).

Key term

Customer charter – a statement of standards and/or procedures that a business agrees will govern the relationship between itself and its customers. A charter can establish standards of service delivery, provision of information to customers, consultation processes, and complaint or dispute resolution mechanisms.

Customer service policy

Many organisations describe their customer service policies in **customer charters**. These might include:

- what information the organisation will provide, how it will provide it, and when

- the performance levels they will aim for, for example punctuality and quality
- their payment and refund policies
- what they will do in the event of a disruption to arrangements, for example delays and cancellations
- the compensation they will provide.

Case study: A customer service commitment

Thomas Cook Airlines have a Customer Service Commitment charter with the following section headings:

- encourage tour operators to offer the lowest fares available for our flights
- honour the agreed fare that has been paid in full
- give customers notice of known delays, cancellations and diversions
- help customers facing delays
- deliver baggage as quickly as possible
- help customers who have special needs, or who need help getting around

- meet customers' essential needs during long delays on aircraft
- try to speed up check-in
- reduce the number of customers not allowed to board
- give customers information on our 'conditions of carriage'
- provide information on carriers
- respond to customers' complaints.

Choose three of these headings. If you were the Customer Service Manager for Thomas Cook Airlines, what processes, or procedures, would you put in place to enable these commitments to be met?

Complaint policy

Organisations want to meet, or exceed, the expectations of their customers. Sometimes they don't achieve it. It is important that organisations handle complaints professionally and fairly. If a customer has had their complaint resolved to their satisfaction, they can be even more loyal to the organisation than someone who has not had cause to complain.

Organisations should make their complaints policy clear to their customers. In that way, the customers know how to complain and what the organisation will do, together with any limitations.

1.3 Processes interaction between the customer and the organisation

The relationship the customer has with the organisation will partly depend upon the interactions between them. This includes the **processes** the organisation uses and the human interaction.

Key term

Processes – tasks and activities needed to accomplish a specific goal.

How an organisation expects its customers to buy and use its products and services also affects the style of customer service it gives them and the amount of human interaction it has with them.

Customer interface

Organisations can interface with their customers in a number of ways:

- *Face to face*: examples of face to face interaction could include a travel consultant in a travel shop, an information assistant in a tourist office, a purser on a cruise ship, or a holiday rep at an overseas resort.

- *Remotely*: many large organisations interface with their customers through call centres. Call centres are large offices in which a company's employees provide information to its customers, or sell or advertise its goods and services by telephone. Imagine working in a tour operator's reservations call centre. The people who call you may not have a brochure, may not have been to that destination or taken that kind of holiday before. You will need to give accurate and honest information to them in an enticing way, so that they decide to buy the holiday from you.

- *I.T. based*: many organisations partially, or totally, depend upon the internet to provide customer service. Increasing numbers of customers are researching information on travel destinations and booking their inclusive holidays, travel arrangements, or accommodation by using the internet. Very few travel and tourism organisations now do not have a website. The design of them and how 'user-friendly' they are, is often critical to an organisation's success.

Case study: Checking-in

Ryanair have withdrawn check-in desks at airports. Passengers must now check-in online, at a cost of £5 per passenger per flight. On-line check-in is available up to four hours before departure. Passengers arriving at the airport without a boarding card must pay a £40 'boarding card re-issue' fee.

What are the customer service advantages and disadvantages of these processes?

Keeping records

Your organisation needs to keep records so that it can operate its business efficiently and effectively. Your customer needs you to keep records about them.

Increasingly, the customer's booking is recorded on a computer. The information will be sent to those who need to take action, for example a customer booking an inclusive holiday will need details of their booking forwarded to the airline to reserve the seats; the hotel to reserve the accommodation; the ground transport company to arrange transfers; the insurers to arrange travel insurance, and so on.

The information must also be available to other departments in your organisation to make arrangements for tickets to be issued and invoices to be sent. Documentation, whether in paper form or computerised, is necessary both for the customer and the organisation. It may include booking forms, customers' records, tickets, invoices, receipts, health and safety records, and records of communications with the customers, contractors and other departments.

Documentation and record keeping needs great care and accuracy as much of it is required, or affected, by legislation, for example the **Data Protection Act 1998** and the **Health and Safety at Work Act 1974**.

Reacting to feedback

Feedback from customers to an organisation, whether it is positive or negative, is important. Your organisation needs to know what it is doing well, what it is not doing so well, and what it needs to improve. Without feedback an organisation cannot improve the services it provides to its customers.

Unfortunately, most people who are unhappy with an organisation don't tell them, they just stop buying from them. If only the organisation had encouraged feedback, they might have been able to keep those customers, and avoided upsetting future customers as well.

Sometimes, it may be that the organisation has provided exactly what it planned to provide, but it no longer suits their customers. Customers build their expectations on experience. If they had a new, good experience, they will want it again. If the customers' circumstances have changed, so might their expectations of your organisation, e.g. if their young children are now teenagers, they will want something different from their holidays. If the situation nationwide has changed, so might the customers' expectations, e.g. if there is a national downturn in the economy, customers may seek cheaper flights and accept they will get a lower service level, like charges for hold-baggage or no in-flight food.

Some organisations are passive and just wait for feedback. Others are proactive and encourage customers and staff to give feedback. Which do you think is the wisest?

Increasing loyalty

Customers must feel that your organisation is a good one to do business with and the organisation must do everything it can to keep all of its customers. Organisations can increase customer loyalty by ensuring the three components of customer service are delivered every time:

- The *product* needs to be what the customer wants, for example a hotel they want to stay in.

Key terms

The Data Protection Act – protects customers' personal data with regard to processing and safe storage of their information.

The Health and Safety at Work Act – ensures that environments are safe and free from hazards for employers, employees and customers.

Case study: Cruise with friends

Saga Cruises cater for those aged 50 or over. They have a loyalty club called Britannia, which has a four-tier membership: bronze, silver, gold, and sapphire. Members move up through the tiers as the number of nights they have cruised for increases. Sapphire members having cruised for more than 500 nights.

Britannia members are given the opportunity to get the lowest rates offered before they are made available to the public. The benefits increase the further up the tiers you go. They include dedicated check-in desks, priority embarkation and disembarkation, discounts for on-board purchases, and free dry cleaning and laundry.

Sapphire members receive all these benefits, plus a chauffeur driven car to, and from, the ship from as far afield as 250 miles, a free cocktail party for up to 16 people and a half-price 16-night cruise.

In small groups discuss:

1 Why would Britannia members like to buy a cruise exclusive to their loyalty club?

2 Why would benefits that sapphire members receive be seen as a benefit?

3 What benefits might you offer loyal customers if you worked for a train company or a hotel?

- The *processes* need to be as hassle-free as possible for the customer, providing choice for them, for example letting them check-in for a ferry crossing through a website.
- **Personal behaviour** needs to be excellent, for example by showing a genuine interest in the customer's comments about the tour they are on.

Many organisations reward their customers for their loyalty and there are many ways they can do this. A common example is that organisations run 'Clubs' for their loyal customers providing facilities such as:

- priority booking
- special reservations and customer service telephone numbers
- guaranteed seat selection
- cabin or car upgrades
- lounges
- club magazines
- discounts on future bookings.

Staff training

Customer service doesn't just happen. An organisation needs to operate and behave in a particular way to deliver its services well. One way to help deliver its services is through continuous investment in staff, to ensure they are *able* to give excellent service and they *want* to give it. That means caring for staff, including providing training which will develop their customer service knowledge and skills – just as this course is aiming to do for you.

Training starts with induction training which all staff receive within the first few days of starting their employment. It is likely to include briefings on legal aspects such as health and safety, on the organisation itself and how it operates and behaves, and training on the general aspects of the job.

Specific training needs also have to be met, not only when staff join the organisation, but also when products, systems or **procedures** change. Such ongoing training refreshes staff, making sure they are up-to-date and can improve their skills and knowledge.

There will also be opportunities for promotion, so developmental training is also valuable to prepare staff for those opportunities. Once promoted, staff will probably have specific training needs again, and so it continues!

If staff experience planned and ongoing training, not only will they improve, but they will also feel more valued and become more loyal to their organisation.

Customer after sales service

Many travel and tourism purchases are made and paid for well before they are used. People book holidays possibly up to a year ahead and business people often book their business trips weeks in advance. So, customer after sales service often starts before the customer has used the product or service they purchased.

Additional purchases might be made later, or changing circumstances may require arrangements to be cancelled or amended. Holidaymakers may book their holidays and later decide they also want to book some tours or hire a car. A businesswoman may find she has to change her travel and hotel arrangements because business meetings have changed. Someone may need to cancel because they are ill, a close relative has died, etc.

After sales service is sometimes provided by call centre staff who will be knowledgeable about how changes can be made and what restrictions there might be.

> **Key term**
>
> **Procedures** – these are a series of steps taken to accomplish a result, for example the driver's procedure for accommodating a passenger in a wheelchair on a coach might use the processes of (i) opening the door, (ii) lowering the floor, (iii) assisting the passenger in wheelchair to the wheelchair position on the coach, (iv) securing safety belts to the wheelchair.

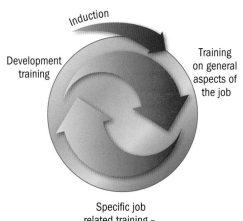

Figure 2.3: Training on a roll

> How can customer after sales service be provided by call centre staff?

Having taken their holiday or business trip, the customer may wish to comment on their experience. Most organisations will accept comments by whatever means the customer wishes, for example by phone (perhaps to a call centre), email, letter, or a personal visit. A few organisations are very restrictive about how they will accept comments and within what time frame. For example, some airlines will only accept complaints in writing, some only by email. Claims for baggage damage are often required to be made in writing within 7 days.

Activity: Customer service through processes

In pairs, choose a local travel and tourism organisation to visit. Design a worksheet under the following headings:

- keeping records
- reacting to feedback
- increasing loyalty
- staff training
- after sales service.

Visit your chosen organisation and discover what processes it has under each of these headings. Record your observations and comments on your worksheet.

In pairs, discuss how effective you think the processes are in providing customer service. What other processes do you think the organisation could have to improve their customer service?

Share your findings with the rest of your class and/or your tutor.

1.4 Resources

Once an organisation has decided upon its policies and processes, it needs to put resources into place.

Staffing

An organisation's decision about its mission statement and policies will have shaped many of its staffing decisions, such as how many staff to employ and with what abilities and temperament. Decisions will need to be made about whether an organisation needs their employees to have relevant qualifications (and if so what type) and previous experience.

Activity: Horses for courses

You are employed by a tour operator and have been assigned to work with the Human Resource Manager as part of your development training. She has asked you to design part of a careers brochure for distribution to schools and colleges. You have to write a brief paragraph describing two roles in your organisation: (i) an I.T. programmer (a day job) and (ii) an overseas resort rep (a shift job). For each of the jobs state the following requirements:

- academic qualifications

- experience
- skills
- personal attributes and temperament
- personal circumstances.

Review what you have written. Are there any differences in your two sets of requirements? Justify the differences between them. Which of the requirements are essential and which are desirable?

When organisation recruit new staff they will usually consider:

- Academic qualifications: the formal qualifications gained at college for example a *BTEC Level 2 First Travel and Tourism*.

- Experience: the knowledge gained as a result of work or personal activity, for example Saturday hotel housekeeping assistant.

- Skills: the abilities and expertise someone has, for example repairing computers, writing reports, organising events.

- Personal attributes: the characteristics and qualities someone has, for example imaginative, analytical, friendly, calm temperament.

- Personal circumstances: the situation or state of affairs necessary for the job, for example must live within 30 minutes of the workplace, must be in possession of a UK work permit.

The organisation's approach to staff

If you want your staff to treat your customers well, you must treat your staff well. They must feel valued and motivated. Sometimes it is assumed that as long as staff get adequate pay, all will be well. Wrong!

Money is just one type of reward. Here are some of the ways in which staff can feel valued and willing to perform even better:

- give staff responsibility

- recognise them when they do a job well

- give them support, guidance and training to help them do their job better and to develop their career

- ask them what they think about their organisation and what can be improved (and take action on what staff say)

- improve their working conditions (perhaps refurbishing their restroom)

- have the occasional celebration (perhaps when the first 1000 holidays have been sold or when it is someone's birthday).

Notice that most of these examples cost little or no money.

Activity: How can I reward you?

Think of three more ways in which organisations in the travel and tourism sector reward their staff.

Financial budgets

Organisations need money to provide a customer service focused business. It costs money to provide and train staff, support staff reward schemes, provide uniforms etc. These costs will be recovered by the extra business which will come from looking after customers and staff well.

Did you know?

A leading management thinker, Frederick Herzberg, studied what made people want to work. His view was that there were maintenance factors such as pay, supervision and procedures which caused dissatisfaction when they fell below acceptable levels, but they didn't motivate people to work. The true motivators came from achievement, personal development, job satisfaction and recognition.

Did you know?

Many organisations conduct staff surveys, to discover their staff's opinions. Issues they ask about might cover their views on:

- how well the organisation supports them in giving customer service

- what is being done well

- what they would like more/less of

- what they are concerned about.

This information enables the organisations to understand what is important to staff, and to meet those needs.

BTEC Assessment activity 2.1 (P1)

You have been asked to carry out research for an article which will examine organisational approaches to customer service in the travel and tourism sector.

1 In preparation for that research, select six travel and tourism organisations across the small, medium and large sized range. Design a grid which identifies, for each organisation:

- whether it is independent, integrated, private, public, or voluntary

- its major method(s) of customer interface.

2 Using those organisations as examples write an article which:

- explains how different mission statements influence the policies and processes which organisations put in place to provide customer service

- explains how resources can be used effectively to provide good customer service.

Grading tips (P1)

- Select your six organisations carefully as they will be the source of your research for the rest of this assessment. Ensure they will be able to provide you with the breadth and depth of information you need.

- Use the European Union (EU) definition when deciding upon size. It is sufficient for the purposes of this activity to just use the headcount measure.

- Make sure that you cover all aspects of *Organisations, Policies, Processes* and *Resources*, about which you have learned so far in this unit.

PLTS

Undertaking research will develop your ability as an **independent enquirer** and **self-manager**. As you write your article, you will develop skills as a **creative thinker** and **reflective learner**.

Functional skills

This assessment activity will develop your skills in using **ICT** systems to find and select information, and develop, present and communicate information, as well as your skills in reading and writing **English**.

1.5 Measuring and monitoring customer service

Activity: What do they think of our customer service?

In small groups, think of as many ways as you can of how organisations can discover what customers think of their customer service.

To assess the quality of customer service provided, organisations must:

- discover what their customers consider are important customer service factors, so that they know what to measure

- monitor their customer service to make sure it is what the customers want, and to the level that they want it

- encourage feedback from their customers, otherwise they will not learn what has gone wrong and will not get the chance to put it right.

Detailed below are some feedback methods.

Comment cards

In its simplest form, a comment card just gives the customer the opportunity to write a compliment or a complaint. This is called qualitative feedback because it will tell you about the customer's feelings or concerns about your service. It might be about a specific incident and need investigation and a response to the customer.

Comment cards may be displayed at the point of sale, for example on the travel consultant's desk in a travel agency, or at the point of use, for example in a hotel bedroom. Sometimes customers may need to ask for them, for example a passenger might ask a cabin crew member for a comment card during their flight.

Customer service questionnaires

Questionnaires are a development of comment cards. They are designed to capture more measurable data. This is called quantitative feedback because it can be measured.

An organisation should first understand what is important to their customers, so that they ask the right questions. There is little point in a hotel asking *Which colour sheets do you prefer?* if that isn't important to its customers. However, it may be valuable to ask *Do you want a minibar in your room?*

When creating a questionnaire, the main criteria should be broken down into specific detail so that decisions can be made on *what* is to be measured and *how*, for example 'Cleanliness' might be a main section. One part of that section could be 'Cleanliness of bedroom'. That might be further broken down into items to be measured, for example 'carpet clean; windows and mirrors mark-free; waste bins empty'. These could be measured by observation and graded, (e.g. 1 to 5 with 1 being very poor and 5 being excellent). In this way, performance can be measured and large quantities of customer service questionnaires can be analysed.

There are many ways in which questionnaires can be provided to customers. They could be:

- handed out by staff, for example by holiday representatives for completion on the homebound flight

- in reading material, for example in in-flight magazines or on display in hotel bedrooms

- through the organisation's website or by email.

Mystery shoppers

Mystery shoppers are employed to visit organisations and report on their experiences of them. The mystery shopper may be employed by that organisation, or by another organisation such as a newspaper or a local authority monitoring a number of organisations. The mystery shopper may be checking on the procedures and standards relating to selling the product or checking on the actual product or service, for example they may stay in a hotel to experience the accommodation, catering and other services.

Travel Trains

Travel Trains welcomes your feedback.

Please tell us of your travel experience with us today.

I was on the 0915 train from Kings Dutton to Stoke Fixton today. Your train conductor George Gould was really charming and helpful. He told me where I would find my bus stop at Stoke Fixton and helped me with my luggage when we arrived. He was interested in why I was travelling today and waved me a cheerful goodbye when we reached Stoke Fixton. Please pass on my compliments to him and to his manager.

Thank you.

Please provide us with your name and contact details so that we can reply to you, which we aim to do within seven days.

Name: *Rachel Head*

Address: *12, The Street, Kings Dutton*

Telephone number:

Email:

Date: *10 April 2010*

Figure 2.4: How can comment cards benefit an organisation?

Case study: Wales mystery shoppers find holiday whoppers

'Nearly a third of North Wales travel agents checked in a new survey were found to be giving incorrect information in their window adverts. In a mystery shopping exercise carried out by Trading Standards in 37 travel agents across North Wales, officers posed as customers and selected holidays advertised in the travel agents' windows.

The officers requested details of the holidays and the full amount they would have to pay to take the holiday. Problems were found in 11 of the agents visited.

Out of the 97 holidays inspected, 18 were no longer available, 13 had increased in price and seven had decreased in price.

Richard Powell, Chair of the North Wales Fair Trading Panel that conducted the survey, said: "It is a cause for concern that nearly a third of those travel agents visited were giving incorrect information in their window adverts.

Currently these problems are being dealt with by way of advice to the traders and we are looking to the trade to co-operate. But if they continue to display misleading adverts in their windows then we will have to consider taking more formal action.

Source: News Wales

In pairs answer these questions.

1 Identify a travel and tourism organisation in your area, other than a travel agency.

2 Design a mystery shopper worksheet covering the product and service you wish to assess.

3 Visit that organisation and make your assessment.

4 Analyse your findings:

- What strengths and weaknesses did you find in what you assessed?

- What changes would you make to the design of your worksheet?

Customer forums/focus groups

Customer forums are small gatherings of potential, current or past customers brought together by the organisation to share their views and experiences of that organisation. Sometimes the term 'focus groups' is used instead of 'customer forums' although focus groups usually consider one particular aspect of the service or product, or one particular type of problem. They are an excellent way of gathering views on customer service issues.

By listening to customers, organisations learn about what is important to the customer and how they are performing in those areas. By open questioning and good listening, the organisation can gather more in-depth views than can be obtained from the ticked boxes and gradings found in some other methods of feedback. Customer forums also stimulate thinking about new ways of doing things.

Customer forums/focus groups can involve people who may not yet have experienced the organisation. This means that they, as well as current or past customers, can tell the organisation what is important to them before they experience the product or service. The organisation can then design the product and service to meet those needs and wishes.

A disadvantage of customer forums/focus groups is that only small numbers of opinions are gained. Increasing use of technology, for example on-line customer forums, is helping to partially overcome this.

Customer reviews

Travel and tourism organisations might seek customer feedback by inviting their customers to provide reviews, which they may post on their website for potential customers to read.

People planning to travel are increasingly using third-party websites (i.e. websites not owned, operated by or in any business relationship with the organisations, destinations etc. being reviewed), to discover other people's views on destinations, airlines, visitor attractions, tour operators etc.

Activity: Using customer reviews

Go to the tripadvisor's travel advice website. To obtain a secure link to this website, see the Hotlinks section on p.x. In the search box, type in your favourite destination and the word 'review'. Read some of the reviews.

1   What are the main travel and tourism segments reviewed, for example attractions, accommodation, restaurants?

2   Do the reviews include any method of grading? If so, what is it?

3   How do you know if they are genuine customer reviews?

Statistics from customer service departments

Customer service departments will receive feedback from many different sources, for example structured questionnaires, letters of compliment and complaint, or telephone calls. Every organisation should have methods to capture and analyse this feedback so that the organisation can make changes to improve their customer service. Trends can be identified by using such statistics.

Front-line staff are a very useful source of information. They experience first-hand what the customers are saying or doing, for example:

- The restaurant staff notice that there is a heavy demand for high chairs.

- Holiday representatives find they are asked a lot of questions about things for which they don't have information.

- Theme park staff notice that one of their colleagues is getting a lot of verbal compliments.

Feeding that information back to their manager, or appropriate department, will enable the right action to be taken. It may be to:

- supply more high chairs

- provide holiday reps with more information

- compliment and reward staff who receive customer compliments.

If you work in a front-line job, always look for clues which could lead to improved customer service. Don't ignore those clues – do something about them! (Also see *Unit 10: Exploring marketing in travel and tourism*.)

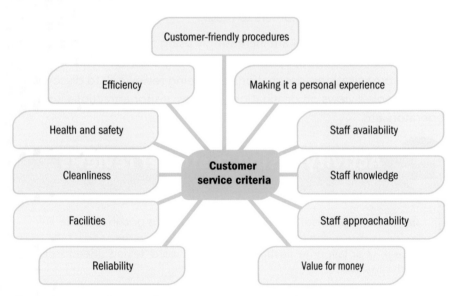

Figure 2.5: Typical criteria for assessing customer service

Assessment activity 2.2 — BTEC — P2

Your manager wishes to review how your organisation monitors and measures its performance. He has asked you to:

1 Obtain copies of comment cards and questionnaires from at least two travel and tourism organisations and describe in which situations they were being used. In what other situations could they be appropriately used?

2 Identify the types of travel and tourism organisation in which you think it is particularly appropriate to use mystery shoppers and describe the information which can be usefully obtained by this method.

3 Describe the strengths and weaknesses of review websites and compare these strengths and weaknesses with the other forms of customer feedback studied in this unit.

Grading tip

• **P2** You could use the organisations identified in assessment activity 2.1 as examples, or choose other organisations.

PLTS

You will be an **independent enquirer** as you investigate how different types of organisations approach customer service.

Functional skills

This activity provides the opportunity to demonstrate the functional skills of using **ICT** systems to find out and select information, and develop, present and communicate information, as well as the skills of writing and, potentially, speaking **English**.

In this first part of Unit 2 you have learned about the various policies, processes, resources and monitoring methods used by the travel and tourism sector to enable good customer service. In the second part of the unit you will learn about the needs and expectations of customers and how to meet them, but before you do, here is a further assessment activity which brings together what you have learned in the first part of the unit.

BTEC Assessment activity 2.3   P1 P2 M1

You work for your County Tourist Office. Your manager is looking for some fresh thinking about how your organisation should operate. He wants to understand how organisations in other sectors of travel and tourism approach customer service. He has asked you to undertake some research and to write a report for him on the subject.

Select two organisations in different sectors of travel and tourism. Visit them and/or research them through other methods and write your report.

1 Outline the policies, processes and resources in those organisations and how they enable the organisations to deliver customer service.

2 Identify the methods by which each organisation measures and monitors customer service and why you believe they use such methods.

Questions 1 and 2 will enable you to achieve **P1** and **P2**.

3 Compare the policies, processes, resources and methods of measuring and monitoring customer service. What similarities and differences are there between the two organisations?

Question 3 will enable you to achieve **M1**.

Grading tips

- Your answers should be comprehensive, covering all the key aspects of what you have studied so far in this unit. The comparisons can be in table form if you wish, but there must be an explanation and not just an identification or description.

- **M1** The report should bring to the attention of the reader the similarities and differences between the two organisations.

PLTS

Your individual activity in research will strengthen your **independent enquirer** and **self-manager** abilities, whilst your collaboration with those in the organisations you visit could identify you as a **team-worker**.

Functional skills

In this activity you can demonstrate the functional skills of using **ICT** systems to develop, present and communicate information, and potentially find and select information, and to write **English** and, potentially, speak it.

2. Understand the needs and expectations of different types of customer

2.1 Different types of customer

To work in the travel and tourism sector you must be willing and able to meet the needs of a wide range of customers.

Key term

Segmentation – this is the grouping of people who have common characteristics, for example a basic segmentation of travellers could be by reason for travel and consist of four segments: business travellers, leisure travellers, those visiting friends and relatives and those travelling for other reasons. These in turn could be segmented further, for example by age.

Segmentation

Whether you refer to your customers as clients, visitors, guests, or passengers, their needs must be understood. To do this people need to be grouped into their common characteristics (see also *Unit 10: Exploring marketing in travel and tourism*).

There are many ways in which customers can be segmented, for example by how much each category of customer spends on a journey and visit. The spider diagram below shows one type of **segmentation**.

Figure 2.6: Segmentation in travel and tourism

Activity: Who is travelling?

The Office for National Statistics *Travel Trends 2008* shows that UK residents took overseas trips for the following reasons (in thousands of trips):

Holidays:	45,531	Business:	8920
Visiting friends/relatives:	12,392	Other reasons:	2168

Create a pie chart to show these statistics graphically.

Working in small groups, gather travel and tourism brochures, website downloads etc. and then identify as many different customer segments of travellers and tourists as you can.

Age groups

In the travel and tourism sector you will meet groups from every age group, ranging from very young children to the centenarian. Children are delighted to have someone they can turn to who can help them have fun and give them assurance at appropriate times. Facilities such as kids clubs in hotel resorts, and play areas in travel agencies are great for children. They also meet a customer service need for adults who can be relieved from looking after them. Some adults without children may also appreciate 'child-free' zones.

The fastest growing age segment travelling overseas is those aged 55 or older. Whilst the number of overseas trips for those in the 0-54 age group went up 15% in 2008, compared with 2000, the growth for those aged 55 or older was 48% (Office for National Statistics – *Travel Trends 2000 and Travel Trends 2008*).

With such growth, you must learn how to give the older age groups customer service they value. They might be more comfortable with a more formal style, for example use their title and surname rather than their first name, and they may be willing to use technology but might want your discreet help.

Don't assume that elderly customers are losing their mental faculties or physical abilities. Saga Holidays caters for those over the age of 50. Their holidays include snorkelling with turtles and sharks in Borneo and trekking in the Nepalese mountains.

Why are the over 55s the fastest growing age segment making overseas trips?

Ethnicity

Ethnicity describes groups with a shared history, sense of identity, or geographical roots. Always be careful to show respect and not give offence, and be mindful of your customer's ethnicity. Recognise that people from different ethnic backgrounds may have different customer needs and wishes from each other.

Culture

Everyone has a set of beliefs, values, behaviours, habits, traditions, and customs which influence their way of life. That is their culture. Their culture may be quite different to other people's. Religion is often a strong feature of culture and can be a particularly sensitive issue. People with different cultures may value different types of customer service.

Working in the travel and tourism sector you are likely to work with people from different ethnic backgrounds, and with different cultures from you, particularly if you work or travel overseas. Respect, learn about, and respond appropriately to their cultures, so that you understand their customer service needs and avoid causing offence.

Why should you always respect other people's culture?

Did you know?

- Muslims and Jews do not eat pork.

- In parts of Asia, it is an offence to pat the head as it is seen as the cleanest and most sacred part of the body. Cabin crew should therefore avoid passing anything over people's heads.

- In northern Europe, greetings are quite formal, for example a handshake. In southern Europe, a greeting is more likely to include hugging and cheek kissing.

Activity: Different ethnic backgrounds and different cultures

Discover if anyone in your group comes from a different ethnic background or culture. What can they tell you about how their ethnic background or culture might affect the service they want when going on holiday?

Special interests

Why, where and how people travel, and the style of customer service they want, is influenced by the interests people have.

Leisure interests

Examples of how people's leisure interests can influence their customer service needs include:

- Someone interested in historic buildings may appreciate an expert on the subject who recognises the customer's interest and knowledge.

- Someone on a surfing holiday may want a guide with local knowledge to tell them where the good surfing conditions are and warn them of the dangers.

- Someone on a gastronomic tour may expect knowledgeable good quality staff at fine dining locations.

Business interests

Business people particularly want speedy, efficient service. They need to have the facilities and support normally available at their office. They welcome a calm airport business lounge with newspapers, computers, and communication facilities. Hotels providing in-room internet resources, same-day laundry facilities, 24-hour room service and express check-in and check-out, are valued. However, even business people need to relax, so they may become leisure tourists as well and expect customer service appropriate to that sector.

Organised groups

Members of organised groups, such as orchestras and youth clubs, often already know each other. They usually have a group leader who may share with you the responsibility of communicating with the group. However, although there will be common needs across the group, each member will have his, or her, own needs and it is important to relate to them.

The other type of group is formed by circumstance. An example could be where the people in a group may all happen to be on the same inclusive holiday or they are all taking the same guided tour. They will probably not know each other and will not have a group leader. You will be asked more questions by such a group as there is a wider range of

Virgin Atlantic's Business Lounge. Why might a customer choose this option?

needs and there is no group leader to help you. This can be challenging and organisations need to be alert to individual needs and make sure that they are met.

Customers with special needs

All customers have needs which are individual to them, but some have additional needs beyond those of most customers. These might arise because the customer:

- has a physical limitation such as being unable to walk or having a hearing or sight impairment

- has a learning disability

- has a language limitation

- is a child on his or her own

- is a parent with a baby or young child

- has a special dietary need.

All staff can help such customers with care, empathy, and a clear understanding of their specific needs. Staff may be given training to help those with special needs, for example learning sign language or how to escort sight-impaired customers.

When caring for a customer with special needs, make sure you introduce yourself to them by name. If you have to pass the customer on to the next person who will look after them, introduce them to each other and explain to your colleague what is needed. Examples of caring for customers with special needs include:

- A car ferry has a special car parking space for people with physical disabilities. It is next to the lift to the main cabin deck. A wheelchair is kept by the parking space. A trained staff member meets the passenger to assist them to the cabin deck.

- An airline has unaccompanied minor escorts at airports and during the flight. There is a special airport lounge with videos, soft drinks, nibbles, and games. In flight, the children are given comics, games and tuck boxes.

- A holiday hotel provides babysitters so that parents can enjoy their evenings knowing their children are being cared for.

Other demographics

Other **demographic** factors also influence the customer service needed, for example, there are often different needs between single people and families, couples and groups, and men and women.

Very Important Persons (VIPs), such as actors or members of a royal family, and Commercially Important Persons (CIPs), such as chairpersons of multi-million pound companies, are very influential people and your organisation may provide specialised staff and procedures to look after them.

Key term

Demographic – this refers to segments of human populations broken down by age, sex, income etc.

2.2 Needs

All customers share a common set of needs. They want you to:

- make them feel important, which means valuing them and treating them as an individual
- know your products and services
- listen, show empathy and understand how they feel.

As the travel and tourism sector is a people business, you will spend much of your time giving information, advice and instructions to your customers.

Accurate information

Customers will expect organisations to be able to answer their questions. The questions are likely to be very varied, for example:

- 'Can you tell me the way to…?'
- 'What are the children's facilities at that hotel?'
- 'How much is a family ticket to your attraction?'
- 'What extra facilities do I get if I pay the Club Class fare?'

Technology helps provide customers with information. Customers can check the internet for directions, timetables, products and services, price and availability, estimated train arrival times etc. In tourist centres, attractions and transport terminals, message displays and touch-screen kiosks provide information. Mobile phones provide information through help lines and internet access.

> **Think about it**
>
> **The customer's lament**
>
> *Hey, I'm ME!*
>
> *I'm not the last customer you had.*
>
> *I'm not the next customer you will have.*
>
> *Please treat me as an individual with my own needs.*
>
> *I'm ME!*

> **Activity: What do the customers want to know?**
>
> For each of the following jobs, list three pieces of information staff are likely to be asked for on a regular basis:
>
> - travel agent
> - hotel receptionist
> - on-board train manager.
> - theme park ride assistant
> - historic house guide
>
> Discuss your list with someone else in your group.

Health, safety and security

The Health and Safety at Work Act (1974) requires employers and employees to ensure a healthy, safe, and secure environment for the public and employees. Your customers and work colleagues expect you and your organisation to do so. Be observant and report anything which could be a hazard, for example a loose carpet in a hotel or trailing wires in an office.

Customers will seek advice on overseas health arrangements. Recent examples have included:

- Severe Acute Respiratory Syndrome (SARS) which spread from China, affected 37 countries in 2002-03, and required health checks at the entry points of many countries around the world.

- Avian flu, first identified in humans in 2003, spread across much of Asia, Europe, and parts of Africa. Poultry was the source. Although transmission to humans was rare, it was sufficient to cause travellers concern.

- Swine flu became widespread in Mexico in 2009 and rapidly spread across much of the world. Airlines increased cabin cleaning and disinfecting and in some cases refused to carry passengers who had signs of the illness. Some airports screened everyone coming into the country.

In all these examples the travel and tourism sector saw a downturn in business. Travellers were concerned about their health and safety. Tour operators, travel agents, airlines, and other organisations needed to be well-informed about risks and travel restrictions around the world. They obtained much of the advice from the World Health Organisation and government health services. Travellers were also able to obtain direct advice from the same sources.

Safety is of vital importance to everyone. Tour operators have a legal responsibility to ensure the safety of all aspects of their customers' holidays. Coach drivers emphasise the need for passengers to wear seat belts; hotels display evacuation procedures in every bedroom; airlines give a mandatory safety briefing before every take-off, etc.

Security is always present in our lives, with access to many tourist attractions, hotels, and transport terminals having security measures such as CCTV cameras, security guards and body and baggage searches.

Why do you need to be careful what is in your hand baggage?

Activity: Foreign and Commonwealth Office advice

Look at the Foreign and Commonwealth Office website. To obtain a secure link to this website, see the Hotlinks section on p.x. Click on the travel advice link and then search for information on France, Kuwait and New Zealand.

What safety, security, and health advice is given for each of those countries? What other types of advice are given?

Assistance

Different types of customers need different types and levels of assistance and often needs change in different circumstances. A passenger may not need help in his home country, but he may need help with the language when he arrives at his overseas destination. Another passenger might not need help when travelling on business, but may need help with his baggage and young children when travelling on holiday.

Activity: Help me!

In small groups list as many situations as you can identify when a family going on holiday might need assistance, from the time they are at their departure airport to the time they arrive overseas at their hotel. Decide what assistance you would give in four of those situations.

How many examples did you think of?

Would you be alert to people who look as though they need help?

Could you tell them what the next stage of their progress through the airport was and where they would need to go?

Does the signage need improving?

Do they need help with the language? Can you speak their language or can you find a colleague who does?

Do they need help with their luggage? Could you find a trolley for them?

Advice

Customers will look to you for advice, for example it may be advice from you as a travel consultant about the suitability of a destination or how to obtain a visa. A holiday rep could be asked about what resort activities they would recommend for a teenage daughter or they could be asked to help solve a problem. This is where you can demonstrate your knowledge, customer service and problem-solving skills.

Products and services

Remember the last time you bought something. You made a choice. If there was only one product on offer, you decided whether or not to buy it. The choice may have been between several types of product. For example, a traveller may decide whether they will make their journey by train or by air.

If there was a choice of several products of the same type, you made a choice between them. Part of that choice may have been because of what it offered you. Just like you, customers have 'needs' and 'wants'. They may *need* a morning train which will get them to their business meeting in time; they may *need* a holiday which is available in the first week of August. They may *want* to be able to use an airport business lounge; they may *want* a hotel room with a sea view.

Customers make judgements about which product meets their needs and their wants best. One example is where a passenger may decide to travel on a budget airline rather than a full-service airline, but this doesn't necessarily mean that the human element of customer service shouldn't still be there. In the USA, Southwest Airlines has shown that it is possible to offer a 'no frills' service yet inject humour and a friendly service through the performance of its staff.

What the customer does expect is that the product, or service, meets their needs and their wants and that the product they purchased delivers what it said it would. The three components of customer service (product, process, personal behaviour) must not fail.

2.3 Identification and recognition of needs

The letter below shows a very clear statement of who the customer is, how he can be contacted, what it is he wants, and his payment details. Sometimes requests are very clear, but sometimes they are not. They may need careful analysis and perhaps more information, to enable you and your organisation to provide what is needed.

Written requests from customers

The first opposite communication your organisation receives may just be an enquiry about what you offer, at what price and whether or not it is available. Your response may be:

- by letter, perhaps supported by a brochure and booking form

- by email, perhaps giving your website address for further information

- by phone call, which would help you learn more about the customer's needs and give you greater opportunity to sell your product.

Activity: Website bookings

Research and select three tour operator websites. Choose a holiday from each website and make a dummy booking to experience the booking process you are taken through. Compare the three processes.

What are the similarities and the differences? What facility was there to identify any extra needs the customer might have?

> 5, Lanark Road,
> Stoke Furness,
> Tel: 01050 923627
>
> 10th August
>
> Please reserve one upper circle seat for me for the 7.30 p.m. performance of 'Hamlet' at your theatre on 17th August. I enclose a cheque for £32.50 which includes booking fee and will collect the ticket from your box office on the night of the performance.
>
> Regards
>
> Mr. F.Harnett

Figure 2.7: A letter booking

Whichever method you use it is an opportunity to sell your organisation's products and services, so it is important to understand what a customer wants and what may appeal to them.

Up until recently tour operators used to include a booking form in their brochures but now many travel and tourism organisations encourage their customers to book on-line. The design of the booking facility on a website needs careful planning. It must take the customer through the process in a logical manner, so that they can make the right choices and provide the organisation with the information it needs.

Concorde **Car Hire** Tramford
01052 072632

Title: (Mr/Mr/Miss/Other)		Hire commencement (Time and date)	
First initial and surname:		Hire termination (Time and date)	
Address:		Type of car (See attached brochure)	
Phone number:		Pick up location (see attached brochure)	
Email contact:		Drop off location (See attached brochure)	
Credit card type: (VISA, MasterCard, Diners and American Express accepted).		Additional requirements (See attached brochure)	
Name on credit card:			
Credit card number:			
Expiry date:			
Security number:			

I have read the terms and conditions in your attached brochure

Signature: Date:

Return booking form to Concorde Car Hire, The Street, Tramford, Wales

Booking confirmation will be sent to you within 3 days of receipt of booking form.

Figure 2.8: What sorts of information should be included in a booking form?

Activity: Davitt's Equestrian Centre booking form

You are the manager of Davitt's Equestrian Centre which offers inclusive holidays for those wishing to learn, or improve, their horse riding skills. The courses are either for three days starting on Friday or four days starting on Monday. The Centre provides three levels of training – Beginners, Intermediate, and Advanced.

The Centre provides three types of accommodation – single ensuite room, twin ensuite room and dormitory with shared bathroom. The holidays are on a full-board basis. A 25% deposit is required at the time of booking which is refundable if the booking is cancelled up to two weeks before the start of the holiday.

Design a booking form which provides the booking information the customer needs and enables them to give you the information you need from them.

Verbal requests from customers

Customers may contact call centres to make enquiries or bookings, resolve problems, etc. This enables the organisation to understand what is required from the customer, explore possibilities and explain things more fully.

Verbal requests will also be made face to face, for example a customer may discuss their needs with a consultant in a travel agency, an airline passenger agent at an airport, or a holiday representative at a resort. All of those staff must be alert to what the customer is telling them and find ways to meet their needs.

Once customers start using the product or service, they are likely to identify different types of needs and use different methods of communication than they would have done prior to using the product or service. For example someone booking a canal boat holiday may have made a written request for a particular type of boat on a particular canal on particular dates. Once they start their holiday, they may ask verbally for instructions on how to operate the boat, for maps, or for recommendations on where to visit.

Recognising unstated needs

This is where your customer skills really come into play – skills which include observation, listening, and problem-solving. Sometimes customers' needs are unstated because they do not recognise the need themselves and sometimes because they feel too sensitive about the need. Two scenarios are outlined below.

You may be a travel consultant booking a holiday in a Caribbean resort for a young couple. They have explained that it will be their honeymoon. They may not have thought about passport requirements for the bride who will be changing her surname, so you may need to think for them and offer advice and help to make any necessary arrangements.

What if you are a receptionist in a hotel and you notice that when someone is checking-in they ask you to repeat everything you say. They could be hard of hearing or perhaps they do not understand your language very well. How could you help them?

Recognising unstated needs is a very powerful demonstration of excellent customer service.

Design a matrix and write supporting information on different types of customer, their stated and unstated needs and how they might be recognised.

1 Copy and complete the following grid. For each of the seven main groups:

- identify two sub-groups, for example for the ethnicity group you might identify (i) French and (ii) Inuit

- select two needs each sub-group might have – one of those two needs should be a need other groups are unlikely to have

- explain how each need might come to your attention.

2 Provide examples of potential unstated needs for:

- an extended family group with young children when they book accommodation in a holiday hotel

- a blind passenger travelling on your ferry

- an overseas visitor who does not understand English well and is visiting a stately home.

3 Identify the skills and attributes needed to help recognise unstated needs.

Group	Sub-group	Needs	Identify the needs
Age	i) ii)	i) ii)	i) ii)
Ethnicity	i) ii)	i) ii)	i) ii)
Culture	i) ii)	i) ii)	i) ii)
Special interests	i) ii)	i) ii)	i) ii)
Organised groups	i) ii)	i) ii)	i) ii)
Customers with special needs	i) ii)	i) ii)	i) ii)
Other demographic (you choose)	i) ii)	i) ii)	i) ii)

Grading tips **P3**

- You can strengthen your answer to question 1 by covering a good range of sub-groups, for example for ethnicity sub-groups, don't just offer countries.

- Your answer to question 1 can be further strengthened by making sure your entries in the 'Needs' and 'How those needs might be identified' columns are well defined and specific.

- When preparing your answers to questions 2 and 3 it may help to think about the situation as if you were the customer.

- Review all you have learned so far in the second part of this unit, to ensure you give comprehensive answers.

PLTS

By providing good examples you can demonstrate your abilities as a **creative thinker**. Thinking about what you have learned and about situations from a customer viewpoint demonstrates your **reflective learner** skills.

Functional skills

This activity gives you the opportunity to demonstrate your skills in using **ICT** systems to develop, present and communicate information and your skills in writing **English**.

2.4 Expectations

Meeting expectations

Having purchased your product, or service, the customer has expectations of you which you must meet if you want them to buy from you again. Remember, in the travel and tourism sector, organisations are largely giving customers dreams and experiences and they are expecting them to be good ones. They expect their flight to operate on time; their hotel room to be clean; their meals to be tasty; their excursions to be fun and interesting.

This takes effort on the part of everyone in an organisation, whether in direct contact with the customer, or working behind the scenes. The hotel's housekeeping staff need a good supply of linen, toiletries, and cleaning materials to make sure the bedrooms are clean and attractive; historic homes guides need to have been trained to make sure visitors get maximum value from their visit; cabin crew must be briefed about the needs of individual passengers, whether it is that the passenger can only eat gluten-free food, or is frightened of flying, etc.

Remember what you learned in the first part of this unit about policies, processes and resources. They need to support staff so that they are able and willing to provide excellent customer service.

Everyone in the organisation is a link in the customer service chain. If one person doesn't do their job properly, the link breaks and the chain will fail to deliver the customer service expected.

Exceeding expectations

To be a customer service star you must try to exceed the customers' expectations. This will ensure the customer keeps buying from you *and* tells other people about how good your organisation is.

You should look for opportunities to anticipate what the customer needs or wants and provide that little bit extra to personalise the service.

Activity: Exceeding expectations

In pairs, write down ways in which you, as customer service agents, could exceed expectations of:

- A passenger whose luggage missed the connecting flight and who must now stay overnight without his belongings and go to a full day of meetings the next day in a nearby city business centre.

- A couple on your train who mentioned in passing to you that they are celebrating their golden wedding anniversary.

- The parents of a 6-year-old boy who has lost his favourite toy in your hotel.

Remember the 'halo effect'. This is the effect you have on people watching you look after your customer, for example if you are talking to a young child going on holiday, you might decide to bend down to her eye level and talk to her about the toy she is hugging, or the holiday on which she is going. People will be watching you and be impressed by how well you relate to the girl's needs and interests.

Exceeding the customers' expectations through your extra effort will not only win over the customers and everyone they tell, but will also make you feel good.

Assessment activity 2.5

BTEC   (P4)

1 In each of the following six scenarios:

   a) explain how the organisation could meet the need of the customer.

   b) explain how the organisation might exceed the customer's expectations.

   Scenarios:

   • A family visits the local tourist office to enquire about overnight accommodation as their car has broken down.

   • A couple arrive at a theme park with their physically handicapped 9-year-old son.

   • A Buddhist monk comes into your travel shop to enquire about flights to Thailand.

   • A Brazilian family visits a castle.

   • A young man tells a holiday representative that he has just had his money and passport stolen.

   • A Finnish businesswoman enquires at the hotel reception desk about car hire.

2 Provide and explain two examples from organisations you have researched, of how they meet and could exceed their customers' expectations.

Grading tip

• (P4) In answering these questions, consider not only what it is the organisation can deliver, but how it can do so. For question 2, you can either use one of the six organisations you researched in assessment activity 2.1, or real case studies. If the latter, you must provide evidence of that case study.

PLTS

Completing your assessment activities on time will give you **self-manager** skills.

Functional skills

In this activity you can use your skills in using **ICT** systems to develop, present and communicate information, as well as your **English** skills of writing and/or speaking.

Case study: Going the extra mile

Passenger agent Maria had a tricky situation at Toronto airport. An elderly couple who had been visiting their son and his family were checking-in to return to the UK. Their son drove them 100 miles (160 kilometres) from his home, left them at the airport, and set off home again. When the couple tried to check-in, they realised they had left their passports in his car.

Maria could have taken the easy way out by telling the couple that they could not travel without their passports but she wanted to help the distraught couple. They couldn't remember their son's mobile phone number so Maria asked if he had the radio on in the car. He had, and they remembered the programme he had been listening to.

Maria called the radio station and asked them to put out a message to the son, to return to the airport.

The son heard it and drove back to the airport just in time for his relieved parents to catch their flight!

The couple were thrilled with the service and so was their family. They told many other friends and relatives. The radio station was so pleased with the part they had played, that they recounted it on air each day of that week. Imagine the value to the airline of all that free advertising time!

1 When have you gone the extra mile to help someone?

2 What did you do?

3 What reaction did you get from the person you were helping?

4 What did you learn from doing it?

5 How did you feel afterwards?

Assessment activity 2.6

(P3) (P4) (M2) (D1)

You have been asked to write a 500-word article for *Customer Service Monthly* entitled 'Customer Needs and Expectations – how they can be met and exceeded in travel and tourism'. Your article should cover:

- A review of the needs of different types of customer and how those needs can be recognised. This will enable you to achieve **P3**.

- An explanation of how travel and tourism organisations meet and exceed customer expectations. This will enable you to achieve **P4**.

- An analysis of how organisations meet and exceed customers' needs and expectations through the recognition of their needs. This brings together all of the second part of this unit and will enable you to achieve **M2**.

- An analysis of how approaches to customer service link to the success of meeting and exceeding customers' needs and expectations. This will enable you to achieve **D1**.

Grading tips

- You can use examples from the organisations you have researched already during this unit or you can choose other travel and tourism organisations.

- **M2** You must analyse (i.e. examine in detail), how organisations achieve the desired customer service levels through accurately recognising needs and finding suitable solutions.

- **D1** You must consider both Part 1 and Part 2 of this unit and clearly explain and analyse the stages examined there and how they form a customer service chain.

PLTS

In this activity you can demonstrate your ability as an **independent enquirer** through your research, and as a **reflective thinker** by reflecting on what you have learned, as well as a **creative thinker** through using effective examples.

Functional skills

This activity gives you the opportunity to demonstrate your skills in using **ICT** to find select information and develop, present and communicate information. You can also use your written **English** skills.

After gaining my Travel and Tourism Diploma, I joined an airline as a Passenger Services Assistant, assisting at check-in; accepting passengers' baggage; boarding departure flights; meeting arrival flights and passenger service functions. But it's not just about carrying out those tasks. It's about providing excellent customer service. The variety of situations we face is immense. We have daily contact with people from all walks of life and from all over the world. On occasions there may be those who'll challenge our ability to stay calm and friendly, but these are very much a minority and that is all part of providing customer service.

Typical day

My day starts with a briefing on operational and customer service issues; what the fleet situation is; if there is any weather or overseas disruption which might affect our flights, and so on. It's then a matter of helping passengers, and resolving the queries, concerns and problems.

Today we were warned of a delay to our flight from Hong Kong because of a typhoon. Our Hong Kong staff and the crew operating the flight kept us up-to-date on the general situation and specific passenger needs. We made new bookings for 18 passengers who had missed onward flights, had wheelchairs ready for three elderly passengers and passed phone messages from passengers to relatives meeting the flight. All departments were aware that this flight was a priority and everyone was at the stand when the aircraft came in. We assisted those passengers we had been alerted to and gave out advice and information.

What's good about the job?

It's hard work and we have to think on our feet, but that's part of the fun of providing customer service. Sometimes I take a quiet moment to watch passengers as they pass through our Terminal and think how lucky I am to be able to make their day for them. It really gives me a buzz, but I couldn't do it without everyone in the airline pulling together.

Think about it!

1 What areas have you covered in this unit that provide you with the background skills and knowledge used by Rolanda? Discuss with your colleagues.

2 What further skills might you need to develop to do Rolanda's job?

Just checking

1 Identify in the correct order, the links (stages) between 'Mission Statement' and 'Measuring and monitoring customer service'.
2 What is the difference between policies and processes?
3 What are the benefits to (a) the organisation and (b) the staff, of a caring approach to staff?
4 Why might third-party customer review websites not be reliable?
5 Why is segmentation of customer types valuable?
6 Which is the fastest growing age group in terms of trips taken?
7 Identify the five main categories of needs.
8 Who is responsible for health and safety?
9 Why might people not state needs they may have?
10 How can you exceed the customer's expectations?

Assignment tips

Success comes with preparation. Several of the assessment activities in this unit require you to do some good research. Here are some suggestions about how to research and prepare your answers:

1 Have a system. How do you plan to collect and organise your notes?

2 Think carefully about how you will answer each question. You may want to make lists or mind-maps identifying the headings and sub-headings you will use.

3 Select your chosen organisations well. Are they likely to be good examples? How easy will it be to gain the information from them in the time available to you?

4 Design any questionnaires, or worksheets, with great care. Check them with your tutor to make sure they meet the need, before you start to use them. Poorly designed questionnaires, or worksheets, may result in you overlooking questions you should have asked, or missing useful information.

5 Don't trust just one source of information. Try to check its accuracy by finding another source.

6 Don't just use the internet. As good a source as it can be, there is little to beat face to face investigation.

7 Provide real examples whenever possible.

8 As you work through this unit you will see links emerging. Recognise those links and how they form a chain of customer service.

3 Understan nature and effects o world travel

It is strange to imagine that while you are reading this, there are people around the world getting up, others going to bed, some are sound asleep and others, probably like you, are part-way through their day.

Weather-wise there are similar contrasts. At any time of the year there will be people around the world facing sub-zero icy blasts while others bask in the tropical sun; there could be a hurricane brewing or torrential rains; in some areas of the world there may be floods while others may have a drought.

Travellers have to take all of these things into account when making their holiday or business travel plans. As a potential employee in the travel and tourism sector, you could be helping people to make the right travel decisions. Your advice could be instrumental in selecting suitable destinations, and your knowledge and understanding of the travellers' world could make the difference between a successful trip or not.

Learning outcomes

After completing this unit you should:

1   be able to identify and locate significant features and major destinations of the world

2   know world climatic conditions affecting travel to worldwide destinations

3   understand the effects of worldwide time on travellers.

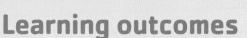

To achieve a **pass** grade the evidence must show that you are able to:	To achieve a **merit** grade the evidence must show that, in addition to the pass criteria, you are able to:	To achieve a **distinction** grade the evidence must show that, in addition to the pass and merit criteria, you are able to:
P1 use resources to identify and locate global aspects, continents and natural features on world maps **Assessment activity 3.1, page 85**	**M1** use resources confidently and efficiently, to identify and locate features and destinations relating to world travel **Assessment activities 3.1, 3.2, page 85 and page 92**	**D1** identify and locate features and destinations relating to world travel independently, with limited use of resources **Assessment activity 3.2, page 92**
P2 use resources to identify and locate holiday destinations and gateways on world maps **Assessment activity 3.2, page 92**		
P3 describe climatic conditions affecting travel to worldwide destinations, identifying seasonal variations **Assessment activity 3.3, page 98**	**M2** explain how seasonal climatic conditions can affect travel to worldwide destinations **Assessment activity 3.3, page 98**	**D2** analyse the effect of extreme or unusual climatic conditions on travel to named worldwide destinations **Assessment activity 3.3, page 98**
P4 explain time zones and their effect on travellers **Assessment activity 3.5, page 104**	**M3** explain how time zones can affect leisure and business travellers when travelling between selected destinations **Assessment activity 3.5, page 104**	
P5 calculate worldwide time differences **Assessment activity 3.4, page 103**		

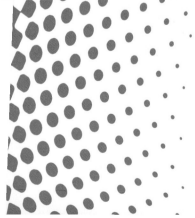

How you will be assessed

his unit will be assessed by one or more internal assignments that will be
marked by your tutor. Your assignments will
Verifier and may al

- written work, for example leaflets and inte

Kate, 22–year–old, long–haul flight attendant

When I started my BTEC Level 2 First Diploma I had set my sights on working as a flight attendant for an airline. Several years later, after also completing the BTEC Level 3 National Diploma and then working for a large hotel chain, I achieved this ambition.

Since gaining my 'wings' my feet have (literally) hardly touched the ground. I now work for a major scheduled airline and travel mainly on transatlantic routes and to the Middle East, to destinations such as New York, Las Vegas and Dubai.

You need to have a lot of stamina to do a job like this. The time differences around the world can play havoc with your body clock. Sometimes I don't know whether it's night or day, especially when I am wide awake at 3 a.m., or eating dinner at what feels like breakfast time!

Having knowledge of world travel destinations, time differences and climate is very useful in this job. You experience all of these things for yourself and it feels good to pass on your knowledge to your passengers too.

Over to you

- Have you travelled to different countries?

- Would you like a job like this one that could take you all over the world?

1. Identify and locate significant features and major destinations of the world

Set off

Spinning around the world

Spin a globe, close your eyes and see where your finger rests when the globe stops spinning. Have you landed in a country? Which country? Which continent is it in? Or have you landed in the middle of a sea or ocean? Which one?

Write your answer onto a sticker and, along with your classmates, place your sticker on the correct location on a large wall map of the world. Your map should now have named stickers dotted all around the world.

Examine holiday brochures to see what types of holiday destinations are featured for any of the countries identified by stickers on the map.

1.1 The world

Resources

As you begin your studies into the nature and effects of world travel you will need to familiarise yourself with different types of resources available to you.

- A globe might seem old-fashioned, but it enables you to see at a glance where continents, countries, seas and oceans are located, to visualise their size and to begin to appreciate the distances involved when travelling around the world. Using a globe will also help you to understand about time differences, seasons and climate as you work through this unit.

- Maps, such as the one in Figure 3.1, are useful for showing you the overall picture. Here you can visualise the extent of the journey you might have to take if you travel from the UK to a country on the other side of the world. Maps become progressively more *localised* and you might, for example, use a map of the USA to help to plan a trip through different states. Even in these days of sat-nav you may find a road map useful when taking a self-drive holiday. You will find pocket maps of destinations useful for helping you to find your way round big cities like New York.

- An atlas is a collection of maps. You will probably use a world atlas containing maps of different continents and countries. Using an atlas effectively is a useful skill to have for the travel industry. It takes practice to become efficient and confident when using a detailed index to find exact locations on different maps.

- The internet has opened up a whole new world of images and information. Google Earth will whizz you off around the world in seconds and give a satellite view of locations all over the world. You can take a street level 'drive' through specific destinations. The internet provides the facility to view maps from all over the world, pinpoint specific destinations, plan routes and access travel and destination information.

- Holiday brochures are very useful for highlighting the main attractions of countries and holiday destinations around the world. They bring a visual element as well as providing useful information to help the reader make decisions about their holiday plans. Even in these days of advanced technology, travel agents have to be competent in using holiday brochures as a sales tool.

- Guide books are handy for carrying out in-depth research into a destination and for taking with you when you travel. They contain lots of information in one book.

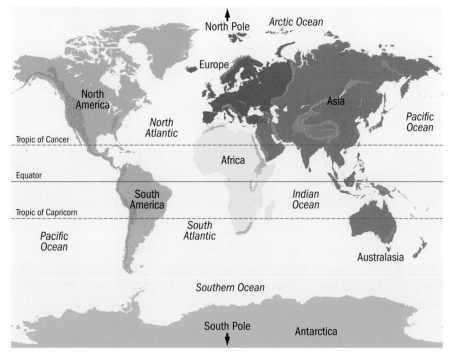

Figure 3.1: Where in the world would you like to visit?

Global aspects

Knowing about different global aspects is a useful starting point when studying the world of travel.

You can see from Figure 3.1 that the imaginary line of the equator divides the world into two halves; these are the northern and southern hemispheres. The UK is in the northern hemisphere and we have our summer from June to August and our winter from December to February.

Think about it

If you are planning a holiday to Australia to visit friends and family for Christmas you will need to pack your sun tan lotion rather than your winter woollies!

Figure 3.2: Find out about how people celebrate Christmas in Australia

In contrast, countries in the southern hemisphere have their winter months from June to August and their summer months from December to February. This means that in the southern hemisphere spring is from September to November and autumn is from March to May.

Running parallel to the equator are lines of latitude. Like the equator, these too are imaginary lines that circle the Earth between east and west. There are five named lines of latitude

- the equator
- the Tropic of Cancer (north of the Equator)
- the Tropic of Capricorn (south of the equator)
- the Arctic Circle
- the Antarctic Circle.

The area between the Tropics of Cancer and Capricorn is characterised by a very hot 'tropical' climate.

The North Pole lies in the middle of the Arctic Ocean in permanently frozen shifting sea ice and is the northernmost point of the Earth, while the South Pole is the southernmost point on Earth and lies in the frozen land mass of Antarctica.

Activity: Using a globe

Use a globe to find the Poles, the Tropics and the equator.

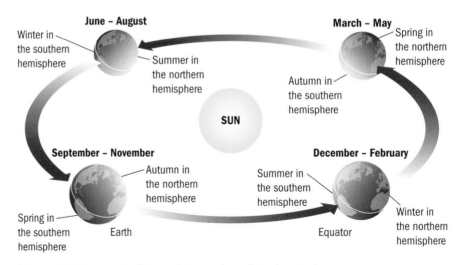

Figure 3.3: Seasons in the northern and southern hemispheres

Case study: Round the world

A relaxing (and luxurious) way to visit different continents is to take a round the world cruise. The cruise line Cunard was the first to offer a world cruise in 1922. Today, a round the world voyage is offered by many major cruise lines. Typically, a world voyage lasts from around 80 to 160 nights and calls at ports in three or four continents. Some voyages travel in an easterly direction around the world and others travel in a westerly direction. Some of the cruise lines who offer round the world trips include Cunard,

Fred Olsen, Holland America, P&O Cruises, Princess Cruises and SAGA.

1 Find out which round the world cruises are currently being advertised by cruise lines.
2 Plot the routes for two round the world cruises using a globe, a world map or using Google Earth on the internet.
3 Compare the routes they take and the different continents included in their itineraries.

Continents

Between them the continents of Europe, North America, South America, Africa, Asia and Australasia offer uniquely different opportunities for travel. History, culture, natural features, climate and location influence the appeal of different continents.

Employees in the travel and tourism sector need to be able to locate continents with confidence and to recognise the features that influence travel, particularly travel times, time differences and climate.

You will be examining the continents and the features influencing travel in more detail later in this chapter.

1.2 Natural features

Natural features attract tourists to many destinations and provide opportunities for both relaxation and adventure.

Oceans

Oceans cover around 70% of the Earth's surface. For many travellers, oceans are viewed only from the air as they fly across the world.

Activity: Ocean appeal

Match the coastal location to the correct ocean in the middle column and then to the correct country in the right hand column.

Location	Ocean	Country
Bondi Beach	South Atlantic	Kenya
Malibu Beach	Indian	Brazil
Copacabana	North Atlantic	Australia
Newquay	Pacific	USA
Mombasa	Pacific	UK

Did you know?

- The Arctic Ocean is the smallest of the world's oceans.

- It is the only place on the Earth where polar bears live.

- Parts of the Arctic Ocean are covered in ice all year round – around 9 million square kilometres in the summer, freezing to 16 million square kilometres in the winter.

- At certain times of the year it is possible to sail by ice breaker through the legendary Northwest Passage from Anadyr in Russia to Resolute in Canada. Check out the route on a map.

How does this location appeal to visitors?

However, exotic ocean beach destinations, such as the idyllic island resorts of the Maldives in the Indian Ocean, attract visitors for relaxation and special occasions, such as honeymoons. For the more active, the Pacific, Atlantic and Indian Oceans offer excellent opportunities for surfing, with Hawaii and Australia boasting some of the best surfing spots in the world. Ocean cruises are also popular, including transatlantic cruises between Southampton and New York, whale-watching cruises in the Pacific Ocean and adventure cruises in the Arctic Circle.

Seas

The Mediterranean and Caribbean Seas are the most popular with British holidaymakers in search of sun, sea and sand. They offer holidays to meet most budgets and to suit different motivations. Many cruise ships alternate between these two seas, spending the summer months in the Mediterranean and then relocating to the Caribbean where the climate is warmer in the winter months.

The inland Black Sea borders Europe and Asia. It has increased in popularity with British holidaymakers, providing some very good value summer sun holidays.

The Red Sea has popular all year round destinations such as Eilat in Israel and Sharm el Sheikh in Egypt. It provides opportunities for some excellent snorkelling and diving.

Did you know?

Some seas link to oceans and some lie within oceans and others are smaller seas within larger seas.

Think about it

Despite their names the Black Sea is not black and the Red Sea is not red! Can you find out how they got their names?

Key term

Expats – this is the shortened term for expatriates or people who have moved to live in a different country.

Activity: Beat the clock

The Mediterranean is the world's largest inland sea and one of the most popular holiday areas for British tourists. Famous for its package holidays, the Mediterranean also has popular cruise areas in the east and west, and is home to many **expats** who have moved from Britain to enjoy the warmer Mediterranean climate. Study a map of the Mediterranean then complete this 30-second test:

Name three islands in the Mediterranean.

Name two continents that border the Mediterranean.

Name three smaller seas that form part of the Mediterranean Sea.

Name six countries with a Mediterranean coastline.

Case study: The Great Lakes

The Great Lakes of Erie, Michigan-Huron, Ontario and Superior are grouped together in North America, flanking the USA and Canada. The area covered by the Great Lakes is similar in size to that of the whole of Continental Europe. They represent the largest expanse of freshwater in the world. Lake Superior is often referred to as the largest freshwater lake in the world, but the lakes of Michigan and Huron are actually one body of water, rather than two as was thought to be the case by original travellers.

The Great Lakes of North America have much to attract the visitor. Outdoor pursuits on the lakes include canoeing, sailing, swimming and fishing, while the surrounding countryside provides opportunities for hiking, golfing, mountain biking, dog sledding and skiing. There are cosmopolitan cities, stylish resorts and small towns with cultural attractions to complete the holiday experience.

1 Locate the Great Lakes on a map.

2 Find examples of cities and holiday resorts that are part of the Great Lakes area.

Rivers

For centuries rivers have been an important lifeline for many communities as a source of food, agriculture and transportation. Many rivers, such as the Nile, are still 'working rivers' today, linking different countries for trade and travel.

At over 4 000 miles in length, the Nile is the longest river in the world. It is a popular destination for river cruises to explore the pyramids and ancient civilisations. The Amazon river is very similar in length and is often referred to as the greatest river on Earth as it carries a greater volume of water than the Nile. Many adventure tourists are attracted to the Amazon to take part in expeditions through the Amazon rainforest.

Closer to home, rivers play their part in adding to the appeal of many tourist destinations, for example the Thames in London, the Seine in Paris and the Rhine in Germany.

Lakes

Lakes provide opportunities for a range of water sports and the chance to relax in beautiful locations. Many lakes are so large that they have several significant destinations on their shores, and they often border different countries.

The largest lakes by continent are:

- Europe – Lake Ladoga

- North America – Lake Michigan-Huron

- South America – Lake Titicaca

- Asia – Lake Baikal

- Africa – Lake Victoria

- Australasia – Lake Eyre.

BTEC BTEC's own resources

Did you know?

- Las Vegas, the 'Entertainment Capital of the World' is situated in the middle of a desert. This is one desert location that attracts millions of visitors each year to gamble and sample its glamorous nightlife.

- According to Rainforest Action Network an area the size of two football fields is lost every second. There are a number of charitable organisations involved in efforts to safeguard the rainforests.

Activity: High spots

In which countries will you find the following mountains?

Mount	Country
Kilimanjaro	
Everest	
Snowdon	
Olympus	
Fuji	
Aconcagua	
Blanc	

Why not use Google Earth to see these mountains at closer quarters? Can you plot them on a map?

Mountains

People are becoming more adventurous and are often looking for a holiday with a challenge. Mountains provide scope for winter sports holidays and adventure holidays, such as climbing and trekking. Less active pursuits are catered for as well, with many mountain locations providing opportunities for relaxation and walking in stunning surroundings. Some mountains are part of major mountain ranges such as the Alps, which provides an excellent range of destinations for winter sports. Others, such as Mount Kilimanjaro, are extinct volcanoes and they often attract people looking for a 'once in a lifetime' adventure.

Deserts

Deserts have tiny amounts of rain and have very little natural vegetation. Deserts do not generally attract mass tourism, as the temperatures are usually extreme, but they do attract people in search of adventure, for example taking a desert safari in the Sahara, Gobi or Mojave deserts.

Rainforests

Tropical rainforests cover around 2% of the Earth's land surface, yet they are said to be home to nearly two-thirds of all living species on the planet. They are an important source of the air we breathe. The largest rainforests are found in the Amazon Basin in South America and also in countries around the equator in West Africa and Southeast Asian countries such as Indonesia.

Unfortunately, rainforests are being destroyed by man at an incredible rate. Tropical rainforests attract travellers who are concerned about the environment, the impact of **deforestation** and the plight of endangered animals. They may travel to destinations to support efforts being made to save endangered species such as the orang-utans of Borneo and the gorillas of Rwanda.

Here today. Gone tomorrow?

Key term

Deforestation – this refers to the cutting, clearing, and removal of rainforest for the purpose of creating land for agriculture, cattle ranching, mines and gas or oil extraction.

BTEC **Assessment activity 3.1** P1 M1

You have started working for a worldwide tour operator. As part of your induction training the manager has asked you have to carry out a number of tasks to show that you have a good awareness of worldwide locations and different features that influence worldwide travel.

1 On a blank map of the world accurately identify:

- the continents of North America, South America, Europe, Africa, Asia and Australasia

- the oceans surrounding the continents

- the imaginary lines of the equator and Tropics of Capricorn and Cancer, showing the Poles, and northern and southern hemispheres.

2 Next, on blank maps of the continents of North America, South America, Europe, Africa, Asia and Australasia identify and locate for each continent:

- at least one major mountain or mountain range

- at least one significant sea, river or large lake

- at least one significant river

- at least one other significant natural feature, for example a desert or a rainforest.

You will be allowed to use resources for these tasks for P1 and M1. This must include the use of an atlas. Keep a record of the resources you have used. Full achievement of M1 will be dependent also on assessment activity 3.2.

Grading tips

- P1 You don't need to complete all of the maps together. Break up the tasks into bite-sized chunks. Use an atlas to check your locations are accurate. Ensure the features you have selected are 'major' or 'significant' in that they attract visitors to an area, for example they may be featured in holiday brochures.

- M1 Ensure that you show that you have used resources efficiently and confidently to identify and locate all items in questions 1 and 2 with minimal supervision.

PLTS

Using resources to identify and locate global aspects, continents and natural features on world maps will help develop your skills as an **independent enquirer**.

1.3 Holiday destinations

In *Unit 1: The UK travel and tourism sector*, pages 5–7 you learned that people travel for different reasons: for leisure, business, visiting friends and relatives (VFR) and other reasons, such as sport, health and education. It is the area of leisure travel where the traveller exercises the greatest degree of personal choice when selecting the destination.

Weather and location are often the key factors influencing customer choice when choosing a holiday. Beach holidays and skiing holidays are equally dependent on particular weather conditions to meet customer expectations and ensure the popularity of destinations. Location is also important as this will impact on the cost of a holiday, transport options and the time it takes to reach the destination.

Capital cities

Many of the capital cities of the world are tourist destinations in their own right, attracting leisure travellers for sightseeing, entertainment and culture. Capital cities are usually significant commercial centres too and they attract many business travellers. If you were to work as cabin crew you might find that many of your flights could be to capital cities around the world.

Activity: Capitals

Match the capital city to the correct country in the middle column and then match the country to the correct continent in the right hand column.

Capital	Country	Continent
Santiago	Denmark	Africa
Canberra	USA	Africa
Wellington	Gambia	North America
Kuala Lumpur	Australia	North America
Nassau	Morocco	South America
Buenos Aires	Malaysia	South America
Banjul	Argentina	Australasia
Bangkok	New Zealand	Australasia
Rabat	Thailand	Europe
Budapest	Bahamas	Europe
Washington DC	Hungary	Asia
Copenhagen	Chile	Asia

Europe

Europe offers great contrasts to the UK, from the cooler climates of Scandinavian countries such as Norway and Sweden, to the warmth of the Mediterranean countries such as Spain and Italy. France, Hungary, Poland and other central European countries offer further contrasts. As well as different climates, European countries also differ in language, history, traditions, landscape, architecture and the way of life. UK and other European holiday destinations are examined in greater depth in *Unit 6: UK Tourism destinations and Unit 7: European holiday destinations.*

Why have European cities become so popular?

North America

The USA and Canada dominate the continent of North America, which also includes the islands of the Caribbean. North America attracts holidaymakers from the UK, and many cities in Canada and the USA also have important business links with the UK.

English is the main language spoken in the USA and Canada, and also in most of the Caribbean countries. This can be a significant plus factor for many UK visitors. In addition, the excellent range of flights makes many North American destinations attractive and accessible to UK holidaymakers.

Activity: Making tracks

Many young people choose an InterRail holiday. This is an excellent way to experience what Europe has to offer. For a set price, you can buy unlimited rail travel throughout Europe for one month. Imagine that you have been offered an InterRail ticket for one month.

Find out which European countries you can travel to with this ticket.

Plan which countries you would like to visit as part of an InterRail holiday (include at least six countries in your plans). Identify the capital cities of those countries and at least one other place you would like to visit in each country.

Plot your trip on a map of Europe.

Activity: North American scramble

Unscramble these islands of the Caribbean and holiday spots in the USA and Canada:

Use holiday brochures to find examples of holidays in these locations and to see what they have to offer the visitor.

Caribbean:			
CAAMJAI DOBSBARA INOCDAINM LECPUIRB		TS TTIKS GAANTIU	
The USA:			
WEN KORY LSA GAVES LANRDOO		HIANGWTONS SNA GOIED	
Canada:			
RMEOANLT WOOTAT		TORTOON COUVVERAN	

South America

South America is located predominantly in the southern hemisphere. It was 'discovered' by the Spanish and Portuguese explorers of the fifteenth century and their influences are still very apparent in the language and architecture of South America today. It has become one of the most popular continents for gap year travellers because of the contrasting range of travel adventures it offers.

Case study: Brazilian adventure

Brazil is a country of great contrasts. Its Portuguese influences are still strong in its language, traditions, architecture and way of life. Brazil's capital Rio de Janeiro comes alive each year with its famous Carnival – an event not to be missed! Rio is an entertaining and lively city where the partying never stops – the New Year's Eve beach party on famous Copacabana beach is an unforgettable experience attracting over two million visitors each year from all over the world.

The huge statue of Christ the Redeemer has become an iconic landmark watching over Rio from the

Corcovado Mountain. The Amazon rainforest provides a sharp contrast to Rio. Visitors can escape the tourist trail, discover the culture and heritage of the Amazon basin and explore the jungle.

Brazil is a perfect choice for a travel adventure, either on its own or as part of a bigger trip to South America.

1 Identify other countries in South America.

2 Compare what other South American countries offer the traveller.

Africa

Much of Africa is part of the developing world and tourism is a very important source of income for African countries. South Africa, home to the World Cup in 2010, regularly hits the 'Top Ten' lists for best destinations and in 2009 Cape Town won Virgin Holidays' 'Best Destination' award. Safari holidays attract many visitors to South Africa and also to other African countries including Kenya, Tanzania, Botswana and Uganda.

The north of the continent is quite a contrast to the south. Tunisia and Morocco feature in a number of package holiday brochures and offer an alternative to Spain for a sunshine holiday. To the east of the continent Egypt is famous for its Nile cruises, taking in ancient Egyptian sights and cities such as Cairo and Luxor.

How does Africa appeal to tourists?

Asia

Thailand, India, China, Japan and Singapore are possibly the best known Asian countries for travellers from the UK. These countries alone offer great contrasts to the visitor in terms of culture, language, religion, traditions and way of life. The UK carries out significant amounts of trade with Asian countries and a high proportion of travel to the continent is for business purposes.

Activity: Asia

Find the capitals for each country and then identify at least one significant resort, or tourist destination, in each country.

Country	Capital	Resorts/tourist destinations
Thailand		
India		
China		
Japan		
Singapore		

Australasia

Australia and New Zealand are the best known countries of Australasia. The surrounding region of the Pacific Ocean, that encompasses Papua New Guinea and the islands of Polynesia, Melanesia and Micronesia, is known as Oceania.

According to Tourism Australia there were nearly 440,600 visitors to Australia from the UK in the nine months to September 2009, while the New Zealand Ministry of Tourism reported that New Zealand welcomed nearly 260,000 visitors from the UK during the same period. To obtain a secure link to the Tourism Australia website and the New Zealand Ministry of Tourism report, see the Hotlinks section on p.x.

Thousands of people have emigrated from the UK to Australia and New Zealand since the 1950s. Many visitors to Australia and New Zealand travel for the purpose of visiting their friends and relatives (VFR) and while they are there many of them take the opportunity to take in some touring and sightseeing. Australia is also very popular with young people visiting as part of a gap year.

Activity: Australian appeal

Australia is a country of contrasts. It is the sixth largest country in the world and is home to world famous attractions including:

- Sydney Opera House and Harbour Bridge
- Ayers Rock (Uluru)
- Great Barrier Reef
- Bondi Beach

Use a guide book to find out about these attractions and locate them on a map of Australia.

1.4 Gateways

Air gateways

Accessibility by air influences the appeal of destinations. When investigating worldwide air travel it is useful to start with identifying **gateway airports**. These are the airports that serve capitals or major cities and typically they will:

- serve worldwide destinations, using scheduled airlines from around the world
- have more than one runway and passenger terminal
- have more than 10 million passengers each year.

Some of these airports may also be hubs. Hubs are airports used by an airline as a transfer point, where passengers transfer from one flight to another flight to reach their final destination.

One important feature of airports is that they have their own unique code. These are depicted as three letters and are used internationally.

Key term

Gateway airports – so called because they are gateways to other areas. You can land there and then transfer to aircraft travelling to different destinations in a country.

In some cases the code is easy to guess, for example Manchester Airport is MAN as there is only one airport in Manchester, UK. London, on the other hand, has several airports and their codes are LCY for London City airport, LGW for London Gatwick and LHR for London Heathrow. Stansted and Luton Airports are also classed as London and their codes are STN and LTN respectively.

Did you know?

There is more than one Manchester Airport in the world so the different codes are especially important so that people are not mistakenly booked on flights to the 'wrong' Manchester. For example Manchester Regional Airport in Boston USA has the code MHT.

Activity: Flying in

For each country identify the correct continent, one major airport for flights from London and its 3 letter airport code.

Country	Continent	Major airport	Airport code
Chile			
Australia			
Botswana			
Norway			
Canada			
Indonesia			
Peru			
Kenya			
USA			
New Zealand			
Greece			
Japan			

Seaports

Seaports are important gateways to many countries, for example thousands of passengers each year choose to travel between the UK and Europe by ferry. There are a number of gateways between Europe and the UK, including Calais, Cherbourg, Rotterdam, Zeebrugge and Santander on the European side and Dover, Portsmouth, Hull and Plymouth on the UK side.

As you will have seen from the earlier case study (see page 81), cruise ports of call can be found all over the world.

Activity: Ship ahoy

Select a cruise ship, for example Queen Mary or Oasis of the Seas. Identify ports of call for three cruises and locate these on a map of the world. Try to select cruises in different cruise areas of the world if you can.

Assessment activity 3.2

This next task focuses on locating popular holiday destinations within the continents of North America, South America, Europe, Africa, Asia and Australasia.

1 On blank maps of the continents of North America, South America, Europe, Africa, Asia and Australasia locate two countries that are popular holiday destinations.

For each country located you must:

- name and locate their capital cities

- name and locate one major passenger seaport if the country has one

- name and locate one major hub or international airport (with its 3 letter code)

- identify and locate two popular holiday resorts or resort areas.

Question 1 will enable you to achieve **P2** and part **M1**.

You will be allowed to use resources for these tasks for **P2** and part **M1**. This must include the use of an atlas. Keep a record of any other resources you have used.

2 To check your awareness of worldwide locations, you have been set a test to see if you can find locations without using resources. This will include the global aspects, natural features and continents that formed activity assessment 3.1, plus two countries in each continent.

Question 2 will enable you to achieve **D1**.

Grading tips

- **P2** You don't need to complete all of the maps together. Break up the tasks into bite-sized chunks, one continent at a time.

- **P2** Use holiday brochures to help you to identify the countries and resorts or resort areas that are popular with holidaymakers.

- **M1** You need to show that you can use resources confidently and efficiently to identify and locate all items for assessment activities 3.1 and 3.2 with minimal supervision.

- **D1** You need to locate all items for assessment activity 3.1 and the countries for assessment activity 3.2 in supervised test conditions without using resources.

PLTS

Using resources to identify and locate holiday destinations and gateways on world maps will help develop your skills as an **independent enquirer**.

2 World climatic conditions affecting travel to worldwide destinations

2.1 Climatic conditions and seasonal variations

Climate plays a big part in influencing travel to particular destinations. Travellers look for different types of climate and conditions depending on the dates and nature of their trip. You can see from the list below that people have different needs and expectations when they travel:

- A group of young people taking a summer beach holiday in the Mediterranean expect hot, sunny weather.

- A family, with young children, also taking a summer beach holiday in the Mediterranean want sunshine but not too hot.

- Experienced skiers want excellent skiing conditions in North America.

- A honeymoon couple are looking for guaranteed sunshine in the winter.

- An elderly couple touring Europe want warm, but not hot weather.

Did you know?

Humidity is a measurement of the amount of water vapour in the air. High humidity combined with high temperatures makes people feel uncomfortable, hot and sticky, whereas low humidity is generally more comfortable, even in high temperatures.

Sun

One of the main reasons for the growth of package holidays to the Mediterranean in the 1970s was that holidaymakers from the UK and Northern Europe were travelling in search of the sun and the Mediterranean offered just that. The Mediterranean climate has long hot sunny days and not much rainfall in the summer months. Low humidity can help to create a very comfortable climate.

Since the 1970s developments in transport and destinations have made it easier to travel beyond Europe in search of sunshine. The Canary Islands have year-round sunshine and are popular for winter holidays, as they are still relatively close to the UK. Further afield, the Caribbean Islands have excellent sunshine records to appeal to visitors. For guaranteed winter sunshine, many travellers from the UK head for destinations closer to the equator or in the southern hemisphere. The tilt of the Earth as it orbits the Sun means that countries around the equator have a steady temperature between 19°C and 27°C. These temperatures remain fairly constant all year round.

Activity: Sun spots

Find five examples of destinations suitable for winter sun in the southern hemisphere.

Why do people choose to holiday in the sunshine?

However, the sun alone does not make for perfect weather conditions. Sunny climates near the equator often have very high humidity which can be very uncomfortable for travellers. In some destinations, such as Dubai, temperatures over 40°C are not uncommon and that is just too hot for many people, especially when combined with high humidity. In desert areas, such as the Sahara, the sun can be dangerous with temperatures rising to 50°C and higher.

Tropical storms

The most dramatic tropical storms affect the areas around the Tropic of Cancer in the northern hemisphere and the Tropic of Capricorn in the southern hemisphere.

The most severe tropical storms are known as **hurricanes**, **cyclones** or **typhoons**, depending on their location.

Tropical storms are seasonal. The hurricane and typhoon seasons are between June and November, particularly August and September. The cyclone season is between November and March.

Some visitors will avoid taking their holidays in risk areas during these times. Tropical storms rarely happen outside the risk seasons, so most visitors will choose to travel when the weather is more favourable. However, hurricanes rarely hit the same area twice and if visitors are willing to risk travelling during the hurricane 'season' they can often find a holiday at an excellent price.

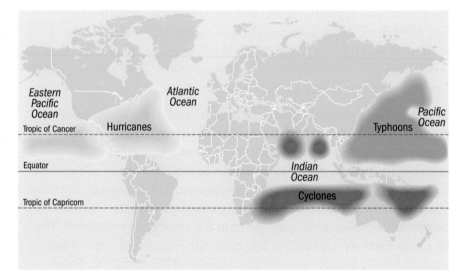

Figure 3.4: Map showing tropical storms seasons

The Saffir–Simpson Hurricane Scale is used to measure the intensity of hurricanes. Table 3.1 shows the maximum wind speed at different levels on the scale and the risk of damage.

Hurricanes can be very destructive. They cause damage to resorts and hotel buildings, can temporarily close airports and roads and affect power supplies. Travel in the area and out of the country can be severely

Key terms

Hurricanes – these occur mainly in the North Atlantic Ocean, especially the Caribbean and the Gulf of Mexico and the north-eastern Pacific Ocean.

Cyclones – these occur mainly in the south-western Pacific Ocean and the Indian Ocean.

Typhoons – these occur mainly in the north-western Pacific Ocean.

Did you know?

Hurricanes are given names chosen from a list selected by the World Meteorological Organisation. The first name on the list begins with A and that name is given to the first hurricane of the season, the next one takes the name beginning with B and so on. There are six lists in existence so the same names can come up again every sixth year. However, when a hurricane has been particularly destructive that name is not used again.

Table 3.1: Saffir–Simpson Hurricane Scale

Scale	Maximum wind speed	Damage
1	74–95 mph	Minimal
2	96–110 mph	Moderate
3	111–130 mph	Extensive
4	131–155 mph	Extreme
5	156+ mph	Catastrophic

disrupted. Holidaymakers caught up in a hurricane, or other severe tropical storms, may suffer disruption to their holiday and prospective holidaymakers may have their holidays cancelled. Holidays may be curtailed and passangers may have to be repatriated. Hurricanes threaten personal safety and can also cause loss of life.

One of the most destructive hurricanes in recent years was Hurricane Katrina.

What happened when Katrina hit New Orleans?

Case study: New Orleans

On 29 August 2005 the eye of Hurricane Katrina passed within 15 miles of the city of New Orleans in the USA and the consequences were devastating. Approximately 80% of the city was flooded, with some parts covered by 4.5m of water, and there was widespread destruction of buildings.

Over one million people had followed the US government's order to evacuate the city, but many refused to do so. Over 1000 people lost their lives.

British tourists enjoying the last few days of their summer holiday were caught up in the aftermath of Hurricane Katrina. New Orleans International Airport closed before the storm, and re-opened for humanitarian aid and rescue flights on 30 August. It did not reopen for commercial passenger flights until 13 September.

Tourists were amongst the 25,000 people evacuated to the New Orleans Superdome, where they were provided with blankets, water and shelter. Conditions soon became overcrowded, squalid and dangerous. There were reports of violence and filthy conditions

and of tourists having to fend for themselves before being taken to safety by the National Guard.

The tourist industry, which had attracted nearly 9 million visitors to New Orleans each year, was devastated by Hurricane Katrina, with hotels, transport networks and attractions destroyed. In 2006 tourist figures dropped to around 3 million visitors. Government aid has been pumped into rebuilding the city. By 2007 over 7 million visitors visited New Orleans. Now find out for yourself:

1 Has New Orleans been affected by hurricanes since 2005?

2 Find another destination where travel has been affected by a hurricane since 2005.

Take it further:

3 There is a new attraction in New Orleans in the form of bus tours around the disaster area, with Gray Line offering a three-hour, $35 tour called 'Hurricane Katrina - America's Worst Catastrophe'. Is it right to turn disaster areas into attractions?

Monsoons

Countries, such as India and the exotic islands of the Maldives, are affected by monsoons. There are two monsoon seasons – a wet season from June to September and a dry season from December to March.

During the wet season monsoon rain can be torrential – it can affect travel and even cause floods. It is said that 80% of India's rain falls during the monsoon months of June to September. The monsoon rains are sudden and can be quickly followed by sunshine.

In the Maldives there is very little difference in temperature between the dry season (north-east monsoon) and wet season (south-west monsoon). It remains at a fairly constant 30°C. The north-east monsoon lasts from January to March and the south-west monsoon from May to November. Even in the 'wet season' the Maldives has sunny spells most days as can be seen in Figure 3.5.

Sudden rains can have a detrimental effect on a holiday and people planning a special holiday, such as a wedding or honeymoon, would need to take this into consideration when choosing dates and destinations.

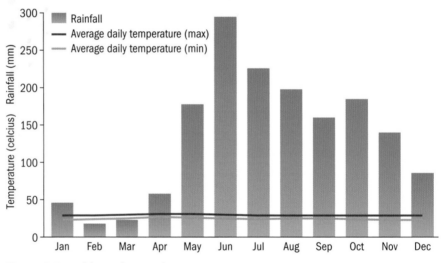

Figure 3.5: Maldives climate chart

Snow

Good snow is essential for winter sports holidays, especially for downhill skiing. The amount of snow depends on the height of the mountains and the direction they face. While there are many excellent areas for snow in Europe, including the Alps and Pyrenees, the snow in destinations such as the Rocky Mountains in North America is more guaranteed, because the mountains are much higher and the snow is deeper.

In the northern hemisphere, for example in Europe, North America and Japan, the main snow season normally starts in November or December and lasts until March or April. However, this depends on how far north the resort is and also on the altitude. The higher the altitude, the better chance of snow and the longer the winter sports season.

In the southern hemisphere, for example New Zealand, the snow season starts in May or June and lasts until until September or October.

Sometimes snow conditions can be very poor and this can seriously affect winter sports holidays. Skiers may have to be bussed to resorts farther up the mountains or they may find themselves skiing on slopes that have been created artificially using snow cannons. Poor snow can result in cancellations, reduced visitor numbers and loss of business for ski schools and hotels.

Occasionally mountain areas and resorts can be prone to avalanches when heavy snow falls onto an unstable base and the snow begins to melt. This can disrupt travel plans and affect safety as roads and resorts can be cut off and avalanches can sometimes cause loss of life. Visitors travelling for winter sports to destinations such as Canada, should expect very cold, freezing temperatures, but they need to be especially careful when temperatures become more extreme and unseasonably cold as this can result in frost nip, frostbite and hypothermia.

Winds

Winds affect climate. Cooling winds can be very beneficial in a hot climate and can give some respite from the heat. The Canary Islands and Caribbean Islands have winds that cool the coast and can make temperatures more bearable in the summer months.

Winds that pass over oceans are rain-bearing as they pick up moisture which turns into rain when they reach land.

2.2 Effects

Some of the effects of extreme weather have already been highlighted in this section. Visitor numbers can drop when a destination has been in the news following particularly adverse weather conditions and some travellers may have to be repatriated back to the UK and others may cancel their holiday plans.

If you are working in the travel industry, perhaps as a travel consultant, you will need to point out to customers the possible risks when travelling to destinations during the hurricane season. You should be aware of the potential disruption to your customers' holidays and give them advice about the best times to travel and those to avoid. While it is impossible to guarantee the weather, always check out the weather charts for destinations at certain times of the year and advise customers of sun, rain and humidity figures to help them to make the best choice for sunshine holidays and snow conditions for winter sports.

Activity: Effects on visitors

Extreme weather can cause disruption to travel, cancelled holidays, repatriation, and influence personal safety. Do some research into the effect that these can have on visitor numbers. Does extreme weather prevent people from travelling to certain locations? What does this mean for the travel and tourism sector?

Assessment activity 3.3

P3 M2 D2

You have completed your induction training with a worldwide tour operator and you have been asked by your manager to make a presentation to your colleagues at the next training and briefing session. The topic you have been asked to research and present is climatic conditions and their effects on travel to worldwide destinations.

1 You must describe:

- at least four different climatic conditions

- how they can affect travel to worldwide destinations

- seasonal variations, including locations and times of the year to avoid and locations and times of the year with favourable conditions

- unusual or extreme conditions.

Include global aspects in your descriptions where applicable (for example, indicate if the destination is close to the equator or the Tropics, northern and southern hemispheres if applicable).

Use PowerPoint and prepare handouts for your colleagues. Keep all your notes in case the tour operator manager has any questions and make sure you reference all sources used.

Question 1 will enable you to achieve P3.

2 The tour operator manager has asked you to also produce information sheets for your colleagues to explain climatic conditions in two destinations of your choice. In these sheets you should explain how seasonal climatic conditions can affect travel to the two destinations.

Question 2 will enable you to achieve M2 .

3 Many of your company's customers book holidays to the Caribbean. Your manager now wants you to complete more in-depth research and to produce a report on the effect of major hurricanes on the Caribbean. You can focus on the Caribbean in general, or choose one, or more, islands or destinations for your research.

Question 3 will enable you to achieve D2.

Grading tips

- P3 The conditions you describe could be positive in attracting people to an area, but negative when the conditions are extreme. Give examples to support your description.

- M2 Make sure that they have different climatic conditions. For each condition you could explain how climate might have a positive effect at certain times of the year, but a negative effect at other times. You could include potential

effects such as reduced or increased visitor numbers, restricted seasons, adverse publicity and potential disruption to travel plans.

- D2 Your report must be analytical. Identify several relevant effects, show how they are linked to travel to the Caribbean and explain the importance of each. Use information from press reports, articles and other sources to support your analysis, with specific examples from within the last ten years.

PLTS

Exploring climatic conditions affecting travel to worldwide destinations and identifying seasonal variations will help develop your skills as a **creative thinker**.

Functional skills

Researching climatic conditions will help you develop your **IT** skills in using ICT systems to find and select information.

Presenting information on climatic conditions will help your **IT** skills to develop, present and communicate information.

Researching and discussing climatic conditions and communicating information will help you to develop your **English** skills in speaking and listening and reading.

3 The effect of worldwide time on travellers

The time differences around the world can be quite confusing for travellers. Employees in the travel and tourism sector need to be aware of different time zones so that they can provide their customers with accurate information and advice.

3.1 Time zones

Greenwich Mean Time

To understand about time zones, and how time differences work, you need to know about Greenwich Mean Time.

The Greenwich Royal Observatory in London is the starting point for all time zones. It is located on the 0° **line of longitude**, also known as the prime meridian. The time in Greenwich is known as Greenwich Mean Time or GMT. It is sometimes referred to as Greenwich Meridian Time. Sometimes you also see GMT listed as UTC or Universal Time Coordinate.

As you travel east, or west, of the Greenwich Meridian you enter different time zones. If you travel approximately 15° east from the Greenwich Meridian you arrive at the next time zone which is one hour ahead of GMT. If you continue east, each time zone is one further hour ahead of GMT. If you travel west, each time zone is one hour behind GMT.

15° West	0° Greenwich Meridian	15° East
11 a.m. ◄───────────	12 noon ───────────►	1 p.m.

You can see time zones of the world in Figure 3.6. There are 24 standard time zones in total. If you travel through 12 time zones to the west of GMT or 12 time zones to the east of GMT, you will reach the **International Date Line**, an imaginary line running through the Pacific Ocean.

You will see from Figure 3.6 that most time zones reflect country boundaries rather than following the line of longitude through a country.

Did you know?

The Greenwich Royal Observatory is now a museum. It has a brass line running through its courtyard at 0° longitude. Tourists like to have their photograph taken straddling the line, with one foot in the eastern hemisphere and one foot in the western hemisphere.

Key terms

Lines of longitude – the imaginary lines that circle the curvature of the Earth, running north and south and converging at the north and south Poles. Try and imagine them like the segments of a peeled orange. They are 15° apart and you will usually be able to see them marked on a globe.

International Date Line – the internationally agreed place where the calendar dates change. The calendar date in the area to the east of the International Date Line is one day earlier than the date in the area to the west of the line.

Think about it

Use a globe alongside your map to track the different time zones. Why do you think time zones do not follow exactly the lines of longitude?

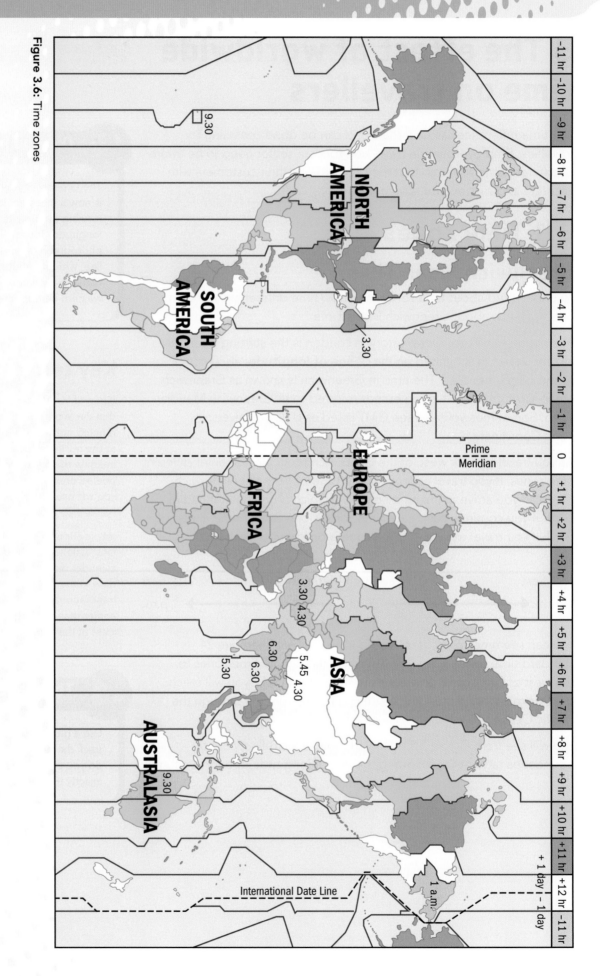

Figure 3.6: Time zones

Some countries, for example Australia and USA, are so large that they have a number of time zones within the same country.

Activity: USA

If you study Figure 3.6 you will see that the USA has six time zones.

Locate a detailed time zone map of the USA using the internet or a world atlas. Starting from the East coast you have Eastern time, then Central, Mountain, Pacific, Alaska and Hawaii-Aleutian. If it is 02.00 GMT in December, what time is it in each of the US time zones?

In which time zone would you find:

- Las Vegas
- San Diego
- Boston
- Chicago.

Did you know?

If you are travelling eastwards across the Pacific Ocean at midday on your birthday, you will go back in time and gain a second birthday when you cross the International Date Line, but if you are travelling westwards you will fast forward to the day after your birthday and will miss out on your celebrations.

Key term

Local time – is the term given to the official time in a particular location.

Case study: European time zones

If you have been on holiday to Spain or France you will have experienced the one hour time difference that exists between the UK and most European countries.

For example, the journey time by ferry from Dover to Calais takes approximately one hour and 30 minutes. If you leave Dover on the 10.00 a.m. sailing you would expect to arrive in France at 11.30 a.m. However, due to the one hour's time difference you must put your watch forward by one hour, making your arrival time 12.30 p.m. and therefore 'losing' one hour of your day.

Coming home, the opposite happens. If you leave Calais on the 9.00 a.m. sailing and the journey again lasts one hour and 30 minutes you would expect to arrive in Dover at 10.30 a.m. However, this time you put your watch back by one hour, meaning that you arrive in Dover at 9.30 a.m. and 'gain' one hour.

On paper this looks as if your journey from Dover to Calais has lasted 2 hours 30 minutes and your journey home has taken only 30 minutes!

The different time zones in Europe are shown in Figure 3.7.

If it is 07.45 GMT in January, what is the local time in:

- Germany
- Greece
- Portugal
- Russia.

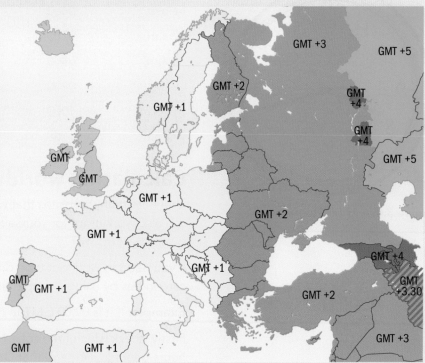

Figure 3.7: Map of European time zones

Daylight Saving Time

Daylight Saving Time is when countries adjust their local time by one hour in the spring to provide extra daylight in the evenings. In Britain this is called British Summer Time (BST).

On the last Sunday in March every year we must move our clocks forward by one hour, so 1.00 a.m. becomes 2.00 a.m. On the last Sunday in October British Summer Time ends and we revert back to GMT by putting our clocks back by one hour, so 1.00 a.m. becomes midnight.

24–hour clock

In the travel and tourism sector the 24-hour clock is used to prevent confusion between night and day times. Whenever you read a timetable or look at times on travel tickets and itineraries the 24-hour clock will be used.

This is how it is used:

Think about it

Using the 24-hour clock. You would refer to 3.00 p.m. as 'fifteen hundred' or 'fifteen hundred hours'; 3.30 p.m. would be 'fifteen thirty' or 'fifteen thirty hours'.

Figure 3.8: A 24-hour clock

12-hour clock	24-hour clock	12-hour clock	24-hour clock
12 am (midnight)	0000	12 p.m. (midday – noon)	1200
1.00 a.m.	0100	1 p.m.	1300
2 a.m.	0200	2 p.m.	1400
3 a.m.	0300	3 p.m.	1500
4 a.m.	0400	4 p.m.	1600
5 a.m.	0500	5 p.m.	1700
6 a.m.	0600	6 p.m.	1800
7 a.m.	0700	7 p.m.	1900
8 a.m.	0800	8 p.m.	2000
9 a.m.	0900	9 p.m.	2100
10 a.m.	1000	10 p.m.	2200
11 a.m.	1100	11 p.m.	2300

Calculating worldwide time

There are many websites that will calculate worldwide time for you. You can also work it out for yourself by counting the hours backwards or forwards from GMT.

If you need to work out time differences between other locations you can do this by using a simple time bar, such as shown in Figure 3.9.

Example: If it is 09.00 GMT in New York what time is it in Dubai?

Firstly, check which time zone New York is in. You will find that it is 5 hours behind GMT, and that Dubai is 4 hours ahead of GMT.

By plotting both of these on the time bar you will then be able to calculate that the time difference between the two is 9 hours. Dubai is 9 hours ahead of New York.

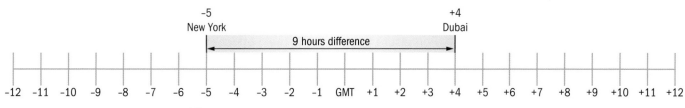

Figure 3.9: How to work out time differences

BTEC **Assessment activity 3.4** **P5**

You have applied to work as a business travel consultant and you have been set an assessment to demonstrate that you can calculate worldwide time differences.

For each of the following scenarios, state the time difference and indicate what the local time it will be on 1 February, using the 24-hour clock:

1 When it is 10.00 London GMT, what time is it in Dubai?
2 When it is 17.00 in Dubai, what time is it in Sydney?
3 When it is 23.00 in Sydney, what time is it in Los Angeles?
4 When it is 04.30 in Los Angeles, what time is it in London GMT?
5 When it is 06.30 in London, what time is it in Chicago?
6 When it is 21.00 in Chicago, what time is it in Hawaii?
7 When it is 15.00 in Hawaii, what time is it in Tokyo
8 When it is 03.15 in Tokyo, what time is it in Rio de Janeiro?
9 When it is 10.15 in London GMT, what time is it in the Gambia?
10 When it is 19.20 in Lisbon, what time is it in Madrid?

This question will enable you to achieve **P5**.

Grading tips

- **P5** Locate the different places on a map with time zones so you can visualise where they are.
- **P5** Use a time bar to help you to calculate the time in different countries.

Activity: Travelling through time zones

Westbound

A business traveller flies from London to New York in November. The flight takes approximately 7 hours. Departing London at 11.00 GMT they would arrive in New York 7 hours later at 18.00 GMT, where the time difference is GMT – 5 hours.

Therefore the local time in New York is 13.00 hours. This means it is early afternoon, but the body clock thinks it is already 18.00.

Eastbound

If a business traveller flies from London to Dubai, the flight takes approximately 7 hours. Departing London at 11.00 GMT they would arrive in Dubai 7 hours later at 18.00 GMT where the time difference is GMT + 4 hours.

Therefore the local time of arrival in Dubai is 22.00 hours. This means it is nearly bedtime when the body clock thinks it is 18.00.

How do you think jet lag might affect the business traveller in these two examples?

3.2 Effect on travellers

Jet lag

Your body is used to a regular routine of light and darkness at certain times of the day. Air travel now allows us to travel quickly across several different time zones in a matter of hours and our body is unable to catch up. This can cause jet lag. The main symptom of jet lag is disturbed sleep, for example feeling tired or awake at the wrong time. This will depend on the direction you have travelled.

PLTS

Calculating and communicating worldwide time differences will help you to develop your **mathematical** skills, to identify and solve problems, find solutions, use checking procedures and draw and communicate conclusions.

Leisure and business travellers

For leisure travellers, the main effect of jet lag is that it might take them a few days to get used to the local time and this could affect their holiday enjoyment. However, the implications for a business traveller might be more serious as they may have important meetings to attend and need to be alert and business-like.

Airline websites contain a lot of good advice about how to avoid jet lag. Some of their recommendations are to:

* avoid drinking alcohol before or during the flight
* drink plenty of water to prevent dehydration
* try to get a good night's sleep prior to the flight
* do some light exercise before the flight
* walk around the cabin from time to time
* set your watch to the local time
* try and go to bed at the correct local time
* aim to arrive at your destination during daylight hours if possible.

Assessment activity 3.5   P4 M3

As a senior travel consultant you have been asked to brief new colleagues on the effect of worldwide time on travellers.

1. Prepare a PowerPoint presentation to explain about time zones and how these can affect travellers. You need to simply, but clearly, explain the following terminology:

   * Greenwich Mean Time (GMT)
   * the location of the Prime Meridian (Greenwich Meridian and the International Date Line)
   * time differences when travelling through the eastern and western hemispheres
   * countries with different time zones
   * Daylight Saving Time (DST).

   You must also explain the effect on leisure and business travellers including:

   * losing, and gaining time, when travelling through different time zones
   * jet lag
   * losing, or gaining, a day when travelling across the international date line.

   Question 1 will enable you to achieve P4.

2. You feel that some of your colleagues may be finding it difficult to understand time differences, so you now provide a step-by-step guide to two specific journeys, one westwards and one eastwards. You explain about the time zones and journey times for the two journeys, clearly illustrating the potential effect on the leisure and business traveller.

   Question 2 will enable you to achieve M3.

Grading tips

* **P4** Make sure you have included all of the listed items and research them carefully to enable you to explain using your own words.

* **M3** Try to imagine yourself taking the journeys. By putting yourself in the traveller's shoes you will be better placed to appreciate the process of time changes and how the journey might affect you when you arrive at the destinations and for the few days after arrival.

WorkSpace Frankie Bales

Travel Consultant

I work for an independent travel agent. We specialise in long-haul holidays, but also offer holidays to Europe and provide business travel arrangements for a number of businesses in the area.

There is no such thing as a typical day in our travel shop as you never know what each customer might want. There are six other staff and I am the youngest and least experienced, so there is always something new to learn every day.

When customers come to the agency I may be the first person they come into contact with. I have to be polite and deal with their enquiry. If they want to book a holiday I have to find out as much as I can about what they want from their holiday and then try and find something to suit them.

The job might sound quite straightforward, but there are a lot of things that can go wrong. People rely on us for accurate information, for example if we are booking a wedding in the Caribbean we have to check that we are not arranging travel in the middle of the hurricane season.

Another aspect we have to be careful about is time differences. If a business person wants to arrive in Istanbul in time for a very important meeting they would not be very happy if we calculated the time differences incorrectly and they arrived after the meeting had taken place. Luckily, the airlines confirm arrival times in local times so that type of mistake is normally picked up before it's too late.

I love the variety of my work and my ambition is to travel to every continent in the world. I've managed Europe and North America so far, so I still have quite a few to look forward to.

Think about it!

1 To what extent do you rely on a travel agent to always give the right information?

2 How would you feel if a travel agent didn't advise you that your dream holiday was going to fall in the middle of the monsoon season?

Just checking

1 Name the ocean lying between Hong Kong and Los Angeles.
2 What is another name for Greenwich Mean Time (GMT)?
3 What time is 20.45 in 12-hour clock time?
4 Is Thailand in the northern or southern hemisphere?
5 Name two countries in South America.
6 Give one side effect of jet lag.
7 Where is the International Date Line?
8 Name a mountain range in Asia.
9 Name a lake in North America.
10 Where is the Great Barrier Reef?
11 Why is it important for travel and tourism employees to know about climate and time differences?
12 How has this chapter helped to develop your knowledge of the world for travellers?
13 What advice would you give to someone who is concerned about suffering from jet lag?
14 How could the skills and knowledge gained be used in different types of jobs in the travel and tourism sector?

Assignment tips

- When you watch live world news try and work out the time difference between the UK and the location – it will often be dark when a report is coming in yet we might have bright sunshine.
- Watch out on the news for extreme weather – we normally hear about this when British tourists have been affected by severe conditions. Remember that British weather too can be very damaging and that travel can be severely disrupted by floods and snow.
- If you have satellite TV you can view the weather forecasts around the world.
- If you want to see the effect of severe storms you will find plenty of clips on YouTube.
- In winter pay particular attention to the ski reports. Find out where the snow is good and where it isn't.
- Google Earth is a great resource to zoom in and gain a bird's eye view of places around the world. Try focusing on mountains and some of the famous natural attractions such as the Grand Canyon.
- Talk to friends and family who have travelled across time zones. How were they affected by jet lag? Did it spoil their holiday?

Credit value: 5

4 Development of the UK travel and tourism sector

UK travel and tourism is a complex and dynamic sector influenced by developments and changing habits. Wider economic, political, environmental and social issues and changes can impact upon organisations operating within the sector, demonstrating the susceptibility of UK travel and tourism to external influences.

Customers are now more demanding than ever. Developments within the travel and tourism sector reflect the diverse and ever-changing needs of the consumer. Technological advances, such as internet booking facilities, have empowered customers to arrange a more customised holiday experience.

This unit explores the development of the UK travel and tourism sector. You will learn about the historical events, developments, changes to tourism habits and other issues that have shaped the UK travel and tourism sector in the past and will continue to shape the sector in the future.

Learning outcomes

After completing this unit you should:

1 know the developments and lifestyle changes that have shaped the UK travel and tourism sector

2 understand how issues have impacted on the travel and tourism sector.

Assessment and grading criteria

This table shows you what you must do in order to achieve a pass, merit or distinction grade, and where you can find activities in this book to help you.

To achieve a **pass** grade the evidence must show that you are able to:	To achieve a **merit** grade the evidence must show that, in addition to the pass criteria, you are able to:	To achieve a **distinction** grade the evidence must show that, in addition to the pass and merit criteria, you are able to:
P1 summarise the developments that have shaped the UK travel and tourism sector **Assessment activity 4.1, page 129**	**M1** explain how the links between developments, lifestyle changes and trends have shaped the UK travel and tourism sector **Assessment activity 4.3, page 135**	
P2 describe lifestyle changes and trends, highlighting links with developments **Assessment activity 4.2, page 135**		
P3 identify issues that have impacted on the UK travel and tourism sector **Assessment activity 4.4, page 139**		**D1** discuss how organisations are responding to the challenges created by the issues **Assessment activity 4.5, page 142**
P4 review how issues have impacted on the UK travel and tourism sector **Assessment activity 4.4, page 139**	**M2** analyse the impact of issues on the UK travel and tourism sector **Assessment activity 4.5, page 142**	

David, 16-year-old learner

This unit helped me to understand more about why the UK travel and tourism sector is like it is today. I think this is really important because I want to work in this sector eventually and I now feel more confident in my knowledge about the developments that have taken place and the factors that have impacted on this area.

There were lots of practical tasks for this unit. I had a lot of fun when my group visited Rhyl in North Wales to complete some field-based research about the decline of traditional seaside resorts.

I also really enjoyed giving an assessed presentation about how developments, along with changes in tourism habits, have helped shape the UK travel and tourism sector. When I was preparing for the presentation I struggled to understand some of the terms that were being used in the assignment brief, like horizontal and vertical integration, but my tutor suggested that I use the index in a textbook to look up these words. When I located the information about these terms in the textbook, I found that the diagrams helped me to understand them more.

Over to you

- How will you prepare for assessed tasks?

- Do you know what sources of help are available to you?

- Do you understand fully what you are being asked to do?

1. Developments and lifestyle changes that have shaped the UK travel and tourism sector

Set off

What is development?

Where have you heard the word development used before? Development is generally about making a change or improvement to an existing product or service, for example Alton Towers introducing a new theme park ride.

Write down six examples of developments that have taken place within the travel and tourism sector (including examples from each of the six component industries making up the travel and tourism sector). Do you agree that each example given can be considered a change or improvement?

Timeline

Key events that have affected the development of the UK travel and tourism sector since 1945 are listed below.

Table 4.1: Key events in the UK travel and tourism sector since 1945

1945	End of Second World War
1946	Heathrow Airport officially opened
1948	Holidays With Pay Act (1938) made effective
1949	National Parks and Access to the Countryside Act passed by Parliament
1950	Vladimir Raitz organised the first overseas package excursion to Corsica
1952	The world's first passenger jet, the De Havilland Comet, went into service
1954	Boeing introduce a new passenger jet, the Boeing 707
1960s	Computer Reservation Systems (CRS) introduced
1965	Lord Thomson founded Thomson Travel Group
1969	Development of Tourism Act passed by Parliament
1970s	Teletext launched
1972	Butlins announced record visitor numbers of over one million
1976	Concorde went into commercial service
1980	Mosney, the first Butlins holiday camp closes
1984	Richard Branson launched Virgin Atlantic
1986	Barry Island, the fifth of the original nine Butlins holiday camps, closes
1990s	Deregulation of European Union airspace

1994	The Channel Tunnel linking England to France opened
1994	easyJet launched
1996	The UK rail network privatised
2001	September 11 terrorist attacks in New York
2005	July 7 terrorist attacks in London
2008	XL, the UK's third largest tour operator, collapsed
2009	Swine flu pandemic
2010	Volcanic ash from Iceland grounds flights across the UK and Europe

1.1 Development of package holidays

Early developments

In 1758 Cox and Kings, widely recognised to be the first travel company, was founded. The initial purpose of the company was to provide a range of services to the military including arranging the payment of officers and men, arranging clothing and, most significantly, organising travel to the Indian subcontinent. Cox and Kings still operate today as an independent tour company based in the United Kingdom, India, USA and Japan.

Thomas Cook founded his travel company in 1841 and is often considered to be the 'father of tourism'. A religious man, Cook believed that many of the problems experienced by working-class people at the time, such as excessive drinking, could be improved through the introduction of mass excursions, using the 'great powers of railways and locomotives'.

A less well known fact is that Cook's initial business running rail excursions was not successful and he was declared bankrupt in 1846. However, Cook persevered and soon organised for over 165,000 people to attend the Great Exhibition of 1851 in London. By 1855 Thomas Cook was organising excursions to Europe. The 'grand circular tour' incorporated Brussels, Cologne, the Rhine, Heidelberg, Baden-Baden, Strasbourg and Paris, returning to London via Le Havre or Dieppe.

Growth of mass market

Before the Second World War **disposable income** for the working classes was limited, although there were efforts from those within the sector to make tourism more affordable for the working-class masses. Billy Butlin introduced the slogan 'A week's holiday for a week's pay!' to promote his new holiday camp in Skegness.

Figure 4.1: The grand circular tour led by Thomas Cook

Did you know?

For one of his 1855 excursions organised from Leicester to Liverpool, Thomas Cook published a handbook outlining details of the journey, a document considered to be a forerunner of the modern holiday brochure.

Key term

Disposable income – the amount of money which an individual has available to spend on non-essential items, after meeting all essential bills.

The Holidays With Pay Act (1938) created a legal obligation for employers to provide holidays with pay. This development in legislation helped to ensure more leisure time for the public to participate in travel and tourism activities, although the onset of the Second World War in 1939 stunted the development of the sector.

In 1950, Vladimir Raitz organised the first overseas package excursion to Corsica, incorporating air travel in a Douglas DC3 aircraft. Developments in aircraft technology led to the introduction of larger commercial airlines, followed by other advances such as the introduction of **Computer Reservation Systems (CRS)** in the 1960s.

By the 1960s, the operation of foreign package tour holidays had become a **mass market** industry, with millions heading to continental destinations such as Spain. Developments in commercial aviation encouraged greater economy by transporting hundreds of passengers at a time. By combining flights, accommodation and transfers, organisations were able to offer foreign package tours at an affordable price. However, mass market tourism was not simply limited to overseas package excursions. In 1972 Butlin's, operating within the UK domestic sector, took over one million bookings. In the 1970s emerging European destinations such as Crete and the Algarve contributed to the growth of the industry, although most package holidays were to Spain and its islands.

Understanding mass market tourism

Mass market tourism is said to evolve through the following stages:

- A few tourists discover a suitable area or destination, commonly a beach resort.

- Recognising the potential for tourism, local business people develop new, or adapt existing, facilities to cater for the needs of the growing number of tourists.

- The government funds improvements to infrastructure to meet the demands of the increasing numbers of tourists.

- Finally mass tourism is developed. Often products are sold through tour operators as a package holiday – mass tourism relies on the large-scale production and sale of package holidays in order to offer customers affordable options.

However, the growth of the internet and the introduction of low-cost airlines in the 1990s has encouraged the growth of new forms of 'specialist holidays' and the popularity of the traditional foreign beach resort is now said to be in decline with certain groups of customer. This may be linked to the fact that people are more aware of the health issues associated with overexposure to the sun than they were in the 1960s and 1970s, and people are more likely to participate in activities that encourage their mental and physical well-being.

Specialist holidays

All-inclusive

All-inclusive holidays offer the holidaymaker flights, accommodation and a range of services and products, such as food and drink within the resort, included at a set price. The advantages of an all-inclusive holiday are that holidaymakers can budget for their holiday without having to spend much money once at the destination. The convenience of having a range of services and products in a relatively safe environment is also appealing. However, the disadvantage of all-inclusive holidays is that there is little motivation for holidaymakers to leave the resort and experience local culture; therefore local businesses do not really benefit.

City breaks

A number of factors, including developments in transport technology and the increasing popularity of **dynamic packaging**, have contributed to changing fashions in short-breaks, including city breaks. The advent of high-speed rail networks and faster ferry crossings has made cities, in places such as Ireland and mainland Europe, more accessible for short-breaks.

The Seacat is capable of reaching Dublin from Holyhead in less than two hours, whilst the Eurostar is able to reach Paris, Lille and Brussels all in less than two hours from London.

Low-cost airlines also offer the opportunity for people to book flights over the internet without the need for a travel agent. Accommodation can also be arranged independently of a travel agent, thus saving money for the consumer and contributing to the popularity of short European city breaks as an affordable option.

Long-haul

Long-haul destinations are resorts and cities that are at least a six-hour flight from the UK. Some of the most popular long-haul destinations are located in North and South America, Australasia and the Caribbean, as well as the many islands in the Pacific and Indian Oceans.

Most long-haul travel is organised by specialist tour operators, some of which have extensive knowledge of tourist provision in certain parts of the world, whilst others have more general knowledge of the main long-haul destinations. Long-haul holidays are seen as expensive and luxurious and are often associated with special events such as weddings and honeymoons.

Cruising

The cruise sector has experienced growth over the past few years. It is estimated that since 1980, the cruise sector has grown at a rate of 8 per cent annually. Once seen as the preserve of the middle and upper classes, cruise holidays now target different market segments, for example the Disney cruise is popular with young families. The most popular cruising areas for UK tourists are the Mediterranean, Scandinavia and the Caribbean.

Key term

Dynamic packaging – when the customer arranges the different elements of a package holiday, including flights and accommodation, independently.

Case study: Queen Mary 2

The world's largest ocean liner, Cunard's *Queen Mary 2* (QM2) entered service in January 2004. At 1132 feet long, the QM2 is five times longer than Cunard's first liner, Britannia (230 ft). The liner is capable of speeds of up to 28.5 knots and has a carrying capacity of over 2500 passengers and 1250 crew. On their website Cunard boast that the Queen Mary 2 is:

- half as long again as the Canary Wharf Tower is high (800 ft)
- three times as long as St Paul's Cathedral is high (366 ft)
- three-and-a-half times as long as the tower of Big Ben is high (310 ft)
- as long as 41 London buses (31.5 ft each)
- twice as long as the Washington Monument is high (555 ft)
- 147 feet longer than the Eiffel Tower is high (984 ft)
- 117 feet shorter than the Empire State Building is high.

1 Why do companies such as Cunard invest so heavily in building such magnificent ships?

2 What is significant about having a high passenger carrying capacity?

3 Why might Cunard want to boast about the scale of Queen Mary 2?

To obtain a secure link to the Cunard website, see the Hotlinks section on p.x.

Dynamic packaging

A common theme running through this chapter is that products and services are shaped to meet customer needs and demands. The development of the internet and low-cost airlines has enabled customers to book individual flights and accommodation to selected destinations. Dynamic packaging empowers the customer as they organise their 'package holiday' independent of the travel agent or tour operator, creating a genuine 'customised' tourism product that meets their individual needs.

1.2 Development of travel agents

A travel agency can be defined as a company that organises personal travel. Although Cox and Kings were formed in 1758, to serve the travel needs of the military among other roles, Thomas Cook is considered to be the first modern travel agency, offering excursions to the public as early as 1841. Other tour companies operating in the nineteenth century included Dean and Dawson, the Polytechnic Touring Association and the Co-operative Wholesale Society.

As the demand for tourism, initially from the middle and upper classes, grew throughout the twentieth century, travel agents became more familiar in the UK. Prior to the Second World War, travel agencies were often limited to more wealthy areas. However, after the war a boom in mass market provision occurred with several agencies located on most UK high streets. This boom in mass market provision occurred from the 1960s onwards for a two important reasons.

Firstly, throughout the 1960s and 1970s a number of larger travel organisations began trading or were created by mergers, for example the Thomson travel group was founded in 1965 following the take over of three smaller travel agents and Britannia Airways by Roy Thomson.

Secondly, alongside the development of travel agencies, technological advances, such as faster commercial airlines with larger carrying capacities and the development of CRS, increased efficiency and enabled organisations to reduce prices for the consumer. In addition to this, social changes increased leisure time and disposable income so people had the time and money needed to participate in tourism activities. These factors encouraged increased volume in sales, which in turn enabled travel organisations to further reduce prices for the consumer.

Multiples

Multiple is a term used to define a travel agency that has more than 50 branches. The majority of travel agents are part of a multiple chain and can be found on most high streets. Examples of multiples include Thomas Cook and TUI.

A travel agent that has between five and fifty branches is called a 'miniple'. Those with fewer than five branches are called 'independents'. Another type of travel agent is one who is based on-line. Some multiples, miniples and independents operate on-line too, but some organisations *only* operate on-line.

Products and services

Travel agents provide a range of products and services aimed at meeting customer's leisure and business travel needs. One of the main services is to act as a link between the customer and the tour operator, although most travel agents also make flight, rail, ferry and coach bookings for customers who wish to travel independently. Travel agents consider the needs of customers and provide advice about tourism products, such as suitable destinations or flights. They are able to make bookings with tour operators using a CRS.

> ### Activity: Types of travel agent
>
> Look around your nearest town or city and list all the different types of travel agents. Identify whether they are multiples, miniples or independent agents. See if you can find four examples of agents who are on-line only.

Figure 4.2: Travel agents offer a range of products

- Inclusive holidays
- Airport car parking
- Air tickets
- Rail tickets
- **Travel agents' products**
- Ferry tickets
- Car hire
- Cruises
- Insurance
- Accommodation

In order to continue to meet the changing needs of leisure and business customers, most travel agents also offer ancillary services such as currency exchange. The exchange is made at the rate for the day, although commission is often charged for the use of this service. Furthermore, travel agents often provide travel insurance, make arrangements for passports and visas, book airport parking and give advice on immunisation.

In order to promote featured holidays effectively, one of the key services provided by travel agents is to display the tour operator's holiday brochures. Although the traditional paper-based brochures are still available, many travel agents also make use of on-line electronic brochures promoted using the internet. As the cost of producing paper-based brochures is astronomical, equating to around £20 for every holiday sold, electronic brochures offer an appealing alternative. They are cheaper to produce, can be amended to reflect changes in holiday prices at little extra cost and are more environmentally friendly as they save on paper usage.

Key term

Chain of distribution – a chain of distribution shows how travel and tourism products are provided to the customer. The traditional chain of distribution shows how the principles of a package holiday – transport and accommodation – are 'packaged' by the tour operator and sold to the customer through a travel agent.

Activity: Adapting products and services

You may have noticed a repetitive theme emerging from this chapter – that the UK travel and tourism sector adapts its products and services to meet customers' needs. What do you think would happen if the sector did not develop its products and services to meet customers' needs? Working in pairs, make a list.

Homeworkers

Advances in communication technologies have increased the opportunities for travel agencies to employ more homeworkers. There are several advantages of employing homeworkers:

- Homeworking reduces the need for expensive retail floor space therefore saving money for the travel agent.

- Homeworking promotes flexible working hours beyond the traditional 9–5 shift, meaning holiday bookings can be made when it is convenient to the consumer.

- Homeworking may meet the needs of employees with families.

1.3 Horizontal and vertical integration

Chain of distribution

A chain of distribution shows how travel and tourism products are provided to the customer. The traditional chain of distribution shows

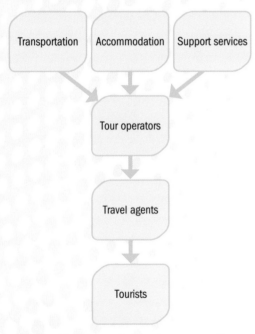

Figure 4.3: The travel and tourism industry buying chain

how the principles of a package holiday, transport and accommodation, are 'packaged' by the tour operator and sold to the customer through a travel agent.

Horizontal integration

Horizontal integration is the merging or takeover of organisations operating at the same level along the chain of distribution, for example the merger of two travel agents, such as TUI Travel and First Choice in 2007. There are a number of advantages and disadvantages of horizontal integration.

Advantages

- Automatically increases the **market share** for the organisation.

- Brings increased profitability, for example TUI Travel estimated that they would save £150 million in staffing costs in 2008 due to the merger with First Choice.

- Enables greater economies of scale to occur.

Disadvantages

- May reduce consumer choice.

- The **Monopolies and Mergers Commission** (MMC) may take action against unequal market influences.

- May lead to large-scale redundancies, for example, when TUI Travel and First Choice merged over 100 high street travel agencies were closed.

Vertical integration

Vertical integration refers to the merging, or takeover, of organisations operating at a different level along the chain of distribution. Vertical integration may be backwards (upstream) integration, for example a tour operator acquiring an airline, or forward (downstream) integration, for example a tour operator buying a travel agency. Thomas Cook AG merged with MyTravel Group PLC in 2008 incorporating MyTravel into the organisation's tour operator products.

Advantages

- Allows travel organisations to retain a greater share of the profits.

- By owning travel organisations operating at different levels along the chain of distribution, tour operators are able to control all aspects of holiday operations, thereby saving money.

- Making savings elsewhere enables tour operators to offer a better price to customers.

Disadvantages

- Smaller travel organisations may be forced out of business.

- An element of financial risk is involved when an organisation invests a lot of money into acquiring new assets.

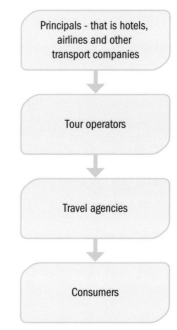

Figure 4.4: An example of full integration

Key terms

Market share – the share of the total sales of brands, or products, for organisations competing in the same market. It is usually expressed in percentage terms.

Monopolies and Mergers Commission (MMC) – an independent public body, established in 1948, which conducts inquiries into mergers, markets and regulation of the major industries in the UK.

Activity: What is a chain of distribution?

The chain of distribution shows how the 'package holiday' product has traditionally been supplied to the customer. Due to developments in booking facilities, chains of distribution are now often much shorter or involve different supply routes. Draw chains of distribution representing the following scenarios:

- A customer using a call centre to purchase a package holiday directly from a tour operator.
- A customer using the internet to purchase a flight directly from the airline.
- A customer referring to a magazine advertisement to contact a hotel directly.

1.4 Technological developments

Computer reservations systems

Prior to the 1950s bookings for holidays were made through the post, or over the telephone, and organised manually using office wall charts. The wall chart method for taking bookings was fairly accurate, but it was not a completely secure system, for example in the event of damage to a chart all bookings details could potentially be lost.

The introduction of CRS in the 1960s was essential in developing airline booking systems. Travel agents and consumers could rely on up-to-date and accurate information about flight availability within the CRS. The CRS also held detailed information about the most appropriate routes for passengers so more complex bookings, such as routes requiring more than one flight, could be secured more efficiently. Other services such as accommodation and car hire could be booked using CRS also.

Teletext

Teletext was developed in the 1970s as a television-based text information service, providing national and international news, sport updates, weather and TV schedules. In the 1980s and 1990s teletext was embraced by travel and tourism organisations. Teletext provided a form of advertising that was more flexible than the traditional brochure, as offers, discounts and last minute deals could be updated regularly. With the internet increasing in popularity throughout the 1990s, Teletext began to operate a web-based service called teletextholidays.co.uk. In 2009, teletextholidays.co.uk was listed in *Marketing Magazine* as one of the top ten most visited online travel agents.

Internet

The expectations and demands of customers have changed, impacting upon the way the travel and tourism sector has developed. New technologies, such as the internet, have provided customers with the opportunity to seek information about activities, destinations, prices and availability without going to a travel agent. The use of the internet for the purpose of travel and tourism in the UK is significant:

- The purchasing of airline tickets is the most frequent online transaction for UK adults, followed by banking, general holiday bookings, supermarket shopping and music downloads.

- Around 22% of UK adults who have internet access use the internet to purchase airline tickets. A further 17% have bought holidays online.

- The majority of travel related bookings (27%) were made by those in the 35-44 age range.

The internet enables travellers to access reliable and accurate information quickly and to save money by making bookings independently. Unfortunately, traditional high street travel agents have struggled to compete with internet services and a number have closed down altogether over the last few years.

1.5 Developments in the airline industry

Aircraft technology

The American-built Douglas DC3, introduced in 1936, is considered to be one of the most influential aircraft in the history of aviation. The Douglas DC3 served the purposes of operating as a military aircraft for the United States during the Second World War, and also as a commercial aircraft transporting passengers internally within the USA. Significantly, the Douglas DC3 became the first aircraft to make a profit from the transport of passengers. More relevant to the development of the UK travel and tourism sector, the aircraft was used by Vladimir Raitz in 1950 for the first UK foreign package excursion to Corsica.

Perhaps the most famous manufacturer of commercial airlines is Boeing. In 1954 Boeing introduced a new passenger jet, the Boeing 707. When the Boeing 707 entered the commercial market in 1959, the main rivals were the Douglas DC8 and the de Havilland Comet. The Boeing 707 became the market leader. In 1960 Boeing announced that they were planning to introduce a new airliner, the Boeing 727. In 1972 the Boeing 727 was the first commercial aircraft to achieve 1000 unit sales, and by 1978 sales of 1500 were achieved. In 1970 the Boeing 747 double-decker 'jumbo jet' went into service; with room for 450 passengers. The 747 held the record for passenger **carrying capacity** for 37 years. At the time the Boeing 747's closest rival was the Douglas DC10, which entered commercial service in 1971, with carrying capacity for 380 passengers.

> **Key term**
>
> **Carrying capacity** – the number of persons that a vehicle, such as an aircraft, can carry per journey.

> The largest commercial airline in current operation – the Airbus A380.

First delivered for commercial use in 2007, the largest commercial airline in current operation is the Airbus A380. The A380 has four engines, twin aisles, a double-deck and 525 seats, although the maximum carrying capacity is 853 if all seats are 'economy'.

Advances in aircraft technology have made it possible to fly further within a shorter time span, making both short-haul and long-haul destinations more accessible to the consumer. Furthermore, increased carrying capacity associated with larger jumbo jets has contributed to a reduction in price per seat, contributing in turn to a cheaper holiday product for the consumer.

Activity: How has airline technology developed?

Airline technology has developed in a number of ways. Perhaps most important, the introduction of the jet engine promoted faster journey times and larger aircraft allowed greater numbers of passengers to be transported at a time.

Using your research skills, find out how one airline, such as British Airways, has used technology to develop in-flight products and services.

Within the UK travel and tourism sector, overall demand for commercial aviation has generally increased over the past ten years. In 2008 around 130 million passengers were 'uplifted' by UK airlines, compared to around 93 million in 1998.

In-flight products and services

As you know, consumers demand quality products and services that meet their needs. In recent years the types of products and services offered by airlines have changed, with the level of service reflecting the 'class' of travel (i.e. first, business, and economy). For airlines, meeting the needs of customers is of paramount importance and the range of products and services offered during flights highlights just how much technology has moved forwards over the past few years. For example, Delta Air Lines offers a diverse range of products and services on many flights:

- in-flight Wi-Fi giving customers wireless access to the internet and email

- in-flight power allowing customers to recharge devices such as mobile phones and laptops

- on-board shopping providing customers with access to a range of goods

- in-flight entertainment showing the latest movie releases and incorporating a state-of-the-art entertainment system.

At the other end of the scale, low-cost airlines limit the number of products and services available to the consumer in order to keep the costs of flights down.

Growth of low-cost airlines

Deregulation of European Union airspace in the 1990s had a significant impact on the operation of airlines throughout Europe. Deregulation meant that EU registered airlines could request an operating licence to base themselves in any EU member country.

The way in which low-cost airlines such as Ryanair, Flybe and easyJet operated was unconventional, signalling a change to traditional ways in which travel products and services were purchased. These airlines offered affordable transport to a wide range of destinations in Europe and beyond, undoubtedly contributing to the growth of the short-break market within many European cities.

Low-cost 'point-to-point' air services were developed by the low-cost airlines, allowing them to offer ground-breaking low prices for a number of reasons:

- no travel agents – all bookings made directly with reservations centre or on-line

- ticketless airlines – the only requirements to travel are a valid passport and order confirmation number

- cheaper, uncongested airports – using mainly regional airports allows more efficient operation

- no meals or snacks – traditional airline meals add to the overall cost of a flight, although most low-cost airlines offer in-flight 'kiosk' points to purchase food and drinks.

> ## Key term
>
> **Deregulation** – the removal of government rules and regulations that may prevent an industry from expanding.

Case study: Flybe

The UK's largest regional airline as of May 2009 was Flybe. Civil Aviation Authority (CAA) statistics demonstrated that the company had achieved the following corporate milestones:

- the Flybe brand carried the largest number of passengers in the UK domestic marketplace

- Flybe carried more domestic passengers to and from London Gatwick than any other airline.

Overall, the Flybe brand carried 26% of the total UK domestic passengers that flew during April 2009, with its closest rival easyJet carrying 23%. For overall passenger numbers Flybe carried 451, which was 413 passengers ahead of all competitors including easyJet, British Airways, the BMI Group and Ryanair.

1 Why do you think that the low-cost airline is so popular in Britain?

2 How has the introduction of low-cost airlines contributed to changes in tourism habits?

There are other types of charter airlines. There are airlines chartered by package tour operators to cover the flight component of their package holiday. They also sell reasonably priced seats on a flight only basis. Thomson Airways is an example of a charter airline. Can you think of any others?

Growth of airports

The popularity of low-cost airlines has contributed to changes in patterns of UK airport usage, significantly the growth of the regional airport. Regional airports can be found close to small cities and large towns, for example Bristol, Exeter, Newquay, Leeds Bradford International Airport and Blackpool. To keep operation costs at a minimum, low-cost airlines tend to offer more flights from regional airports. The advantage for the consumer is that regional airports are often closer to home, less busy and offer a more personalised service. A survey by the Civil Aviation Authority in 2007 showed that regional airports were experiencing larger rates of growth than bigger airports such as Heathrow.

However, the development of airports is not limited to regional airports. Over the last few years some of the larger airports have undergone extensive developments, for example in 2008 Terminal 5 was opened at Heathrow Airport at a cost of £4.3 billion.

Figure 4.6: How has the growth of regional airports affected the travel and tourism sector?

1.6 Other developments in transport

Rail transport

The nineteenth century saw the railway system established at a surprising speed. In 1850 it was estimated that 80 million passenger journeys were made by railway each year. Rail travel became more affordable between 1840 and 1860, with excursion trains becoming a feature of life. Excursion trains facilitated the mass movement of people to popular destinations, for example in 1845 15,000 passengers were transported from Manchester to various locations around the Northwest of England and Wales.

Thomas Cook embraced the railway when introducing his organised excursions in the 1840s. The early steam railways were important in providing a link between the cities, where the majority of the population lived, and destinations. The most popular destinations were undoubtedly the seaside resorts, which were beginning to develop attractions such as piers, pier-theatres, peep shows and amusement arcades, specifically to attract tourists. Throughout the 1880s and 1890s rail trips were organised from many of the Lancashire weaving towns to the seaside resorts of Blackpool, Rhyl and Skegness.

Modern rail travel provides an alternative to car travel. The UK rail network was **privatised** in the mid-1990s. Now Network Rail owns and operates Britain's rail **infrastructure**. Network Rail's main customers are from the private sector, known as train operating companies (TOCs). They are responsible for passenger transport and include companies such as Virgin Trains, Arriva and ScotRail. The TOCs offer a range of products and services to meet the needs of their customers. These may include first class, group, advanced purchase and concessionary tickets.

More recently, the Southeastern train company has planned to introduce Japanese bullet trains to the UK. The 140 mph (225 km/h) six-car Hitachi Class 395 train will connect the final section of the Channel Tunnel Rail Link from Kent to central London. There are also plans to use the trains to transport spectators to and from the London 2012 Olympic site.

Channel Tunnel

A survey conducted in the 1980s predicted that cross-channel traffic between the UK and France would more than double between 1983 and 2003. In 1987 the governments of Britain and France agreed to build an underground rail tunnel to connect the two countries, offering an alternative form of cross-channel travel. After many delays the Channel Tunnel was finally opened in May 1994. The Channel Tunnel is about 50 km long and runs between rail terminals at Folkestone and Calais. There are two separate rail tunnels with a service tunnel between them. The journey time is about 35 minutes from Folkestone to Calais and a train departs every 10–15 minutes.

Key terms

Privatised – where the state sells assets previously in the public sector to the private sector in order to raise money.

Infrastructure – the physical services and facilities, such as transport networks and communication systems, needed by a community to function.

Did you know?

Due to the growth of car ownership over the last 50 years, cars are the most important means of transport for UK domestic tourism.

123

Sea transport

One of the most important forms of sea travel is by ferry. The main sea routes from the UK are from the west coast to the Republic of Ireland and Northern Ireland, from the east coast to Scandinavia, and from the south coast to France and Spain. On many of the routes passengers can travel as foot passengers or they can take their car on board. Over recent years the quality of the products and services provided on ferries has improved dramatically with many offering catering facilities, entertainment and accommodation.

1.7 Developments in legislation

Package Travel, Package Holidays and Package Tours Regulations 1992

The Package Travel, Package Holidays and Package Tours Regulations 1992 were devised in response to an EU directive to standardise consumer rights in relation to package holiday contracts. The legislation has had a significant impact on the rights of consumers within the UK. In brief the regulations cover the consumer against:

*   misleading descriptions of products and services
*   changes in agreed prices
*   the right to cancel the holiday
*   liability of the travel company
*   failure of the travel company.

To ensure that consumers are financially protected, all travel agents and tour operators selling package holidays must be bonded. Providing a bond is a condition of membership for the Association of British Travel Agents (ABTA) and Air Travel Organisers' Licensing (ATOL). A bond is like an insurance policy, and in the event of a travel agent or tour operator going bust, customers who would otherwise lose money which they had paid are given a refund.

Working time and paid holidays

Working Time Directive 1993

The Working Time Directive introduced within the European Union in 1993 is a set of regulations relating to hours of work. The main aims of the directive were to ensure the health and safety of workers and improve working conditions. The directive states that the maximum length of a working week should be 48 hours in 7 days, and that a minimum rest period of 11 hours should be had every 24 hours. In 1998 the Working Times Regulations Act was passed making it a legal requirement that employees should only work a maximum of 48 hours per week averaged over any 17-week period.

Work and Families Act 2006

The Work and Families Act 2006 was passed to enhance the rights of employees with young families in relation to a number of areas, including:

- maternity and adoption pay extended from six to nine months from April 2007

- the right to request flexible working time arrangements

- giving fathers the right to request up to 26 weeks' additional paternity leave, with partial pay, if the mother returns to work.

Other legislation

Disability Discrimination Act (1995 and 2005)

The Disability Discrimination Act (1995 and 2005) makes it illegal to discriminate against disabled people in connection with employment, or the providing of goods and services. One of the key aims of the act was to establish a National Disability Council in order to look after the interests of people with disabilities. The implications of this act for the travel and tourism sector were that service providers were required to make 'reasonable adjustments' to ensure that all facilities were accessible by those with sensory, physical or mental disability which affects their day-to-day activities.

The Countryside Rights of Way Act 2000

The National Parks and Access to the Countryside Act was passed in 1949. Under the act, open country was defined as mountain, moor, heath, down, cliff and foreshore. In 1968 a new Countryside Act sought to broaden the effectiveness of the 1949 Act by incorporating woodland and riverside within the definition of open country.

More recently the Countryside and Rights of Way Act was passed in 2000, giving new rights to people to roam in areas of open countryside and common land in England and Wales.

Aviation regulations

The Civil Aviation Authority (CAA) is the UK's specialist aviation authority. The specific responsibilities of the CAA include air safety, economic regulation, airspace regulation, consumer protection and environmental research. Similar to other regulatory bodies, the CAA requires a bond to be placed with them by the travel company. This means that if the company fails then the CAA will either refund the passengers or arrange transport home.

Did you know?

In 1932 six people were sent to jail for holding a mass trespass on Kinder Scout moorlands in the Peak District. This was seen as an overly harsh punishment by many, and the campaign for established rights of way and the freedom to roam gained support from the British public.

Case study: The Disability Discrimination Act (1995 and 2005)

According to the Directgov website, organisations must make the following reasonable adjustments to cater for the needs of disabled customers:

- using large print for registration and guest information

- ensuring that at least one copy of the fixed menu is in Braille

- providing phones with large buttons

- providing portable vibrating alarms for guests who will not be able to hear an audible fire alarm

- where a low reception desk is not available, providing an alternative low desk for wheelchair users

- sending staff on a disability-awareness training course to increase awareness of common disability-related issues.

1 What are the implications of the Disability Discrimination Act for the travel and tourism sector?

2 How have developments in legislation improved accessibility to travel and tourism products and services for all customers?

Activity: Key legislation

Developments in key legislation have promoted access to the travel and tourism sector for all. Copy out the table below and match the text extracts to the appropriate legislation or organisation.

The implications of this act for the travel and tourism sector were that service providers were required to make 'reasonable adjustments' to ensure that all facilities were accessible.	Annual leave entitlement
Further Bank Holiday Acts were passed in 1871 and 1875 in recognition of the need for the working classes to experience leisure time.	Package travel regulations
The legislation states that the maximum length of a working week should be 48 hours in 7 days, and that a minimum rest period of 11 hours should be had every 24 hours.	Civil Aviation Authority
This legislation was devised in response to numerous complaints about the lack of consumer rights in relation to a package holiday contract.	Disability Discrimination Act
The specific responsibilities of this organisation include air safety, economic regulation, airspace regulation, consumer protection and environmental research.	Working Time Directive 1993

1.8 Development at destinations and resorts

Development of purpose–built resorts

A purpose-built resort is a destination that has been developed specifically for tourism. A number of purpose-built resorts have been developed within the UK travel and tourism sector. Between 1936 and 1966, for example, nine Butlins holiday camps were built at locations such as Ayr, Barry Island and Clacton. In the 1980s Center Parcs was introduced to the UK at locations including Nottinghamshire, Suffolk, Wiltshire and Cumbria.

The significance of purpose-built resorts to the UK travel and tourism sector is not just limited to UK resorts. In the 1950s, the Spanish government began to develop small coastal towns as purpose-built resorts, for example Torremolinos was a small fishing village until it became the first resort to be developed along the Costa del Sol. Seen initially as sustainable developments, one of the main aims of these resorts was to attract tourists from northern European countries, including the UK. Others followed suit, leading to the development of purpose-built resorts in locations such as Greece and Portugal which attracted customers from the UK.

Decline and regeneration of traditional seaside resorts

Due to improvements in social and economic conditions, health awareness, and transport during the eighteenth and nineteenth centuries, seaside resorts attracted visitors from the middle and working classes. The popularity of seaside resorts continued well in to the twentieth century, but the offer of affordable package tours to foreign holiday destinations triggered the demise of the British seaside

Did you know?

The very earliest seaside resorts developed as a result of health awareness. Many believed that seawater held therapeutic properties and doctors at the time promoted the benefits of cold seawater bathing.

What evidence is there of decline in seaside resorts?

Case study: Center Parcs

Originally based in Holland, Center Parcs was first introduced to the UK in 1987, offering short-break holidays year-round. Center Parcs is the leader in the UK short-break holiday market, with a consistent annual occupancy rate averaging at over 90%. Center Parcs operates four resorts in the UK: Sherwood Forest in Nottinghamshire, Elveden Forest in Suffolk, Longleat Forest in Wiltshire and Whinfell Forest in Cumbria. Center Parcs' philosophy involves the idea of an active holiday with resorts offering a range of sporting activities and outdoor pursuits. Although the facilities differ from resort to resort, all locations offer a subtropical swimming pool.

1 When Center Parcs was introduced to the UK in 1987, how did the product on offer differ from other purpose-built attractions, such as Butlins?

2 Why are activity-based holidays more popular now than they were 20 years ago?

3 What factors contribute to Center Parcs maintaining an occupancy rate of over 90%?

resort. In the 1960s many people began to holiday overseas; in response British seaside resorts went downmarket, offering cut-price deals. Current government statistics show that some of the most deprived areas of the UK are seaside towns such as Rhyl, Skegness, Blackpool and New Brighton. In New Brighton unemployment is relatively high when compared to the rest of the country and the former visitor attractions such as the tower, ballroom, amusement park, pier and open-air pool have shut down and not been replaced.

However, some evidence shows resurgence in the popularity of the British seaside resort. English Heritage has identified that the heritage aspects of seaside destinations can be used to promote **regeneration**. They highlight 15 examples across England where features such as hotels, fisherman's cottages and harbours are being used to promote business and tourism activity. A survey conducted by English Heritage in 2009 highlighted that people perceive seaside resorts as having nostalgic appeal and historic character (77%), although many respondents (75%) felt that seaside resorts were 'shabby and run down'. According to English Heritage, investment in the preservation and restoration of historic buildings and places of interest is crucial in order to encourage businesses to invest and seaside resorts.

Key terms

regeneration – the improvement or development of derelict land for residential or commercial purposes.

Development of themed destinations

Themed destinations or attractions are usually all-in-one complexes offering family-centred entertainment and leisure. These attractions often include adventure playgrounds, amusement arcades and thrill rides. Throughout the 1990s and 2000s this component of the travel and tourism sector experienced large growth, reflecting the needs of the customer for a 'thrilling' experience. Part of the success of themed destinations is down to the ever-changing products on offer and the large financial investments in creating world-class rides, for example the Nemesis ride at Alton Towers cost £10 million to build, while the Pepsi Max Big one rollercoaster at Blackpool pleasure beach cost £12 million to build.

1.9 Lifestyle changes and trends

Increases in paid holidays

It is widely recognised that the growth of mass tourism occurred after the Second World War, though large groups of working-class people were participating in tourism before this. A survey conducted in York in 1901 revealed that around 50% of the working-class population took short summer holidays away from the city. Two important factors led to this trend:

* the Bank Holiday Act (1871)
* Holiday Extension Act (1875)

Assessment activity 4.1

BTEC

P1

A local Tourist Information Centre (TIC) has asked you to produce a display illustrating the key developments, lifestyle changes and trends that have shaped the sector. You should work in small groups to prepare your display.

Summarise the key developments that have shaped the UK travel and tourism sector. You should include:

- development of package holidays
- development of travel agents

- horizontal and vertical integration
- technological developments
- developments in the airline industry
- other developments in transport
- developments in legislation
- development at destinations and resort.

Grading tip

P1 Make sure you that you provide a brief summary of the key (significant) developments listed, giving specific examples where appropriate. You only need to know the basics of integration, as this is quite a complex topic. For the developments in legislation you should summarise only the parts from this chapter that relate directly to the travel and tourism sector.

PLTS

When you explore the developments that have shaped the travel and tourism sector for this activity, it will help to develop your skills as an **independent enquirer** and **creative thinker**.

Prior to the Second World War the Holidays with Pay Act was introduced to secure holidays with pay for workers in all industries. This Act initiated the growth of mass-market tourism although due to the outbreak of the Second World War it was not developed until after the war ended in 1945. Many of the returning troops had experienced foreign soil for the first time during the war, and in some ways this stimulated the desire to travel abroad. Now most UK employees receive at least four weeks' holiday a year.

More disposable income

As early as the nineteenth century people were budgeting for holidays. In the 1880s 'going off' clubs were founded in many northwest industrial towns. In 1889 Oldham's going off club took a full week's holiday in the summer and approximately £40,000 was saved through all of the clubs combined.

Activity: Rising costs of holidays

Recent trends show that because of factors such as rising oil prices and a weak pound, the relative price of a foreign holiday is increasing, at a time that coincides with economic recession. How do you think this will affect the UK travel and tourism sector in the future?

Case study: Flexible working time

Common types of flexible working include:

- part-time: working less than the normal hours, perhaps by working fewer days per week
- flexi-time: choosing when to work agreed hours
- compressed hours: working agreed hours over fewer days
- staggered hours: different starting, break and finishing times for employees in the same workplace
- job sharing: sharing a job designed for one person with someone else
- homeworking: working from home.

1 What are the implications of flexible working time legislation for travel and tourism organisations?

2 How might flexible working time legislation contribute to changes in the way travel and tourism organisations sell their products?

Living in the twenty-first century we are wealthier than ever before, with the average family having approximately £1700 per year to spend after covering essential bills. This is significant as VisitBritain estimated that UK domestic tourism, combining overnight domestic trips and day visits, was worth around £65 billion in 2008.

Unlike previous generations most people living in the UK today have taken a foreign holiday at some time in their lives, with many people taking a foreign holiday each year.

Flexible working patterns

The government has recently introduced a flexible working scheme giving parents of children under 16, or disabled children under 18, the right to request flexible working.

Cash–rich, time–poor

The saying 'cash-rich, time-poor' refers to the idea that some people have experienced a relative increase in disposable income over the last few years though they are limited in the amount of time they have to enjoy their wealth.

Within the UK travel and tourism sector the prime cash-rich, time-poor market are the professional classes, such as lawyers, doctors and tutors. Although those with cash-rich, time-poor needs are likely to take at least two-weekly holidays per year, many also enjoy extended weekend breaks to both domestic and outbound destinations.

The needs of the cash-rich, time-poor reflect that this group have limited time for leisure pursuits and are likely to exploit time-saving measures. Internet booking, as opposed to visiting travel agents in person, allows people to arrange flights, accommodation and transport without leaving their house. The cash-rich, time-poor are also likely to use other time-saving services once at their destination, such as personal concierge which may include making restaurant reservations, arranging for spa services, recommending nightclubs, booking transportation, organising tickets to special events and arranging tours of local attractions.

Increase in leisure time

Legislative acts such as the Working Time Directive (1993) and the Working Times Regulations Act (1998) have contributed to an increase in people's leisure time.

Advances in domestic technology have also contributed to an increase in leisure time. Labour-saving devices such as automatic washing machines were introduced in the 1930s, dishwashers with electric drying elements were introduced in the 1940s, and vacuum cleaners were commonplace in middle-class homes towards the end of the 1940s. The time saved by using these labour-saving devices meant that people had more time, especially at weekends, to enjoy leisure pursuits.

Trends

Sports tourism

Sports tourism is a growing element of the UK travel and tourism sector. Generally sports tourism involves travelling or touring domestically or abroad to participate in a sporting activity, for example a golfing holiday, or travelling to watch a sporting event, for example travelling to Moscow to watch Manchester United in the Champions League final. Many tour operators are aware of the significance of sports tourism and some offer tailor-made excursions for sports fans, for example a tour operator called 'World Sports Travel' offers specific Champions League football tours that include one or two nights' stay in a 4-star hotel and tickets to a Champions League game.

There are five specific areas of sports tourism:

- sports tourism attractions, for example Wembley Stadium in England
- sports tourism resorts, for example Gleneagles in Scotland
- sporting tours, for example the Australian cricket team tour of the UK for the Ashes series
- event sport tourism, for example the FIFA World Cup
- adventure sport tourism, for example surfing holidays in the Outer Hebrides in Scotland.

Growth of short-breaks

Short-breaks are leisure excursions that usually last between one and three nights. The short-break is a growing market, involving both domestic and outbound tourism. Research by VisitEngland shows that 63% of the British population expected to take a short-break or holiday in England before the end of 2009. In order to promote the domestic market, VisitEngland launched a £3 million advertising campaign in April 2009. Although domestic short-breaks are a larger market, research shows that outbound short-breaks to Europe are ever-increasing in popularity.

> **Why is sports tourism a growth area?**

VisitEngland™

The growth of budget airlines has made very cheap travel to Europe a reality. As many low-cost airlines operate independently customers have become more familiar with using the internet for flight bookings, as well as to arrange accommodation, entertainment and transport once at the destination. These changes highlight the growing trend for the 'unpackaging' of traditional package holidays.

Access to regional flights

The growth of regional airports has been important, especially when considering the development of flights within the UK. Regional airports, such as Exeter, Newquay, Bristol, Liverpool and Blackpool, are well supported by low-cost airlines offering internal flights. Compared to certain countries with highly developed regional flight networks, such as the USA, Canada or Australia, travel within the UK involves relatively short distances, but flying can still be a time-saving and cost-effective and method of travel.

Scotland's main airports (Edinburgh, Glasgow and Aberdeen) can be reached in an hour from the London area airports. Apex (or advance purchase) tickets, available on all flights, can be cost-effective. However, the full airfare must be paid at least two weeks before the flight. Special offer tickets sold at least three days in advance of a flight can also be cost-effective, although these often involve flights at unsocial hours.

Internet bookings

In April 2009 the Office for National Statistics reported that around 18.3 million households (70% of the UK population) had access to the internet from home. Internet technology is significant for the UK travel and tourism sector as internet booking systems are now widely used to support a number of component industries. Tour operators, travel agents, transport providers and accommodation services rely on the sales generated through internet booking facilities. Examples include, the internet systems that are used to distribute airline seats form an essential part of an airline's operation; airlines use the internet to manage online reservations and distribute 'printable' versions of tickets electronically.

Tour operators have embraced internet booking systems when offering certain specialist products such as customised packages where the customer can put together all of the components of the holiday. All of the major tour operators now also offer on-line brochures. These are beneficial to the tour operator as they save the costs of manually printing the holiday brochures and details, such as changes to prices, can be amended easily and at little cost.

Did you know?

Hotels often use a network-based Property Management Systems (PMS) to mange 'front' and 'back' of house effectively by having access to all essential information, such as reservations and sales, on one system. However, the PMS is expensive and only really benefits the operation of large chained hotels as opposed to small individually owned hotels.

Overseas second home ownership

Owning a second home was originally the preserve of the upper classes. However, towards the end of the twentieth century, the popularity of second home ownership spread to a wider cross-section of society. The reasons why people wish to own a second home overseas are varied and may include using it:

- as a holiday 'retreat'

- for the financial gains that might be acquired through letting the property out

- as a potential retirement property

- for the challenge of renovating a run-down property.

Adventure tourism

Adventure tourism is about participation in activities that involve perceived risk. The natural features of some destinations make them ideal for adventure tourism, for example the mountainous regions of Switzerland, Austria, Germany and France make them ideal for climbing activities. In the Canary Islands, Fuerteventura is exposed to the southwesterly winds blowing from the Atlantic, making an ideal destination for kitesurfers and windsurfers. Wave swell pounds the Atlantic coastlines of Portugal, Spain, France, Ireland and the UK making them ideal surfing destinations. Some tour operators specialise in adventure tourism, offering a range of products and services to the customer.

Case study: Gap adventures

'Gap Adventures have been a world leader and innovator in sustainable adventure travel since 1990. We invite you to explore a world of tours infused with inspiration and excitement that will take you off the beaten track into the real heart of the destination. Our approach to travel provides small groups and independent travellers the rare opportunity to connect with nature and local cultures.' To obtain a secure link to Gap Adventures website, see the Hotlinks section on p.x.

1 What is the appeal of adventure tourism?

2 Why do some tourists want to 'connect with nature and local culture'?

1.10 Links between lifestyle changes and travel and tourism

Throughout this chapter, numerous references are made to the ways that lifestyle changes have affected developments and trends within the travel and tourism sector. This table summarises some of these links:

Lifestyle changes and developments	Trends and developments
Increases in paid holidays and the growth of package holidays • Increases in paid holidays and the introduction of legislation relating to holidays and pay contributed to the growth of package holidays. • Throughout the 1950s and 1960s people found they had more leisure time and more disposable income than ever before. • Travel operators at the time, such as Thomas Cook, recognised the potential of package holidays as a growth market. • Technological developments in commercial airline technology meant that larger numbers of customers could be transported abroad at a time, thus encouraging the mass-market tourism associated with package holidays.	**PC ownership for internet bookings and the growth of budget airlines** • PC ownership and access to the internet opened up a new market for travel and tourism organisations to exploit. • Many of the original budget airlines such as easyJet and Ryanair found that they could shorten the chain of distribution, thus saving money for the organisation and customer, by offering products and services exclusively over the internet. • Internet booking systems meant that customers could organise flights and accommodation on-line, without the need for a travel agent. • This type of 'dynamic packaging' is growing in popularity and highlights how internet booking has helped to shape the sector.
Increases in paid holidays and the development of purpose-built resorts • Legislation relating to holidays and pay introduced in the 1950s and 1960s led to increases in paid holidays. This contributed to the development of purpose-built resorts, as people found they had more disposable income to spend on holidays. • Some of the most popular early package holiday destinations were in Spain. • At the time the Spanish government recognised the potential of tourism and promoted the development of purpose-built resorts.	**Adventure tourism and the growth of specialist adventure tour operators** • Customers are more demanding than ever, requiring products and services matched to their specific needs. • Due to ever-increasing health awareness, many see the benefits of participating in active, 'adrenalin rush' holiday activities. • The trend for this type of tourism has led to a demand for adventure products and services and subsequently for adventure tour operators, who often specialise in particular areas of adventure tourism.

Assessment activities ⓟ2 Ⓜ1

Assessment activity 4.2 ⓟ2

For your Tourist Information Centre display describe lifestyle changes and trends, highlighting links with developments. You should refer to examples in relation to:

- links between various lifestyle changes and developments
- links between various trends and developments.

Grading tips ⓟ2

Think about these examples:

- For lifestyle changes and developments, there are links between the increases in paid holidays and legislation relating to holiday pay and the subsequent growth of package holidays.

- For trends and developments there are links between PC ownership and the increase in internet bookings, and the subsequent growth of budget airlines.

At this level you should highlight the links, but they do not need to be explained.

- Why do you think people's tastes change?

- What do you think would happen if travel and tourism products and services did not adapt to meet customer needs?

Assessment activity 4.3 Ⓜ1

For your Tourist Information Centre display explain how the links between developments, lifestyle changes and trends have shaped the UK travel and tourism sector. You should link at least three developments to three lifestyle changes, or trends, and provide a full and detailed explanation.

Grading tips Ⓜ1

- You should build on the summaries provided for assessment activities 4.1 and 4.2 and explain clearly how the links between developments, lifestyle changes and trends have shaped the sector. An example could be how PC ownership and the use of the internet have allowed customers to make their own independent travel arrangements with the ever-increasing number of low-cost airlines and internet travel and accommodation options.

- How has increased competition from the internet contributed to tour operators and airlines adapting their products and services?

PLTS

When exploring the developments that have shaped the UK travel and tourism sector, you will develop skills as an **independent enquirer** and **creative thinker**.

Functional skills

When you present information for the assement of the unit you will use skills in **ICT** – develop, present and communicate information.

2 How issues have impacted on the travel and tourism sector

2.1 Issues affecting the travel and tourism sector

Economic issues

In 2008, the UK went into economic **recession**. What were the implications of this for the UK travel and tourism sector? A recession can have a significant impact on the commercial sector, although the travel and tourism sector has been widely recognised in the past as having been able to continue its development throughout periods of recession. However, certain component industries that make up the sector have experienced difficulties, including falling sales and a decrease in revenue.

Collapse of airlines

The airline industry has been especially hard-hit with many airlines experiencing a drop in sales in 2008 and 2009. XL Airways collapsed in 2008, leaving around 80,000 passengers stranded overseas and disrupting the travel arrangements of many more holidaymakers.

Collapse of tour operators

Some tour operators have also been affected by the global recession. In September of 2008, XL Holidays, (incorporating XL Airways), the UK's third largest tour operator collapsed. The collapse of XL coincided with a surge of bookings for holidays with Thomas Cook and TUI Travel. Reasons for this included the withdrawal of XL from the tour operations market and the fact that both Thomas Cook and TUI Travel offer inclusive consumer protection.

> ### Key term
>
> Recession – slowdown in economic activity measured over a significant period of time.

Case study: The collapse of XL Holidays

In September 2008, XL Holidays the UK's third largest tour operator collapsed. Fluctuations in oil prices, unfavourable currency exchange conditions, threat of economic recession and falling sales contributed to the difficulties faced by XL.

A spokesman for the Civil Aviation Authority (CAA) said that the collapse was huge, in fact the biggest since ILG 20 years ago. For the CAA, the organisation accountable for regulating the aviation industry, the

major short-term impact of the collapse was the stranding of thousands of British holidaymakers.

1 What were the factors that contributed to the collapse of XL?

2 How might the government have helped to prevent the collapse of XL?

3 What are the advantages and disadvantages of the collapse for other UK tour operators?

Oil prices

The price of oil is also a significant economic factor. Airlines, already under pressure due to the global economic recession, are at the mercy of rising oil prices. Boeing, one of the main aircraft manufacturers, attempted to adapt aircraft to allow their operation to be more profitable and economical. New seats designed with more streamlined backs will allow Boeing to increase the number of seats on a 737 aircraft by six, bringing the total to 156. These six extra seats mean that airlines can potentially earn more money for the same amount of fuel used if the aircraft is operated at full carrying capacity.

Changing currency exchange rates

Tour operators' decisions about the price of holiday products are affected by ever-changing exchange rates. In the case of foreign package holidays, accommodation, transfer costs and resort costs are usually paid for by the tour operator in foreign currency. One of the key challenges faced by tour operators when setting prices for holidays is allowing for changing exchange rates. This is because holiday brochures are produced months before the advertised holiday can be taken, and therefore tour operators have to forecast any changes in exchange rates that might occur. Exchange rates may also impact upon the spending decisions made by the tourists themselves.

> **Did you know?**
>
> The UK travel and tourism sector does not always gain from the tourist activities of the UK population. If you go on holiday to Florida and spend your money in Florida, then the American travel and tourism sector gains revenue from the UK economy.

Political issues

Political unrest

Recent political unrest in countries such as Thailand and Kenya has affected the UK travel and tourism sector. In 2008 protesters calling for the resignation of Prime Minister Somchai Wongsawat of Thailand blockaded Bangkok airport. Due to the threat to the security of British travellers, the UK government issued a travel warning for Thailand. The resultant impacts for the UK travel and tourism sector were that flights were diverted and holiday bookings were cancelled.

In January 2008 Kenya also experienced severe political unrest. As a result UK tour companies suspended visits to Kenya. The country experienced a 73% fall in visitor numbers for the first three months of 2008. When the country was deemed safe for visitors again in May 2008, Richard Branson, owner of Virgin Atlantic, became involved in the promotion of the country as a tourist destination.

War

War can have a devastating effect on tourism. Many parts of Africa and the Middle East have been dangerous for many years, especially for western tourists. Frustratingly, countries at war such as Afghanistan and Iraq would make excellent tourist destinations as they are rich in culture and have fascinating historical links to Britain,

Activity: Terrorism

A report by the London Chamber of Commerce and Industry showed that, in the wake of the devastating bombings in central London on 7 July 2005, the resulting fall in tourism could cost in excess of £300 million. It was mainly city centre attractions, such as the Tower of London and Madame Tussauds, which experienced a fall in visitor numbers of up to 15%, when compared to the previous year. On a positive note, in the year after the bombing outer London attractions such as Kew Gardens reported an increase in revenue of 10%, whilst RAF Hendon reported an increase in visitor numbers of up to 14%.

Why did central London attractions experience a fall in visitor numbers in the wake of the bomb attacks in July 2005, whilst outer London attractions reported an increase in visitor numbers?

Environmental issues

Climate change

Climate change for the UK travel and tourism sector has significant implications. The development of travel and tourism in the UK, and travel and tourism on a global scale, has impacted upon the environment. Factors such as the **carbon footprint** left by commercial aircraft, have contributed to global warming. Global warming, linked to melting polar ice-caps, may result in the raising of the Earth's sea levels. This may have disastrous results for tourist destinations located in coastal, wetland and low-lying island areas. Damage to the ozone layer and reduction of its ultraviolet (UV) light-filtering properties is linked to increases in skin cancer rates caused by overexposure to UV rays.

Natural disasters

In the event of natural disasters, such as hurricanes, volcanic eruptions and earthquakes, tourism is disrupted and often the infrastructure supporting tourism is destroyed. Many of the world's less developed countries rely on tourism income to support the economy; however many of these countries are located in hazard zones, such as tropical areas.

Key term

Carbon footprint – according to the UK Carbon Trust, a carbon footprint is the total greenhouse gas emissions caused directly and indirectly by an individual, organisation, event or product.

What is the carbon footprint of commercial aviation?

Case study: Boscastle flash floods

UK natural disasters only really affect the UK travel and tourism sector at a local level. When Boscastle in Cornwall was hit by flash floods during the peak tourist season in August 2004, millions of pounds' worth of damage was caused to local properties and businesses. As the village's infrastructure was severely damaged, tourism in the short term suffered.

1 Why might the impacts of natural disasters in the UK be felt mainly at a local level?

2 What were the short-term impacts of the flood, and why?

Pandemics

Pandemics (global outbreaks of disease) such as the swine flu outbreak in 2009 can have potentially devastating effects for tourism. In the UK there was a decline in overseas visitors due to fears over swine flu. However, as the outbreak was recognised as a pandemic that began in Mexico, the World Health Organisation felt that restricting foreign travel to and from the UK was unnecessary. This factor highlights that the UK travel and tourism sector can be affected by global issues.

Social issues

Unemployment and recession

One significant impact of the global recession has been increased unemployment within certain component industries making up the UK travel and tourism sector. The social implications of unemployment are many and can include family tensions, loss of housing, loss of confidence and self-esteem, and perhaps most significantly an increase in crime.

However, a scheme launched by the government in 2009 aimed to use tourism as a tool to reduce unemployment among 18–25-year-olds. The government invested £1 billion into the scheme creating 47,000 jobs, including tourism ambassadors, to be made available to 18–25-year-olds out of work for at least a year.

BTEC Assessment activity 4.4   P3 P4 M2

A tour operator has asked you to prepare a PowerPoint presentation to a panel of industry representatives about issues that have impacted on the travel and tourism sector and how organisations are responding to the challenges involved.

Identify, and then review, how issues have impacted on the UK travel and tourism sector. You should select one issue that has had a significant impact on the sector from each of these four areas:

- economic issues
- political issues
- environmental issues
- social issues. P3 P4

Analyse the impact of three of these issues on the UK travel and tourism sector. M2.

Grading tips

- **P3** The issues which affect the travel and tourism industry today can be classified as economic, political, environmental and social. For this task you only need to select one issue from each of these areas. It is important to remember that these issues are often interlinked; for example economic recession can lead to social issues such as unemployment.

- **P4** Think about what the actual impacts of these issues are; they may include increases in prices, withdrawal of destinations, disruption to travel, growth in sales, and decline in sales.

- **M2** You need to expand on the evidence gained for P4, detailing how and why these issues have had such significant impact.

PLTS

When you identify and review how issues have impacted on the travel and tourism sector, you will develop your skills as an **independent enquirer**.

Functional skills

This activity will help you develop your **ICT** skills by using ICT systems, finding and selecting information. It will also use your **English** skills in reading and writing.

2.2 Impact of issues on the travel and tourism sector

Increase in prices

For organisations within the travel and tourism sector to operate, the pricing policies must reflect the quality of the products and services on offer. In the UK travel and tourism sector a market leader has often set prices which other organisations follow, but to gain a competitive advantage discounts and undercutting of rivals prices is common.

Factors outside the control of travel organisations can impact drastically upon the sector. In order to compensate for fluctuations in the cost of oil, airlines have increased prices of flights. In 2004, Virgin Atlantic and British Airways developed new 'surcharge' pricing policies supposedly to cover the cost of airline fuel. However, in 2008 British Airways and Virgin were fined £100 million for fixing the price of the 'surcharge' levy. Despite this, fuel surcharges are commonplace within the airline industry and ferry companies are also asking passengers to pay a surcharge to cover the cost of fuel for the first time.

Withdrawal of destinations

Sometimes holiday destinations are withdrawn because they are no longer economically viable to run, often because they no longer meet the ever-changing and more demanding needs of the consumer market and therefore spiral into decline. One market hit especially hard by the desire of the British public to holiday abroad on foreign package tours, was the traditional British seaside holiday camp.

Case study: Closure of Butlins holiday camps

Between 1936 and 1966 nine Butlins holiday camps were built at locations throughout the UK. During the 1980s and 1990s six of the nine camps were closed, with only Bognor Regis, Minehead and Skegness remaining open. Many of the closed camps have since been bought and reopened under a different name, for example former Butlins camp at Ayr was reopened in 1998 as a Haven Park.

1 Why did demand for Butlins holiday camps decline?

2 Why might the camps have since reopened under a different name?

Repatriation of customers

Repatriation means to return to your original country. In a number of instances it has been necessary for travel companies to repatriate customers. This might be for reasons of war, political unrest, pandemic outbreaks or economic reasons such as the collapse of organisations. The collapse of XL Holidays had implications for thousands of British tourists who were stranded on foreign soil.

To repatriate the stranded tourists the Civil Aviation Authority (CAA) launched Britain's largest ever 'peace-time' airlift. Over 85,000 tourists were left stranded and the initial 94 CAA flights repatriated 22,000 people within the first 48 hours of the operation.

In 2009, after the outbreak of swine flu, a number of British tourists were repatriated. Thomson Airways, under the instruction of TUI Travel, operated a special flight to allow British tourists in Mexico to return home early.

Disruption to travel

Disruption to travel can occur for many reasons, including poor weather, accidents, terror alerts, traffic congestion and strike action. Disruptions occurring during the peak seasons of July and August can be especially costly for the UK travel and tourism sector. In August 2005, British Airways was forced to cancel all flights out of Heathrow because of an unofficial strike from British Airways staff. This action left 70,000 passengers stranded and was estimated to have cost British Airways £10–15 million pounds. In 2007, British Airways was forced to cancel 1280 flights between 10 and 17 August due to a terror alert. The £40 million cost of the cancellations was equivalent to about a fifth of the company's pre-tax profits for the three months before August. Furthermore, British Airways reported that the disruption had some impact on future bookings.

Think about it

1. In March 2010, British Airways was forced to cancel thousands of flights when cabin crew went on strike. How did these strikes affect holidaymakers?

2. In April 2010, flights across the UK and Europe were grounded due to volcanic ash from Iceland. What was the impact on the travel and tourism sector?

Decline in sales

Decline in sales could occur because of the development of a new or improved product or service available elsewhere, because changing trends make certain products unfashionable or because issues such as the threat of terrorism knock consumer confidence.

Activity: Outside factors

It is clear that the UK travel and tourism market is sensitive to factors beyond its control. In groups, discuss why this is the case. Give some examples of global events that have impacted upon the UK travel and tourism sector.

Growth in sales

Many of the factors that we have looked at in this chapter may be considered to have a negative impact upon the development of the UK travel and tourism sector. However, certain factors have had a positive impact: the threats of terrorism associated with flying, the fears that arise from global pandemics such as swine flu, and falling disposable income caused by mass unemployment and the freeze in public sector pay scales have all contributed to the appeal of the UK as an affordable and relatively 'safe' domestic tourist destination. Traditional UK destinations, such as seaside resorts have experienced a resurgence, while city breaks to places such as York, London, Bath and Chester are as popular as ever.

Case study: Dark tourism

'Dark' tourism is a component of the special interest market, a growth area within the UK travel and tourism sector. It involves visiting places where natural disasters, political unrest or war may have occurred, such as memorials, battlegrounds, and places of horrific crime and suffering. Although currently representing a small element of the special interest market, 'dark' tourism is seen as an area of tourism that will experience a growth in sales in the future.

1 Why might people want to visit such 'dark' sites?
2 What sort of people might want to participate in 'dark' tourism?
3 Some people might think it is wrong to promote tourism in places where tragedies have occurred; what is your opinion about 'dark' tourism?

BTEC Assessment activity 4.5 D1

For your tour operator presentation discuss how organisations are responding to the challenges created by the issues that you have looked at. You should bring together all of the knowledge that you gained by completing assessment activities 4.4 and 4.5, then select and discuss how organisations are responding to the challenges created by the issues.

This question will enable you to achieve D1.

Grading tips D1

- Think about the economic, political, environmental and social issues that you have learned about. Impacts on the various organisations should be fully analysed and discussed and you should explain how organisations are responding to the challenges they are facing.

- Can you think of recent examples where a single issue has had a massive impact on a number of organisations operating within the sector?

- You should choose issues which have happened within the last two years.

- Support your discussions with data, statistics, articles and interviews with travel specialists.

- Your discussion could be in a written or a verbal format.

I'm part of a team of three people working for an independent travel agent located within a local shopping centre. My responsibilities include:

- contributing to the daily running and operation of the travel agent, including replenishing brochures and keeping the display areas clean and tidy
- checking the system for late holiday deals, cheap flights and other offers to put in the window displays
- helping customers to find the best holidays, including flights, accommodation, car hire and insurance, for themselves and their travel companions.

How have recent developments affected your role?

There is no question that internet bookings are more popular now than they were ten years ago. People now book traditional package holidays on-line, but also organise dynamic package holidays by arranging accommodation and flights separately.

Some low-cost airlines sell tickets only via the internet. The way I see it is that this is bad news for the high street travel agent. You hear on the news about stores being shut and jobs being lost all the time, but then again, I've just heard that Teletext is planning to open a load of high street travel agents.

All this competition means that as a high street travel agent, value for money is crucial, especially because of the credit crunch. We rely on new and repeat business, so we have to provide customers with the best deals and a personalised service.

Also, not everyone likes the internet; one customer recently commented that they spent hours trying to cost a package holiday to Turkey using the internet, but to no avail. Within five minutes of their enquiry, I provided the same customer with full details about the costs of the holiday and information about suitable travel arrangements.

Think about it!

1 Why might the development of internet bookings be considered bad news for high street travel agents? Create a mindmap of the problems and compare it with your peers' mindmaps.

2 Why might it be important for a travel agent to be familiar with the development of the UK travel and tourism sector and up to date with current issues? Make a note of some reasons and discuss in groups.

Just checking

1 What does the term 'multiple' mean?
2 A city break is a type of specialist holiday. Give three other examples of specialist holidays.
3 Draw a simple diagram representing horizontal and vertical integration.
4 How have technological developments made booking a holiday easier?
5 Why did many traditional seaside resorts decline?
6 Why are themed destinations increasing popularity?
7 Give three lifestyle changes that have contributed to changes in tourism habits.
8 Give an example of a global event that has impacted upon the UK travel and tourism sector.
9 How might the global recession impact upon the UK travel and tourism sector?
10 What is 'dark' tourism?

Assignment tips

When completing assignments, plan your time carefully:

- Plan a schedule of fixed working times into your week. For example, if you play sports on Monday and Wednesday, then keep Tuesday and Friday free for assignment work.

- Keep a record of the individual tasks that you have completed and tasks you still need to finish in a notebook or diary. Make sure that you note down any important dates such as assignment and individual task deadlines.

- Always allow yourself extra time to complete assignments. Do not leave everything to the last minute!

- Try to prioritise your workload – complete tasks in order of size and deadlines. Treat yourself when you meet a tough deadline.

- Be disciplined. Remember that if you want to complete the course successfully there may be times when you have to work, even if you don't want to.

- Don't forget to stay up-to-date with the developments and issues affecting the industry. Newspaper travel supplements, travel journals and various internet websites contain loads of useful information.

5 Developing customer service skills in travel and tourism

In Unit 2 you learned the different approaches organisations take to providing customer service and the needs and expectations of customers.

You are the person who will bring that alive for the customer, by using what you learn in this unit. You will have the opportunity to learn methods, skills and techniques of giving good customer service, and then putting them into practice. You will learn of the importance of first impressions and effective communication and techniques for providing them. You will learn how to present information and sell products and services. There will be plenty of opportunity to role-play with your class colleagues and tutor, to help you develop your skills.

The service you provide will improve the customers' travel and tourism experiences. Your excellent customer service skills will result in loyal customers and repeat business.

Learning outcomes

After completing this unit you should:

1 understand the methods, skills and techniques needed to provide good customer service in the travel and tourism sector

2 be able to demonstrate customer service skills and techniques in travel and tourism situations.

Assessment and grading criteria

This table shows you what you must do in order to achieve a pass, merit or distinction grade, and where you can find activities in this book to help you.

To achieve a **pass** grade the evidence must show that you are able to:	To achieve a **merit** grade the evidence must show that, in addition to the pass criteria, you are able to:	To achieve a **distinction** grade the evidence must show that, in addition to the pass and merit criteria, you are able to:
P1 explain how a positive image can be created in travel and tourism situations **Assessment activity 5.1, page 152**	**M1** explain how different methods and techniques contribute to the delivery of good customer service **Assessment activity 5.2, page 167**	**D1** provide excellent customer service in travel and tourism situations linking own performance to customer service methods, skills and techniques **Assessment activities 5.3, 5.4, 5.5, 5.6, 5.7, pages 178, 179, 179, 180, 180**
P2 describe methods, skills and techniques required to deliver good customer service **Assessment activity 5.2, page 167**		
P3 use skills and techniques to provide customer service in travel and tourism situations **Assessment activities 5.3, 5.4, 5.5, pages 178, 179, 179**	**M2** use skills and techniques confidently with customers in travel and tourism situations to provide good customer service **Assessment activities 5.3, 5.4, 5.5, 5.6, page 178, 179, 179, 180**	
P4 demonstrate selling skills and techniques in a travel and tourism situation **Assessment activity 5.6, page 180**		

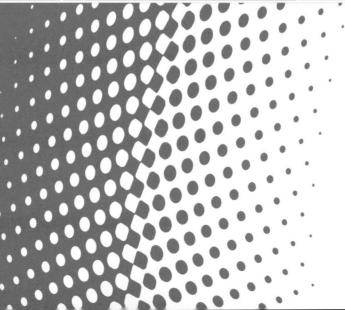

Kevin, 16-year-old learner

I found this unit really turned theories into practice for me. It made me think about what I was seeing and hearing every day in customer service situations and it helped me identify the skills and techniques used by people who are great at giving excellent customer service.

I then got the chance to practise those skills and techniques with friends in my group. We had some good fun and I gained confidence in what I was doing.

I started to use those skills and techniques in my part-time job and found they really worked! The customers appreciated what I was doing and I felt good about it.

Over to you

- What customer service skills and experience do you have before you start this unit?

- What customer service skills do you hope to learn or develop by studying this unit?

1. Methods, skills and techniques needed to provide good customer service in the travel and tourism sector

In this first part of this unit you will focus upon creating a positive image, communication methods, communication skills and techniques, customer service skills and techniques, and selling skills and techniques.

Set off

Draw your own conclusions!

In pairs, using two sheets of A3 paper and felt pens, draw two cartoons of a travel and tourism employee with one or more customers in situations of your choosing:

- In the first, draw a scene which demonstrates as many examples of *poor* customer service as you can.

- In the second, draw a scene which demonstrates as many examples of *good* customer service as you can.

Share your cartoons with the rest of the group. How many examples could you think of? See how many you covered as you work through this part of Unit 5.

1.1 Creating a positive image

Creating a positive image is vital to the success of your organisation, and your personal success as a customer service professional. The customer must feel you are part of a great organisation with whom to do business. Whenever they think of you and your organisation, they must have a positive and pleasant mental picture in their mind. They must be impressed by the positive caring and 'Can do' attitude they experience.

It is the approach your organisation takes to customer service which will determine whether its premises, staff, products and services are presented in a positive and pleasing way. Without that, the organisation is unlikely to win new customers or keep existing ones.

First impressions

First impressions are so important. The first few seconds of coming into contact with you and your organisation can influence a customer as to whether or not to even enter your shop or start a conversation with you. If the first impression isn't positive and the customer walks away, that is the *only* impression they have of you, so they are unlikely ever to come back.

Case study: Moments of truth

Jan Carlzon was the Chief Executive Officer of Scandinavian Airlines System (SAS). He realised that the reputation and success of SAS depended upon how highly the passengers judged their contact with SAS staff, for example when a passenger made a reservation, checked-in at the airport, boarded the aircraft, spoke to the cabin crew or retrieved their luggage. Contact with SAS staff could be for any reason and by any method, lasting for several minutes or just a few seconds.

He called these contacts 'Moments of truth'. He recognised that the airline had to do everything it could to make those 'Moments of truth' successful. He said: 'These "Moments of truth" are the moments that ultimately determine whether SAS will succeed or fail as a company.'

What did Jan Carlzon mean by a 'moment of truth'?

Personal presentation

Dress and grooming

Customers will judge you and your organisation on the image you present. Many travel and tourism organisations require staff to wear a uniform. This promotes the organisation and presents a powerful image. It makes it easier for customers to find a staff member when they need help, advice or assistance. It can also give the staff member a feeling of professionalism, belonging and pride. The organisation should give a demonstration and written briefing on how to wear the uniform and rules and guidance about grooming, including information on acceptable hairstyles, make-up, tattoos, jewellery, etc. Look your best by making sure you and your clothes are clean and smart.

Personal hygiene

Good personal hygiene is essential. Take regular showers or baths. Use deodorants and perfumes appropriately. Make sure your teeth are clean and your breath smells fresh. You may be working in difficult environments, for example in high temperatures, crowded aircraft cabins or non-air conditioned call centres, so it is a good idea to take hygiene products with you to use throughout the day.

Voice

How you use your voice will influence the customers' response and views about you and, therefore, your organisation. Use your voice in a friendly and positive manner. You will learn more voice techniques later in this unit.

Female uniform
Jacket

- To be worn fastened.
- **Cabin crew** – the decision on whether the jacket is worn for pax boarding, deplaning and transportation to and from the aircraft is made by the FSM.
- **Ground staff** – the Ground Supervisor makes the decision on whether the jacket is worn by all female staff on duty.
- An "all on" or "all off" policy should be adopted.

Scarves
Cabin crew – must be worn

- Worn tucked into neck of shirt.
- To be worn at all times on the ground and for boarding.
- The scarf should be removed on doors closing for departure and replaced again for landing and disembarkation.
- Uniform issue only.
- Purple to be worn foremost.
- Can be worn without jacket in warm conditions, at the discretion of FSM.
- An "all on" or "all off" policy must be adopted.

Extract from Virgin Atlantic grooming guide

Environment

What impression would you get if you walked into a travel shop and found empty brochure racks, paperwork stacked high on desks, litter on the floor or customers waiting whilst staff chatted to each other? What if you boarded an aircraft and found the cabin was cold, the crew were all having coffee in one of the galleys and the seats had litter on them? What if you visited a hotel and found yesterday's newspapers on the reception desk, dirty glasses on a table or blaring music playing?

You would probably want to leave as quickly as possible and take your business somewhere else!

Organisations, and everyone working in them, must monitor the appearance of the work environment and take action to ensure the best impression is given to the customer. You have a personal responsibility to do this – don't leave it to other people. You may not have dropped that paper on the floor. You may be tempted to leave it to someone else to pick up but, as long as it is on the floor, it is creating a bad impression for the customer who may decide to take their business elsewhere. The act of picking it up actually creates a positive impression for the customer – here is an employee and an organisation that cares.

Activity: Creating impressions

Look around you at the room you are in and the people in it. If you were a customer, or a stranger, walking into the room now, what would create a good impression and what would create a bad impression?

Meeting and greeting

First impressions count. It is important to think about how you meet and greet people. Customers need to know right from the start that you are professional and care about them. If you are in the public eye, customers will see you and form an impression about you and your organisation before they even speak to you. That is why you must *look* smart and *behave* smart. What your body is doing is very important. Have an approachable appearance by standing or sitting straight, by not leaning against the wall, and by not having arms folded across your chest or chewing.

Choose your first words carefully. This will depend both upon the type of organisation you work for and the situation you are in, as well as the type of customer involved. 'Hi!', 'Good morning sir' or 'Hello, Mr Smith' can all be appropriate depending upon the circumstance.

Make the greeting professional, yet personal. Remember the customer's lament in Unit 2? (*Hey, I'm me!*). Treat them as an individual. There is nothing as personal to each of us as our name, so try to use the customer's name as soon as you can. You will often be given the opportunity to discover it. They may give you their ticket or credit card, have a baggage label on their luggage or even tell you what their name is. Use it.

Case study: Use my name

Feargal Quinn founded the Irish supermarket chain Superquinn. He believes in spending time with his customers. Once, he was assisting staff when a man, a woman and their son came to the check-out desks. He bagged their goods and said, 'Thank you Mrs. Connolly for shopping at Superquinn.'

Minutes later, the customer returned to ask Feargal to explain to her husband that they had never met before. He happily did so, and was asked how he knew the wife's name. He explained that he had noticed the boy's name on a name tag on his scarf. How's that for observation!

Can you recall anyone using your name when you were a customer?

Try to find something to say which relates to your customer and their situation:

• 'I see you have a lot of luggage, sir. Are you going away for long?'

• 'It looks as though it's raining pretty heavily, Mrs Lawrence. Let's get you checked in to your room quickly so that you can get into some dry clothes.'

• 'Hi Lily! What's your teddy's name?'

• 'It's nice to see you staying with us again, Mr Williams.'

Activity: Greetings!

Ask your friends, tutors, parents and grandparents how they like to be greeted by customer service staff. What other ways can you think of to make the customer feel welcome?

Brand identity

Organisations spend enormous amounts of money creating their brand name and logo, which they then use on everything from website pages to letter headings, from uniforms to cutlery.

That brand image must be protected and used in the most positive way. If it is welcomed and valued by the customer, they will repeatedly buy from the organisation. If it is not used in a positive way, the customer will think it is of no value and, therefore, that the organisation is not worth dealing with. So, wherever you work, make sure your organisation's brand identity is shown in the best way possible. It should be displayed neatly in travel shop windows, on brochures, and on all other materials and equipment seen by the customer. Travel documents should be presented to the customer in a branded wallet. Anything bearing the brand logo must not be dirty, torn, scribbled on or damaged in any way. The customer must form a positive image of your organisation whenever they see your brand name and logo.

Activity: Brand logo

What designs or emblems do the following travel and tourism organisations use in their brand logos?

• Alton Towers

• British Airways

• TUI

• P&O Ferries

• Sheraton Hotels and Resorts

Influencing the customer's decision

Paying attention to your appearance and hygiene, your environment, how you greet customers and your brand identity will all influence your customer's decision to purchase, or repurchase, from you. If you present and use your product and services in a positive way, the customer will recognise the value of your products and services.

A positive image will make customers more comfortable with dealing with you and more confident that your products and services will deliver their promise.

Travel and tourism work situations

Creating a positive image is about appropriately using some or all of those methods in your work situations. Some examples of how you can help create a positive image are:

- as a travel consultant, by ensuring your window displays are attractive and up-to-date; your shop is inviting; and your brochure racks are well stocked.

- as a holiday representative, by greeting your clients in a friendly way; showing you are knowledgeable about your resort; giving them guidance; and resolving their problems.

- as cabin crew by being very presentable; observant; interested; pro-active; caring, and putting your passengers at ease.

Assessment activity 5.1

BTEC P1

You work with a consultancy which specialises in the travel and tourism sector. You have been asked to write a 500-word brief to be used on a course being given to new travel and tourism managers.

The brief is to be entitled 'Creating a positive image'.

It should explain how a positive image can be created in a range of travel and tourism situations, to enhance the delivery of customer service.

All items in the content must be covered within travel and tourism working situations.

Grading tips P1

- Review what you have learned in this unit so far about creating a positive image and refer to all of those items in your answer.

- Give examples across a good representative range of the travel and tourism sector.

- Make sure your brief highlights the impact a positive image will have on the customer's decision to use an organisation.

 PLTS

Describing methods, skills and techniques required to deliver good customer service will help you to develop skills as an **independent enquirer**.

Functional skills

This activity will develop your **ICT** skills by developing, presenting and communicating information. It will also use your **English** skills both in reading and writing.

1.2 Communication methods

Why do people communicate?

People communicate with others to:

- inform
- instruct
- seek information
- motivate.

Inform

You may be a cruise ship purser telling your customers when the ship will depart. You may be a hotel receptionist and need to leave a written message for one of your guests to tell them when their taxi will collect them.

Instruct

You may be cabin crew giving a safety briefing. You may be designing a notice for passengers telling them what they cannot carry in their hand-baggage.

Seek information

You may need to verbally ask questions of your customer so that you can respond to their needs. You may need to write to a hotel to find out if special arrangements can be made for one of your customers.

Motivate

You may want to verbally encourage your customers to go on an excursion. You may want to write to one of your staff to compliment them on their good work.

 Activity: Motivating staff

Some words and phrases are motivational – they can make people feel good when used about them. Here are some examples:

- caring
- concerned
- friendly
- helpful
- knowledgeable
- polite
- committed
- confident
- good-humoured
- kind
- patient
- 'went the extra mile'.

Choose some of these words and phrases to complete the following letter to an employee.

Dear Sameera,

I had a phone call from Mrs Simpson this morning, telling me how _____ you had been when she made a booking with you.

She told me she was travelling to visit a sick relative and was very uncertain about the flight arrangements she needed to make. She said you were _____ and _____ and helped her in a very _____ manner. You were very _____ about Switzerland and _____ about what you were doing. Once you had helped her decide which city to fly to and had booked her flight, you _____ and found details of the train connection she needed to make.

Clearly, you were very _____ and _____ to help Mrs Simpson. I am very pleased to add my thanks to hers. Keep up the good work!

Formal and informal

People use different styles of communication depending upon whether they are talking or writing to a friend, a tutor or a grandparent. Sometimes your style will be informal, sometimes formal. Different customers and situations also require different styles.

Written

We are all familiar with letter writing. Business letters need to be well structured.

Figure 5.1 is very clearly a business letter. It identifies the name and contact of the organisation, together with the name and position of the person sending it and the date it was written. It identifies the name and contact of the person to whom it is being sent and includes a reference number to ensure accurate records. The first paragraph sets out the context of the letter. The middle paragraphs deal with the subject matter. The final paragraph closes the letter by looking to the future (and future business). It is written in a formal but friendly style.

Even though much of our written communication is moving away from letters, documents, brochures etc. and towards electronic methods, writing skills remain important.

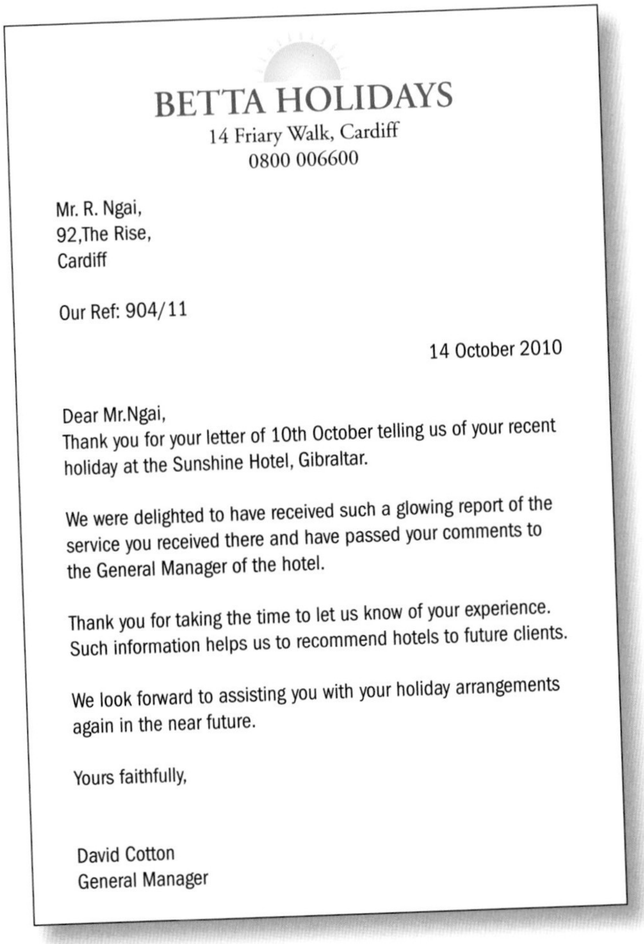

Did you know?

Electronic communication is increasingly being used to provide customer service, as this example demonstrates:

'Air Malta has launched free mobile phone boarding for all its flights out of Malta International Airport enabling passengers with internet-enabled mobile phones to check-in and select their seats. A special bar-coded boarding pass is delivered to their mobile phone in an image format that can be processed by airline staff.'
Source: Airliner World. October 2009

BETTA HOLIDAYS
14 Friary Walk, Cardiff
0800 006600

Mr. R. Ngai,
92,The Rise,
Cardiff

Our Ref: 904/11

14 October 2010

Dear Mr.Ngai,
Thank you for your letter of 10th October telling us of your recent holiday at the Sunshine Hotel, Gibraltar.

We were delighted to have received such a glowing report of the service you received there and have passed your comments to the General Manager of the hotel.

Thank you for taking the time to let us know of your experience. Such information helps us to recommend hotels to future clients.

We look forward to assisting you with your holiday arrangements again in the near future.

Yours faithfully,

David Cotton
General Manager

Figure 5.1: What is good about this letter?

Activity: The written word

Write down as many examples as you can of written communications used by travel and tourism organisations, for example letters and timetables. How many did you come up with? Did your list include:

- text messages
- brochures
- tickets
- emails
- menus
- signs
- invoices
- itineraries
- moving message boards?

The customer will judge an organisation, and you, on the style and accuracy of what is written in its communications. Has it got an easy and pleasant style to it? Can they clearly understand what it is saying? Is it free of errors? Is it well presented, whether it be a website or on a piece of paper?

A useful aid to language is the use of symbols. They are often universal so will be understood in any country.

Case study: They are symbolic

There are 50 international symbols which are widely used at transport locations and elsewhere across the world, designed to be understood by people of different languages, cultures and age groups.

What do the following symbols mean?

How many more can you think of?

To obtain a secure link to a website with further details of symbols, see the Hotlinks section on p.x.

Verbal

Many travel and tourism jobs involve face to face communication with customers. Many other travel and tourism jobs involve communicating by telephone. This is more challenging because your message is entirely dependent upon your words and your voice.

Whether you are face to face with the customer, or talking to them on the telephone, you need to make sure you are talking in a way with which the customer feels comfortable (for example, formally or informally) and in a way which makes it easy for them to understand what you are trying to communicate.

Communicating in writing is likely to be more formal than communicating verbally. Indeed, it is often the case that a verbal conversation will be confirmed in writing, for example your telephone booking will be confirmed in writing, perhaps in a letter or perhaps by email.

Did you know?

A skill is a practised ability, or the ability to do something the way it ought to be done. A technique is a systematic method, routine or procedure by which a task can be accomplished.

Words – what we say

Music – pitch of and tone of voice (how we say things)

Dance – our body language

Figure 5.2: Words–Music–Dance

Key terms

Body language – bodily movement, or posture, which transmits a message to the observer.

Phonetic alphabet – code words for identifying letters in voice communication.

1.3 Communication skills and techniques

People tend to think that the important thing to do when communicating is to use the right words. In truth, the words that are used are only one part of communicating and in fact are the part which has the least impact!

- The words that people use account for around 10% of the impact of communication.

- Pitch and tone of the voice account for 30% – this can be called 'the music'.

- The part which has the most impact, around 60%, is the *body language* – this can be called 'the dance'.

Think about what you say, how you speak and what your body is doing. Ask a friend if you have any mannerisms (we all have!). Do you 'um' and 'er'? Do you use slang phrases like 'Gotcha!' or 'Y'know'? Do you put your hand in front of your mouth when speaking, or stand on one leg? Stop it!

Verbal

Face-to-face and telephone

It is important to choose the right words to create the right impression. You need to make sure your customer can understand you, so you need to use words and phrases they can understand. Don't use long, complicated words and phrases just to impress people. Don't use

Case study: Phonetic alphabet

Some letters sound like others, e.g. 'm' and 'n', and 'b', 'v' and 'p'. With increased use of radios and telephones in the twentieth century, the military and aviation industry developed a universal phonetic alphabet. This is used throughout the world in the aviation sector and across most travel and tourism organisations. It is important that you learn it off by heart.

A:	Alpha	J:	Juliet	S:	Sierra
B:	Bravo	K:	Kilo	T:	Tango
C:	Charlie	L:	Lima	U:	Uniform
D:	Delta	M:	Mike	V:	Victor
E:	Echo	N:	November	W:	Whisky
F:	Foxtrot	O:	Oscar	X:	X-ray
G:	Golf	P:	Papa	Y:	Yankee
H:	Hotel	Q:	Quebec	Z:	Zulu
I:	India	R:	Romeo		

Use it to spell words verbally, for example if you were spelling David over the telephone or radio, you would say:

"David, spelt 'D' for Delta, 'A' for Alpha, 'V' for Victor, 'I' for India, 'D' for David".

1 Spell your name phonetically out loud.

2 In pairs, choose some words and ask your partner to spell them phonetically.

jargon – there is a lot of it in the travel and tourism industry. Certainly do not use slang.

The other travel and tourism standardisation across the world is the use of the 24-hour clock. This avoids confusion. When you say 9 o'clock, do you mean 9 o'clock in the morning or 9 o'clock in the evening? If your customer needs to catch a train, they need to know which it is!

The music

The effectiveness of your verbal communication is powerfully altered by the pitch and tone of your voice – the 'music'. Sometimes it can even change the meaning of the message you want to get across. Varied pitch and tone demonstrates interest. Flat pitch and tone demonstrates boredom and disinterest. You can vary the volume of your voice to create an effect. You might use a loud voice to communicate an instruction in an emergency or a soft voice to encourage a calm atmosphere.

If you are communicating by telephone, the words you choose and the pitch and tone of your voice become even more important because you do not have the 60% impact which body language provides. Standing when talking tends to give you more oxygen and improve your voice.

Pronounce words correctly. If unsure, check in advance if you know you are likely to be using a particular word or phrase. If necessary, try to find an alternative word or phrase. Don't put on a 'posh' voice, but talk clearly and naturally.

Have you ever listened to someone who is mumbling? You strain to hear what they are saying. You guess at some of the words. You probably lose interest. Don't mumble; learn to project your voice. That doesn't mean shouting, it does mean speaking clearly, using the pitch and tone of your voice so that everyone listening to you can clearly hear and understand you.

Non-verbal

The dance

What your body is doing – the dance – has the biggest communication impact. Look around you now. Do you see enthusiasm, boredom, anger, puzzlement or happiness?

How would you feel if the escort on your excursion trip leant against the coach door with his arms folded? He is presenting a 'closed' style. You might assume he is bored and not about to give you a fun journey.

What if the escort is standing up straight, greets you with good eye contact and a smile? He is presenting an 'open' style. You will probably feel he is demonstrating interest, warmth and confidence and this should be a fun journey.

Figure 5.3: Always use the 24-hour clock

Actively listening

We aren't good at listening – we need to work at it! Do you interrupt? Do you look around the room when 'listening' to someone? Do you do other things whilst they are talking to you? Do your eyes glaze over? If so, you are not actively listening. You miss important information – they can feel annoyed and undervalued.

Demonstrate that you are listening, by using verbal and non-verbal techniques. You might nod your head whilst saying 'ah-ha' or 'I understand'. You might repeat key words and statements, for example 'You said you left your passport at the check-in desk'. You might ask questions that demonstrate you are listening and want more information, for example 'Can you remember which desk you left it at?' Sit or stand in a way that the customer can see you clearly and which demonstrates attentiveness. Use eye contact.

Activity: Are you really listening?

Work in pairs for this activity, which is in three parts. Work with someone you don't know very well. Someone, perhaps your tutor, should act as timekeeper.

1   One person is the speaker, one is the listener.

The speaker should talk for two minutes about the last holiday they had.

For the first minute, the listener should listen but use poor attention skills, for example stare out of the window, tie up shoe lace, shuffle books.

For the second minute, the listener should listen but use good attention skills.

2   Reverse the roles and run the exercise again.

3   Review the exercise.

How did it feel when you were the speaker, when the listener was not paying attention?

How did it feel when you were the speaker, when the listener was paying attention?

Presentations

Many employees in the travel and tourism industry speak in public, for example, holiday representatives, guides and cabin crew. These may be formal presentations or informal announcements, to small or large groups.

Prepare well

- Always think about what you are going to say and how you are going to say it.

- Plan a logical structure to your presentation.

- Prompt cards are useful but don't stand in front of your audience reading them. They didn't come to see the top of your head and to have to strain to hear what you are saying.

- Practice your presentation. Get a friend to give you feedback.

- Check the location is suitable.

- Decide what to wear and make sure it is clean and smart.

In what type of job role might you have to make a presentation?

Nerves

- Calm your nerves by rehearsing.

- Have a 'Plan B' in case anything goes wrong, for example if the projector fails.

- Take deep breaths.

- Tell yourself you look good and that your presentation will go well.

- Think of your audience as your friends.

- Go out there and enjoy it!

Presentation

- The first few seconds of your presentation will be the most powerful. Make sure your appearance and what you say in your opening sentences create a positive impression. Learn the first few sentences off by heart.

- Speak confidently. Make sure you are clear, both in what you say and how you say it.

- Avoid speech mannerisms.

- Use the pitch and tone – the music – of your voice, to keep the audience interested.

- If you are using a microphone, don't put it in front of your face. The audience want to see you, not a metal stick. Hold it a couple of centimetres below your chin and don't shout.

- Use your body language to create a confident image. That will impress your audience and have a positive effect on you.

- Scan the audience and make brief eye contact with the people in it.

Remember

When giving a presentation make sure everyone can hear you. Pace what you have to say. Don't rush. It can be easy to speed through a presentation so take care to get the right speed, tone and pitch.

Activity: 'Ladies and gentlemen...'

This exercise includes individual, small group and large group activity. Preferably, a microphone should be used. Get into groups of three.

Choose one of the following scenarios for your own presentation. Make sure each exercise is chosen by someone in your group.

• Individually plan a one-minute announcement based upon the scenario.

• Make the announcement to the full class.

• Within your small group of three, provide feedback to the presenter on what they did well, what they should not do or what they should do less of, and any other techniques which might further improve their presentation.

Scenario A

You are a holiday representative in Ibiza. Your clients have just landed from Manchester. The flight arrived two hours late. You are going to make a PA announcement on the coach whilst they are travelling to their hotels, which must include:

• mention of the delay and how the passengers may be feeling

• information about where the coach is going and how long it will take to get there

• information about where and when they can find you at the resort.

Scenario B

You are a tour guide at an historic castle. You have just met a group of 12 people. You are going to make an announcement to:

• welcome them to the castle

• establish who needs help

• outline what they will see and how long the tour will take.

Scenario C

You are a cabin crew member making a PA announcement once everybody has boarded the aircraft. Your welcoming message must:

• welcome passengers on board, linking the welcome to what your name is and who you are, as well as mentioning the Captain's name

• explain that a safety briefing will be given shortly and encourage people to pay attention to it

• inform the passengers that a meal will be served during the flight.

Written reports and forms

The same principles apply to written communication as they do to verbal communication. Think about what you want to communicate and who you are communicating with, and choose an appropriate style.

Many people in the travel and tourism sector have to write reports. They range from lengthy documents, perhaps recommending the launch of a new product, to brief handover logs between shifts. They all need to be legible, accurate and complete, and all need to have correct spelling and grammar. All these aspects are important, as others will probably need to read and understand them and some documents and reports might, for example, have to be used in court cases.

When communicating in writing, always:

• think first about what you want to say – make rough notes, using bullet points

• put what you want to say into a logical order

- write it in an appropriate style
- check for spelling mistakes, grammatical errors and punctuation
- check that you have covered all the points you wished to mention
- read it again before sending it.

Activity: Punctuation please!

Use punctuation to give opposite meanings to this statement:
The woman said the man ate the sandwich

Different types of written communication are suitable for different situations, for example emails can be used for speedy communication but they are less formal than a letter, so should not be used to respond to complaints. Memos and adhesive notes are only appropriate for use within the organisation.

The travel and tourism sector still uses a lot of forms, although they may be electronic rather than paper. Forms are used for a variety of purposes, for example holiday booking forms, car hire rentals, and incident reports. The forms should be designed to make sure they contain all the information the sender and recipient need and should be laid out in a logical sequence and in an appropriate style.

Did you know?

Guidance on email etiquette can be found on many internet websites; just type 'email etiquette' into a search engine. To obtain a secure link to some useful websites, see the Hotlinks section on p.x.

Case study: Shift report

You are an assistant in your local tourist office and are just coming to the end of your shift. It has been a busy morning. You remember, in no particular order, that:

- Mid-morning you had to call the computer engineer because of a fault. He corrected it remotely.

- Your area office wants someone to call them at 5.00 p.m. to tell them how much revenue your office has taken this week.

- A lady, whose name and telephone number you have written on a scrap of paper, is going to call back to confirm whether she wants to book two rooms tonight at Willow Farm.

- You opened the office on time but found several people already waiting. You have noticed this has happened several times recently.

- You sold several books and maps on the district and made seven accommodation bookings for clients.

Your late shift colleague takes over in a few minutes. Write the shift handover report.

There has been a revolution in written communication in the past few years, through the use of email. It is a useful and speedy method of communicating. However, emails are not confidential and can be misinterpreted, with the reader assuming a tougher, less polite message than the sender intended. Beware of this and learn email etiquette.

Confidentiality

Whatever type of communication you use always be aware of the need for confidentiality.

Customers expect organisations to treat information about them in confidence. This means not discussing any details about them or their arrangements with anyone unless for valid business reasons.

Case study: An expensive mistake!

A particularly difficult passenger made a booking with a ferry line call centre. He annoyed the agent so much that she wrote 'Be afraid – this is the passenger from Hell!' on the booking. When the passenger got to the ferry port, he decided to change his return booking, which he did at the ticket desk.

He asked for a printout of the booking. The agent gave it to him, without thinking about what was written in it! The customer sued the ferry company.

Who was at fault and why?

Do not make casual comments about your customers or release information to anyone asking about them. Airline staff are sometimes asked if a certain person is on a flight. The caller might, for example, say he is the person's husband and she has asked him to meet her from the flight. Staff will not release the information. That might seem unfair, but how do they know the caller really is the passenger's husband or that she wants her husband to know where she is?

Customers' confidentially is protected by law. The Data Protection Act 1998 protects individuals from the misuse of computer data which is held about them. They have right of access to that data, rights of compensation for inaccuracies or wrongful disclosure, and the right to have inaccuracies corrected.

If you think communication is all talk, you haven't been listening!

1.4 Customer service skills and techniques

Now that you know the skills and techniques of good communication, you can use them to meet the needs of the customer.

Case study: Back to the shop floor

Deepa Chauhan and Sarah Cooper are new to easyJet as Human Resources Business Partners, working with the cabin crew and ground operation communities respectively. Within weeks of starting their new roles, they were given the opportunity to 'go back to the shop floor' by attending a full day on-board with the flight and cabin crew.

Source: easyJet

What do you think the benefits are of this type of programme to:

* the organisation
* the staff visiting others' jobs
* the staff being visited
* the customers?

Providing up–to–date and accurate information on products and services

Providing up-to-date and accurate information is not easy in the fast-moving environment of the travel and tourism sector. For tour operators and travel agents, the products may only change by the season, but their availability and prices change by the minute. The transport sector experiences changes very quickly and for a wide range of reasons, for example departure and arrival times affected by road conditions, weather or technical problems. Customers will expect you to give up-to-date and accurate information. You need to know the answers or where to find them quickly.

The probability is that much of this information will be available to you through I.T. facilities, which may include your organisation's operational systems, databases, an intranet and the internet.

Think about the complexity of communicating up-to-date and accurate information if a train is delayed by a signalling fault. The train driver and on-board manager need to be told, the train operations department needs to know, as do the en-route and arrival stations, any organisations supplying catering or fuel to the train, and so on. Passengers on the train, and those meeting the train, also need to know. Other trains may need to be allocated to different platforms to accommodate the late train. The crewing department may need to assign the crew's next journey to another crew because they will be late for their next service. All of this communication needs to be repeatedly updated until the train finally arrives at its destination. Often I.T. is the only way that accurate and up-to-date information can be communicated in time to all those needing the information.

Activity: Timely information

In pairs or small groups, visit a local transport facility, for example an airport, a railway station or a ferry port. By observation and asking questions, discover the methods used to communicate to passengers. List every method and note what purpose it is serving. On your return, discuss your findings with your group.

Being on time and available

If you are standing in a long queue, five minutes can feel like 20 minutes. Your customers expect you and your products and services to be on time. Always aim to be early. This allows you time to prepare yourself and allows for any small delays you might experience. One airline advanced all of its clocks by five minutes. Staff worked to those clocks so that they were always where they should be, and completed their tasks, a few minutes ahead of time. The airline's punctuality – a critical customer service measure – improved greatly.

Being a few minutes early also means you can get those little jobs done in advance so that you are available when the customer arrives. They won't have to wait for you to finish stacking those brochures or switching your computer on. You will also be ready to greet the customer warmly and enthusiastically, rather than as an interruption.

Being welcoming and approachable

Use your communication skills to make your customer welcome. Your body language, opening words and tone of voice should warmly welcome your customer. If the situation allows, avoid having a barrier, such as a desk or counter, between you and your customer. Walk towards them to greet them. Even if you are seated at a desk, you can be approachable by demonstrating the right attitude, standing up and showing you are ready to assist and that your environment is also in a state of readiness (computer working, brochures available, writing materials to hand, labels in order and so on).

Recognising and responding to needs

Customers need information, advice and instructions. To provide that in timely and appropriate ways, you need to be alert to what is happening around you and to the clues the customer is giving you.

- If you are a guide in a medieval castle and you notice some Japanese visitors, you might approach them with a leaflet on the castle in Japanese and personal audio equipment which provides commentary in their language.

- If you are a theme park assistant and it looks as though it is going to rain heavily, you might advise visitors to go first to those rides and shows which are indoors.

- If you are a cabin crew member and notice a mother with a baby, you might approach her to ask if she needs any help.

Customers may have other needs:

- If you are a hotel duty manager expecting a coach party to arrive for lunch, and it suddenly gets colder and starts to rain, you might recognise the need to adjust the heating, increase the available hot drinks and hot meals, ensure the coach can park directly outside the hotel entrance and have staff on hand with umbrellas.

- If you are a cabin crew member on a long flight and see a family board with several young children, you might check to make sure you have sufficient children's games and meals on the aircraft.

- If you are a travel consultant selling a holiday to an elderly couple who appear to be slow walkers, you might recognise the need to offer a hotel with few steps or steep slopes.

> **Remember**
>
> Being a customer service professional means you must have good antennae to be alert to what is happening and to pick up the clues!

1.5 Selling skills and techniques

The eight stages of selling

There are eight stages of selling as detailed below:

1 Creating an image

Make sure you and your environment are creating the right image to attract the customer:

- Is your appearance smart?

- Is your work area clean and tidy?

- Are the goods you want to sell or the brochures you want to offer in good condition and easily available?

2 Establishing a rapport

Create a favourable first impression. Be warm and sincere. Personalise the experience. Pay attention to how you communicate, particularly your body language. Don't get distracted.

3 Identifying needs

Find out what the customer wants by asking appropriate questions.

- Start with **open questions** (i.e. questions which start with *what*, *why*, and *how*). These will give you a lot of information, for example, 'What interests does your daughter have?'

- Continue with **leading questions**. These will narrow down the subject to give you more information, for example, 'You say she likes travelling. Where does she like to go?'

- Move on to **closed questions**. These will give you specific information or confirm something, for example, 'Has she been to France?'

Key terms

Open questions – questions worded so that they will probably produce a long answer.

Leading questions – questions worded so as to gain particular information, or a particular answer.

Closed questions – questions which can be answered with a single word or short phrase.

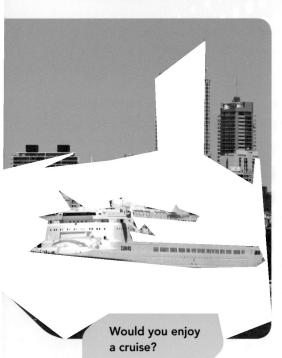

Would you enjoy a cruise?

4 Actively listen

Demonstrate you are listening and have understood what has been said. Use your body language, for example by nodding. Repeat key words and statements, for example, 'You said you like cruises, but only if you visit a different port each day.' Say encouraging things, such as 'Since you have already taken a cruise on the Queen Victoria, you know how enjoyable cruises can be.'

5 Matching products and services to customers' needs and wants

By now you should have a clear idea of your customers' needs and wants. Know your products. Select one product to offer your customer. Choose two or three features which you feel will particularly appeal to the customer. Sell the benefits, for example 'This ship is a bit smaller, so it can get into some really interesting ports larger ships are unable to visit.'

Customers' 'wants' or 'desires' are influenced by a lot of factors including social class, peer pressure, attitudes and aspirations. Once you have established the customer's needs and 'hooked' them onto a product, or service, you may be able to increase the sale by having them consider how their other desires might be met. One way this could work is if your customer has decided, for example, to take a cruise you offered, you might be able to sell them the additional benefits of upgrading to a deluxe cabin – 'This ship has some superb deluxe cabins which are much larger, have picture windows so that you can see the passing coastline, and offer the choice of twin or double beds. Deluxe cabin passengers are also invited to the Captain's cocktail party.' You might add, 'There is a special deal at present offering deluxe cabins for just £200 more than a standard cabin.'

A further way in which you can increase the sale is to sell 'add-ons'. Continuing our cruise example, add-ons might be shore excursions. Sell the benefits, for example. 'You wouldn't want to miss visiting the Sydney Opera House whilst in Sydney. There is an excellent shore excursion available which gives you a behind-the-scenes tour and includes stall seats at an evening production. This tour sells very fast, so I would recommend you book it now.' You have now reached the stage where you can use other techniques.

6 Handling objections

Don't tell the customer that he or she is wrong, but overcome the objection by finding something positive to say which addresses it, for example 'I understand why you feel you might be seasick in a smaller ship, but don't worry because this is a modern ship fitted with the latest design of stabilisers.'

7 Closing the sale

Watch for clues that the customer is ready to buy, for example the customer might say 'That seems like the holiday I am looking for,' or 'Do you need a deposit?' When that happens, re-emphasise the benefits to reinforce the customer's comfort about buying and ask how the customer wants to pay.

8 Providing after-sales service

Ask the customer if there is anything else that he or she would like to purchase, for example shore excursions or foreign currency. Remind the customer about when the balance is due. Tell them about guarantees etc. Package the purchase well; even if it is only a ticket, present it with a flourish in a wallet. Follow-up after the customer has used the product to enquire if it was as they wished and to encourage them to think about the next purchase.

Activity: Overcoming objections

Work in pairs on this exercise. Think of objections that might be raised by a customer thinking of buying a holiday. Tell your colleague what your objection is. Your colleague must offer a positive reply to overcome the objection.

BTEC Assessment activity 5.2

You are the Assistant Training Officer for a large tour operator, based in the UK, which markets worldwide holidays. Your organisation is recruiting people to become resort representatives. Excellent customer service is considered vital by your organisation.

1   Prepare a presentation for the new staff which describes the various communication methods, the customer service, the selling skills and the techniques required to deliver such service. **P2**

2   Explain in your presentation, how the different methods, skills and techniques you identified contribute to the delivery of excellent customer service. **M1**

You can prepare this as a PowerPoint presentation or as a hard copy of bullet point slides and accompanying notes.

Grading tips **P2 M1**

- Make sure you describe all of the methods, skills and techniques so far covered in this Unit. Support them by using examples relating to customer service from the travel and tourism sector in the form of quotes from articles, photos, news items, data and statistics.

- Strengthen your answer by drawing upon real examples of these methods, skills and techniques being used appropriately or inappropriately (perhaps from your own experience, or from TV or magazine articles).

PLTS

Describing methods, skills and techniques required to deliver good customer service will develop your skills as an **independent enquirer**.

Functional skills

You will use **ICT** skills to find and select information and then develop, present and communicate it. You will develop your **English** skills both in reading and in writing and, if you decide upon a verbal presentation, in speaking.

2 Customer service skills and techniques in travel and tourism situations

How, and when, you use these skills and techniques for delivering good customer service will depend upon the customer and the situation.

Activity: Assessment worksheets

You are a travel and tourism recruitment consultant. You will be selecting candidates this week for customer service roles for a train company. They will be assessed in customer service situations which are (i) face to face, (ii) in writing, (iii) on the telephone.

Observers will record the communication and customer service skills and techniques used by each candidate.

Your task is to design three assessment sheets, one for each of those scenarios, which list the communication and customer service skills and techniques which should be observed.

2.1 Customer types and disposition

A wide variety of customer service situations require skills, techniques and initiative, often in unplanned, fast-moving situations. Customers will have a range of experiences which affect their moods and attitudes. Great if they are happy – work with them to keep them that way! Unfortunately, some customers may have different dispositions, so how can you best manage the situation?

Aggressive customers

Customers may become aggressive because something has gone wrong or because they are in a situation which they find frightening, confusing or worrying. Some people get upset when they feel they don't have control over the situation. Anger can turn to aggression, which needs a calm, but firm, response. Stay in control and get assistance if necessary. If other customers see that staff are in control and looking after the interests of all the customers, they will be less likely to become angry themselves and more likely to support the staff.

Of course, your customer service antennae will hopefully have alerted you to the situation at an early stage, so that you can take corrective action before customers start to become worried and upset.

Customers with complaints

However hard you and your organisation try, things will occasionally not go to plan. Problems will arise. Sometimes they may be caused by the organisation (perhaps they have been unable to obtain accommodation) or the customer (perhaps they forgot to renew their passport), or by external factors (perhaps bad weather is delaying flights). By using your initiative and problem-solving skills you will almost always be able to find solutions, or reduce the impact, to the satisfaction of the customer.

Even so, there will be a few occasions when solutions are not to the liking of the customer. Some customers are less able to handle unexpected situations than others, and they may turn their concerns into complaints.

Few people like dealing with complaints, but if you have the right attitude and use the right skills and techniques, the customer can be satisfied. Surveys show that customers who have been handled well after something has gone wrong can become the most loyal of customers.

Distressed customers

Dealing with distressed customers requires a calm approach, with patience, empathy and gentle questioning to find out what is causing the distress, so that the problem can be resolved. Imagining yourself in the customer's situation will help understand what the cause might be and how they may feel.

Non-English speaking customers

Sometimes people assume that others can (and should!) speak their language. This shows disrespect to customers. Be patient, look for clues as to what the customer is saying and what language they may speak. Try to speak their language or find someone who can, such as a work colleague or perhaps another customer. Offer appropriate leaflets etc. in their language.

Be careful to use clear diction (speak clearly) and do not speak too quickly. Avoid the temptation to raise your voice. Use your body language or even quick drawings to communicate.

Throughout your communication, think about what you want to say and how you will say it. Use short sentences and check for understanding before moving on to the next sentence. Structure helps you manage the communication and demonstrates knowledge and confidence.

Customers with different cultures

Working in the travel and tourism sector gives you wonderful opportunities to witness and work with people from different cultures. It may be that you are working:

- in this country and dealing with customers from this country

In what situations might you work with people from different cultures?

- in this country and dealing with visitors from overseas
- overseas and dealing with visitors from this country and with nationals of the country in which you are working.

The type and style of customer service you give will be influenced by the cultures of your customers, whether they are UK customers travelling overseas, or overseas customers visiting the UK, and the environment you work in. That is because tastes, preferences and opinions will be shaped by those cultures.

Be sensitive about how you ask for, and use, people's names. It is better to ask a customer for their surname and first name, than for their surname and Christian name. Buddhists and Hindus would prefer to be asked for their surname and personal name. Muslims have a religious name, a personal name and a hereditary name. It is polite to address a Muslim by his/her personal and religious name.

These religious cultures are not exclusive to particular countries. People from such cultures could live in any country. However, knowing the country your customer lives in can be a clue as to which culture he, or she, has. For example, over 70% of those living in Bhutan, Cambodia, Myanmar, Sri Lanka and Thailand follow the Buddhist faith; over 70% of those living in India and Nepal are Hindu; over 70% of those living in much of the Middle East, many African countries, Bangladesh and Pakistan are Muslim.

Why might customers want to experience different languages and cultures?

You need to adjust to other cultures and, if you are working overseas, you may also need to give guidance to visitors on what is, and what is not, appropriate. Culture can have a very wide range of influence on behaviour. The shops in many Mediterranean countries close during the hottest part of the day (siesta time). Entering places of worship for most religions requires covering of the body, sometimes the legs and arms and sometimes the head. The Islamic culture often requires that women cover themselves from head to foot by wearing full-length dresses, head covering and veils (burkha), and also may expect women and men to be in separate groups. Many cultures have restrictions on what food and drink can be consumed and how it must be prepared. Your customers will expect you to be aware of cultural needs and to provide for them.

Groups

When you are providing customer service to an organised group, seek out a group leader who can tell you the group's needs and assist you in communicating to the group. This person might also be the keeper of the group's tickets and passports and also be the one who makes sure all the people in the group are in the right place at the right time. Finding the group leader, or selecting one, and using their support will assist you greatly, but remember that every member of the group has individual needs, so you must meet those needs as well.

Some groups don't have leaders, for example those who happen to be on the same inclusive holiday or visitor attraction tour. You need to be alert to their individual needs, so watch for those who seem to be confused, concerned or wishing to ask a question. Also make sure you don't lose anyone. There is a range of techniques you can use for this for example;

- If you are a holiday rep you might have a list of the customers you are meeting at the destination airport to take them to various hotels. Use that list to tick them off when they join you at the airport and when they leave you at the hotel. Do a headcount when they have boarded their coach. Try to remember their names.

- If you are a tourist attraction guide, remember how many are in your group and check you have the same number as your tour progresses. Watch for those who linger or divert away from the group. Try to remember what those in your group look like, perhaps by linking them to others in the group, for example 'The elderly lady in the red dress is with the man wearing a blue blazer, there are two Japanese ladies in the group and the little boy is with the young couple who are wearing shorts'.

Individuals

Don't forget those who are travelling on their own. If proposing holiday options, discover whether they wish to be on their own or to be with others. Select the type of holiday and facilities carefully to reflect their needs and wishes. If on holiday, they may appreciate you talking with them from time to time. They might welcome you introducing them to others or asking them about their interests.

> **Why is it important to ensure special needs are met?**

Special needs

In the broadest sense of the term, special needs can include a very wide range of customers, including children travelling unaccompanied, those who have special dietary needs and those who do not have English as their first language.

The Disability Discrimination Act 1995 has been significantly extended, including by the Disability Discrimination Act 2005. It defines those with disability as 'having a physical or mental impairment that has a substantial and long-term adverse effect on his or her ability to carry out normal day-to-day activities'.

The extended Disability Discrimination Act now gives disabled people rights in many areas, including access to goods, facilities and services. This has meant a review across the travel and tourism sector to ensure the requirements of the Act are met and that special needs customers receive the customer service they should.

Part of your role in this is to be alert to their needs and how they may best be met. So you must also be aware of the environment you are in and of anything in that environment which might create a danger or problems for the special needs person.

2.2 Situations

Providing customer service is complex:

- You will be providing it to different types of customer who have different types of needs.

- You may be informing, instructing, seeking information or motivating.

- You may be solving problems or dealing with complaints.

- You may be providing service face to face, by telephone or in writing.

- You may be providing service indoors, outdoors, or on moving vehicles.

- You may be in a quiet or a noisy environment.

For each of these situations and combinations you need to consider how best to provide customer service.

Let's look at some situations.

Face-to-face

Being face to face with your customer gives you the opportunity to use your full range of communication skills: words, voice and body language – the words, music and dance. It also enables you to pick up clues about what the customer might need. Their dress might, for example, give you clues as to their culture. Their body language might indicate whether they are happy or unhappy. From such clues you can anticipate what needs they might have.

Use your body language to support your discussion with them, for example:

- If they have a problem, show concern, perhaps by inclining your head to one side, staying quiet, keeping eye contact and having a serious face.

- If they are seeking directions you might reach forward to touch their elbow lightly, whilst pointing to where they need to go.

- If they are referring to a leaflet in their hand, you might stand by their side so that you can both read it, and turn your face to them at appropriate moments.

- If you are talking to a group, make sure they can all see you, perhaps by standing on a step. Ask if they can all hear you. Project your voice.

Written

Almost every customer will have seen something in writing from your organisation, whether it is a website, a brochure, an itinerary, an invoice, a ticket, a resort information leaflet, etc.

You will need skills in writing the appropriate type of document in a suitable user-friendly style, without any errors in spelling or grammar.

Accuracy is very important. If you need to record something which is supposed to be factual, make sure it is correct.

Make sure that what you have written cannot be misunderstood. Whenever possible, have someone else read it to make sure they interpret what you have said in the way you wanted.

Telephone

The customer cannot see you if you are talking to them on the telephone, so you have to be skilled in questioning, answering clearly and logically and using your voice to help get the message across. Think about what you want to communicate and who you are communicating with and choose an appropriate style.

Speak clearly. Don't eat or drink during the call. Standing or sitting comfortably, upright and alert, will affect the way you speak.

It can be very helpful if you jot down the key points of what a customer is asking, so that you don't forget to respond to all their points. If you are being asked to take a message for someone, write down the full details of the message, including;

* the time at which you took the call
* who it was who called
* how and when they can be contacted
* what the message is
* who you are and how you can be contacted.

Complaints

Remember this five stage plan when dealing with a complaining customer:

Stage 1 Don't take complaints personally
Hopefully, the customer is complaining about a situation, rather than about you. However, you represent the organisation with which the customer is dissatisfied, therefore you have to take ownership of resolving the problem. Adopt a friendly, helpful, but assertive manner. Being assertive means explaining your position whilst respecting the other person's feelings and situation. It enables you both to feel OK and valued.

Stage 2 Listen
Initially, the customer will be climbing the Anger Mountain, pouring out to you what went wrong and how appalling your organisation is. It is important to stay quiet at this stage. If you try to interrupt, give reasons or excuses why something happened, the Anger Mountain is likely to keep growing and the customer will continue to complain angrily and perhaps increase his or her demands.

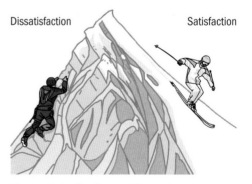

Figure 5.4: The Anger Mountain

Show that you are listening by using your body language effectively, for example nodding and adding the occasional 'Ah-ha' or 'I see'. Wait until the customer reaches the top of the Anger Mountain. By doing so, you will have allowed him, or her, the opportunity to tell you what went wrong and to calm down.

If dealing with a written complaint, don't jump to conclusions, or think of responses, until you have read the entire letter.

Stage 3 Clarify

Then it's your time to speak. Apologise and make it clear that you aim to find a solution. Don't blame others in the organisation, 'Oh, the invoice department is always making mistakes'. To the customer, you *are* the organisation, so say 'we', not 'they'.

Ask questions as this demonstrates that you have been listening and also gives you the opportunity to get the detail you need, for example, 'You told me you travelled last month. Can you give me the exact dates?' Imagine yourself in the customer's situation (known as 'putting yourself in John Brown's shoes' or 'seeing it through the customer's eyes'). That will help you understand how the customer feels and to understand how the situation may have arisen. If dealing with a written complaint, re-read to check you have understood accurately.

Stage 4 Investigate and resolve

By now you will have found out most of the information you need, so that you can investigate and resolve the situation. Once satisfied that you have the best solution, offer it in a positive way to the customer, emphasising the benefits. It can help if you give the customer a choice of solutions as this shows you are trying to meet their needs. It also helps move them from thinking about what went wrong to thinking about what choice to make.

If dealing with a written complaint, it is probable that the customer has already moved on from their initial annoyance and just wants to bring the matter to a conclusion. Therefore, offering choices in a letter is usually less appropriate, as it further delays bringing the matter to a close.

Stage 5 Ensure it doesn't happen again

If further investigation is needed, take a contact for the customer so that your organisation can respond later. Make sure that whatever went wrong doesn't happen again, either to this customer or to any other. The same applies whether you're responding to a face-to-face or written complaint. An example is if a train passenger complains that a wheelchair is not available at the departure station, tell the staff at the destination station so that the passenger does not have a repeat problem, and tell your manager so that he, or she, can make sure it doesn't happen again.

Selling

Everyone has the opportunity to sell, whether it is formally, or 'unconsciously' encouraging someone to consider buying something, by seeing what you are doing or how you are behaving. Here are just a few examples:

- selling a holiday to a customer in a travel shop
- selling a holiday, or a flight, in a call centre
- selling an excursion whilst at a resort or on a ship
- selling catering or gifts onboard a train, ship or aircraft
- selling souvenirs at a tourist attraction
- selling accommodation in a hotel or a guest house.

Activity: Selling opportunities

Think of as many other situations as you can in the travel and tourism sector when there are opportunities to sell.

Providing advice

Your customers will look to you as being the expert to whom they can turn for advice on a wide range of issues from where to go, when to go, how to go, what to eat, what to do, what to wear and so on. You might be in a tourist information office being asked about accommodation, in a travel shop being asked about a flight, or in a resort being asked about getting medical treatment.

To give good customer service you need to be knowledgeable about issues likely to arise and willing to find the answers to any question. Your organisation should support you with an information store, electronic or manual, with answers to likely questions and contacts to use to find any other answers.

Remember to phrase your responses to the questions suitably. You are giving advice not instruction, so you might start your reply with 'I would suggest...' or 'You might like to try...'

Dealing with problems

The travel and tourism sector is complex. Teamwork is important, both between colleagues within organisations and between organisations. Problems are a part of the daily fare for anyone in the travel and tourism sector. By working together, these problems can be resolved.

There are two types of problem – the problem the customer doesn't know about and the problem the customer does know about.

You might be a resort rep who has just received the guest list for next week and you are trying to allocate rooms. You notice that one couple wants a standard category ground floor room because they are elderly, but you don't have one available. You might upgrade a customer, to whom you were going to allocate a ground floor room, to a deluxe room on the first floor. Problem solved and the customers didn't even know there had been one.

You might be cabin crew and have a passenger who wants a chicken dinner but they have all gone. The offer of beef instead, but with a free glass of wine, might be enough to overcome the problem. The customer knew there was a problem, but it has been resolved.

Sometimes problems are easy to resolve, sometimes they are not. Sometimes a compromise might be needed, for example how do you solve the problem if a customer needs to cancel their holiday, but does not have any travel insurance to cover cancellation?

It helps to have a framework to solve problems. This diagram demonstrates one problem-solving technique.

Figure 5.5: A problem-solving technique

What is the problem? At present there may not be one. All we know so far is that the passenger has to cancel his holiday. Not a problem, he can do so, even if he has no travel insurance.

- However, the *problem* is that he doesn't want to lose the money he has paid which he may do because he has no travel insurance.
- That also defines the *objective* – not to lose the money paid.

- Now generate some potential solutions. Perhaps seek a full refund from the tour operator, delay the holiday or let a friend or relative travel instead. Further investigation might result in discovering real solutions – perhaps he could have a 25% refund or delay the holiday for up to two months for a fee of £50, or have a friend or relative travel instead for a £25 name change per person.

- Now the customer can evaluate the options.

- The final stage is for the customer to select the preferred solution.

2.3 Demonstrating skills and techniques

Unit 2: Understanding customer service in travel and tourism helped you understand the different approaches organisations bring to customer service and the needs and expectations of different types of customer. This unit has helped you understand some of the methods, skills and techniques you can use to provide good customer service. You should now be able to bring this knowledge together to practise and demonstrate customer skills and techniques.

Appropriate to the situation

Remember that you need to select the customer service skills and techniques which are appropriate to the situation you have. What is the situation? What communication method must you use? What combination of skills and techniques in your customer service tool-bag can you use?

Appropriate to the type of customer

You have learned that customers' needs and expectations can be different, depending upon the customer and the circumstance. What are the needs and wants of the customer? What communication method is appropriate? What combination of skills and techniques will you use?

Effectively utilised and demonstrated

You will need to demonstrate that you have used those skills and techniques effectively, in other words, did using them result in the desired outcome? Could other skills and techniques have been more effective?

Assessment activity 5.3

P3 M2 D1

Your airline has received the following complaint:

Your investigation has identified:

- The vegetarian meal request had been noted on the original booking, but the passenger had phoned to change his flight and the request had not been transferred to the new booking.

- The passenger's flight arrived in Munich at 17:45.

- The cabin crew say he had been very angry and pompous.

- He is travelling on your flight 345 from Southampton to Zurich on 12 December.

Write a reply to the passenger including all, some, or none of your investigation, together with some recompense if you think it is appropriate.

This activity will enable you to achieve P3 (part 1 of 3), M2 (part 1 of 4) and D1 (part 1 of 4). See also assessment activities 5.4 and 5.5.

> 12, Sunny Way,
> Doddle,
> Dorset,
> 18 April 2010
>
> Dear Sir/Madam,
>
> I must bring to your attention the appalling service I received on your flight from Southampton to Munich last Saturday.
>
> The flight was supposed to depart at 1400, but it did not leave until 1500. This delay caused me great inconvenience as we did not arrive at Munich until 1745. As a direct result, I had to pay for a taxi to get me to my hotel, so that I could get to the evening performance of 'La Tosca' in time.
>
> As if this was not bad enough, I expressly told your lady when I booked my flight on the phone that I cannot eat meat, so must have a vegetarian meal. Through sheer incompetence, your Cabin Crew said they didn't have it on board. The stewardess put a few lettuce leaves and fruit etc. on the plate, but I still felt treated like a second class citizen whilst the other passengers enjoyed their steaks.
>
> I know your Chairman personally as we served in the same regiment. Unless I get suitable recompense, I shall be addressing my complaints directly to him the next time we meet in the Club. I suggest a free return ticket and a couple of bottles of the finest champers would meet the need.
>
> I look forward to an early and satisfactory reply.
>
> Yours truly,
>
>
> Marmaduke Fitzgerald,
> (Colonel, retired)

Grading tips

- P3 Remember the objective of achieving a good recovery from a poor situation. Look for opportunities to ensure that the customer continues to buy from you. Make sure you cover all the points you feel are appropriate to cover, in a clear and logical manner. Make sure there are no errors in facts, spelling or grammar.

- If your style demonstrates confident professionalism, it will move you towards M2 (part 1 of 4).

See also assessment activities 5.4, 5.5 and 5.6.

- To partially achieve D1, you must demonstrate that you can use skills and techniques to provide excellent customer service across the four scenarios you will undertake. Make notes for use later, which analyse your performance in this written scenario. This analysis will form the remaining part of the D1 requirement. See also assessment activities 5.4, 5.5, 5.6 and 5.7.

PLTS

When you use skills and techniques to provide customer service in travel and tourism situations you will develop skills as a **reflective learner**, **self-manager** and **effective participator**.

Functional skills

Once again you will use your **ICT** skills to develop, present and communicate information, and your **English** skills, both in reading and speaking.

BTEC Assessment activity 5.4 — P3 M2 D1

This is a role-play assessment. Your tutor will give you information on a tourist destination in advance of this assessment and will tell you how it will be assessed and conducted. You should make yourself familiar with the tourist destination information before the assessment.

For your assessment, you will be asked to give advice on the telephone to a caller who may be from overseas and/or have a particular cultural background.

This activity will enable you to achieve **P3 (part 2 of 3)**, **M2 (part 2 of 4)** and **D1 (part 2 of 4)**. See, also assessment activities 5.3 and 5.5.

Grading tips

- **P3** One of the skills in giving advice is to know what you are talking about, so use the knowledge you have and relate it to the needs of the customer seeking advice. Use the telephone techniques you have read about in this unit. Don't forget to listen carefully and check you have understood correctly.

- If your style demonstrates confident professionalism, it will move you towards **M2 (part 2 of 4)**. See also assessment activities 5.3, 5.5 and 5.6.

- To partially achieve **D1**, you must demonstrate that you can use skills and techniques to provide excellent customer service across the four scenarios you will undertake in 5.3, 5.4, 5.5 and 5.6. Make notes for use later, which analyse your performance in this telephone scenario. This analysis will form the fifth of five parts of the **D1** requirement. See also assessment activities 5.3, 5.5, 5.6 and 5.7.

PLTS

When you use your skills and techniques to provide customer service in travel and tourism situations you will develop skills as a **reflective learner**.

Functional skills

In this activity you will use your **English** skills in reading, and most particularly, in listening and speaking.

BTEC Assessment activity 5.5 — P3 M2 D1

This assessment activity is a face to face role-play. Your tutor will tell you how it will be assessed and conducted.

You are a holiday representative making a hotel visit, when you are approached by a distraught elderly gentleman and his wife who are staying on one of your organisation's holidays. They have some problems and need you to solve them **P3** and deal with them **M2 D1**.

This activity will enable you to achieve **P3 (part 3 of 3)**, **M2 (part 3 of 4)** and **D1 (part 3 of 4)**. See also assessment activities 5.3 and 5.4.

Grading tips

- **P3** Remember the problem-solving model. Empathise but stay calm and be positive.

- If your style demonstrates confident professionalism, it will move you towards **M2 (part 3 of 4)**. See also assessment activities 5.3, 5.4 and 5.6.

- To partially achieve **D1**, you must demonstrate that you can use skills and techniques to provide excellent customer service across the four scenarios you will undertake in 5.3, 5.4, 5.5 and 5.6. Make notes for use later, which analyse your performance in this face to face scenario. This analysis will form the fifth of five parts of the **D1** requirement. See also assessment activities 5.3, 5.4, 5.6 and 5.7.

Assessment activity 5.6

P4 M2 D1

This assessment activity is a face to face role-play. Before your assessment you should spend some time obtaining product information and prices from car rental offices or websites. Your tutor will tell you how the role-play will be assessed and conducted.

You are a car rental sales assistant. A man approaches your desk with his wife and a child, who is 7–9 years old, and a baby, who is 1–2 years old. Rent him a car.

This activity will enable you to achieve P4, M2 (part 4 of 4) and D1 (part 4 of 4).

Grading tips

- P4 Remember the eight stages of selling. Use them appropriately.

- M2 If your style demonstrates confident professionalism, it will move you towards M2 (part 4 of 4). See also assessment activities 5.3, 5.4 and 5.5.

- D1 To partially achieve D1, you must demonstrate that you can use skills and techniques to provide excellent customer service across the four scenarios you will undertake in 5.3, 5.4, 5.5 and 5.6. Make notes for use later, which analyse your performance in this face-to-face scenario. This analysis will form the fifth of five parts of the D1 requirement. See also assessment activities 5.3, 5.4, 5.5 and 5.7.

PLTS

As an **independent enquirer** you can identify questions to answer and problems to resolve, and analyse and evaluate information. As a **self-manager** and **effective participator** you will use skills and techniques to provide customer service in travel and tourism situations.

Functional skills

This is an opportunity to develop your **ICT** skills in finding and selecting information, and your **English** skills in reading, listening and speaking.

Assessment activity 5.7

D1

Reflect on your performance in the four assessment scenarios (5.3, 5.4, 5.5 and 5.6). Write a report analysing your performance. What went well and why? What would you do differently? What would you do more of, or less of, and why? Highlight the links between

the customer service you provided and the skills and techniques you used.

Combined with the D1 requirements of 5.3, 5.4, 5.5 and 5.6 this activity will enable you to achieve D1.

Grading tip D1

- Think about your performance and collate the notes you took at the end of each of the assessments

to identify any themes which influenced your performance.

PLTS

Here you can particularly develop your skill as a **reflective learner**, by assessing yourself, evaluating experiences and identifying opportunities for improvement.

Functional skills

This is your final opportunity in this unit to develop your **ICT** skills in finding and selecting information and developing, presenting and communicating information. It is also another opportunity to develop your written **English** skills.

I work for a Tour Operator in their call centre and I am responsible for responding to our customers' needs after they have made their bookings. My job is to provide the finishing touches and resolve any problems, so that the customers have wonderful holidays.

I work shifts because the call centre is open from 0800–2200 every day of the week. We have job rotation, so some days I am dealing with tailor-made arrangements and sales, and other days I am dealing with operational issues.

Typical day

I spoke to a customer this morning whose daughter is getting married in Barbados. The gentleman wanted to surprise his daughter by flying her best childhood friend to the wedding from Canada. That was a bit challenging, but really interesting, finding flights for her and arranging accommodation, whilst making sure they wouldn't see each other until the big day.

Later, I had a call from a lady who was very upset. Her daughter was on one of our Swiss skiing holidays, but she had a skiing accident and needed to be flown back to the UK with a medical escort. We managed to sort it all out and the daughter will fly home tomorrow. The mother was very relieved and thanked me for all my help.

What's good about the job?

I've just had a meal break with some of my team and we were exchanging stories about the calls we had taken and the help we had given. There were some really funny stories to tell, and some sad ones, but we all agreed that it was a really satisfying job. We feel good when there is a successful outcome, and even better when the customers thank us, which they usually do.

Think about it!

1 Which communication and customer service skills do you think Parveen and her colleagues use in their day-to-day work?

2 What knowledge and skills do you think you have gained on this course so far which would help you as a travel and tourism customer service advisor in a call centre?

Just checking

1 Give three reasons why organisations might have their staff wear uniforms.

2 Which is the best way to respond to a letter of complaint:
   - by letter
   - by email
   - by telephone?

3 Spell 'travel' and 'tourism' phonetically.

4 Using the 24-hour clock method, write out:
   - nine twenty in the morning
   - eight fifty in the evening.
   - a quarter to twelve in the morning
   - four thirty in the afternoon.

5 List three 'open' styles and three 'closed' styles of body language.

6 What methods can a tour operator use to make sure the holidaymaker is provided with up-to-date information on their holiday arrangements?

7 Name the eight stages of selling.

8 Give three examples of open questions.

9 What is the difference between a problem and a complaint?

10 With which of the following types of customer would you use listening skills:
   - complaining
   - non-English speaking
   - groups
   - special needs?

Assignment tips

- This unit had an emphasis on developing and using methods, skills and techniques to provide good customer service.

- The more you observe others in customer service situations and think about what they are doing, and why, the more you will able to build your customer service 'toolbox' and select appropriate methods and techniques.

- The more you practise using your customer service methods and techniques, the more skilled you will become. Work with a friend to practise role-plays and give each other useful feedback.

- Find time to visit travel and tourism locations (e.g. travel agencies, theme parks, transport hubs) and observe. What do you notice about the customers? How do they behave? What do they ask? What do the organisations you visit and their staff do to give excellent customer service?

6 UK tourism destinations

Have you ever thought about the appeal of the United Kingdom (UK) as a destination? Where do people go and how do they get there? Where have they come from? The UK can offer a vast range of destinations to appeal to everyone, from business groups to parents with young families. The UK may be relatively small, but the tourist industry is BIG on variety. Domestic visitors made over 21,000 trips within the UK in 2008, and together with overseas visitors, account for a total spend of £86.3 billion in the visitor economy (source: VisitBritain).

Understanding the appeal of the UK to different types of visitor is an essential starting point for anyone who wants to work in the travel and tourism sector. This unit will help you to develop your knowledge of selected UK destinations and increase your skills in using different sources of information to locate key tourist destinations and the transport gateways where the tourist experience starts.

The unit has links with *Unit 1: The UK travel and tourism sector Unit 9: Holiday planning* and *Unit 13: Organising a travel and tourism study visit.*

Learning outcomes

After completing this unit you should:

1 know the location of significant UK travel and tourism destinations and gateways

2 know the appeal of UK tourism destinations for different types of visitor

3 be able to use sources of information to find out about UK destinations.

Assessment and grading criteria

This table shows you what you must do in order do achieve a pass, merit or distinction grade, and where you can find activities in this book to help you.

To achieve a **pass** grade the evidence must show that you are able to:	To achieve a **merit** grade the evidence must show that, in addition to the pass criteria, you are able to:	To achieve a **distinction** grade the evidence must show that, in addition to the pass and merit criteria, you are able to:
P1 locate significant UK travel and tourism destinations, airports and seaports **Assessment activity 6.1, page 192**		
P2 describe the appeal of one UK town or city destination, one seaside resort and one countryside area, each focusing on the appeal for a different type of visitor **Assessment activity 6.2, page 208**	**M1** assess, giving detailed examples, the strongest aspects of appeal of each destination for one type of visitor **Assessment activity 6.2, page 208**	**D1** use analysis of the overall strength of appeal of one UK destination for one type of visitor to identify any gaps in provision **Assessment activity 6.2, page 208**
P3 use appropriate sources of information to find out about the location and appeal of UK destinations **Assessment activity 6.2, page 208**	**M2** work independently when researching destinations, using different sources of information that are clearly referenced in work that is presented clearly, logically and coherently **Assessment activity 6.2, page 208**	

Charlotte, 16-year-old learner

My grandparents live by the sea, and we often visit them. I didn't take much notice of the town before doing this unit, but now I look at it with new eyes – I didn't realise how much the resort relies on tourism and the effort it goes to make tourists welcome.

I went in to the Tourist Office, and picked up a lot of leaflets. The people in there were very helpful and gave me lots of ideas. I looked through the information and picked out the bits that were relevant to my assignment and I went round the town imagining that I had a small child with me. There were a lot of places aimed at children, with activities throughout the school holidays. I really enjoyed talking to people in attractions to find out what they can do with kids on a rainy day. There were a lot of students working during the holidays as well and that's what I would like to do. Some said they had worked in cities too where it was very different, but just as interesting with a lot of different people around.

I know I am lucky to be able to visit a resort, but there is a lot of information available for others because they want people to come here and have a good time. I found it very interesting and can't wait to get a part-time job.

Over to you

- What challenges might you face in doing research for this unit?

- What can you do now to prepare for this unit?

- Who can you talk to about what they look for in a destination?

1 The location of significant UK travel and tourism destinations and gateways

Where would I like to go?

Imagine you have been offered a day out, all expenses paid, with a couple of friends. You can go wherever you want, as long as it is within the UK. Where would you like to go? Would you go to the city or to the countryside? Clubbing or canoeing? Seaside or seal sanctuary? Write down your chosen destination and the 'selling points' you might need to persuade your friends to go there. Discuss this with your friends and see which destination wins!

1.1 UK travel and tourism destinations

Capital cities

In order to understand UK travel destinations, you will have to know where they are! The UK is made up of England, Scotland, Wales and Northern Ireland. Each of these countries has a capital city which is visited by thousands of tourists every year, as well as being a cultural and commercial centre.

How would you sell these holidays to your friends?

Activity: Countries in the UK

In groups of four, each of you research one of the countries of the UK. Find out how many visitors each country received the previous year. Discuss why the volume of visitors may vary from country to country. Locate the country on a map, and add the capital city. Cut out the country shape, and put all four together to make a UK map.

Seaside resorts

Going to the seaside has been a traditional activity since the mid to late nineteenth century. Many resorts date from that time and rely on visitors for their local economy to prosper. Look at the amount of coastline around the UK – there is a lot to choose from!

Activity: Seaside

Locate the following seaside resorts and mark on a blank map.

- South coast, Brighton – a traditional resort, but with international and artistic atmosphere.
- West coast, Newquay – currently a popular place for young people and for surfing.
- Wales, Tenby – a beautiful sandy beach.
- Scotland, Ayr – an elegant resort on the west coast.
- East coast, Great Yarmouth – a traditional resort with many activities.
- Isle of Wight – popular for families.

Spa towns

Towns with healing springs have attracted visitors for thousands of years and many tourists still visit to 'take the waters'. Towns gradually built up as it became fashionable to be seen at these destinations. The towns often became cultural centres for music, theatres and dancing. In the eighteenth century, rich and influential people often built grand houses and squares.

One of the most famous spa towns is Bath, where a new spa resort has opened near the original Roman baths.

Activity: Spa towns

On a blank map, add the following spa towns:

Bath, Tunbridge Wells, Harrogate, Leamington Spa, Matlock Bath and Wells.

Figure 6.1: Countries and capital cities of the UK

Figure 6.2: Seaside resorts in the UK

Countryside areas

The UK is known for the variety of its countryside such as hills, moors, lakes and coasts, and the beauty of many unspoilt areas despite being a relatively small area compared with many other European countries. The UK is lucky to have such a variety of scenery from mountain ranges, such as the Grampians in Scotland, to gentle rolling downlands such as the South Downs in Sussex.

National Parks

Each of the National Parks has been awarded its status to preserve the countryside within it for the future and for the public to enjoy.

The UK is densely populated and guards its countryside areas against inappropriate development. One of the most effective ways of ensuring that countryside areas have controlled development is through the National Park system. There are ten National Parks in England, three in Wales and two in Scotland. Much of the land is still privately owned, but it is protected by legislation against unsuitable building projects, the use of insecticides, etc. The National Parks are also required to encourage visitors so that everyone may enjoy the beautiful scenery.

Did you know?

The Scottish Highlands include some of the highest mountains in the UK, such as Ben Nevis, and are home to ski resorts, such as Aviemore.

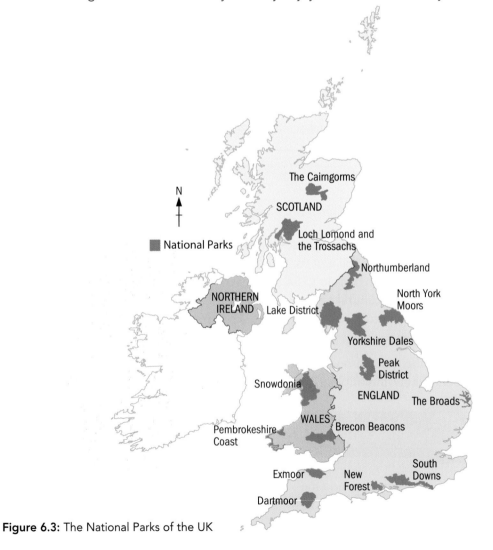

Figure 6.3: The National Parks of the UK

Coastal areas

The UK coastline covers 11,000 miles. Much of it is built-up with towns, resorts and caravan/camping sites where visitors can enjoy traditional 'bucket and spade' holidays. Part of the coast is owned by the National Trust, which preserves it from over-development by restricting building activities. The National Trust protects over 600 miles of coastline, keeping it accessible to the public and helping to keep it in its natural state. Other parts of the coast, such as the Pembrokeshire Coast National Park, are also protected against development. Thousands of visitors each year also walk along long-distance trails, such as the South West Coast Path.

Activity: Identifying areas

Research at least two countryside, or coastal areas, and locate them on your map. Then, in pairs, produce posters advertising the activities that can be done in these areas. Make them as exciting as possible, including all the information that visitors would need to know.

Cultural and historic towns and cities

There are many cultural and historic towns and cities throughout the UK – you need to know about the range of towns and cities available. Towns and cities may be connected to a famous person, for example Howarth is linked with the Bronte sisters, or may be popular for other reasons. Bath, for example, is visited for its Roman and Georgian architecture and Windsor has many visitors to its famous castle.

Islands

There are many islands off the coast of the UK. Each of them has its own significance and receives many visitors every year.

Activity: Marking maps

1 On a map of the UK mark the South West Coast Path and the Pembrokeshire long distance coast paths.

2 In pairs, discuss a town or city that you have visited. Describe why you went there and what you did, and then locate it and mark it on your map.

Find the following historic towns, and mark them on your blank map.

- Stratford-upon-Avon – famous as Shakespeare's birthplace.
- Glasgow – European Capital of Culture in 1990.
- York – Roman and Viking city.
- Chester – half-timbered houses and cathedral.
- Caernavon – castle and ancient city.
- Warwick – castle and river.

3 Research reasons why these cities are popular with tourists.

Add the following to your maps:

- Isle of Wight – traditional family 'bucket and spade' venue.
- Isle of Man – famous for motorbike 'TT' races.
- Scilly Isles – unspoilt countryside and mild climate.
- Channel Islands – a 'French' flavour, and governed separately.
- Isle of Skye – beautiful area, renowned as the hiding place of Bonnie Prince Charlie.
- Shetland Islands – remote islands popular as cruise destinations.

Research some other islands off the coast of the UK and explore why they are popular as a tourist destination.

1.2 Airports

Types

Every major city in the UK, including London, Edinburgh, Birmingham, Cardiff, Bristol and Manchester, has an airport. Most of them are classed as 'international' airports where visitors can officially enter the country. London alone has five airports – Heathrow, Gatwick, Stansted, Luton and London City. Some airports are positioned so they can serve a whole area, such as Leeds/Bradford or East Midlands and are usually referred to as 'regional'. Other airports, such as Exeter, are usually referred to as 'local'.

All airports are allocated 3-letter codes that are used internationally. The larger airports have easily identifiable ones; smaller ones tend to have less easily recognised codes. Examples include:

* London Heathrow – LHR

* London Gatwick – LGW

* Manchester – MAN

* Belfast – BFS.

These codes are used on airline tickets and baggage labels. Next time you go to an airport, look at the codes on your documents.

Did you know?

* The international language of air travel is English.

* Nearly 14 million passengers and 3 million tourist cars used the port of Dover in 2008.
  (Source: Port of Dover)

Figure 6.4: Main airports in the UK

1.3 Seaports

Ports

The UK is home to some of the busiest ports in Europe and hosts hundreds of thousands of tourists from home and abroad every year. These ports have grown and developed into international and domestic points of embarkation and disembarkation. Examples are Dover, Holyhead, Penzance, Poole, Portsmouth and Larne. The port of Dover recently celebrated 400 years as a ferry port.

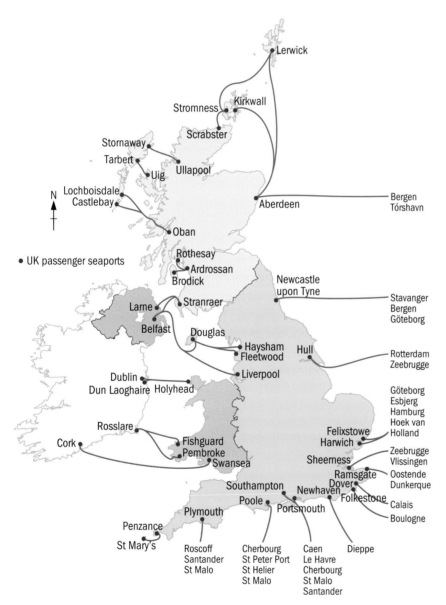

Figure 6.5: Main seaports and sea routes of the UK

Activity: Sea routes

In groups, draw a poster for one of these routes:

- UK to Ireland (Northern Ireland and Eire)
- UK to France
- UK to Netherlands and Scandinavia.

You could use a travel atlas or ferry timetables and brochures. You could look at Stena Line, SeaFrance, Brittany Ferries or Caledonian MacBrayne.

Routes

In general, the main routes serviced by the seaports are:

- ports on the south coast of England – servicing ferry crossings to France, the Channel Islands and Spain
- the west coast of the UK – servicing ferry crossings to Ireland
- the east coast of the UK – servicing ferry crossings to the Netherlands and Scandinavia.

There are also many smaller ferry routes between the mainland and islands, for example the Wightlink between Portsmouth and the Isle of Wight.

Assessment activity 6.1

P2 P3 P4 M2 P1

On blank UK maps, mark and clearly label the following:

- countries of the UK and their capital cities
- at least six seaside resorts (try to identify these from different countries)
- at least six cultural or historic towns or cities
- at least six countryside or coastal areas (these should include some National Parks)
- at least six spa towns
- at least six islands
- at least six major or regional airports (with 3-letter codes)
- at least six seaports, indicating a typical route (make sure you include routes within the UK, UK to Republic of Ireland and to mainland Europe.

Ensure you include a 'key' to identify each type of destination.

Grading tip P1

- You must present your own maps, using a pre-printed outline, for your assessment. You should not use maps which are copied or download maps with locations already printed.

PLTS

If you complete your assessment tasks on time, you will be a self-manager.

Functional skills

You will use your ICT skills to find and select information.

2 The appeal of UK tourism destinations for different types of visitor

2.1 Different types of visitor

Earlier in this unit you have seen a few examples of why visitors from within the UK (**domestic visitors**) or from other countries (**inbound visitors**) travel to different destinations. They could be going to towns or cities, a seaside resort or a countryside area. People will choose to go to different places because they want different things from their trip. Remember that you need to think of these destinations from the point of view of a tourist.

There are different kinds of visitor to the UK and each of them will have different reasons to choose the UK as their holiday destination and will have different needs. The reasons for choosing a holiday are as individual as people: one visitor's ideal may be totally wrong for another person.

> ## Key terms
>
> Domestic visitors – visitors from within the same country.
>
> Inbound visitors – visitors from another country

Figure 6.6: Types of visitor

Families

Parents principally need to keep the children happy and occupied while trying to have a relaxing time themselves! Some families will look at destinations which provide activities on-site or within their price range and such destinations could include a Butlins or Haven holiday. Destinations such as Center Parcs provide a safe environment for participating in sporting activities and an all-year-round swimming zone. If the weather is good, then families might be happy making sandcastles on a safe beach. There are many family resorts around the UK that provide a variety of all-weather activities, as well as traditional 'bucket and spade' holidays. Examples include Weston-super-Mare, Cleethorpes and Portrush.

Retired people

Retired people may also be looking for activities with other retired people – ballroom dancing weekends or painting holidays are popular. Sometimes older people may simply want the opportunity to sightsee in peace! Increasingly, older people are also taking advantage of better health in retirement to undertake activities such as sailing or hiking. Golf and other sporting activities are popular and retired people will often have the time available to be able to go on holiday to enjoy their hobbies.

Activity: Types of visitor

In groups, take one of the types of visitor. Using brochures, leaflets and guides, design a collage of destinations and attractions suitable for the specific group of visitors you have chosen.

Young adults

Young adults usually like to have plenty of opportunity to meet others so look for clubs, bars and other places to meet. They may well want to have activities during the day in order to socialise. Some destinations, such as Newquay, have surfing and other watersports, as well as a variety of bars and clubs. Destinations such as Blackpool often host 'hen' and 'stag' parties, and are particularly popular during the 'illuminations' season in the autumn. University towns and cities, such as York or Brighton, are also very popular with young adults and have a 'cosmopolitan' feel.

People with special needs

There are many organisations which specially organise holidays for people with special needs. To obtain a secure link to a website listing such organisations, see the Hotlinks section on p.x.

Tourism for All UK is one source in the UK of holiday and travel information for disabled people and their carers. They can help with information on accessible accommodation, visitor attractions and transport. They can also help to organise activity holidays for people with disabilities, holidays for children with disabilities, respite care establishments and accessible overseas destinations. To obtain a secure link to the Tourism for All UK website, see the Hotlinks section on p.x.

The special needs may be physical or may include a learning difficulty or disability. Visitors may be wheelchair users, or their hearing or sight may be impaired. Reasonable adjustments have to be made in order to accommodate these needs and organisations are required by law to make adjustments, such as providing ramps for wheelchairs, induction loops for hearing-impaired people or enlarged print for sight-impaired people.

Activity: Local attractions

Look at an attraction or hotel near you. Find out what provision it has for people with special needs.

Inbound tourists

Inbound tourists may need some help at attractions or on guided tours. The provision of leaflets in foreign languages, multi-language signs or bilingual guides (guides who speak more than one language) is useful. Some attractions have audio guides, where the visitor can listen to a pre-recorded soundtrack in their own language. The Pavilion in Brighton, for instance, has hand-held audio guides, similar to a large mobile phone, which provides information as visitors reach certain points on the tour.

Inbound tourists are particularly interested in history and heritage. Many countries are fascinated by our royal family and will visit palaces such as Hampton Court or Windsor Castle, both within 30 minutes of London. Destinations such as Stonehenge in Wiltshire, or Bath, with its Roman remains and elegant architecture, are also popular.

Many inbound tourists are also interested in seeing where their families originated from. Scotland has run a marketing campaign based on the idea of returning 'home'. Above all, inbound tourists are usually looking for something different from the things they have at home.

School groups

School groups are often key visitors to attractions and destinations outside the main summer season. Their curriculum often means that they go out to look at natural features, such as lakes or the seashore, as well as science museums and other attractions. Very often the destination will provide study guides specifically linked to the curriculum and have study areas to accommodate the groups. Cities will provide guides written specifically to inspire children.

2.2 Range of destinations

The decision where to go on holiday is sometimes said to be the 'pull factor'. Below we will look at some of the factors that pull visitors to particular places.

Town or city

The different towns and cities in the UK appeal to visitors for a variety of reasons. Many have universities, for example Oxford and Cambridge, shops, entertainment, business facilities, or historical buildings which appeal to many types of visitor. One example is York where

Case study: The sights and smells of history

York is the county town of Yorkshire. There has been a city here for thousands of years. The Romans had their settlement of Eboracum and the Vikings built Jorvik on its ruins. The medieval city of York can still be seen in the 'snickleways' (alleys) and 'bars' (gateways) in the Roman-based walls.

The Jorvik Museum can take you back in time to AD 975 on a ride through the sights and smells of the excavated Viking town. This was where the famous York Helmet was found, one of the finest eighth century Anglo-Saxon helmets discovered in the UK. The museum tries to appeal to those interested in history, as well as provide a 'fun' attraction. Children can beat a 'Viking' coin, or take part in activities with 'Vikings' – actors who bring the past to life. You can find out more about The Jorvik Viking Centre on-line. To obtain a secure link to their website, see the Hotlinks section on p.x.

There are many other heritage attractions in the city of York, such as Clifford's Tower and the Castle Museum,

as well as the beautiful York Minster cathedral. Visitors can enjoy a trip to the Railway Museum or a boat trip along the river. There are also many concerts and other cultural activities available to the tourist.

There are many bars, restaurants and clubs and the university and colleges ensure that there is plenty for young people to do as well. There are individual shops as well as the usual range of department stores. A visit to the tea rooms is a treat not to be missed!

1 List four attractions in York and identify who you think would be interested in visiting each of them, for example, children, young people or couples, etc.

2 Locate York on a map and draw in:
   • the nearest airport (Leeds/Bradford)
   • the main roads to York
   • the railway lines to London and Edinburgh.

thousands of visitors visit every year to view its heritage and historical buildings. Destinations such as these have easy access via trains, coaches, motorways or even airports, and they will also have a range of accommodation available from guest houses to luxury hotels.

Activity: Tourist towns

Research at least three tourist towns and find out why people go there. Mark them on a blank map with a suitable symbol. Save your map for future activities – you might like to use it again!

Seaside resorts

Towns, usually referred to as 'resorts', have often grown up next to beaches to provide accommodation and other facilities for tourists.

Seaside resorts vary from small villages in coves, such as Porthcurno in Cornwall, to large towns with miles of flat sandy beaches, such as Torquay on the English Riviera on the south coast. There are traditional 'bucket and spade' resorts with piers and candyfloss, crazy golf and arcade games when it rains. Families visit seaside resorts year after year, as children can spend hours making sandcastles and paddling in the waves. Visitors find the ever-changing sea relaxing and walks along the 'promenade' can be exhilarating, even in winter. During the off-season seaside resorts are particularly popular with different groups such as school groups and retired people, as well as ramblers and those who are interested in natural history.

However, resorts in England find it difficult to compete with the sun of the Mediterranean, so they have developed other ways to encourage tourists. Examples include Blackpool which has casinos, its world famous illuminations and the Pleasure Beach theme park, and Bournemouth which has increased its conference and exhibition facilities.

Activity: Seaside resorts

In groups, discuss the UK seaside resorts you have visited and put them on the map. What do they have to offer visitors during bad weather/outside the summer season? List the type of visitors who would be attracted to these seaside resorts.

Countryside areas

The countryside of the UK is varied and can provide activities for all ages, tastes and needs. There are imposing mountains such as the Scottish Highlands with its ski resorts, rolling hills such as the Cotswolds, and peat marshes such as Romney Marsh. Visitors come to 'get away from it all' and to pursue leisure activities such as horse riding and hiking.

You have looked in the previous section at National Parks and the part they play in conserving the countryside for visitors. There are many other areas renowned for their scenery, such as the Areas of Outstanding Natural Beauty, for example the Wye valley, one of the finest lowland landscapes in Britain. Cornwall is also well known for its fine coastal scenery.

In addition to this, many people walk the Long Distance Paths, such as the Pennine Way or Offa's Dyke. Others may visit countryside areas for sporting activities, such as mountain biking or watersports.

2.3 Natural features

Many places attract visitors because of their natural features, such as rivers, lakes, valleys, hills and mountains.

Mountains

Some people visit mountainous areas for climbing or skiing. The Scottish Highlands are the scene of ski-resorts, such as Aviemore in the winter, and are popular with mountain climbers in the summer. The Yorkshire Moors are visited because of the opportunity to go fell-walking (hiking in mountainous terrain). Even children can walk up Snowdon in Wales – and can go up by mountain railway (the funicular) if they are feeling tired!

Lakes

Lakes are popular with a wide variety of tourists. There may be watersports such as sailing, waterskiing and sailboarding available. Some lakes are also ideal for swimming and paddling. Other people are happy just to hike around the lake and look at the scenery. Scottish lakes are called 'lochs' similar to the Irish 'lough' The most famous loch is probably Loch Ness, home to the 'monster'. One of the most visited lake attractions in the UK are the cruises on Lake Windermere in the Lake District.

What kind of activities can you enjoy on a lake?

Beaches and coasts

Some areas of the UK are known for their beaches. Blackpool has miles of sand and Holkham beach in Norfolk was been named as one of the best beaches in the UK by The Times in 2009. Some beaches remain unspoilt and people visit them to hike or just to watch the waves. Areas such as the Pembrokeshire Coast National Park contain many isolated and peaceful beaches.

Rivers

Many people like to holiday on rivers as well – boating up the Thames or the Grand Union canal system can be a relaxing holiday. The Norfolk Broads has a whole industry based on the rivers and waterways of East Anglia. Boats of all shapes and sizes can be hired by individuals or large parties.

Activity: Inland waterways

Look at a map of inland waterways and rivers in the UK. In groups, investigate one of the waterways and find out what activities you can do there. Present your findings to the rest of the group.

2.4 Visitor attractions

You have already looked at a number of different reasons why visitors may choose a particular place – one of the main draws is what there is available to do. Visitor attractions can be almost anything people can enjoy looking around or learning more about. Attractions can be built, for example a castle, or a natural attraction, such as a lake. Attractions may be found in towns, cities, seaside resorts or countryside areas.

The National Trust and English Heritage

You may think that only older people are interested in historical properties but both the National Trust and English Heritage work hard to encourage visitors of all ages and provide special activities for children and school parties.

Case study: Visitor attractions

The National Trust

The National Trust is a huge organisation. It has 3.4 million members and owns hundreds of historic houses.

The National Trust's core purpose is 'to look after special places for ever, for everyone'. There are National Trust properties all over England, Wales and Northern Ireland and there is an equivalent organisation in Scotland (National Trust for Scotland). The National Trust is a charity and is therefore dependent on membership fees, entry fees and donations to carry on its work.

1   Look at the National Trust and the National Trust for Scotland websites and find three national properties, one in England, one in Wales and one in Scotland. To obtain a secure link to these websites, see the Hotlinks section on p.x

2   Search for a property closest to your home. Perhaps you have been there? Discuss with a group why you might want to visit it.

English Heritage

English Heritage is a public body with responsibility for all aspects of protecting and promoting the historic environment. They look after more than 400 historic properties and monuments including Stonehenge, Dover Castle and parts of Hadrian's Wall. You can find out more about the work of English Heritage by visiting their website. To obtain a secure link to their website, see the Hotlinks section on p.x.

1   From where does English Heritage obtain its funding?

2   Research one property and design a poster to encourage visitors.

ENGLISH HERITAGE

Both the National Trust and English Heritage encourage visitors, but they also aim to preserve land and buildings from destruction by developers and natural decline.

Theme parks

Theme parks can range from large parks with different themed areas, such as Thorpe Park in Surrey, to parks where the whole attraction is based around a particular theme, such as Flamingo Land in North Yorkshire. These parks usually have rides and attractions included in the entry price. Some of the rides can be thrilling or frightening, depending on your point of view, and are known as 'white knuckle' rides because of the way riders grip the handlebars!

Activity: Theme parks

What are the theme parks in your local area or the nearest holiday region? Investigate:

• the main theme or themes

• who the main customers are.

Historical and heritage sites

Historical and heritage sites concentrate on looking at traditional or ancient buildings and activities. They can also be to do with social history, such as how we lived in the war (for example the Cabinet War Rooms in London) or industrial heritage, such as Wigan Pier in Lancashire.

One of Shropshire's top attractions is the heritage site of Ironbridge Gorge, which is known as the birthplace of the Industrial Revolution. Today, the area is far from industrial. Although the revolution started here, most of the factories are long gone and the natural beauty of the gorge has been restored.

Figure 6.7: Attractions in the UK

Museums

Many modern museums are interactive, using technology to enable special effects such as erupting volcanoes and earthquakes. There are many new museums that have been given Millennium Funding – money provided by the European and UK governments for special projects. These include Magna near Sheffield, as well as some of the great London museums such as the Science Museum or the Victoria and Albert Museum.

Many visitors are also attracted to the Victorian themed museums at Ironbridge Gorge, which are operated by the Ironbridge Gorge Museum Trust.

Activity: Top museums

Using the VisitBritain website, which provides statistics on tourism in the UK, look at the top museums and the number of visitors they attract. Draw a graph comparing the number of visitors to the top ten museums. To obtain a secure link to their website, see the Hotlinks section on p.x.

Wildlife parks and zoos

There are many attractions which provide the opportunity to see animals in the UK, such as Monkeyworld in Dorset or Drusilla's Zoo in East Sussex. Many of these are also concerned about conservation and breeding, as well as just showing the animals off. Some attractions have animals living 'in the wild' in enclosures, such as at Longleat Safari Park in Wiltshire. Many of these attractions have facilities to appeal to families, but attract people of all ages, particularly because of their conservation work.

2.5 Range of accommodation

Types of accommodation available

Many tourist destinations provide a variety of accommodation, from guest houses to large hotels with bars and restaurants. There may also be a range of self-catering accommodation from converted farmhouses to lighthouses and stables.

Some people, particularly families, prefer self-catering because of the freedom it allows in terms of meal times and children may be happier eating familiar food. Self-catering also tends to be cheaper than hotel accommodation generally, although some self-catering is very luxurious.

Guest house accommodation is often good value for money and particularly suitable for people who are staying a short time or

Did you know?

It is very easy to assess the level of quality and service you can expect from hotels and other guest accommodation using the 5-star rating system agreed by VisitBritain, VisitScotland and Visit Wales together with the AA. The same standards are used across these regions, allowing for different categories of self-catering and hotels.

are touring. Hotels usually have many more leisure facilities and encourage guests to use their bars and restaurants. Hotels can range from inexpensive to luxurious accommodation at city or 'country house' hotels.

Holiday parks, such as Butlins or Center Parcs, offer self-catering chalet accommodation which can be quite basic. They do, however, offer cafes and restaurants on-site, together with a huge variety of activities, many of which are included in the price. This is often ideal for families, particularly if there is a large heated pool for when the weather is disappointing.

Camping and caravanning is also very popular and can be available in a variety of places, from the corner of a farmer's field, to a campsite with swimming pools and electricity.

Boats provide a different kind of accommodation. There may be houseboats or cruisers available and they can sleep anything from a few people to large numbers of people, depending on the number of berths.

Activity: Boating in the UK

Visit the Hoseasons website or your local travel agent for a brochure or information on boating holidays in the UK.

Name three areas in the UK where you could take a boating holiday. What types of people do you think would enjoy living on a boat?

To obtain a secure link to this website, see the Hotlinks section on p.x.

2.6 Facilities

The weather can be unpredictable in the UK, so it is important that destinations have a range of facilities available that do not depend on the weather for visitors' enjoyment.

Shopping

A popular way of passing the time is to go shopping – this can be at purpose-built shopping malls, such as Bluewater in Kent, or individual craft and art shops in town centres. Many visitors buy souvenirs of their visit and one of the joys of being somewhere different is the range of different food and produce available. Devon cream or Bakewell tarts can make a welcome gift.

Activity: Metrocentre, Gateshead

Visit the website of the Gateshead Metrocentre.

Who do you think is Metrocentre's main client group? What facilities are there as well as the shops? How do these encourage a range of clients?

To obtain a secure link to this website, see the Hotlinks section on p.x.

Sports and leisure

A destination will often provide sport and leisure facilities. Many resorts have swimming pools, and some use seawater, such as the Plymouth Lido. Boating and sailing are part of the British way of life and many resorts, such as Cowes on the Isle of Wight, hold sailing regattas.

Newquay, and neighbouring resorts on the north Devon and Cornish coast, are known for their surfing and bodyboarding activities on the Atlantic Ocean. These sports are becoming more and more popular, particularly with young people.

Towns have also invested in leisure facilities. At the Snowdome near Milton Keynes visitors can hire equipment and ski down the artificial ski slope; they can even use a ski lift to reach the top. Many places will have indoor bowling or skating rinks available.

Activity: Nearest towns

Research your nearest town. What leisure facilities are available? Are these suitable for visitors as well as residents?

2.7 Arts and entertainment

Arts and entertainment can bring in visitors from all over the UK and from many other countries. Think of the Glastonbury music festival (usually noted for its mud!) or the Edinburgh Festival where established acts perform alongside the 'fringe' acts.

Art galleries and exhibitions

Art galleries receive thousands of visitors a year. Many galleries have specific activities for children during the holiday period and may have special exhibitions to entice visitors. The Tate Modern in London has an education office which welcomes families. There have also been Tate galleries opened recently at St Ives and Liverpool.

Activity: Arts and attractions in your town

Research the facilities available for a school group at a local art gallery, or choose a city gallery to explore.

In pairs, choose a local town or city. Research the theatres, art galleries, exhibitions and local events available. Describe the three top attractions in that location for the next month. Who will these attractions appeal to?

Theatres, local festivals and events

London is known worldwide for its theatre district and has world renowned shows and film premieres. Many UK towns and cities have their own programmes of events, some even have festivals dedicated to art, music and literature, such as the Cheltenham Literature Festival. Glasgow is host to the internationally renowned T-Music festival each year, while other towns may host small niche festivals dedicated to classical music, crafts or literature.

2.8 Sightseeing

When visitors have reached their destination, there are many ways they can get to know it better.

Why are land trains so popular in resorts?

In many towns and country areas, there are often guided walks led by authorised 'Blue Badge' guides or countryside rangers. These can be very informative and may happen all year round at different times allowing tourists to see different aspects of an area or location. Another popular activity is to go on a 'ghost walk' during which visitors are taken on a walk through dark areas of the city as ghostly tales are told (this is often led by someone in a black cloak and a large hat).

Another way of seeing a destination is to go on a sightseeing boat trip – many towns and cities, including London, offer such trips and multi-lingual commentaries are often available.

Many resorts also have road trains or mini-trains available, often with commentaries, so that tourists can see the sights from the relative comfort of an open-air seat. Bournemouth, Weymouth and Swansea are all resorts that operate road trains along the coast. Open-topped buses are very popular in larger destinations, such as Brighton or Bath. Again, they will often have commentaries, from guides or on headphones, describing what the visitor can see. These can be very useful in helping visitors to get a feel of a new destination.

2.9 Transport links

You will remember that we started this unit looking at the location of different destinations. The location is very important, because visitors need to be able to reach it safely and conveniently. Many domestic visitors will travel by car, but not all areas are close to major road links such as motorways and some areas have notoriously narrow roads. Not all tourism takes place in the summer – consider the problems visitors may have reaching ski resorts in Scotland.

Many people travel by train – tickets can be cheaper if booked well in advance and this method of travel may be much quicker than other forms of transport. Some people choose coach travel, for example National Express runs a network of coach routes all over the UK. This method may be longer than the train but is often cheaper.

You have looked in the first section at the airports in the UK. These are important both for ensuring inbound visitors are able to access destinations, but also for enabling people to travel within the UK quickly. Many domestic routes connect cities, such as Edinburgh and London, as well as smaller holiday routes, such as that between Penzance and the Scilly Isles.

Seaports are also important for inbound and domestic visitors. The southeast of England receives many visitors from mainland Europe, particularly France through seaports such as Dover and Newhaven. Sea routes are also important for visitors to Northern Ireland, through Larne or Belfast, and to the Scottish Isles, such as Skye and the Hebrides.

When looking at a destination, you must consider all the methods of transport to and from the centre. However exciting the destination, it is no good if people can't get there.

Figure 6.8: The motorway system in the UK

3 Sources of information to find out about UK destinations

You must make sure that you use a range of information sources to find out about UK destinations. The use of the internet alone is not enough. A great deal of information on different UK destinations is available – after all, they need to market themselves to their visitors! Some sources of information include:

- VisitBritain, the official tourist office for those visiting the UK
- Tourist Information Centres (local ones will probably have information on the whole of the UK)
- holiday brochures/coach tour brochures
- television programmes about holidays in the UK
- regional websites, for example Tourism South East
- town and borough council websites, for example Devon County Council
- guide books, for example, *The Rough Guide to England (Ordnance Survey/AA Leisure Guides)*
- promotional videos, leaflets and newspaper travel supplements
- trade journals, for example *Travel Trade Gazette*
- atlases, for example the Columbus Travel Atlas
- libraries and other educational resources.

Assessment activity 6.2

P2 P3 M1 M2 D1

1 Research three tourist destinations in the UK. These must include one UK town or city, one seaside resort and one countryside area.

Choose a different visitor type for each destination and produce a visitor leaflet aimed at encouraging them to visit. You must include visitor attractions, natural features, a range of accommodation and facilities, for example shopping, sport and leisure, arts and entertainment, sightseeing and transport links. Make sure you are clearly aiming at your chosen visitor type.

Use appropriate sources of information to find out about these destinations. **P2 P3**

2 Using the same destinations, as in the previous question, provide a display giving more information on at least three of the most important aspects of appeal (visitor attractions, natural features, range of accommodation, facilities for your visitor type)

for each destination. Give specific examples from your research and use visual aids to make this more effective. You are trying to 'sell' this destination to your visitors.

Work independently and use different sources of information that are clearly referenced **M1 M2**.

3 You are working for a destination tourist board. You have been asked to provide a report on how well your chosen destination appeals to one type of visitor. You could break down a type further, for example the family market could include families with small children, families with school-aged children and families with teenaged children. Examine this in detail, reporting on how well each aspect succeeds in providing what the types need. Where you identify a gap in the market suggest how this may be filled. **D1**.

Grading tips

- **P2** You must focus clearly on aspects of appeal for your chosen type of visitor. General descriptions that do not focus on the appeal for the visitor type would not meet P2.

- **P3** You must provide full details of information sources used in your research. You could do this by providing a bibliography with copies of leaflets and articles attached as appendices.

- **M1** is a progression from P2, and you must assess the strongest aspects of appeal for your visitor types. You should give specified detailed examples as supporting evidence.

- **M2** You need to show that you have worked independently. You should show that you have used at least three different types of information sources.

Using the internet alone would not be sufficient. You must also provide evidence of working independently, such as an observation sheet and/or self-evaluation sheet. You should include a clear and comprehensive bibliography, and include reference to sources throughout the work. You must make sure that your work is clear and logically presented and that you have used your own words to describe the destinations.

- **D1** You need to analyse the strength of appeal of one UK destination for one type of visitor. You should determine how well this destination caters for this type of visitor and where it could improve. At distinction level you could break the visitor type down in to further sub-sections (see above).

PLTS

When you use appropriate sources of information to find out about the location and appeal of UK destinations, you will develop skills as an **independent enquirer**.

Functional skills

You will use your **ICT** skills to communicate and exchange information safely, responsibly and effectively, including the storing of messages and contact lists.

I work for an Incoming Tour Operator specialising in school groups. We arrange for school parties to come to the UK, usually for cultural visits. The groups can be anything from 10 to 100 at a time and often arrive in coaches from mainland Europe.

We arrange the channel crossing, accommodation, visits and transport for the groups. They often want local guides who speak the same language. I speak Italian so I often deal with groups from Italy.

Typical day

I work in central London, so I usually start at 9 a.m. The first thing I do is check the emails and messages from bookings I have begun to arrange, and check on the progress of group requirements. These change regularly as people become ill, change their mind or leave the schools! Then I will check on any groups that are due in that day, and double check all the arrangements are made. It only needs a major disaster in one area to disrupt all the arrangements for the week.

I often have people coming back year after year. They will ring and book with us because they had such a good experience before. It is important to find out exactly what each group requires, and to make sure that we provide good value, while being realistic about the cost of staying in a capital city. I need to find exactly the right 'fit'.

The best thing about the job

I enjoy using my knowledge of the products we offer to find exactly the right one for each group. I can go out and visit accommodation and attractions, so that I know precisely what it is I am recommending. It is really great to have thank you cards from visitors, knowing they have had a great time.

Think about it!

1 What have you covered in this chapter that would help you find the information you need to advise visitors? Which ones did you find most useful?

2 If you had to advise a visiting school or college trip from Europe, where would you suggest they go? Discuss with friends and put together an itinerary.

Just checking

1 Name the four countries that make up the UK and their capital cities.

2 What might be the appeal of a) seaside resorts, b) cities and c) countryside areas to families and/or a group of young people?

3 What are National Parks, and who is allowed to go to them?

4 What is a 'spa' town and why do people visit them?

5 Identify five different types of visitor and name four different facilities they might need.

6 How do the National Trust and English Heritage encourage visitors to historic properties?

7 Name three islands off the coast of the UK and give one reason why people visit each of them.

8 Name three cathedral cities and explain why people might want to visit them.

9 Name two towns connected to authors and explain why people might want to visit them.

10 Give two reasons why tourism is important to the UK.

Assignment tips

- Use a variety of sources to find your information – each of the destinations produces a variety of marketing material because it wants to encourage people to go there, so make the most of this.

- Write down each source of information as you find it, particularly websites. You can write each one on an index card and keep it safe. This is much easier than trying to remember everything at the end.

- Choose places to study that you have a connection with – somewhere you would like to go, or have been to on holiday, or have relatives.

- If you are looking at destinations for a specific visitor type ask someone you know who fits into that type. For example, ask a young family what they would like to do, and the sorts of things they look for in a destination. Make the most of your friends and family as sources of information, rather than just trying to work it out for yourself.

7 European holiday destinations

Many people travel all over Europe for many different reasons. It could be for business or for a holiday, such as a city break, camping or skiing. Europe has a huge variety of destinations and can cater for all tastes and needs. Working in mainland Europe would give you the chance to experience many different ways of life. Knowledge of European resorts and how to reach them is also essential for those who want to work for tour operators or in retail travel.

Tourism in Europe is important, for example 14 million visits were made by UK tourists to Spain 2008, spending £6.5 billion (Source: *UK National Statistics*). France is consistently the most popular destination each year, receiving 79.3 million international arrivals in 2008, followed by Spain (57.3 million) and Italy (42.7 million) (Source: *World Tourism Organisation*).

Learning outcomes

After completing this unit you should:

1 be able to locate major European holiday destinations and gateways

2 know the accessibility of European destinations for visitors from the UK

3 understand features influencing the appeal of different types of European holiday destination.

Assessment and grading criteria

This table shows you what you must do in order to achieve a pass, merit or distinction grade, and where you can find activities in this book to help you.

To achieve a **pass** grade the evidence must show that you are able to:	To achieve a **merit** grade the evidence must show that, in addition to the pass criteria, you are able to:	To achieve a **distinction** grade the evidence must show that, in addition to the pass and merit criteria, you are able to:
P1 locate major European holiday destinations and their gateways **Assessment activity 7.1, page 220**		
P2 describe accessibility from the UK to two European destinations **Assessment activity 7.2, page 223**	**M1** assess how accessibility contributes to the appeal of two European destinations for visitors from the UK **Assessment activity 7.2, page 223**	
P3 review, with examples, features that contribute to the appeal of different types of European holiday destinations **Assessment activity 7.3, page 232**	**M2** explain how different features combine to create the appeal of two European holiday destinations **Assessment activity 7.3, page 232**	**D1** analyse the main features that contribute to the appeal of one European holiday destination **Assessment activity 7.3, page 232**

James, 16–year-old learner

I want to work as a tour rep in Spain eventually, but I will probably work for a tour operator first in the UK. This unit has been very useful because I didn't know there were so many different types of holiday destination. My family often go on beach holidays, but I hadn't thought about skiing or walking in the mountains. I know that a lot of people rely on specialist information when they book holidays. This unit has helped me get a grip on where the most popular resorts are and the best ways of getting there. It's really made me think that I could do a lot of different things, rather than just go to a beach resort. It was useful looking at maps, because you don't really know where you are going when you fly everywhere.

We were able to talk to each other about where we had been and it was very interesting.

Over to you

- Ask friends and family what they look for when choosing a destination.

- What ideas about European holidays can you get from watching television programmes?

1 Locate the major European holiday destinations and gateways

Set off

Where have you been?

In groups of four, describe a European destination that you have been to, or that you know, but without saying the name itself. Ask the other three in the group to guess the destination. The first person in each group to get it right gains a point. The person in the class who gets the most points is the winner.

1.1 Countries

For the purposes of this unit, Europe is considered to be all of continental Europe, west of the Urals and including the Republic of Ireland, the Canary Islands, the Azores and Cyprus. 'Europe' is often as far as tourists want to go on short-haul flights (under 4 hours).

Activity: Locating countries

On a blank map of Europe locate and name the following countries, and mark their capital cities:

Austria, Belgium, Czech Republic, Denmark, France, Germany, Greece, Hungary, Italy, Portugal, Spain, The Netherlands.

Figure 7.1: Map of Europe

Most visitors travel either on 'city breaks' to capitals and other major cities, to resorts around the Mediterranean Sea or into mountain areas. Some countryside areas, particularly in France, are popular for leisure activities such as hiking and boating. The Alps and Pyrenees are centres for skiing in the winter. If you want to work in the travel industry, you should know the locations of these destinations.

1.2 Holiday destinations

Summer sun

The Mediterranean is the main summer sun region for visitors from the UK. The Mediterranean coasts of Spain, Portugal, Greece and France are very popular destinations, as are the Balearic Islands of Majorca, Ibiza and Menorca. The weather is hot and sunny for most of the summer and the sea is warm. Many of the big resorts, such as Torremolinos in Spain, were once fishing villages, but now have all the leisure attractions to keep visitors occupied. As well as almost guaranteed sunshine and high temperatures from April to October, food and drink tends to be relatively cheap and there are many facilities such as golf courses and water sports. There are also bars, restaurants and clubs to ensure an interesting nightlife!

Did you know?

'Mediterranean' in Latin means 'the middle of the earth'

Activity: Summer sun

In groups, discuss any summer sun destinations you may have visited. Draw up a list of attractions and facilities found at these resorts and display them on a poster. Why have these resorts been so successful?

Why do so many people prefer to holiday at these resorts rather than in the UK?

On a blank map of Europe, locate and label the following destinations:

Crete, Rhodes (Greece); Majorca (Balearics); Benidorm, Torremolinos (Spain); Bordeaux, Nice (France); Praia da Rocha (Portugal); Sicily (Italy); Madeira, Tenerife (Canary Islands); Cyprus, Gibraltar.

Add any summer sun resorts you have been to in the last few years.

Figure 7.2: European Mediterranean coast and resorts

Winter sun

Many Mediterranean countries are not very warm in the winter, apart from the very south of Spain and Cote d' Azur (France) and more southerly islands such as Malta or Cyprus. People have to travel further south to find warmth during the winter months. The Canary Islands and Madeira, which are closer to the African coast, are very popular.

Case study: Tenerife

Tenerife, one of the Canary Islands, is situated off the coast of Africa, near the equator. This means that Tenerife has warm weather and sunshine all year round and is very popular as a winter sun destination. The beaches in the south are soft and sandy, but in a dramatic contrast, the north has dark, volcanic beaches created by the dormant volcano, Mount Teide, a major tourist attraction.

There are many resorts, such as Playa de Las Americas, which are lively and cosmopolitan and offer a wide choice of bars, discos and nightclubs. The resorts also have a range of shops and boutiques selling international, as well as Spanish, goods. There are restaurants and cafés which serve a variety of food. The atmosphere is lively and appeals to a wide range of people from young families and teenagers to older travellers. There are also many water sports facilities

from water-skiing, to scuba diving off the golden sandy beaches.

There are also smaller resorts such as La Caleta, which was a picturesque fishing village and still retains much of its character. Here there are small bars and restaurants, without the hustle and bustle of the larger resorts. This would be ideal for families with small children or those looking for a peaceful getaway. Resorts like Puerto de Santiago are in the steep hilly area, perfect for walkers and nature lovers.

Using a tour operator's brochure, find a resort on Tenerife which would be suitable for:

- **a group of young singles who enjoy water sports**
- **a middle-aged couple looking for a peaceful walking holiday.**

Key term

Après-ski – (literally 'after ski-ing') – means any of the entertainment or relaxing activities available in ski resorts. These could be tobogganing by torchlight, a sleigh ride or bowling while drinking schnapps (strong alcoholic drink similar to gin).

Winter sports

Of course, some people don't want to spend their winter holiday in sunshine, but in snow! Skiing can be an exhilarating experience in the sunshine and crystal clear air and once people have experienced the freedom they are often hooked. Snowboarding has become a popular winter sport, particularly among younger people and ski resorts offer their own culture of clothing, music and **après-ski**.

Europe has two main mountain regions where ski resorts have been built especially for the sport — the Alps, that sweep in an arc across France, Italy, Switzerland, Austria and Slovenia and the Pyrenees, that divide Spain and France.

Case study: Valloire

Valloire is situated in the French Alps. It has been a winter ski and summer walking destination for many years and grew out of a farming community in the lush river valley.

There are year-round ski lifts to take people to the mountain top. In the winter, a number of lifts mean that people of all abilities can ski down the sides of the valley and in summer the walkers are accompanied by herds of cows with tinkling cowbells eating the lush grass and flowers.

The village has many bars and restaurants where visitors can relax in the evening – in winter this is known as **après-ski** where *vin chaud* (warmed, mulled

wine) soothes aching muscles. There are also bars and restaurants on the mountains to refresh skiers as they ski down the pre-prepared runs, or *pistes*. There are many shops which cater for skiers, climbers and walkers, where boots, skis and snowboards can be hired in winter and hiking and climbing equipment in summer. There is also a swimming and sports complex, and children's playground. In winter a ski-school operates, with a children's section.

1 Why do you think Valloire is successful as a ski resort? What facilities does it have for skiers?

2 Look at a ski brochure. Find out what the different colours on the *pistes* mean.

Figure 7.3: The Alps and the Pyrenees

Activity: Mountains

Locate, and label, the following destinations on your blank map:

Seefeld, Zell-am Zee (Austria); St. Moritz (Switzerland); Ardèche, Chamonix, the Dordogne river (France); Bormio, Courmayeur, Lake Garda (Italy); Sol-y-nieve (Spain), Black Forest (Germany), Andorra.

Countryside areas

The winter sports destinations above can also be countryside destinations in the summer. Many tourists use the lifts to access hiking trails and sporting activities.

The great river valleys and lakes of Europe also provide opportunities to explore the countryside and engage in watersports. Forests often have sporting activities and picnic/recreation areas.

City breaks

Many cities are popular with tourists and they have a wealth of culture and heritage.

Activity: City breaks

Add the following to your map of Europe:

Florence (Italy), Amsterdam (Netherlands), Salzburg (Austria).

Case study: Budapest

Budapest is the capital of Hungary and is just a two-hour flight from London. Since emerging from communist rule the city has become a very popular destination.

The river Danube flows between the old centres of Buda and Pest, which merged in 1873. Buda has a medieval city with palaces and churches on top of Castle Hill, a limestone crag overlooking the river. Pest is much flatter on the river plain, with boulevards, shops and grand buildings.

The city is full of bars and restaurants, art galleries and museums of local Magyar heritage. There are many natural hot water springs where people can swim in indoor or outdoor pools. In the winter, you can skate in the City Park or in summer travel on the children's railway from Moskvater. For music lovers there is the Liszt Academy and the Autumn Festival in October.

The city has a definite eastern European feel, but with modern comfort and facilities.

1 Why is Budapest suitable to visit all year round?

2 What is the difference between the two halves of the city?

Activity: European cities

In small groups, draw a spider diagram of your images of a European city. You may like to look at Paris, Amsterdam, Rome or Venice, etc. Just write down the first things which come into your head about the chosen city, for example Venice might be gondolas and singing gondoliers!

Cruise areas

The Mediterranean provides a popular destination for cruise ships. These may be 'fly cruises', where passengers fly to a port, such as Palma or Majorca and then cruise from there. Other cruises may start from the UK, and sail to the Mediterranean. The Baltic is also popular for cruises, visiting cities such as St. Petersburg or Tallin. The rivers of Europe are often called their 'arteries' and many have river cruises sailing from one country to another, stopping at ports such as Budapest or Vienna.

Increasingly, there are many younger people going on cruises, which previously had a rather 'stuffy' image. The introduction of easyCruise with its orange livery has opened up the market, providing inexpensive basic cruising with add-ons – rather like the low-cost airlines.

What activities are available in Budapest?

Activity: Cruising

On a map, locate the rivers Danube, Rhine and Rhone. Use cruise brochures, or the internet, to find at least three Mediterranean cruise itineraries and mark them on your map.

1.3 European gateways

Airports

All of Europe's capital cities have at least one airport and some, such as Paris or Milan, have more than one. Each airport is allocated an individual 3-letter code, which is used internationally (see page 91 and 190 for further information). The code is often the same as the city code if there is only one airport. Many other cities will also have their own airport, or provide transport from a nearby airport. An example of this is Florence, which has excellent train connections to Pisa airport.

Activity: Airports

Using timetables, or the internet, look at the routes offered by European airlines. Find six airports (each in a different country) which are accessed from at least three UK airports.

Mark these on a map of Europe and add their 3-letter code. Indicate on the map from which UK airports they can be accessed, for example Paris Charles de Gaulle airport (CDG), accessed from LON, BHX, EDI.

Passenger ferry ports

UK tourists can also access Europe by sea (look at the map on pages 191–192 in chapter 6). Many tourists take their car on European roads; France in particular has many links to UK ports.

Channel Tunnel

Many passengers take their car on the train that uses the Channel Tunnel from Folkestone to Sangatte, just outside Calais. The cars travel in special drive-on/drive-off carriages and the driver and passengers stay in, or beside, their vehicles during the short journey.

Activity: Ferry ports

On a map of Europe, add six ferry ports that passengers can travel to if they are travelling from the UK. For each of these, draw the route to a named UK port.

Mark the Channel Tunnel terminals on a map. Look at a timetable or a brochure and find out how long the journey takes under the channel.

Have you, or anyone you know, been through the Channel Tunnel? What are the advantages and disadvantages of each way of travelling? In a group, discuss whether you would prefer to go on a ferry or through the Channel Tunnel.

Eurostar terminals

The Eurostar passenger train has recently changed its London terminal to St. Pancras from Waterloo. From here, passengers can board the train (which is very similar to a UK train) which will use the Channel Tunnel crossing to France. Trains will go direct to central Brussels or Paris, from where passengers can connect to the European high-speed train network.

Although the journey itself is longer than an air journey, the time taken from city centre to city centre can be the same, or less, than flying.

Assessment activity 7.1

BTEC

Your office manager wants to produce an 'easy-reference' file for the office showing the location of popular destinations. They would like you to contribute to the file by producing a series of maps. You may use an atlas to help you.

1 On a blank map of Europe, accurately locate at least six destinations for each of the following types of holiday:

- summer sun
- winter sun
- winter sports
- countryside areas
- city break
- cruise areas.

Ensure each destination is used only once, and each destination within each 'type' must be in a different country. The same country can feature the different 'types' of destination.

2 Locate at least six European airports used by UK holidaymakers (with their 3-letter code). Ensure that each airport is in a different country and can be accessed from at least three named UK airports.

3 Locate six European ferry ports. For each port, identify at least one route from the UK, naming the UK port.

4 Add the Channel Tunnel route and terminals to the map.

5 Name two Eurostar passenger train terminals in Europe.

Grading tip

P1 Make sure that you accurately locate at least six destinations for each holiday type. Do not use a location more than once. Each of the six destinations, within a holiday type, needs to be in a different country.

PLTS

When you organise your time and resources to complete the activity you will develop skills as a **self-manager**.

Functional skills

You will use your **ICT** skills to identify and locate destinations for this activity.

You will develop your **English** skills in reading to compare, select, read and understand texts and use them to gather information, ideas, arguments and opinions.

2 Know the accessibility of European destinations for visitors from the UK

For many years, people have travelled to Europe from the UK because it is relatively easy to get to. In 2008, 81% of UK passengers travelled by air (Source: *UK Tourist Survey*) but France, for instance, is also easily accessed by ferry and high-speed train. Passengers may find that it is quicker, door-to-door, to travel on Eurostar from central London to central Paris, rather than taking an hour flight to airports some distance from the centre of the city.

Main entry gateways

The entry point to a country or area is known as the 'gateway'. This may be a port, city, airport, or train terminal. Passengers may travel from this 'gateway' to their final destination or destinations within that area.

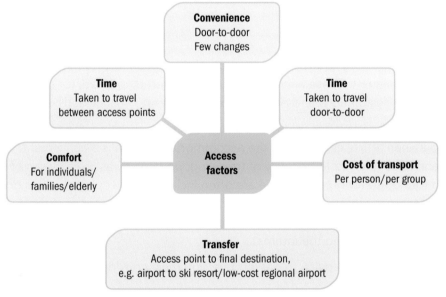

Figure 7.4: Factors in choosing access methods

Ease and cost of travel to destination.

There are many different ways of reaching destinations in Europe and the one you choose depends on a number of factors. For example, a businessman may be happy to pay quite a lot in order to reach his destination in comfort. On the other hand, a student with little money might be happy to spend two days on a coach if it means that the fare is cheap. Convenience, cost and speed may all be taken into account when deciding the best way to travel.

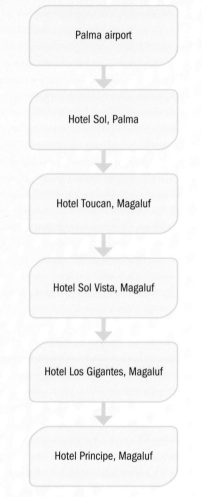

Figure 7.5: Transfer times can be lengthy, especially if the bus to your hotel has to make many stops!

Travel and transfer times

When looking at destinations, it is important that access to the destination is considered. Some ski resorts, for example, have a four-hour coach transfer from the nearest airport, since airports are not usually located in mountainous regions. You might prefer to travel by 'snowtrain' to avoid this, because train stations tend to be much closer to the ski resorts, for example Moutiers in France is closer to the Three Valleys ski resorts than the nearest airports of Chambery and Grenoble.

The low-cost airlines, such as easyJet, Ryanair and bmibaby, have greatly increased the number of provincial airports in Europe and decreased the cost of travelling by air. However, these airports may be some distance from the city.

Activity: Airports

Look at the websites for easyJet, Ryanair and bmibaby. Plot the airports these airlines use, both in the UK and Europe, on a blank map.

Of course, many tourists travelling to holiday beach resorts travel by charter aircraft. These aircraft have been chartered, or hired, for specific holiday destinations and durations by tour operators, such as Thomson.

Package holidays are sold with transport, accommodation and transfers between arrival airports and the accommodation. This is a convenient and relatively hassle-free way of travelling, particularly as the services of a tour operator representative are often included. However, travellers do sometimes feel that they are 'herded' and may prefer to put together their own independent holiday. It is easier than ever to put together all the elements using the internet.

If you are giving advice to passengers, you must consider all these aspects carefully.

Assessment activity 7.2

BTEC

P2 **M1**

Your office manager has asked you to help make sure that everyone is aware of the range of access options available when customers are travelling to Europe.

1 Choose two European holiday destinations and describe their accessibility. You have been asked to provide a display describing the cost and ease of reaching each destination, including travel and transfer times.

Include information about the following:

• Choice of options by air from UK airports to the nearest airports for the destination.

• Choice of rail/sea options to the nearest gateways for the destination.

• Cost of travel to the gateway(s) and transfer to destination.

• Travel times to the gateway(s) and transfer times to the destination.

• Convenience of the different choices.

You may use maps, information leaflets and timetables to illustrate your findings, but your evidence must describe the accessibility of the destinations.

2 Assess how the accessibility of the two destinations selected contributes to the overall appeal of the destinations. Include ease of access from different parts of the UK, as well as the cost and transfer times. This should be presented in the form of a leaflet for each destination.

Question 1 will enable you to achieve **P2** and question 2 will enable you to achieve **M1**.

Grading tips

• **P2** Ensure you describe the access options and the ease of accessibility from different parts of the UK.

• **M1** The choice of destinations to research is crucial. Make sure that you select destinations that will allow you to provide evidence for all the requirements above and to easily describe and assess accessibility. Check this before you research destinations that may not be suitable.

PLTS

Describing accessibility from the UK to two European destinations will develop your skills as an **independent enquirer** and **creative thinker**.

Functional skills

You will use your **ICT** skills to find and select information.

You will use your **English** skills in reading to compare, select, read and understand texts and use them to gather information, ideas, arguments and opinions.

3 Understand features influencing the appeal of different types of European holiday destination

3.1 Types of destination

In this section you will look at the appeal of different types of holiday destination in Europe. The types of destination range from places visited for summer and winter sun, winter sports, countryside locations, towns and cities.

3.2 Natural features

Mountains

The most obvious natural features of Europe are the mountain ranges of the Alps and Pyrenees. Where there are facilities for skiing there will also be the infrastructure for summer sport activities, such as climbing and walking.

Lakes and rivers

Lakes often are part of a mountain landscape and British tourists have been visiting the Italian and Swiss lakes for centuries for water sports and walking. Lake Garda (Italy) has a Mediterranean climate because of its position nestling beneath the mountains. More water sports, such

What activities could you do in a location like this?

as rafting, can be pursued in rivers such as the Dordogne (France). The great rivers of mainland Europe, such as the Rhine, have cruisers from which passengers can watch the beautiful scenery.

Forests and woods

Forests and woods also provide opportunities for activities, such as riding and mountain biking, and are popular 'back to nature' holidays. Some people stay in lodges or cabins within the woods and enjoy the peace and tranquillity. Long distance paths, such as those of the 'Grande randonnée' in France take walkers through stunning scenery.

Beaches

The beaches of Europe, particularly on the Mediterranean, are renowned for their beauty. They can range from the rocky (Praia da Rocha in Portugal) to fine sand (Skiathos in Greece) and can be tiny fishing hamlets to huge purpose-built resorts. Some people prefer small coves with hardly anyone else within sight, while others prefer larger public beaches where facilities are close at hand.

3.3 Local attractions

Destinations, such as cities, are visited because of their attractions. Many resorts offer coach-trip excursions to local attractions.These can include historical sites, heritage sites, religious sites, theme parks, museums and aqua parks. Some examples are given below.

Historical sites and museums

Historical sites are extremely important and give visitors a sense of linking with the past.

- There are prehistoric caves, many thousands of years old, in Rocamadour in the Dordogne area of France.

- There are architectural and artistic treasures in the Renaissance cities of Italy, such as Florence, as well as Roman remains such as the Coliseum and Forum in Rome.

- Some areas are designated World Heritage Sites, such as the Acropolis in Athens.

- Sometimes whole towns or cities are protected as World Heritage Sites. Many of these sites have museums.

- The capital cities of Europe are home to museums full of national and international objects and art. These include the Louvre in Paris, the Prado in Madrid and the Uffizi Gallery in Florence.

What other World Heritage Sites in Europe can you think of?

Activity: World Heritage Sites

In pairs, find information on World Heritage Sites in a chosen country and make a collage of images.

Theme parks

At the other end of the scale, European theme parks are much enjoyed by 'children' aged from 8 to 80 years! There are many such parks with various themes all over Europe. These are sometimes geared to younger children such as Efterling in the Netherlands or Disneyland Paris. There are also other theme parks, such as Futuroscope at Poitiers, France, with a science theme or Parc Asterix in France, which is named after the comic strip character.

There are many aqua parks, particularly in southern Europe. In Spain, these include the aqua park at Universal Mediterranea, Port Aventura and those in the major resorts at Torremolinos and Magaluf.

3.4 Range of accommodation

There is a huge range of accommodation available across Europe, from the very basic to 5-star deluxe hotels. Each country has its own method of grading accommodation, so many tour operators have had to use their own criteria so that their grading of accommodation is consistent.

Accommodation on the mainland of Europe tends to be less expensive than in the UK and there are a variety of different types available to tourists. Sometimes there are state-run hotels (*paradors*) in Spain and Portugal, which are converted castles and monasteries, or *gîtes* in France (rural cottages and converted farm buildings) available for self-catering hire.

Self-catering is increasingly popular for families, and many resorts provide self-catering apartments. Some can be found in 'aparthotels', which give guests the option of eating in restaurants and using other facilities that you would expect to find in an hotel. Villas (self-contained accommodation), often set in the countryside with a private pool can also be popular with families, but tend to be more expensive.

Camping is also very popular, particularly with families. Many operators, for example Eurocamp, offer pre-erected tents on sites, as well as caravans. Both are supplied with equipment to save tourists having to bring equipment with them. Campsites often have pools, playgrounds and food outlets.

Think about it

In groups, try and think of different places you could stay, such as in a caravan.

Did you know?

'All- inclusive' accommodation includes all food, drink, clubs and most activities within the cost.

Activity: Hotel grading

Look at some major tour operators' brochures. Do they have their own method of grading hotels? Can you find the same hotel in different brochures and if so, is the grading similar?

3.5 Facilities

Local transport

Local transport is often used by tourists, particularly if they arrive by air. Travelling on local transport can be an exciting part of the holiday, for example journeying by tram in the Czech Republic when unable to read any signs can prove very interesting! Many European destinations have subsidised local transport, and this can include small railways or funicular (mountain) railways, as well as trams and trolleys. Many destinations have land trains which take tourists around resorts or towns. There may also be bicycle taxis, or horse-drawn carriages, which can be an exciting and alternative means of getting around.

> What other ways can you get around a location?

Shopping

This can be an exciting way to spend your time. Visitors are often entranced by foreign markets with unfamiliar local goods and different colours and by the smells of local food. Goods such as leather and jewellery in Italy and Spain can be excellent value for money.

Nightlife

The quality of nightlife can be very important to young people and can in some cases be the main reason for choosing a resort. Some areas, such as Ayia Napa in Cyprus or Ibiza in Spain, are extremely popular with clubbers and can attract DJs from the UK and United States. Cities, such as Prague, are popular for hen and stag nights with relatively cheap clubs and bars. For other people, more sophisticated pursuits such as theatres or concerts are sought. The New Year's Eve ball in Vienna is an example of an internationally renowned event.

Sport and leisure

Some destinations are chosen because of their links with sport. Fans will travel to important matches, such as the European Cup Final or Winter Olympics, in order to watch first class sport. The Commonwealth Games and Olympics attract thousands of tourists.

Others may travel in order to pursue their sport, such as white water rafting, pot-holing in the Dordogne or horse riding in the Black Forest. Many people travel to the Mediterranean coasts to play tennis and golf, particularly on the Costa del Sol in Spain and the Algarve in Portugal.

3.6 Traditions and cultural aspects

Many European destinations are now dependent on tourism and so make sure their welcome encourages visitors to return. However, some resorts, particularly in Eastern Europe, have expanded very quickly and some local people find the sudden appearance of plane loads of (comparatively) wealthy tourists confusing and may resent this change. You should be aware of local customs, including festivals, local cuisine, siestas, religious practices and pilgrimages as well as of values and tradition. Some examples of where it's important not to cause offence and to be aware of what is acceptable locally are given below.

In Eastern Europe it is much less acceptable, even now, for young people to be alone together before marriage, and young men and women are expected to behave appropriately. 'Binge-drinking' is also much less common, as wine is usually drunk with food and children are often given a little with water. Some resorts are no longer willing to clear up after British 'lager-louts' and are making sure that all visitors are aware they may be arrested for drunkenness.

In Islamic countries, for example Bosnia, women are protected by their dress and may be expected to be escorted in public. Consequently, female western visitors may feel uncomfortable in some areas if unaccompanied, particularly if their head and shoulders are uncovered and shorts, or short skirts, are worn.

Countries retain their traditional cuisine dishes. Many people find buying food from markets and local restaurants a most enjoyable part of a holiday and are eager to try unusual dishes and ways of eating.

Most cities will have a cathedral, mosque, synagogue or other religious building. Tourists may wish to visit holy sites, but will need to be flexible because different religions will need to be able to worship in their holy places at various times of the day. Muslims, for example, pray regularly throughout the day. There may be many local festivals, often linked to religious celebrations. The period around Easter is often a time of religious processions and festivals in southern Europe.

Did you know?

'Culture' in this context means the way people live. It could be their art, music, traditions and beliefs; essentially what makes each area or destination unique.

Activity: Festivals

Using the internet, find out about ten different festivals and fairs that are held in Europe.

3.7 Climate

People travel to different places for a number of reasons. One of these is to experience different climatic conditions. Major destinations tend to be warmer climates with long hours of average daily sunshine, although popular ski resorts rely on an abundance of snow.

A destination's climate depends on many factors:

- its distance from the equator (the further north or south you go from the equator, the greater the temperature variation)

- its distance from the oceans (the further away, the more extreme the temperature and the less rainfall)

- its height (the higher the destination above sea level, the cooler it will be)

- whether the destination is in a prevailing wind area (temperatures will be moderated).

While seasons can be predicted, there may be natural disasters such as earthquakes, droughts and floods, which can happen at any time. There is always a risk to travel and visitors will need to be aware of these forces of nature.

The amount of snow for winter sports is governed by the height of the mountains and their aspect, that is whether the slopes are south-facing (facing the sun). There is sometimes concern that the Alps and Pyrenees won't have enough snow during the winter sports season. The higher the resort, the more likely it is to have reliable snow – and it will be correspondingly more expensive!

Information on climate, average rainfall and temperatures is available from tour operators' brochures, the *World Travel Guide* and internet sources. Tourists ought to be aware of the bitterly cold eastern European winters, the blazing hot Mediterranean summers and how these variations might affect what they want to do.

Did you know?

It is important for you to know something about the seasonal climatic conditions of popular European tourist destinations when advising customers on their holiday choices. Remember: not every visitor wants hot sunshine.

Barcelona, Spain

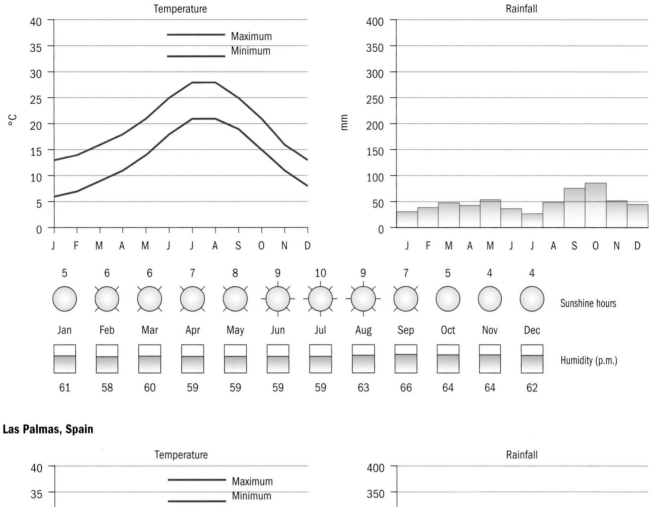

Las Palmas, Spain

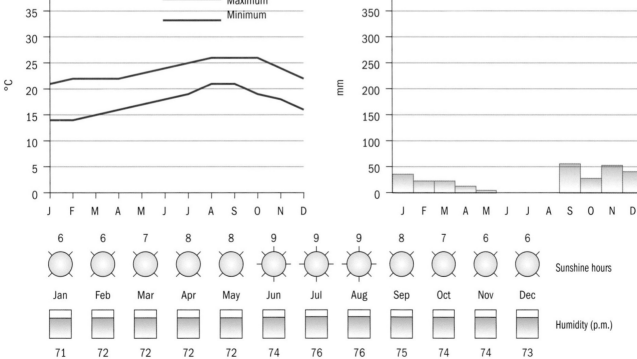

Figure 7.6: The climates of Barcelona and Las Palmas

Assessment activity 7.3

1 Produce a presentation, using visual aids, to review the features that contribute to the appeal of European destinations. You should look to include at least the following:

- natural features including lakes, rivers, forests and beaches
- local attractions
- range of accommodation
- facilities
- traditions and culture
- climate.

You should use specific examples of appropriate destinations to review and illustrate these features and outline the types of visitor these destinations might appeal to. The destinations should be from summer sun, winter sun, winter sports, countryside areas and city areas.

This will enable you to achieve **P3**.

2 Conduct research into two different types of European holiday destination (for example a summer sun and a city break destination) in two different countries. Produce an article, or booklet, to explain how the various features contribute to the destination's specific appeal.

This will enable you to achieve **M2**.

3 Select one of the two destinations from question 2 and analyse the main features that contribute to the appeal of that destination. Produce a written analysis making judgements on what draws UK visitors to that destination.

This will enable you to achieve **D1**.

Grading tips

- **P3** Make sure that your destinations cover all the requirements *before you continue with research on a destination that may not be suitable.* Remember that Europe has enormous variations and make sure you bring this out in your presentation!

- **M2** You should research widely before selecting destinations.

- **D1** Make judgements about the reasons for the appeal of the destination based on the evidence you have available. Remember that the appeal of different destinations may vary from season to season.

PLTS

Reviewing features that contribute to the appeal of different types of European holiday destinations will develop your skills as an **independent enquirer** and **creative thinker**. As you organise your time and resources to carry out the assessment activity, you will be a **self-manager**.

Functional skills

You will use your **ICT** skills to find and select information.

You will use your **English** skills in reading to compare, select, read and understand texts and use them to gather information, ideas, arguments and opinions (researching appeal features P3 and M2; using information to form opinions on significance of appeal features D1).

I work with a team of people on a shift system, as we have to cover weekends and evenings. I answer the phone to people who want to visit cities, but are not confident about booking things independently. I give advice on suitable accommodation and the best way to travel. I will also suggest pre-booked excursions and visits, to save them time when they arrive and I'll give them a breakdown of the cost, advice on climate etc. I am there to sell the package on behalf of the company, but it is really important to find out exactly what the customer wants. There is no point in selling something you know is not suitable or they will never come back.

Typical day

I spend a lot of the day on the phone, answering calls and booking new holidays. I spend quite a lot of time on each call, as it is quite complicated to put a package together for each individual customer group – there are so many choices. Large groups are the worst as they always change their minds several times!

I often follow up bookings, for example I may have to ask an hotel for particular information, and then pass it on to the customer. I also attend briefings about new or different options available.

The best thing about the job

The best thing about the job is that I go to visit the destinations on 'familiarisation trips' as it's easier to sell something you know. I also get many customers coming back to me because they have appreciated the service. It is good to know I helped them have a good time.

Think about it!

1   What skills do you think Richard needs?

2   What knowledge is helpful to Richard in his role? How doe
    he keep up to date?

Just checking

1 On a blank map, mark the major UK tourist-receiving countries of France, Spain, Greece, Italy, Portugal and the Netherlands.
2 Add the capital city, one airport and at least one major destination for each country.
3 Add the Alps and the Pyrenees, with a key explaining what activities can be found there.
4 List the types of destination found in Europe, and link each to a customer type. Add a few sentences explaining your choice.
5 Apart from the internet, list six other sources of information about European destinations.

Assignment tips

- Watch travel programmes on television – they are meant to be entertainment, as well as informative.

- Look at the travel supplements in weekend newspapers – they will give a real flavour of destinations as well as the selling points. They often have articles aimed specifically at families or couples, for instance.

- Pick up brochures from travel agents (but be aware that these are their selling tools and don't take more than you need). These will be helpful for pictures/local information and are travel orientated, unlike some websites.

- Always check that the destination that you have chosen to study is appropriate – ask your tutor before doing research which may be a waste of time.

- Beware of using encyclopaedias, particularly on-line ones. Use country tourist offices, for example the Spanish Tourist Office or specialist tour operators for tourism specific information.

8 Worldwide holiday destinations

"If I won the lottery I would travel the world." You have probably heard people say this many times, but stop for a moment and consider, if you were given the opportunity, where in the world would you like to travel?

Would you choose to join in the excitement of Florida's theme parks? Maybe you would prefer the hustle and bustle of Hong Kong or the opportunity to explore the underwater world of the Great Barrier Reef.

Your career in the travel and tourism sector could open up the world of travel to you. Knowing about worldwide destinations and their locations and being able to select holidays to meet customer needs is highly regarded by many employers and is the main focus of this unit. You will also develop your knowledge of factors that can affect travel to holiday destinations around the world.

This unit has a lot of practical elements and everything is relevant for worldwide travel, whether for your future career or your own travels. So if you think you have no interest in visiting Borneo, Boston or Bora Bora, now's the time to find out about them, and think again. You might surprise yourself.

Learning outcomes

After completing this unit you should:

1 be able to locate worldwide destinations for different types of holiday

2 be able to select worldwide destinations to meet customer needs

3 know about factors that can impact on travel to worldwide destinations.

235

Assessment and grading criteria

This table shows you what you must do in order to achieve a pass, merit or distinction grade, and where you can find activities in this book to help you.

To achieve a **pass** grade the evidence must show that you are able to:	To achieve a **merit** grade the evidence must show that, in addition to the pass criteria, you are able to:	To achieve a **distinction** grade the evidence must show that, in addition to the pass and merit criteria, you are able to:
P1 identify and locate worldwide destinations for different types of holiday **Assessment activity 8.1, page 243**		
P2 select worldwide destinations to meet specific customer needs **Assessment activity 8.2, page 246**	**M1** justify the choice of destinations, explaining how they meet specific customer needs **Assessment activity 8.2, page 246**	
P3 describe factors that impact on travel to worldwide destinations, giving relevant examples **Assessment activity 8.3, page 252**	**M2** explain how different factors impact on travel to a selected worldwide destination **Assessment activity 8.3, page 252**	**D1** assess the impact of two factors on travel to worldwide destinations within the last five years **Assessment activity 8.3, page 252**

For the purposes of this unit worldwide destinations include those in the area east of the Urals, and in Africa, North America, South America, Asia and Australasia. Due to its political ties to Europe, Turkey has been included in Unit 7 European holiday destinations.

Nathan, 19-year-old

I must admit that when I started my travel and tourism course I was not really aware of many places outside Europe. As a football fan I knew about World Cup hosts like Japan, South Korea and South Africa, and also about the skills of footballers from Brazil and Senegal, but I knew nothing about those countries. I had no idea why people might want to visit them or what sort of holiday destinations they offered.

I'm now working in a job where these places feature in my day-to-day routine. Every customer is different and when they walk into the travel agency I have no idea what their request will be. It's great that I can now put my knowledge of worldwide destinations into practice. No one expects me to know about every holiday destination in the world, but you can imagine that it's embarrassing if you haven't heard of places or can't locate them, so I try to improve my knowledge by watching travel programmes and looking through the latest holiday brochures.

Over to you

- Have you travelled to any worldwide destinations?

- Are there any worldwide destinations that particularly appeal to you?

1 Locate worldwide destinations for different types of holiday

Set off

Where in the world?

Imagine you have the chance to travel absolutely anywhere in the world. Consider areas of the world that may have grabbed your attention in the movies, on TV, in books, in magazines or maybe after seeing some great photographs from someone's holiday.

Flick through some worldwide holiday brochures. Write down five destinations you would like to visit and the reasons why.

Discuss your 'wish lists' in small groups. Compare your choices and the reasons for selecting these destinations.

Figure 8.1: World continents

Figure 8.2: What type of holiday could you have in Australia?

1.1 Worldwide destinations

Destinations

Worldwide destinations offer scope for virtually any kind of holiday imaginable. You will find many contrasts between destinations in different continents (see also *Unit 3: Understanding the nature and effects of world travel* influenced by diverse cultures, varied history, natural features and climate.

Visitors are attracted to different types of holiday destination for different reasons:

- **Towns and cities** will often be busy and exciting with sightseeing opportunities, shopping and entertainment.
- **Beach resorts** range from remote and relaxing tropical paradises to lively, fun holiday hotspots.
- **Islands** can be large or small and can offer complete contrasts. They may be chosen by visitors who want the variety of beach and countryside, maybe with traditional towns and villages too.

Some destinations are known for their *natural significance*, such as safari parks or rainforests, while others have *historical significance*, with links to historical events or providing an insight into ancient civilisations.

As you can see from figure 8.2, countries like Australia offer a wide choice of destinations.

1.2 Different types of holiday

History and culture

One of the main reasons people like to travel is to see places of historical significance and to experience different cultures. Many visitors will be attracted to destinations because of their links to ancient civilisations, such as the Aztecs or the Incas.

Activity: Historical sites

Match the historical sites to the country. Then use holiday brochures and websites to find examples of holidays featuring these historical sites.

Chichen Itza	China
Taj Mahal	Peru
Machu Picchu	Cambodia
Great Pyramid of Khufu	Mexico
Terracotta Warriors	India
Angkor Wat	Egypt

History and culture are often intertwined, for example the history of early settlers to Australia and the USA will link to the history and culture of the Aborigine and Native American populations. The ways that these cultures have been preserved will be of interest to many visitors.

For many people a holiday overseas is an opportunity to learn about different cultures. This can be expressed in the way people dress, their food, traditional dances, art, music, religion, rituals and customs.

Have you ever experienced different world cultures?

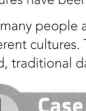

Case study: Aloha

Lying in the middle of the Pacific Ocean, Hawaii is well known for its relaxed and welcoming way of life.

Visitors to Hawaii are welcomed with a flower *lei*, a garland worn around the neck. The lei custom was introduced to Hawaii by the Polynesians and it is still used as a symbol of celebration for the locals. For tourists, the giving of a lei has become the symbol of *aloha*, a term of greeting. Family life is very important to the islanders of Hawaii, and visitors are honoured if they are invited to a *luau*, a great feast of celebration with dance, song and offering of foods as thanksgiving to the ancestral gods. The *hula* dance has religious origins but has now become a form of entertainment, long associated with the wearing of a grass skirt and coconut bra. Each movement has a specific meaning and a chant is used with the hands to tell a story.

1 Research local culture and traditions in other areas of the world.

2 How do they attract visitors?

Why do you think people choose to marry abroad?

Did you know?

You can tie the knot in some unusual venues around the world:

- whilst scuba diving off the Great Barrier Reef in Australia
- on the bridge of the Starship Enterprise, in a Star Trek themed wedding in Las Vegas
- on a ski slope in Virginia, USA
- in a chapel made of ice in Alaska
- on the back of an elephant in Sri Lanka
- attached to a safety rope on the top of Sydney Harbour Bridge, Australia
- in a South African safari park
- 55 floors above the streets of New York at the top of the Empire State Building.

Beach relaxation

Holidaymakers are often tempted to travel beyond Europe to soak up out-of-season sunshine or to relax in more exotic surroundings. Beach holidays that also combine snorkelling, diving or spa therapies are becoming very popular, while many beach resorts in Australia, South Africa and the Americas have excellent surfing.

Some beach destinations, such as those of the Maldives in the Indian Ocean, are remote and exclusive, offering luxury in idyllic, tranquil surroundings. In contrast, the beach resorts of Goa in India have laid-back hostels, beach bars and restaurants that attract many backpackers for long stays, whereas Brazil's Copacabana beach attracts international jetsetters and sun-worshippers in their thousands.

The time of the year is a very important consideration when selecting a worldwide beach destination, as this type of destination can be affected by seasonal weather conditions such as tropical storms.

Weddings and honeymoons

The average cost of a wedding in the UK is now estimated to be over £20,000. It's no wonder that many couples decide to tie the knot overseas, where they can combine the wedding ceremony with a honeymoon.

Beach weddings are particularly popular and there are many exotic locations where couples can get married on a beautiful palm-fringed beach surrounded by friends and family. It can be less stressful too as someone else takes care of all the arrangements. Tour operators offer tailor-made wedding holidays where the customer selects the destination and accommodation, and the tour operator's wedding coordinator in the resort puts together all the finishing touches, organises the paperwork and makes sure the wedding day is perfect and unique to that customer.

Most wedding packages also incorporate a honeymoon, but for couples getting married in the UK an exotic honeymoon overseas is a chance to relax after the wedding celebrations. Many hotels offer special extras for honeymooners, such as a free room upgrade, champagne, flowers, a celebration dinner or a complimentary spa treatment or massage.

Activity: Top ten honeymoons

These worldwide destinations feature in many 'top ten' honeymoon lists:

Bahamas	Fiji	Mauritius	St Lucia
Barbados	Hawaii	New York	
Dubai	Maldives	Seychelles	

Use holiday brochures to find an example of a typical honeymoon in one of the destinations.

Leisure and entertainment

Some of the best-known leisure destinations are the Disney resorts around the world. The original – Disneyland in Anaheim, California – opened in 1955 and was billed 'The happiest place on earth'. There are now also Disney resorts in Florida, Hong Kong and Tokyo.

Orlando in Florida has become one of the leisure magnets of the world. In addition to Walt Disney World, you will find Universal Studios, Islands of Adventure and lush tropical resorts such as Discovery Cove where you can swim with dolphins.

Some worldwide destinations are so famous for their entertainment that people are willing to travel thousands of miles to hit the bright lights, see spectacular shows and sample the nightlife. Examples include Las Vegas, known as the 'entertainment capital of the world', and New York, the 'city that never sleeps', with its hit Broadway shows and megastar concerts at Madison Square Gardens.

Activity: Carnival time

Rio de Janeiro's Carnival has become a world famous, artistic and cultural event that entertains people from all over the world.

Carry out research to find out:

- What are the origins of Rio's Carnival?
- When does it take place?

Did you know?

- Over 37.5 million people visit Las Vegas each year.
- The famous Las Vegas Strip is four miles long.
- There are 197,144 slot machines in Las Vegas.
- The average visitor to Las Vegas spends 3.8 hours gambling each day.
- There are 15,000 miles of neon tubing on the Strip and Downtown Las Vegas.
- 15 of the 20 biggest hotels in the world are located within a two-mile radius in Las Vegas.
- The biggest hotel in Las Vegas is the MGM Grand with 5690 rooms.
- On average 15,000 pillowcases are washed each day in the MGM Grand.
- The laser light that shines from the top of the pyramid on the Luxor Hotel is visible from space.

Winter sports

For British winter sports enthusiasts there are a number of worldwide destinations beyond Europe that offer first-class snow conditions for a range of winter sports activities.

Activity: Snowbound

The Winter Olympic Games have taken place in a number of worldwide locations including:

1960 – Squaw Valley	1998 – Nagano
1972 – Sapporo	2002 – Salt Lake City
1980 – Lake Placid	2010 – Vancouver
1988 – Calgary	

Identify the country, and location in that country, of each of these Olympic venues.

Why do people like to experience a carnival?

Natural world

Many people travel to destinations around the world to view the wildlife, marvel at natural wonders, and enjoy beautiful or unusual natural surroundings for relaxation or adventure. Safari holidays take visitors on an overland adventure, travelling with experienced guides to observe big game and wildlife in Africa. Mountains, jungles, deserts and forests open up the natural world on guided trekking holidays, while lakes, waterfalls and other natural attractions can provide awesome scenery.

Activity: Natural attractions

Match each natural attraction to the correct country:

Grand Canyon	South Africa
Ayers Rock	Zambia/Zimbabwe
Amazon Rainforest	Ecuador
Kruger National Park	USA
Victoria Falls	Australia
Galapagos Islands	Australia
Great Barrier Reef	Nepal/Tibet
Mount Everest	Brazil

Locate these attractions on a map. Find examples of them in holiday brochures

Where can you go to experience the natural world?

Did you know?

Exodus Holidays is one of the biggest operators of adventure holidays. To obtain a secure link to this website, see the Hotlinks section on p.x.

Think about it

Does tourism have a positive or negative impact on the natural environments of the world?

Adventure

Adventure travel means different things to different people. Most adventure holidays are linked to the natural world and can involve diverse activities such as trekking through the Himalayas, white water rafting in New Zealand, exploring the glacial landscapes of southern Chile, trekking in the ancient jungles of Borneo or riding elephants in northern Thailand. Specialist tour operators now exist to put together a huge range of holidays catering for increasingly adventurous travellers.

Many young people take a gap year between school or college and university. Setting off from the UK with a round-the-world ticket can become a big adventure in itself as they come to terms with different cultures, landscapes and experiences.

Gap year destinations

Figure 8.3: What would be your choice of destinations for a gap year? Is there anywhere not on the map you would go?

Assessment activity 8.1

P1

As part of your training to become a travel consultant you will be assessed to show that you can use holiday brochures and atlases to accurately locate a wide range of destinations that are suitable for specific types of holiday.

1 You must identify at least two worldwide destinations (outside Europe) that are suitable for each of the seven types of holiday listed below. Of the 14 destinations you identify, there must be at least one in each continent and they must include at least ten different countries. The holiday types are:

* history and culture

* beach relaxation

* weddings and honeymoons

* leisure and entertainment

* winter sports

* natural world

* adventure.

2 Use an atlas to help you accurately locate these destinations on blank maps of the world. Colour-code the destinations to show the type of holiday they represent.

Grading tips

Make up a checklist to record that you have located:

* two suitable destinations for each holiday type, i.e. 14 different destinations in all

* destinations in at least ten different countries

* at least one destination in each continent (North America, South America, Africa, Asia,

Australasia). Note that the Caribbean is within the continent of North America for the purposes of this assessment.

Colour-code your maps to show the type of holiday each destination represents.

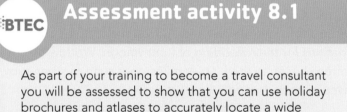

PLTS

This activity will help you to develop your skills as an **independent enquirer**.

Functional skills

Identifying and locating worldwide destinations will help you to develop your **ICT** skills to use IT systems to find and select information.

2 Select worldwide destinations to meet customer needs

2.1 Worldwide destinations

Worldwide destinations offer holidays to suit all tastes, budgets and interests. To be successful, tour operators and travel agents must recognise the needs of their customers and select holiday destinations to meet those needs. Unless the customer is specific about where they want to travel, keep an open mind and consider how worldwide destinations in different continents might meet their needs.

2.2 Types of customer

Couples

Many couples plan a holiday to a worldwide destination to celebrate a special occasion. You have already seen how some couples choose faraway destinations for their wedding or honeymoon. Worldwide holidays are often chosen to mark other milestones such as silver, ruby, golden and even diamond wedding anniversaries.

Young couples often travel the world when they have no ties, while older couples may treat themselves to worldwide travel when their children have left home.

Singles

People travelling on their own will usually look for destinations where there is plenty to do and where they can join in organised trips and activities.

Families

Families have different needs depending on the age of the children. A family with babies and very young children might try to avoid extreme temperatures. They are likely to be attracted by safe, sandy beaches and a good standard of family-friendly accommodation. Health, safety and security will be key priorities for families when selecting a worldwide destination.

Groups

There are many different types of group. Some have common interests such as groups of skiers, climbers and divers while other groups could include those attending a wedding or taking part in a pre-wedding stag or hen break. Educational visits by schools and colleges may venture to worldwide destinations, while major sporting events, such as the soccer and rugby World Cups, the Olympic Games and cricket test matches, will also appeal to groups of supporters and participants.

Did you know?

For the ultimate stag or hen party, tour operators can organise a pre-wedding break in exciting destinations like New York, Dubai, Las Vegas, Rio de Janeiro and Cape Town.

Differing ages

Many young people travelling worldwide do so as part of a gap year. Backpackers tend to focus on countries where the culture and way of life is very different from the UK. Older, retired people are increasingly adventurous when travelling overseas. They have the time to take longer holidays at any time of the year and many have good private pensions to be able to afford to do so.

2.3 Customer needs

In order to meet customer needs it is important to establish the main motivation for a planned holiday. Sales consultants working in travel agencies and with tour operators do this by asking questions to find out about the purpose of the planned holiday. It could be to celebrate a special occasion, to follow the England Rugby squad, to rescue orang-utans or perhaps to relax?

Activity: Spotlight on Dubai

Dubai has become one of the fastest growing holiday destinations in recent times. Situated on the Persian Gulf, this desert oasis boasts some of the world's most luxurious hotels and many attractions. Part of Dubai's appeal is that it does have something for everyone.

Carry out some research into Dubai to find examples of how it could meet different motivations. Record your findings in a diagram such as Figure 8.4.

Once the motivation for the holiday has been established, other questions need to be posed. For example:

- When would you like to travel?
- Are your dates flexible?
- Where would you like to fly or sail from?
- What class of travel would you like?
- What standard or type of accommodation would you like, for example deluxe or traditional?
- What board arrangements do you want?
- Do you have any special requests?
- What type of weather are you hoping for?
- Do you have any special considerations, for example proximity to local attractions, things to do?
- Do you have a maximum budget?

It is the job of the sales consultant to meet these needs.

Did you know?

SAGA Holidays is the market leader in holidays for the over 50s. Find out more about their extensive range of worldwide holidays by visiting their website. To obtain a secure link to this website, see the Hotlinks section on p.x.

Figure 8.4: What motivations do customers have?

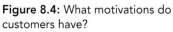

Think about it

Why is it so important to meet customer needs?

Assessment activity 8.2

1   You are working as a travel consultant and have two enquiries to deal with. For each of these you must select two destinations (in different continents) that would meet the customers' needs. You must prepare written proposals for your supervisor.

Enquiry 1: A couple wants to book a 14-night honeymoon in early April. They are looking for sunshine and a relaxed, romantic beach location, ideally no more than 12 hours' flight time from London. They would like the accommodation to be something special. They are not too bothered about having lots of activities, but they do like water sports and would like to have a few places to visit that would give them a feel for the country, for example heritage and sightseeing opportunities.

Enquiry 2: A group of six friends, all keen skiers, want to ski somewhere with good snow and conditions for experienced skiers. They would like to have the chance to try heli-skiing if possible. They want to travel outside of Europe for seven nights in February. They would like bed and breakfast accommodation and flights from London.

For each enquiry you should select two destinations in different continents to meet these needs, Provide full details of the destinations for the customers highlighting how they address their needs.

Question 1 will enable you to achieve **P2**.

2   Produce a written justification for the destinations you have selected in task 1 to show that you have taken the customers' needs into account. You must clearly explain how the recommended destinations meet all the specific needs of the customers.

Question 2 will enable you to achieve **M1**.

Grading tips

P2 Keep and attach records of all sources of information used, for example brochure pages and screen shots of web pages, to support your proposals. List the needs that have been included in the enquiries and make sure that you have responded to all of these needs in your proposals.

M1 Think about why you have made the choices, and double check your proposals so you can justify (give good explanations for) how the destinations you have selected fully meet the customers' needs

Functional skills

Researching destinations will help you to develop your **IT** skills to select, interact and use IT systems to find and select information.

Storing information about worldwide destinations will help you to develop your **IT** skills to manage information storage to enable efficient retrieval.

Presenting information about worldwide destinations will help you to develop your **English** skills to enter, develop and format information independently and to bring it together to suit its meaning, purpose and audience.

Figure 8.5 Where in the world could you go? What will you have to consider?

3 Factors that can impact on travel to worldwide destinations

3.1 Factors

If you've made plans to travel to a faraway location you would be very disappointed if things didn't go to plan. Unfortunately there are many factors that can impact on your plans, and frustratingly these are usually outside your control.

Foreign and Commonwealth Office (FCO)

The Foreign and Commonwealth Office (FCO) is a government department. Part of its role is to provide a service to advise British nationals about travel safety overseas. Up-to-date travel information is provided on its website and contains advice for travel to different countries, including health, safety, extreme weather, etc. The FCO plays a key role when deciding whether or not it is safe for British nationals to travel to individual countries. To obtain a secure link to this website, see the Hotlinks section on p.x.

Extreme weather

When you travel to many worldwide destinations you can encounter extreme weather conditions. Depending on the type of holiday you have chosen, this could have a major impact on your holiday enjoyment. After all, a beach holiday on a beautiful remote island in the Seychelles would be completely ruined if it poured down all day, every day.

If you're planning to travel, or if you are in a job where you are advising others, it's important to find out about seasonal and potentially extreme weather conditions, such as the monsoon season and tropical storms.

You can read more about extreme weather and how it can affect your holiday in *Unit 3: Understanding the nature and effects of world travel* pages 94–97.

Monsoon season
The monsoon season brings torrential downpours that can cause flooding and disruption to travel plans. It affects mainly India, but also Australia, the Americas and East Asia.

Tropical storms
Tropical storms are seasonal and can vary in intensity. Extreme tropical storms like hurricanes can cause widespread damage to buildings, flooding and loss of life. Even when seasonal tropical storms do not develop into hurricanes they can seriously affect holiday enjoyment. Holidaymakers planning a trip to a 'hurricane area' would be well advised to check out the risk season before they book.

How can extreme weather affect where tourists choose to go?

Health issues

Pandemics

A pandemic is when an infectious disease exceeds **epidemic** proportions and spreads through human populations in large areas, for example across continents and even across the world. There have been a number of pandemics in recent years including bird flu in 2005, swine flu in 2009 and HIV which has been ongoing for decades, particularly in parts of Africa. Sometimes travel restrictions are imposed as a result of pandemics, and even when there are no restrictions, many people are wary of visiting a destination for leisure purposes where infectious disease is rampant.

Malaria

Malaria is a potentially fatal tropical disease that is spread through the bite of an infected mosquito. It occurs in hot, humid climates, such as in Africa and Asia. Travellers should make sure they take precautions to avoid mosquito bites and take a course of preventative medicine if they are travelling to an area considered to be of significant risk.

Safety

Staying safe should be central to any worldwide travel planning. The FCO publishes advice and tips for staying safe when travelling to different countries of the world.

Activity: Travel checklist

Using the FCO and Caroline's Rainbow Foundation websites, produce a travel checklist aimed at young people setting off on a gap year trip around the world.

Crime

Crime exists in virtually every country in the world. Tourists are targeted by pickpockets because they are usually carrying sums of money, credit cards and passports. The Caribbean has received negative press in the past because of the serious crimes on islands such as Jamaica. Although, in these cases, tourists are not the main target, they sometimes are caught up in violence and there have been a number of murders in recent years. Such incidents are not common but they do create negative publicity and can put holidaymakers off travelling to a destination. Tourists must take care not to venture into unsafe areas, especially at night.

Terrorism

Terrorist activities usually take the form of deadly bombs being activated, sometimes in tourist areas, for example the 2009 attacks on the luxury Ritz-Carlton and Marriott Hotels in Jakarta, Indonesia.

Key term

epidemic – is when a disease is transmitted amongst humans at a rate that is significantly higher than the expected rate.

Think about it

Don't travel overseas without making sure you are adequately insured for medical cover and make sure your insurance covers you for any extreme sports or hazardous activities.

Did you know?

Caroline's Rainbow Foundation is a charity set up to raise young people's awareness of travel safety. To obtain a secure link to this website, see the Hotlinks section on p.x.

Although they can cause loss of life and disruption, attacks usually happen without warning and do not usually have a long-term effect on travel planning. However terrorist atrocities such as 9/11 have been responsible for long-term measures of improved security, particularly for international air travel.

Unrest

Dissatisfaction with governments can result in riots, unrest and civil war. It can be a frightening experience for tourists caught up in riots and unrest. The FCO monitors events and in serious cases will advise against travel to destinations until the situation has calmed down.

Case study: Sri Lanka

Sri Lanka has idyllic beaches and seven World Heritage Sites. For over 25 years tourism to this beautiful island was affected by civil war. In May 2009 the Sri Lankan government formally declared an end to the war after the army took control of the entire island and killed the leader of the rebel Tamil Tigers. Tourism to Sri Lanka had also been hit hard by the 2004 tsunami and the ongoing civil war seriously affected its recovery. However by July 2009 it was

reported that tourism arrivals had jumped by 28% compared to the previous year.

1 Check out the current travel advice for Sri Lanka. Has the situation changed since May 2009?

2 Check out FCO advice and find an example of a country where the FCO currently advises against all but essential travel as a result of unrest.

Social conditions

Tourism is important to **third world** countries. Visitors spend money and help to create new jobs and opportunities for small businesses. Many travellers are attracted to visiting countries that are not 'touristy', but they may have to be prepared to witness extreme poverty and hardship.

Poverty

Coming face to face with poverty can be an uncomfortable experience. You don't have to travel into the slums to experience poverty; in many worldwide destinations beggars surround tour buses when they stop at hotels and attractions, making many western visitors feel guilty about their comparative wealth, especially when they see vulnerable children living in squalid conditions.

Key term

Third world – this is the term given to the less developed and developing countries in Latin America, Asia and Africa.

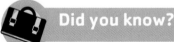

Did you know?

Mumbai does not have the largest slum in the world. Mexico City's Neza-Chalco-Itza barrio is bigger, as is Karachi's Orangi Township.

Case study: Mumbai

Mumbai features in many tours to India. It is the financial capital of India and draws many business travellers. It is estimated that there are some 7 million slum dwellers living in terrible conditions, as shown in the film *Slumdog Millionaire*. The Dharavi slum lacks water, sewage and waste disposal. Overcrowding is rife and infant mortality is high. When the monsoon

rains come the slums can become submerged in feet of water and diseases are rampant.

1 Find out what attracts tourists to Mumbai.

2 How do you think tourism can help the slum dwellers of Mumbai?

Entry and exit requirements

Visas

A visa is a permit issued by a country to allow you to visit, stay or work in the country. Different types of visa are issued for the different purposes. Countries can refuse to issue a visa and this would mean that a visitor would be denied entry to that country. Travel agents are required to advise their customers about visa regulations and, as the requirements change from time to time, they must gain up-to-date information from the FCO or from the Embassies of the countries concerned.

Vaccination certificates

A yellow fever vaccination certificate is required for entry into some countries. Yellow fever is a non-treatable deadly disease caused by a bite from an infected mosquito. The main risk countries are the tropical parts of Africa and South America, and some of the cities of West Africa. Travellers entering other countries from a risk area will usually have to prove that they have been vaccinated against the disease.

Some countries also have additional requirements for vaccinations. When travelling to worldwide destinations you should always check current requirements at least six weeks before the planned date of departure as many treatments are given in doses over a period of time. Some travellers leave it too late and then have to change their holiday plans.

Departure tax

Many countries, particularly in Latin America, Asia and Africa, impose a departure tax which must be paid when you leave a country.

Departure taxes can be confusing. Sometimes they are included in the price of your air ticket; sometimes they are payable in local currency at the departure airport; sometimes they are payable in US dollars. They can be expensive and could add over £100 to the holiday cost for a family of four. High departure taxes can put people off travelling to a particular destination, especially as some impose an arrival tax too.

Activity: Entry and exit

Visit the FCO website and find five examples of worldwide countries that:

- require UK citizens to obtain an entry visa
- require vaccination certificates
- impose a departure tax.

To obtain a secure link to this website, see the Hotlinks section on p.x.

World economy

What happens in the financial capitals of the world can have an impact on the price of holidays and personal finances.

Recession

A recession is when there is an economic slump. It can bring about unemployment and concerns about job security. During a recession people tend to spend their money more carefully and this can mean deciding to miss out on a holiday or to 'downsize' to a cheaper kind of holiday or one closer to home. Both of these can have an impact on travel to worldwide destinations. However, hoteliers and transport providers rely on tourism to support their local economies and they often come up with some excellent special offers and inclusive deals in order to encourage bookings during a recession.

Exchange rates

The value of the pound sterling, particularly against the US dollar, can impact on travel to worldwide destinations. Oil is priced in US dollars and this can affect the price of flying. When the pound is strong, holidays to worldwide destinations can represent good value for money.

Activity: Dollar value

Imagine you have booked a flight to the USA and you are now organising your accommodation. You have found a lovely hotel that is quoting a $2500 inclusive rate for the whole family for two weeks. However, as the exchange rates have been fluctuating you are trying to work out whether to book now or hope for a better exchange rate nearer the time.

Calculate how much the hotel will cost when the exchange rate is:

- £1 = $1.50
- £1 = $1.30
- £1 = $1.70

It is not just the US dollar that can impact on the price of your holiday. When travelling to worldwide destinations you will have to get used to using different currencies. Find out what currency is used in the following countries and the current rate of exchange against the pound sterling (£).

Country	Currency	Rate of exchange
Australia		
Japan		
Chile		
South Africa		
China		

Assessment activity 8.3

P3 M2 D1

1 You are working as a travel consultant and have been asked to produce a written guide for travellers containing descriptions of the factors that can impact on worldwide travel. You must include:

- extreme weather, for example hurricanes and the monsoon season
- health issues in the destination, for example. pandemics, malaria, HIV
- safety, for example terrorism and crime
- unrest, for example riots and war
- social conditions, for example poverty in the destination
- entry or exit requirements, for example visas, vaccination certificates and departure tax
- world economy, for example exchange rates and recession
- the role of the FCO.

Provide at least one example of a worldwide destination affected by each factor within the last five years.

Question 1 will enable you to achieve P3.

2 One of your customers is interested in travelling to Bangkok. Write to them explaining how different factors might affect travel to Bangkok. Include all relevant factors.

Question 2 will enable you to achieve M2.

3 Some customers have asked for reassurance regarding the possibility of encountering extreme weather and unrest. They have asked you to assess the impact of these two factors on travel to worldwide destinations during the last five years. Provide them with a written assessment of your findings. Include examples of at least two worldwide destinations for each factor.

Question 3 will enable you to achieve D1.

Grading tips

P3 Look out in the news for factors that are affecting worldwide travel; it can be useful to build up a file with copies of newspaper cuttings in readiness for assessment. For each factor you describe make sure you have found an example (from within the last five years) that has affected a worldwide destination and indicate the main impact on travel. Keep records of all the useful sources you have found in case you need to go back to them for the higher grades.

M2 Choose a worldwide destination that has been in the news due to significant factors such as unrest, health issues, severe weather, etc. Check on the FCO website to see what other factors might be relevant. The choice of destination is important so it is worth spending time

finding one that will give you lots of material. You need to explain how the different factors might affect travel to the destination. This could include negative publicity, FCO warnings, cancellation of holidays, it being unsafe to travel, disinclination to travel, prohibitive cost.

D1 To 'assess' you need to weigh up the impact of two factors. This means working out the extent of the impact. For example you will need to consider whether the factors had a long term effect on travel to a destination. How quickly have destinations recovered from, say, the aftermath of hurricanes or terrorist activity? Has the FCO warned against travel to the destinations? Are any restrictions still in place? Is there on-going negative publicity?

PLTS

Describing factors that impact on travel to worldwide destinations will help develop your skills as an **independent enquirer**.

Functional skills

Presenting information on travel factors will help your **English** skills to develop, present and communicate information.

Researching and discussing travel factors and communicating information will help you to develop your **English** skills in speaking and listening, reading and speaking.

I work for a small specialist tour operator. We offer holidays to the Caribbean and South America, and specialise in escorted multi-centre tours using expert local guides. There are five of us in the tours department. I am responsible for:

- dealing with customer enquiries
- giving travel advice
- producing tour itineraries
- sending out travel documentation to passengers
- sending passenger lists to our overseas agents
- dealing with special requests.

Typical day

A typical day for me involves arriving at the office and checking emails. The destinations we deal with are between three and five hours behind GMT so there will usually be some messages from our local agents. Accuracy is important in my work because if I give someone inaccurate information about visas or put inaccurate timings on an itinerary this could have disastrous consequences for someone's holiday. I have to be very organised making sure that I send out travel documentation to passengers and information to our overseas agents in good time.

Is the work challenging?

It can be. One day a hurricane was heading for Cuba where we had a number of holidaymakers. We had to liaise with our overseas agent and make sure that everything was being done to keep our customers safe because flights to and from the island had been halted. It was nail-biting watching the satellite images of the hurricane moving across the Atlantic but luckily it passed just north of Cuba and, apart from a nasty 24-hour storm, the holiday continued without major disruption.

The best thing about the job

I like working through the arrangements for holidays. It is nice to build up a rapport with customers, particularly when helping to fulfil any special requests. It gives me a great sense of satisfaction when people enjoy their holiday.

Think about it!

What would be the potential 'disastrous consequences' of:

- giving a customer the wrong information about entry requirements?
- putting the wrong timings on an itinerary?
- sending incorrect information about passenger numbers to the overseas agents?

Why is it important for travel organisers to have good knowledge of worldwide destinations?

Just checking

1 How can the FCO assist British citizens?
2 Name the garland presented to visitors to Hawaii.
3 Where is Machu Picchu?
4 Where is Kruger National Park?
5 Name a holiday company that specialises in adventure holidays
6 What is a pandemic?
7 When should you find out about requirements for vaccinations?
8 How can exchange rates affect travel to worldwide destinations?
9 What is Caroline's Rainbow Foundation?
10 Name a holiday company that specialises in holidays for the over 50s.

Assignment tips

- Talk to friends and relatives who have been on a worldwide holiday. What did they like and dislike? How was the weather? What did they see and do? What types of people would their holiday appeal to?

- There are many TV programmes set overseas; these can give you the 'flavour' of different countries around the world. Documentaries can be particularly informative; try and make a point of watching some to broaden your awareness of worldwide destinations.

- Google Earth is a great resource that lets you zoom in and gain a bird's-eye view of places around the world.

- Visit a large travel agency to have a look at the wide range of brochures available to promote worldwide destinations. These are an expensive resource so don't collect brochures indiscriminately, but if you have a word with the agency manager they may be able to supply you with spare copies or brochures that are coming to the end of their shelf life.

- Watch the news and read newspapers to see what's happening around the world. If you hear of severe weather, unrest or disruption in different countries, check the FCO website to see what advice they are offering potential travellers.

9 Holiday planning

Going on holiday is one of the most exciting and interesting aspects of the travel and tourism sector. Many holidaymakers are now able to research and book their own holidays on-line or by telephone. There are also a range of employment opportunities in the travel and tourism sector, which involve planning holidays to meet customers' specific requirements. Those wishing to work in retail travel, transport operations and tour operating will need to have the necessary skills in order to plan holidays and provide information and advice which meet all of their customers' needs.

This unit will introduce you to the practical task of planning holidays in the UK and abroad. You will explore different sources of information, both paper-based and online, in order to research, plan and propose suitable holidays to meet the needs of different customers. You will learn how to use brochures, timetables and websites to plan holidays and select the most suitable holiday arrangements.

You will also investigate the pre-holiday information and advice needs of customers who are travelling overseas, for example requests relating to travel health, documentation and currency exchange.

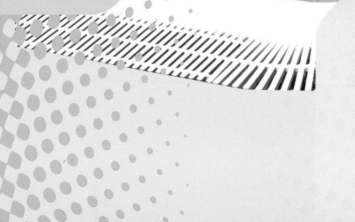

Learning outcomes

After completing this unit you should:

1   be able to plan journeys within the UK

2   be able to use different sources to select and cost holidays outside the UK

3   be able to provide information and advice to customers travelling to an overseas holiday destination.

255

To achieve a **pass** grade the evidence must show that you are able to:	To achieve a **merit** grade the evidence must show that, in addition to the pass criteria, you are able to:	To achieve a **distinction** grade the evidence must show that, in addition to the pass and merit criteria, you are able to:
P1 use different sources of information to plan simple journeys in the UK by rail, coach, air and car **Assessment activity 9.1, page 271**	**M1** compare simple journeys in the UK in terms of time, cost and convenience **Assessment activity 9.1, page 271**	
P2 use holiday brochures to select and cost and overseas package holiday to meet a given customer brief **Assessment activity 9.2, page 277**	**M2** explain how the selected holidays meet the customer brief **Assessment activity 9.2, page 277**	**D1** work independently to select and cost holidays, presenting the information coherently and accurately **Assessment activity 9.2, page 277**
P3 use the internet to select the best value overseas package holiday to meet a given customer brief **Assessment activity 9.2, page 277**		
P4 independently put together and cost individual components to create an overseas holiday to meet a given customer brief **Assessment activity 9.2, page 277**		
P5 provide information and advice to customers travelling to an overseas destination **Assessment activity 9.3, page 284**		

Jess, 16–year-old learner

I really enjoyed this unit as it helped me improve my practical skills in planning holidays. When I have been on holiday before with my parents, we usually look at the holiday brochure and go to the local high street travel agent to make our booking. This unit has given me a better understanding of the role of a travel consultant, and also of the fact that many holidays are now booked online using the internet. I have explored many different holiday websites, such as those from a tour operator and those where you book all the different components separately, like your hotel room, your flight and your car hire.

The best part of this unit for me was taking part in the holiday planning role-plays, where I took the role of a travel agent and used the internet to book a holiday which met my customer's needs. My tutor played the part of the customer and I asked lots of questions to understand the type of holiday they wanted. I also used a travel website to find out the total costs. It was quite a realistic situation and I was nervous about getting it right. I was pleased that my tutor liked the holiday I had planned for them and said I had good customer service skills.

It was also interesting to look at all the different travel advice questions that holidaymakers might have, such as what you are allowed to take on-board an aircraft and the difference between travel insurance and the European Health Insurance Card. I would definitely feel more confident booking my own holiday now.

Over to you

* What areas of this unit might you find the most challenging?

* Which section of the unit are you most looking forward to?

* What preparation can you do in readiness for the unit assessment(s)?

1 Journeys within the UK

How do you plan yours?

On your own, think about any holidays you have taken in the last couple of years with family or friends, and answer the following questions:

1 How did you, or the person making the booking, plan and book your holiday?

2 Did you use the services of a travel agent? If yes, was this in a high street shop or on the telephone? Was the agency part of a chain (multiple) or independent?

3 Did you use the internet and which site(s) did you use?

4 Why did you choose to plan and book your holiday in this way?

Compare your answers with a partner.

1.1 Journeys

There are many ways to make a journey in the UK, for example by rail, air, coach and car. There are also many different ways to plan your journey, depending on your method of transport. You might choose to use paper-based sources of information, such as timetables, or travel planning websites. For further information about different types of transport see *Unit 1: The UK travel and tourism sector*.

Rail journeys

Rail travel can provide a fast and convenient way to travel around Great Britain, whether making a local or national journey. The National Rail network covers approximately 9000 miles of track. Great Britain has a number of main routes, including the East and West Coast Mainlines which connect London with Scotland. Northern Ireland has its own rail network.

Planning a rail journey is often done using paper-based timetables. Timetables for specific routes are produced by train operating companies (TOCs), such as Virgin Trains or South West Trains, and are generally available from train stations and Tourist Information Centres (TICs). The National Rail timetable is also produced by Network Rail which covers all of the passenger rail services in Great Britain. This is a large document (almost 3000 pages) and is available to download from the Network Rail website or to buy as a printed copy. Most routes usually offer a main summer and winter timetable.

Rail timetables can be complicated documents and most feature a range of symbols and codes. It is very important that those planning journeys understand the different signs and symbols featured in the timetables, to make sure that travellers receive the correct information.

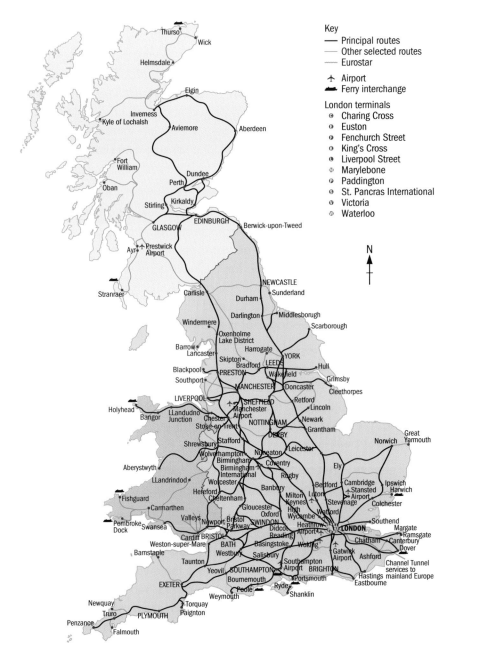

Figure 9.1: The national railway network. Can you identify the main East and West Coast Mainlines?

Key term

Passenger assistance – the term used by transport providers for the additional services offered to passengers with specific and additional needs, often relating to those with a disability or limited mobility. Transport providers may provide a member of staff to accompany travellers at stations and airports from arrival until they are safely on-board.

The onboard shop offered to customers on many train journeys

Did you know?

Network Rail run, maintain and develop Britain's tracks, signalling system, rail bridges, tunnels, level crossings, viaducts and 18 key stations, including London Euston, Manchester Piccadilly, Leeds and Birmingham New Street.

Rail services

When planning a rail journey, it is important to understand the needs of the traveller and to find services which meet the required level of service, facilities, comfort and convenience. Some travellers may require information relating to direct services only or those which do not require a change of trains. Other passengers may have specific needs and require wheelchair access, bike storage or **passenger assistance** at departure and arrival stations.

Many rail services offer passengers a First and Standard Class service. First class tickets are more expensive, but offer travellers a range of additional services often including larger seats, more legroom, at-seat meal service, complimentary newspapers and wireless internet access. Rail travel can be attractive for business travellers who are able to work and communicate whilst on the move. Large tables provide a convenient working space for laptops and First Class lounges at large stations often provide meeting rooms and Wifi facilities.

On busy services, seat reservations are often recommended or sometimes compulsory with certain ticket types, e.g. advence tickets. Passengers are given the number of the carriage (sometimes called the coach number) and the seat that they have been allocated. Travelling without a seat reservation may result in passengers having to stand for long periods at peak-times.

Some rail services are timetabled to connect with certain ferry and shipping services. Passengers are able to continue their journey to selected UK islands and Ireland.

Some rail services offer catering options to passengers, from a full meal and wine service for First Class passengers to an 'at-seat trolley service' where a member of the on-board crew makes their way through the carriages serving a selection of hot and cold drinks, sandwiches and snacks. Some rail operators provide an 'on-board shop' where passengers can also purchase books and magazines as well as food and drink.

Activity: All aboard

Working in pairs, use the extract from the National Rail timetable to answer the following questions. You will need to refer to the key to railway symbols in Figure 9.2 to help you.

- Mrs Liu would like to travel from London Euston to Glasgow Central. Identify the departure times of the three direct services from London Euston.

- Mr Duggan would like to make a connecting service at Manchester Piccadilly. What is the minimum interchange time for a connecting service at this station?

- Which two stations on the timetable are shown to have a connecting tram/metro interchange?

- Which three stations on the timetable are shown to have an airport link?

Case study: Railcards

Travel on trains in Great Britain can cost you one-third less if you have a Railcard. Railcards are available to selected groups of passengers who meet certain eligibility criteria and can be used on most rail services in Great Britain, although some specific terms and conditions including time restrictions and minimum fares may apply.

Available railcards currently include:

- **16–25 Railcards:** Available to those aged 16–25 and full-time students aged 26 and over.

- **Family and Friends Railcard:** For anyone travelling with at least one child aged between 5 and 15 years.

- **Senior Railcard:** Available to those aged 60 and over.

- **Disabled Persons Railcard:** Discounted travel for passengers with certain disabilities and their companions.

- **Network Railcard:** Those regularly travelling in the South East of England can save money on their rail travel, after 10 a.m. Monday–Friday and at weekends.

- **HM Forces Railcard:** For members of the Regular Armed Forces and their partners.

To obtain a secure link to these websites, see the Hotlinks section on p.x

In pairs, choose one type of railcard and find out the minimum fare which applies. How much does each Railcard cost?

References and Symbols used in this Timetable

Date and Time Symbols
a   Arrival time.
d   Departure time.
p   Previous night.
s   Stops to set down only.
u   Stops to pick up only.
x   Stops on request. Customers wishing to alight must inform the on-train staff, prior to departure from the previous station, and those wishing to join must give a clear hand signal to the driver.

M   Monday.
T   Tuesday.
W   Wednesday.
Th Thursday.
F   Friday.
S   Saturday.
Su Sunday.
- Adding **'O'** to the abbreviation for the day or days (eg **WO**) means the train runs **only** on the day or days preceding the **'O'**.
- Adding **'X'** to the abbreviation for the day or days (eg **FX**) means the train runs on all the days in this section of the timetable **except** the day or days preceding the **'X'**.

{   Wavy line between train times indicates that this train does **not** run during the full period of the timetable on which the train is shown.

BHX Does not run on designated Bank Holidays 25, 26 December, 1 January, 2, 5 April and 3 May.
→   Train continued in a later column.
←   Train continued from an earlier column.

Station Symbols
⊖   Stations having interchange with London Underground services.
10 Figure in box indicates the minimum Interchange Time in minutes to allow between trains at this station; example shows 10 minutes—see also **Connections** page.
⚓   Shipping service.
✈   Airport Link – station for interchange. See also Airport Links pages.
⛴   Hovercraft, Catamaran or Hydrofoil.
⇄   Tram/Metro Interchange.

Accommodation
All services shown in this timetable convey Standard accommodation only unless otherwise shown.

Train Numbers
On certain tables, mainly in South East England, route codes are shown as part of the column heading information. These codes correspond with numbers that will be displayed on trains which are equipped to display such information.

Train Symbols
Catering Symbols
Services are available for First and Standard Class ticket holders, for all or part of the journey, unless otherwise shown.
Alterations may apply at Bank Holiday periods. See the directory of Train Operators for further information and availability of complimentary refreshments.
✕   A restaurant (for First Class ticket holders) and a buffet service of hot snacks, sandwiches, hot and cold drinks are provided.
✕   A restaurant (for First Class ticket holders, also Standard Class ticket holders if accommodation is available), and a buffet service of hot snacks, sandwiches, hot and cold drinks are provided.
Ø   A service of hot or light meals and a buffet service of hot snacks, sandwiches, hot and cold drinks are provided.
⊐   A buffet service of hot snacks, sandwiches and hot and cold drinks is provided.
⊼   An at-seat trolley service of cold snacks, sandwiches and hot and cold drinks is provided.
Other Symbols
Ⓡ   Seat reservations recommended. See also **Reservations** page.
Ⓡ   Seat reservations compulsory. See also **Reservations** page.
◇   Seat reservations available. See also **Reservations** page.
1   Also conveys First Class accommodation. On some services such accommodation may be described as Business Class.
🚌   Bus service - heavy luggage, prams, bicycles, etc. may not be conveyed.

References and Symbols used in this Timetable

Date and Time Symbols
a   Arrival time.
d   Departure time.
p   Previous night.
s   Stops to set down only.
u   Stops to pick up only.
x   Stops on request. Customers wishing to alight must inform the on-train staff, prior to departure from the previous station, and those wishing to join must give a clear hand signal to the driver.

M   Monday.
T   Tuesday.
W   Wednesday.
Th Thursday.
F   Friday.
S   Saturday.
Su Sunday.
- Adding **'O'** to the abbreviation for the day or days (eg **WO**) means the train runs **only** on the day or days preceding the **'O'**.
- Adding **'X'** to the abbreviation for the day or days (eg **FX**) means the train runs on all the days in this section of the timetable **except** the day or days preceding the **'X'**.

| Wavy line between train times indicates that this train does **not** run during the full period of the timetable on which the train is shown.

BHX Does not run on designated Bank Holidays 25, 26 December, 1 January, 2, 5 April and 3 May.
→   Train continued in a later column.
←   Train continued from an earlier column.

Station Symbols
⊖   Stations having interchange with London Underground services.
10 Figure in box indicates the minimum Interchange Time in minutes to allow between trains at this station; example shows 10 minutes—see also **Connections** page.
⚓   Shipping service.
✈   Airport Link – station for interchange. See also Airport Links pages.
⛴   Hovercraft, Catamaran or Hydrofoil.
⇄   Tram/Metro Interchange.

Accommodation
All services shown in this timetable convey Standard accommodation only unless otherwise shown.

Train Numbers
On certain tables, mainly in South East England, route codes are shown as part of the column heading information. These codes correspond with numbers that will be displayed on trains which are equipped to display such information.

Train Symbols
Catering Symbols
Services are available for First and Standard Class ticket holders, for all or part of the journey, unless otherwise shown.
Alterations may apply at Bank Holiday periods. See the directory of Train Operators for further information and availability of complimentary refreshments.
✕   A restaurant (for First Class ticket holders) and a buffet service of hot snacks, sandwiches, hot and cold drinks are provided.
✕   A restaurant (for First Class ticket holders, also Standard Class ticket holders if accommodation is available), and a buffet service of hot snacks, sandwiches, hot and cold drinks are provided.
Ø   A service of hot or light meals and a buffet service of hot snacks, sandwiches, hot and cold drinks are provided.
⊐   A buffet service of hot snacks, sandwiches and hot and cold drinks is provided.
⊼   An at-seat trolley service of cold snacks, sandwiches and hot and cold drinks is provided.
Other Symbols
Ⓡ   Seat reservations recommended. See also **Reservations** page.
Ⓡ   Seat reservations compulsory. See also **Reservations** page.
◇   Seat reservations available. See also **Reservations** page.
1   Also conveys First Class accommodation. On some services such accommodation may be described as Business Class.
🚌   Bus service - heavy luggage, prams, bicycles, etc. may not be conveyed.

Figure 9.2: Key to railways symbols

Source: National Rail Timetable

Figure 9.3: Extract from the National Rail timetable

Rail planning websites

As well as using printed timetables to plan rail journeys, many passengers now find the internet a more convenient way to plan and book their rail travel.

The National Rail Enquiries (NRE) website provides an excellent information source for the latest train times, including delays, cancellations and planned maintenance work. It also features useful details of services and facilities at most UK train stations, including opening times, disabled access and local transport links.

Other sites, such as thetrainline.com provide rail times and fares as well as allowing customers to book tickets for all train companies. In addition, sites such as megatrain.co.uk offer a few limited services at discounted rates, with some fares starting at just £1.

Most train operating companies also have the option to buy tickets online direct from their own company websites, such as Virgin Trains, First Great Western, Cross Country, London Midland, Scot Rail and Arriva. To obtain a secure link to these websites, see the Hotlinks section on p.x.

Case study: National Rail Enquiries

National Rail Enquiries (NRE) is a service run by the Association of Train Operating Companies (ATOC) and provides information for all passenger rail services on the National Rail network in England, Wales and Scotland.

NRE handles an average of 1.3 million journey enquiries every day, either through their telephone contact centres or website. Introduced in 2003, the NRE website offers a journey planning service, as well as timetable and fares information. The site can also provide passengers with 'Live Departure Board' information, which includes 'real-time' information on the running of most train services, including delays and cancellations.

NRE also provides the automated 'TrainTracker' service, which uses speech-recognition software to provide train times over the telephone, and a text-messaging service where details of train times for a particular service can be sent directly to your mobile phone.

NRE have also made available an application for the Apple iPhone, which allows users to quickly find their next train home as well as plan other journeys on the move.

How do National Rail enquiries benefit travellers?

To obtain a secure link to the National Rail Enquiries website, see the Hotlinks section on page.xx.

Did you know?

ATOC — stands for the Association of Train Operating Companies and is the trade body which represents the needs of train operators to the government and regulators. ATOC provides the National Rail Enquiries service and promotes the national railcard schemes. ATOC also licenses travel agents to sell rail tickets.

Journeys by air

By far the most convenient way to plan travel by air is now through the internet, although some travel agents will also be able to provide domestic UK flight information. UK domestic air travel has become easier and more attractive in recent years, due to the increase in the number of regional airports and the number of internal flights offered by 'no-frills' or low-cost scheduled airlines. The cost of flights can often be cheaper than travelling by rail, and sometimes road, and taking a flight is often the fastest way to travel.

Most full-service, and low-cost, scheduled airlines give you the ability to research flight timetables, routes, destinations and prices direct from their websites, help you to plan your journey. They also offer the option of buying your ticket direct, paying on-line with a credit or debit card.

Examples of airlines offering UK domestic flight information and ticket bookings include British Airways, bmi, Flybe, Jet2.com, easyJet, Ryanair and Aer Lingus. (To obtain a secure link to these websites, see the Hotlinks section on p.x.)

Some airports also provide information on scheduled flight times.

Many low-cost airlines now provide passengers with the options to check-in on-line, pre-book specific seats and additional legroom, book an in-flight meal and receive priority boarding. All these options come at an extra cost – this is how the low-cost airlines generate most of their revenue.

As well as booking direct with a specific airline, passengers can go to other travel websites that provide flight times and prices for multiple airlines. This can often save time, without the need to search many different airline websites.

Example of websites which search a range of airlines to find flight details include Skyscanner, Expedia, Opodo and CheapFlights. To obtain a secure link to these websites, see the Hotlinks section on p.x.)

Functional skills

Using the internet to carry out research will help you develop your ICT skills in finding and selecting information.

Activity: Come fly with me

Working in pairs and using one of the flight search websites:

- List the names of airlines providing direct flights from any London airport to Edinburgh.

- Identify the cheapest flight found by the search website for a one-way flight leaving on Monday. Make a note of the airline and the cost.

- Go direct to the airline's own website and search for the same flight and compare the prices. Are they the same? If not, why do you think this is?

Did you know?

'On-airport' parking is where the car park is within the airport grounds, often quite a short distance from the terminal buildings and often operated by the airport itself. 'Off-airport' car parks are on other private land and operated by private providers. These car parks can often be cheaper, but are usually further away from the terminal buildings.

Parking is often categorised in three different ways: drop-off/pick-up; short-term and long-term. Drop-off/pick-up parking is usually free for around 20 minutes and is great for friends and relatives dropping-off or collecting passengers. Short-term parking is appropriate for passengers making a return journey in the same day, for example commuters. Long-term parking is generally for stays of over 24 hours.

When planning to travel by air, passengers have to consider how they are going to get to, and from, the airport. Many airports have parking facilities, but at larger airports car parks can get full very quickly and often parking facilities are 'off-airport' and quite a distance from the terminal buildings. A park and ride scheme is often available for those using off-airport car parks, when a shuttle bus service will transfer passengers to the terminal building. Passengers should ensure that they consider the transfer time from an off-airport car park to the departures terminal.

Case study: Manchester Airport

As well as having plenty of car parking, Manchester Airport welcomes passengers travelling by public transport. 'The Station', Manchester Airport's integrated transport hub, offers frequent train, bus and coach services linking the airport with hundreds of destinations across the North of England and nationally.

Frequent direct rail services run to and from Sheffield, York, Newcastle, Leeds, Huddersfield, Bolton, Preston, Blackpool and the Lake District. Many of these services now run 24 hours a day, 7 days a week. There are also up to six trains an hour linking the airport to Manchester Piccadilly station in the city centre.

In addition a large number of national coach and bus services connect the airport with the local region and other national cities. There are also future plans to link the airport to the Metrolink tram system.

Once passengers arrive at The Station, it is easy for them to reach the terminal buildings using the Skylink moving walkways, making Manchester Airport one of the UK's most accessible international gateways.

(For more information about Manchester Airport and to obtain a secure link to their website, see the Hotlinks section on p.x.)

1   Do you think that transport links influence a traveller's decision on which airport to fly from?

2   How do you think Manchester Airport might further improve its accessibility?

Travelling to the airport by coach, or rail, can often be more convenient and cost-effective than travelling by car. Most airports have a choice of public transport options for passengers wishing to travel this way. After arriving at the airport, passengers often have the option to take connecting coach or rail services. The Stansted, Heathrow and Gatwick Express rail services provide a fast and direct link between central London and each airport.

Functional skills

Using the internet to carry out research will help you develop your ICT skills in finding and selecting information.

Activity: Airport links

Working in pairs, use the internet to research how passengers would travel into the city by public transport from each of these airports: London Heathrow, Manchester, Liverpool and Newcastle. Make a note of the means of transport and the approximate prices.

Journeys by coach

There are various national coach companies that provide coach travel across the UK. Coach travel can be less expensive than rail and air, but journey times are often much longer. Some coach companies still publish paper-based timetables, but often the most convenient way to plan a coach journey is via the internet, through the local Tourist Information Centre (TIC) or a transport information office.

Examples of coach providers offering intercity UK travel nationwide include National Express and Megabus. (To obtain a secure link to these websites, see the Hotlinks section on p.x.)

Other coach providers also provide more regional services, or offer links with airports and the city, for example easyBus, Green Line and

Terravision. (To obtain a secure link to these websites, see the Hotlinks section on p.x.)

Each company has a 'journey planner' option on their website to help make travel planning quick and easy.

Case study: National Express

National Express is the largest scheduled coach service provider in Europe. In the UK, National Express coaches operate to 1700 destinations and carry over 18 million customers each year.

Like the railcard system available for train travel, National Express offers its customers a range of discounts on standard coach prices, including:

- 16-26 Coachcard – available to those aged 16-26 and full-time students aged 26 and over, offering a 30% discount on standard prices.

- Family Coachcard – free travel for children travelling with each full paying adult.

- Over 60s discount –travellers over 60 automatically qualify for a 50% reduction on standard ticket prices.

All-inclusive passes are also available for those travelling around the UK over 7, 14 or 28 days.

An explorer pass can be very cost-effective for passengers choosing coach travel to tour the country.

Passengers can buy their National Express tickets through travel offices, Tourist Information Centres or on-line. You can choose to print an 'e-ticket' from your computer or receive an 'm-ticket' as a text-message on your mobile phone – you just show it to the driver, no printing is required.

In the UK National Express has a network of larger 'interchange-hubs': London Victoria Coach Station, Birmingham Digbeth, Manchester Chorlton Street. These are all large stations that provide passengers with toilets, refreshments and places to change coaches for a longer onward journey.

1 Why do people choose to travel by bus?

2 What other offers do National Express have?

National Express operate an inter-city national coach service across the UK

Notes

Please be aware that the clocks go forward by one hour on the last Sunday in March and back by one hour on the last Sunday in October. Please contact us to see how the change of hour might affect your journey.

25 December – No service

1	Does not operate 24 December.
2	24 December departure from London terminates at Glasgow.
a	Arrival time.
d	Departure time.
k	Operates 15 minutes later Fridays.
(30)R	30 minutes refreshment stop.
(45)R	45 minutes refreshment stop.

Activity: Coach trip

Working in pairs, use the extract from the National Express timetable in Figure 9.4, to answer the following questions. You will need to refer to the notes section to help you.

- Becca would like to travel from London to Inverness. At which station must she change coaches?

- Adam has a ticket for the 592 service from London to Dundee. Where will the coach stop for refreshments and for how long?

- Which days of the week does the 588 service from London to Inverness run?

Did you know?

The sat-nav system we currently use depends on a network of 26 United States satellites which orbit around the Earth. This is known as the global positioning system (GPS). GPS is run by the US military and is currently the only fully functional Global Navigation Satellite System (GNSS) in the world. For more information, go to the British National Space Centre website. (To obtain a secure link to this website, see the Hotlinks section on p.x.)

London to Glasgow, Aberdeen & Inverness

Service number		500	538	592	592	588
Period of operation			1	2	•	2
Days of operation		Daily	Daily	Daily	Daily	Daily
London, Victoria Coach Station		0900	–	2230	2300	2300
London (Golders Green), Bus Station		0935	–	–	–	2325
Heathrow Airport, Central Bus Station		–	–	2305	–	–
Toddington, Services, M1 Motorway		–	–	–	–	2359
Milton Keynes, Campbell Park, Silbury Boulevard		1040	–	–	–	0015
Knutsford Services, M6 Motorway		(45)R	–	(30)R	(30)R	(30)R
Penrith, Rail Station		–	–	–	–	0505
Carlisle, Bus Station, Lonsdale Road		1555	–	0505	–	–
Lockerbie, outside Semple and Fergusson		–	–	–	–	0555
Abington, M74 Service Area, Coach Park		–	–	–	–	0630
Hamilton, Bus Station		1725	–	0635	–	–
Glasgow, Buchanan Bus Station	a	1755	↘	0705	0705	0715
Glasgow, Buchanan Bus Station	d	1815	1830	0715	0715	0730
Stirling, Bus Station, Goosecroft Road		–	1910	–	–	0813
Perth, Leonard Street, Bus Station		1930	–	–	0840	0856
Dundee, Seagate Bus Station		2000	–	0900	0910	–
Aberdeen, Guild Street, Bus Station		2120	–	1025	–	–
Pitlochry (Aldour), Bus Stop		–	2030	–	–	0935
Pitlochry, Fishers Hotel		–	2035	–	–	0940
Aviemore, Cairngorm Hotel, opposite Rail Station		–	2150	–	–	1055
Inverness, Farraline Park Bus Station		–	2230	–	–	1135

Figure 9.4: Extract from the National Express timetable

Journeys by car

Despite more reliable and frequent public transport, for some travellers the car is still the most convenient choice for certain journeys. When travelling with a group of people, the costs of car travel can often be cheaper than paying for rail, flight or coach tickets.

Travellers often enjoy greater flexibility and choice when travelling by car. They can choose when to set off, where to stop for refreshments and how long to travel. However, road works, traffic jams and accidents can all cause long delays for car travellers.

When planning a journey by car, an essential source of information is a road atlas. Road atlases provide clear maps of all the UK's major road networks, including motorways, toll-roads, dual-carriageways, 'A' and 'B' roads and most minor roads.

Satellite navigation (sat-nav) systems have also become very popular in helping drivers to navigate their way through the UK's road and motorway network. Journeys can be programmed into the system, often by postcode, and audible instructions and on-screen maps help drivers get to their destinations. Popular sat-nav systems include TomTom, Garmin and Navman. Many mobile phones now have a global positioning system (GPS) receiver which allows travellers to track their locations and plan journeys wherever they are.

Activity: Navigation

Compare and contrast using a traditional road atlas and a sat-nav system to plan a road journey. What are the advantages and disadvantages of each method?

There are various websites which can help with planning a car journey, providing route instructions, maps and details on estimated journey times, fuel costs and even levels of **CO_2 emissions**.

Example of car journey planning websites include the AA, the RAC, ViaMichelin, Transport Direct and Green Flag. (To obtain a secure link to these websites, see the Hotlinks section on p.x.)

Key term

CO_2 emissions – it is widely accepted that the main greenhouse gas responsible for recent climate change is carbon dioxide (CO_2). This has been released in huge quantities by our modern way of life, including our use of cars, train, coaches and planes. Large increases in man-made CO_2 are thought to contribute to the greenhouse effect on the planet and to have led to global warming and climate change. (To obtain a secure link to a website, see the Hotlinks section on p.x.)

Activity: Planning road journeys

Using a road atlas, make a note of the motorways a car driver would take, travelling the most direct route between the destinations listed below:

- Birmingham to Exeter
- Carlisle to Birmingham
- London to Sheffield
- Manchester to Leeds.

Did you know?

The first motorway in Britain was the Preston Bypass in Lancashire, opened in 1958 and now part of the M6 motorway. The M6 is Britain's longest (236 miles) and busiest motorway. In 2003, the M6 Toll was opened, Britain's first motorway toll-road, and provides an alternative route around Birmingham.

Figure 9.5: The UK motorway network *Source: Highways Agency*

Case study: Highways Agency

The Highways Agency was established in 1994 and is an executive agency of the Department for Transport. The Highways Agency is responsible for operating, maintaining and improving England's motorways and trunk roads. Its main roles are to manage traffic, tackle congestion, provide information to road users and improve safety and journey time reliability.

The Highways Agency operate the National Traffic Control Centre, which controls over 300 roadside traffic signs and provides up-to-date information through their real-time traffic website for the latest information on the flow of traffic throughout England's road network.

The Highways Agency also provide a network of Traffic Officers who attend to motorway incidents and assist car travellers with accidents.

1   How does the Highways Agency improve England's roads?
2   How might the network of Traffic Officers improve journeys by car for travellers?

(To obtain a secure link to this website, see the Hotlinks section on p.x.)

Motorways

England has a network of over 2025 miles of motorway, providing car and coach travellers with links to most major towns and cities. A network of motorway service stations keep travellers refreshed and on the move, providing a range of services, many 24 hours a day, which may include provision of fuel, food and drink, shops, toilet facilities, overnight accommodation, outdoor areas and traveller information.

Many travellers are now becoming more environmentally aware and are concerned about the impact their travel and choice of transport are having on the environment. Travelling by air and car can often have the biggest effect on the environment, producing the largest amount of CO_2 emissions. Some passengers are trying to reduce the amount of unnecessary journeys they take by choosing different methods of transport which are more 'green', or have less negative effects on the environment. The government is also actively encouraging more travellers to consider public transport options, rather than taking the car for every journey.

Public transport planning

Transport offices, County Information Centres and Tourist Information Centres can all help when planning a journey by public transport. Various websites are also available to assist with journey planning, giving travellers comparisons between different forms of transport and their associated duration and cost.

Examples of public transport planning websites include Traveline, Traveline Scotland, Traveline Cymru, Transport Direct and Transport for London. (To obtain a secure link to these websites, see the Hotlinks section on p.x.)

Case study: Transport Direct

Transport Direct is a non-profit service funded by the UK Department for Transport, the Welsh Assembly Government and the Scottish Government. The website offers information for door-to-door travel for both public transport and car journeys around Britain.

At the Transport Direct website, you can:

- Compare public transport options with a car route to find a way of travelling which best suits your needs.

- Obtain a car route that takes into account predicted traffic levels at different times of the day, so that you can make informed decisions about when to travel.

- Get an estimate of the cost of a car journey.

- Buy train and coach tickets from retail sites without having to re-enter your details.

- Use Personal Digital Assistants (PDAs) and mobile phones to find out departure and arrival times for railway stations throughout Britain and for some bus or coach stops.

- Calculate CO_2 emissions for a car or public transport for a specified journey.

Transport Direct is the world's first website to provide national coverage for information about all types of transport.

1 **What are the benefits of websites such as Transport Direct for those planning journeys?**

2 **Can you think of any other useful services that the Transport Direct website could introduce in the future?**

To obtain a secure link to the Transport Direct website, see the Hotlinks section on page.x.

Different methods of transport

Each method of travel has its own advantages and disadvantages, such as the cost, the level of convenience for the traveller and the time it takes (duration) of the journey.

Cost

The cost of a journey may well have an impact on the traveller's decision to use that particular method. Cheap flights and rail tickets can often be purchased if passengers are able to book in advance, although last minute bookings can be much more expensive. Car journeys can work out expensive for a single traveller but can be more economical if more people are travelling in the same vehicle. The cost of fuel can also have a large impact on the overall cost for a journey.

Convenience

Different methods of transport might be more convenient in certain circumstances and for different types of traveller. Travellers may choose a particular type of transport because of the level of services and facilities it offers, the level of comfort, how accessible it is and the impact on the environment.

Time

The duration of a journey may well be an important factor for some travellers in choosing which method of transport to use. Business travellers, for example, may be on a tight schedule, attending meetings and meeting clients. For these passengers, the quickest method of transport may be the most important factor, even if the cost is much higher. Leisure travellers may have much more time on their hands and be happy to take a slower method of transport, particularly if the costs are lower.

Table 9.1: Comparing different methods of transport

	Cost	Convenience	Time
Rail	Different fares available depending on the class of travel, the time of booking and the use of railcards.	Often frequent journeys from larger stations, but services from smaller stations may be less frequent and subject to changes. Range of on-board services and facilities.	Relatively quick way to travel depending on the number of station stops and any delays on the line.
Air	Lower fares often available for low-cost scheduled airlines, advance booking and amount of checked baggage.	Different airports offer different routes. Getting to, and from, the airport may be difficult from regional airports. Range of on-board services and facilities dependent on type of airline.	Fast travel but check-in time, security procedures, waiting for baggage and getting to and from the airport can add hours to total journey time.
Coach	Often very economical, with cheap fares booked in advance. Railcard discounts available.	Often services available from a local coach station, but may involve changes. Limited on-board services available.	Journeys can sometimes be slow and subject to traffic delays, particularly at peak times.
Car	Dependent on fuel prices, type of vehicle and contents of the car.	Maximum control for the driver. Door-to-door travel with limited on-board services such as radio, MP3 player. Motorway services offer additional facilities en-route.	Travel times variable, due to time of travel, traffic delays, road works and speed restrictions.

Activity: Compare and contrast

In small groups, use the Transport Direct website to plan a journey from London Heathrow Terminal 5 to central Manchester. Compare the different options presented for rail, coach and car. Make sure you compare:

- journey time
- cost
- CO_2 emissions.
- number of connections
- facilities and services

Based on your findings, discuss which method of transport you would choose and your reasons why.

BTEC **Assessment activity 9.1**　　　　　　　　　**P1** **M1**

You are working in the local Transport Office. Mrs Anderson would like to take her husband and two children (aged 10 and 12) on holiday to Newquay, in the second week of July for 7 nights. The Anderson family live in Leeds and have not yet decided how they will travel. They would like information on journeys from Leeds to Newquay by rail, coach, air and car.

1　You should carry out research in order to provide Mrs Anderson with a full breakdown for **each** journey option, to include:

- service provider
- journey times
- costs
- departure and arrival points
- details of changes and connections

Question 1 will enable you to achieve **P1**.

2　You should then present your findings to Mrs Anderson after comparing each option. You should provide advice on the advantages and disadvantages of each option.

Question 2 will enable you to achieve **M1**.

Grading tips

P1 Have you considered the cost discounts a family railcard would offer?

Remember to keep any research evidence you use throughout your research, such as print-outs, timetables and a list of websites used.

M1 Have you considered check-in times and the time it takes to travel to coach stations and airports in your recommendations to Mrs Anderson?

PLTS

When you carry out the assessment activity and complete this on time you will develop skills as a **self-manager**.

Functional skills

When you present your findings, you will develop skills in **English** – writing. When you cost the journey options you will develop skills in **Mathematics** – select and apply a range of skills to find solutions.

2 Different sources for selecting and costing holidays outside the UK

2.1 Different sources of holiday information

When planning a holiday overseas, there are many useful information sources that can be used to gain all the required information, such as paper-based tour operator brochures and websites. (Types of travel agent and tour operators are covered in more detail in *Unit 1: The UK travel and tourism sector*.)

Paper-based tour operator brochures

A visit to any local travel agent will find a range of traditional travel brochures from a variety of tour operators, all featuring comprehensive information on destinations, accommodation options, additional excursions and extras, as well as prices and supplements. The brochures are free and are attractively designed to promote the different destinations and services for specific types of customers.

Web-based travel retailers

While many tourists enjoy the services of an experienced travel agent to help them plan and book their next holiday, more and more people are choosing to book their holidays themselves by using the internet. The opportunity to explore different holiday options, compare prices and read on-line accommodation reviews are just some of the reasons why people often prefer to plan and book holidays independently.

Some tour operators do not publish travel brochures, or have high street shops, but offer all holiday information over the telephone or their website. Web-based travel retailers include Expedia, Opodo, Travelocity, eBookers and lastminute.com. (To obtain a secure link to these websites, see the Hotlinks section on p.x.)

These websites offer travellers the option to book transport, accommodation, excursions and travel insurance all from one site. This is often quite a simple process and provides one point of contact if there are any issues, problems or questions with the booking. Most websites also offer multiple discounts if more than one holiday component is booked at the same time.

Tour operator websites

As well as offering paper-based brochures and information, most large tour operators also have their own websites for those wishing to use the internet to plan and book their holidays. Examples of tour operators producing holiday brochures and offering direct website bookings include Thomson, Thomas Cook, First Choice, Olympic Holidays, Virgin Holidays and Titan Travel. (To obtain a secure link to these websites, see the Hotlinks section on p.x.)

On-line information can be easily updated and amended, but brochure information cannot and it is therefore very important that details such as prices, times and dates are always confirmed directly with the tour operator at the time of booking.

Websites for individual components

Some tourists, however, prefer to be completely independent, using a variety of different websites to separately book the best options for each component. This approach gives travellers the most flexibility in choosing options to meet their specific needs, but it can be more difficult to arrange and modify.

There are hundreds of independent websites offering different specific holiday components, such as accommodation or travel insurance. Other websites, such as those of low-cost scheduled airlines, provide travellers with the option of booking their hotel, transfers, car hire and insurance cover, direct from their own website. This allows the traveller to create their own **dynamic package** of holiday options to meet their particular needs and **budget**.

2.2 The customer brief

When planning holidays, it is important to understand the specific requirements of the customer. This is to ensure that all the holiday options meet customers' needs, as this will in turn lead to greater levels of customer satisfaction.

Travel agents have particular skills in understanding their customers' needs and often use a customer enquiry form to record all the necessary information. The benefits of meeting customer needs are explored in *Unit 5: Developing customer service skills in travel and tourism*.

Type of customer

Who is travelling? A family, a retired couple or a group of students might all choose very different holidays. Certain groups of customers may typically choose similar types of destination or types of holiday, for example a family with small children may wish to avoid a very lively and busy clubbing resort, such as Ayia Napa in Cyprus, although this may appeal to a group of students.

Party size

How many people are travelling? There may be discounts available for groups or families with children. Many package holidays are sold on a basis of four or six people sharing the accommodation.

Budget

What is the customer's budget? This is very important information in being able to match the most appropriate holiday options to the available budget. It is important to check if the budget price is per person or for the total trip, and whether any extras are expected to be included in that price.

Travel dates and duration

Are the dates fixed or flexible? There may be better value options if the customer can be flexible as to when they go. Many summer package deals are set for 7, 10 or 14 nights, although many other options and short-breaks will also be available.

> ## Key terms
>
> **Dynamic package** – mainly completed on-line, dynamic packaging is a term used to describe the process of tourists selecting different holiday components to create their own tailored holiday package. Unlike a traditional package holiday, the tourist has more control in selecting the different components that meet their specific needs and budgets.
>
> **Budget** – how much money the customers have available to spend.

Destination

Does the customer have a specific resort, destination or region in mind, or a particular type of holiday, for example beach, ski, city break or clubbing? Different destinations can be more popular at different times of the year, depending on, for example the weather, the season and the rate of currency exchange.

Travel requirements

Is the customer travelling by air, sea or rail? Would they like to fly from a regional airport? Smaller regional airports do not always fly to as many different destinations as larger ones, but can be very convenient.

Type of accommodation

Does the customer want a specific type of accommodation – hotel, apartment or villa? As well as the type of accommodation, there are often many different options for the type of room and meal basis. It is important to check whether accommodation is offered on a double, twin or family room basis. Sometimes holiday packages are sold with accommodation which is '**allocated-on-arrival**'.

- **All inclusive (AI)** – Your accommodation also includes all, or most, meals and drinks for the duration of you holiday. Always check the small print however, as some deals have restrictions.

- **Full-board (FB)** – This option includes your room, plus breakfast, lunch and evening meal.

- **Half-board (HB)** – This is the same as full-board, but without your lunch provided.

- **Bed and breakfast (B&B)** – This provides you with a room plus a continental, or full-cooked, breakfast.

- **Self-catering (SC)** – No meals are included with this option, but your accommodation includes a kitchen and a dining area, so you can cook and eat your own meals.

- **Room only (RO)** – This is just a standard bedroom without meals or cooking facilities.

Key term

Allocated-on-arrival – a term used by tour operators where customers are given details of their accommodation, and sometimes holiday resort, only on arrival in the holiday destination. These deals are then often offered at a discount to customers and allows tour operators to be more flexible and to maximise their bookings.

A typical self-catering apartment

Extras

As well as the standard holiday components of transport and accommodation, customers may also wish to book extras, or upgrade their holiday booking, for an additional **supplement** or extra charge.

- **Room with a view** – Hotels may charge an additional supplement for their rooms with the very best sea or mountain views.

- **Regional flights** – Depending on the destination, a connecting regional flight may be available to a larger international airport.

- **Superior rooms** – Bigger beds, better views and more facilities may be an option for customers happy to pay for a superior room upgrade.

- **Meals** – Customers may wish to upgrade their meal basis to a half- or full-board option. Many charter airlines do not include an in-flight meal as standard and this may often be added as an additional extra.

- **Priority and premium upgrades** – For those customers who don't like waiting in line, priority check-in and boarding upgrades are sometimes available. Those requiring extra legroom can often upgrade to premium seats.

- **Additional luggage allowance** – With tight restrictions on the maximum weight of luggage allowed per person, some operators offer passengers upgrade packages with an additional luggage allowance.

Key term

Supplement – an additional charge on the standard price of a holiday booking which takes into account any additional upgrades or extras. A supplement may also be applied to cover any fees lost on the price of a standard booking, such as a single person travelling alone staying in a room for two people.

Other ancillary products and services

Customers may also wish to book a range of other services and holiday options to complete their total holiday package. These might include:

- insurance
- transfers
- car hire
- car parking
- airport hotels
- access to airport lounges
- tours and excursions
- tickets for theatre shows and attractions
- pet sitting and kennel services.

Most travel agents are able to add these ancillary products and services to the main booking. There are often incentives and commissions available for travel consultants who are able to sell these additions to holidaymakers. For customers making independent holiday bookings, most large tour operators' websites also offer a range of additional products and services, often at discounted rates. There are also a number of specialist websites which offer independent travellers holiday extras, such as holidayextras, skiholidayextras, dosomethingdifferent and mytravelextras. (To obtain a secure link to these websites, see the Hotlinks section on p.x.)

2.3 Select and cost a package holiday using a brochure

With so many different elements, planning and booking a package holiday to meet the specific needs of customers can be quite a complex process. Whether using a traditional printed brochure, a tour operator's website or a variety of different websites for independent travel companies, you must be careful to select the holiday elements that meet the customer's requirements.

The tour operator's brochure provides lots of information for holidaymakers planning their next trip. Brochures usually feature details about destinations and resorts, types of accommodation, places to go and things to do, average temperatures and details about kids clubs and children's activities.

Brochures also feature pricing information so you can work out the approximate cost of your holiday, depending on your group size, accommodation choice, departure date and meal basis. Planning holidays using a brochure can be a little complicated and you must be careful to include any supplements or discounts which may be applied.

- **Under-occupancy supplement** – when the number of adults sharing is less than the standard room occupancy basis.

- **Over-occupancy reduction** – when the number of adults sharing is more than the standard room occupancy basis.

- **Flight supplements** – depending on the departure airport, the time and date of the flight chosen and the level of services on-board.

- **Adding holiday extras** – additional supplements, or discounts, may apply for sea or mountain views, superior rooms or changes to the standard meal basis.

- **Child and group discounts** – special deals may apply, depending on the time of booking and the number of people in the party, for example free child places or one free place in every ten for larger groups.

- **Taxes** – a range of taxes may affect the final price of a holiday, including air passenger duty, security and fuel taxes.

Functional skills

Calculating costs will help you to improve your functional skills in mathematics.

2.4 Select and cost a package holiday using a web-based travel company

Using the website of an on-line travel company can often be easier than using a brochure, as all the calculations are made for you, any supplements and discounts should be automatically applied, and availability is often right up-to-date. Be sure to double-check all the essential holiday details you enter, such as passenger names, holiday dates and duration of stay.

2.5 Independently select and cost a package holiday

This is often the most flexible option for booking a holiday. By creating your own package of individual holiday elements, you can choose products and services that meet all your customer's needs. There can be price savings to be had too, by carefully comparing different companies and the level of services and facilities each one offers. This option needs some very careful planning, however, to make sure you are able to book your chosen flight, accommodation, transfers and extras.

PLTS

Putting together an itinerary for an overseas holiday for a customer, will help to develop your skills as an **independent enquirer** and **creative thinker.**

BTEC **Assessment activity 9.2**   P2 P3 P4 M2 D1

Customer Information Form

Customer Details

Party name:	Elliott Family	Contact number:	0161 199255
Party size:	3	Adults	2
Budget	£1000 in total	Children	1 (aged 6)

Travel Details

Preferred destination:	Cyprus	Departure date:	20 – Jul
Departure point:	Manchester	Duration:	7 nights

Accommodation Details

Room type:	Apartment / Family room	Preferred meal basis:	Self-catering
Special requests:	Sea view room, with air conditioning		

Specific Needs:

Lively		Swimming pool	✔	Excursions	✔	Nightlife	
Quiet		Car hire	✔	Beach	✔	Kids Club	✔

Other:
Hire of small car for three days
Require insurance

What would the customer like to see and do on their holiday?

Relax
Visit the beach
Go on a few family excursions – zoos or water park
Travel round the resort by hire-car

You are required to select and cost a holiday that will meet the Elliott family's requirements. You should select suitable accommodation and transport options and plan the holiday in three different ways:

1   Using holiday brochures provide a full written breakdown of your selected package holiday. You must show your calculations and mark the relevant brochure pages.

Question 1 will enable you to achieve **P2**.

2   Using two web-based travel organisers provide a full written breakdown of the selected package holidays. You should include print-outs to show the costs and holiday components from both websites. You should select the holiday option which best meets the needs of the Elliott family.

Question 2 will enable you to achieve **P3**.

3   Using the internet to book each component independently you should provide a full written breakdown on the selected holiday and calculate the total price. You should include print-outs to show each of your holiday components and the websites used.

Question 3 will enable you to achieve **P4**.

4   You should continue by justifying to the Elliott family how the holidays you have selected meet their needs.

Question 4 will enable you to achieve **M2**.

5   Finally, you should evaluate each of the three different methods of holiday planning, assessing the positive and negative aspects of each method.

Question 5 will enable you to achieve **D1**.

Grading tips

P2 You need to apply at least one supplement and add at least one ancillary product or service

M2 P3 P4 Remember to keep your research evidence, such as print-outs, brochures, list of websites used to help you justify your selections

D1 When considering the advantages and disadvantages of each method, think about:

*   how accurate the information was?
*   which was the easiest to use?
*   did each method take the same amount of time?

3 Information and advice for customers travelling to an overseas holiday destination

As well as being able to plan and book all the necessary holiday options, being able to provide customers with appropriate travel information and advice is also very important. Travellers often need specific information and advice before they travel, including:

- travel and accommodation documentation
- travel health, insurance and vaccination information
- holiday money and currency
- other information, such as how to stay in touch with friends and family in the UK.

3.1 Pre-holiday information and advice

Travel and accommodation documentation

At one time, all holidaymakers received their travel tickets from a travel agent or collected them at the airport. Today, more and more people are using electronic bookings (e-tickets) or mobile bookings (m-tickets) for their travel requirements, particularly if booking over the telephone or internet.

E-tickets are really only reference numbers that the holiday company allocates to their customers in order to track their booking. All of the personal information and holiday details are stored on computer reservation systems. M-tickets are stored on your mobile phone and also record the required booking reference numbers in order to find your booking details. When booking on the internet, confirmation of the booking together with booking details and the reference number is available to download or print out. Confirmation is also sent to the customer's email address. In some cases, such as hotel bookings and car hire, a voucher is provided and this is either printed out from the website or sent to the customer's email address. These vouchers must be presented on arrival at the hotel or car hire desk.

Customers should be advised to carry relevant photographic identification when travelling. For most places, a valid photocard driving licence or passport are the only acceptable forms of identification. A passport is generally required when travelling outside the UK. These are available in advance from the Identity and Passport Service. (To obtain a secure link to these websites, see the Hotlinks section on p.x.).

Did you know?

Since April 2007, UK adults requiring their first passport now need to have an interview before a passport can be issued. The Identity and Passport Service has set up a network of Passport Interview Offices across the country. The 30-minute interview is designed to stop identity fraud.

Health, insurance and vaccination information

It is highly recommended, and often a condition of travel, that holidaymakers have appropriate travel insurance to cover them in the event of an accident, incident, or in some cases death, while overseas. The cost of medical care when abroad can be very expensive and most travel insurance will provide cover to travellers in the event of:

- medical emergencies and accidents
- loss of baggage
- personal liability
- cancelled or delayed travel
- loss or theft of passport, personal money and possessions.

Other insurance policies can also provide protection for those taking part in sports.

Vaccinations and preventative medicines are often required for travellers going to destinations further afield, particularly tropical countries. Holiday vaccinations are often available from your local GP surgery or health clinic, where a charge is normally made. Customers booking holidays to certain destinations should be given information and advice on possible vaccinations they may need before travelling.

Vaccinations and preventative medicines given before travel to some destinations could include:

- Malaria
- Typhoid
- Hepatitis A
- Hepatitis B
- Diphtheria

- Tuberculosis
- Rabies
- Cholera
- Yellow fever

For more information, check out the travel health section of the Foreign and Commonwealth website. To obtain a secure link to the FCO website, see the Hotlinks section on p.x.

Did you know?

- Under The Package Travel, Package Holidays and Package Tours Regulations 1992, it is a legal requirement for holiday organisers to provide customers with information on passport, visa and health information.

- Malaria is a potentially deadly tropical disease that is caused by a parasite and is often spread by mosquitoes. Malaria can cause serious medical problems and sometimes death. Around 1500 people each year return to the UK with malaria, and of these, an average of 12 will die. Malaria can be prevented by taking medicines before and during travel to tropical countries and by using mosquito nets, sprays and creams.

Protect yourself – why should a traveller take necessary precautions to protect against mosquito bites?

Case study: European Health Insurance Card

The European Health Insurance Card (EHIC) allows you access to the same state-provided healthcare as a resident of the country you are visiting in all European Economic Area (EEA) countries, and Switzerland, at a reduced cost or sometimes free of charge.

All UK residents are advised to carry a valid EHIC card when travelling abroad. Cards are free and valid for up to five years. The EHIC is not an alternative to travel insurance and will not cover any private medical healthcare, lost and stolen property or delays to travel. (To obtain a secure link to the EHIC website, see the Hotlinks section on p.x.)

Holiday money and currency

Customers planning and booking their holidays may well need information about the local currency and currency exchange rates. Many travel agencies also have currency exchange bureaux in their high street branches.

Tourists may choose to take foreign currency, traveller's cheques, a pre-paid currency card, or a combination on their holiday abroad. Traveller's cheques provide greater security if lost or stolen, but require tourists to carry identification when using them to pay for goods or exchanging them for local currency. Pre-paid currency cards are becoming more popular and work like a cash card at ATMs. They can be quickly replaced if lost or stolen, but they do charge a fee for each withdrawal.

Standard debit and credit cards are also generally accepted for buying goods and services overseas, but most also charge the user a fee with each transaction. These fees can soon mount up and be an additional cost to your holiday. Most banks and credit card companies closely monitor card transactions in foreign countries to prevent fraud and it is often a good idea to let your bank know that you will be using your card abroad.

Staying in touch back home

Holiday customers may also require information on how to stay in touch with friends and family back home in the UK. International phone cards, available from many hotels and newsagents, are often a convenient and cost-effective way to make telephone calls back home.

Mobile phone users are charged 'roaming fees' when using their phones abroad. These are fees charged to make and receive calls and text messages. Different operators in different countries often charge different rates for mobile phone services and it is often advisable to check on these before travelling.

Other information

Travellers may also appreciate other information relating to their holiday destination such as:

- the local weather conditions and average temperatures
- electrical voltage and information on appliance adapters
- information regarding local customs, traditions and religions
- advice on **carbon-offsetting** and being a responsible traveller.

3.2 Travel information

As well as general information about travelling overseas, customers, planning and booking their holidays, will also need to be aware of more specific terms and conditions relating to their holiday, the holiday company and transport provider. These booking agreements can

Key terms

Roaming fees – when you travel your mobile phone keeps working while you are roaming. You can make and receive mobile phone calls, write text messages (SMS) and access the internet on some phones even while abroad. The foreign network operator charges your home operator and this additional cost is passed on to you. When roaming in Europe, there are now regulations which limit the charges that operators can charge. To obtain a secure link to the European Union website, where more information can be accessed, see the Hotlinks section on p.x.

Carbon-offsetting – even one flight can produce lots of carbon dioxide, which can be harmful to the environment. Many travellers are now looking at ways to reduce this negative effect by contributing to schemes which have a positive effect on the environment and reduce carbon emissions, such as using renewable energy sources, tree planting and providing education about climate change. 'Reduce My Footprint' (to obtain a secure link to the website, see the Hotlinks section on p.x.) is a carbon reduction programme set up by ABTA – The Travel Association with the Association of Independent Tour Operators (AITO).

often be found at the back of holiday brochures, or on the terms and conditions pages of travel websites. Often referred to as 'the small-print', it is essential that these terms and conditions are followed and understood in order for holiday plans to run smoothly and without complications.

Common terms and conditions often refer to:

- the holiday booking contract and agreement
- accuracy of information featured in the brochure and online
- price of the holiday package and surcharges
- changes to your booking and booking cancellations
- travel insurance and documentation
- conditions of carriage, baggage allowances, delays and cancellations
- accommodation conditions
- how to make a complaint.

Amendment and cancellation policy

The booking terms and conditions of a package holiday will outline what happens if the customer, or the holiday company, need to make any amendments to the booking or to cancel the holiday altogether. If the customer needs to change any of the details of the booking, such as the names of passengers travelling, the time, date of departure and the destination airport, they may be charged an amendment fee.

If the customer needs to cancel the booking, they will almost certainly be charged a cancellation fee. This fee is usually a percentage of the total booking price and will often increase the closer it is to the departure date. Many bookings cancelled with less than 7 days notice will lose the total amount paid. Customers with comprehensive travel insurance may be able to claim some of this money back, depending on the circumstances.

If the tour operator has to make any changes to a booking, such as a change to the accommodation, holiday destination or departure airport, they may pay compensation to each passenger. Details of the specific terms and conditions and compensation available will be found in the small-print at the back of holiday brochures, or on the internet.

For independent travellers, who have booked the different components of their holiday separately, there may well be different terms and conditions relating to the flight, the accommodation and any other services they have booked. Low-cost scheduled airlines often have very strict amendment and cancellation policies, making a significant charge if passengers need to change any details of the booking, for example the names of the passengers. Most low-cost scheduled airline tickets are non-refundable. Full-service scheduled airlines will often have a range of conditions relating to the amendment and cancellation of tickets depending on the type of ticket purchased.

Case study: Ryanair – terms and conditions

Ryanair provide travellers with flights, often at incredibly low prices. They also have a range of terms and conditions that apply to flight bookings, which include flight and name changes. Flight dates, times and routes are changeable (subject to seat availability). If booked online the change rate of £25/€25 per one-way flight/per person applies.

In addition to these flight change fees, any price difference between the original total price paid and the lowest total price available at the time of the flight change is charged. If the total price on the new flight is lower, no refund will be made. A passenger name can be changed on-line at the rate of £100/€100.

Source: Ryan Air November 2009

1 **What impact do you think the amendment terms and conditions have on passengers?**

2 **Do you think that the amendment fees charged are reasonable? Explain your response.**

Activity: The small–print

Working in pairs, use two holiday brochures, from two different tour operators, to compare and contrast the terms and conditions for customers who need to make an amendment to the details of their booking. Are the fees the same or different? Would different terms and conditions affect who you made a holiday booking with in the future?

The Moss Family have booked a two-week holiday to Portugal, costing £1400. Due to personal circumstances, they now need to cancel their holiday, 30 days before departure.

Using the two different operators identified earlier calculate the cancellation charge they would impose and how much the Moss Family would be refunded.

Functional skills

Calculating costs will help you to improve your functional skills in mathematics.

Hotels also have terms and conditions relating to the booking of their rooms. Many hotel rooms are able to be cancelled up to a certain time on the day of arrival, for example 2 p.m., although other terms and conditions can apply, particularly if the room was booked in advance at a discounted rate. Holiday planners should always check the small-print at the time of booking.

Checking-in

Most tour operators and airlines publish specific instructions regarding the check-in procedure for their flights. This is to ensure there is enough time to process the security and baggage checks necessary before take-off. Many airlines are now offering online check-in, and priority check-in services, to reduce the long queues often found at airports in the busy summer season.

Restricted items

What is and isn't permitted, on-board the aircraft is an essential piece of travel information. Different rules apply for **hand-** and **hold-luggage**.

What cannot be taken as hand-luggage?

- Toy or replica guns and catapults.
- Razor blades, Swiss Army knives, pen knives and knives with blades of any length.

Key term

Hand- and hold-luggage – hand-luggage are items that are allowed in the cabin of the aircraft with the passenger. This is usually limited to one small bag containing personal items required throughout the flight. Hold-baggage is checked-in luggage and is stored in the hold of the aircraft. Specific conditions apply to the maximum size and weight of hold-baggage, often with specific variations for each airline.

- Scissors (with blades more than 6 cm), corkscrews and metal cutlery (except teaspoons).

- Hypodermic syringes (except for medical use).

- Darts or knitting needles.

- Sporting bats and billiard, snooker or pool cues.

- Tradesmen's tools (such as hammers, screwdrivers, drills).

- Any liquids in quantities greater than 100 ml, including:

  - all drinks, including water, soups and syrups

  - perfumes, lotions, oils and mascara

  - pressurised containers, including shaving foam and spray deodorant

  - pastes, including toothpastes

  - hair and shower gels

  - lip gloss

  - any other solutions and items of similar consistency.

There are also special rules regarding baby food, medicines and the storage of liquids. All passengers should be advised to check the latest information before travel.

Prohibited items

Prohibited items are those which are not allow on any aircraft. These are restricted under section four of the Aviation Security Act 1982, which prevents passengers from taking guns, firearms and weapons, explosives, flammable substances, chemical and toxic substances and any other items that can cause injury or damage to themselves and other passengers.

Rules and regulations regarding hand-luggage can be complicated

Baggage allowances

Different airlines will often have different restrictions and allowances on the size, weight and number of bags that passengers are allowed to take on-board. When planning and booking holidays, this is an important piece of information to pass on to customers so they can pack their luggage appropriately.

The Department for Transport has set the maximum size for an item of hand-baggage as 56 cm × 45 cm × 25 cm. However, some airlines may only allow smaller bags, so it is always advisable to check with individual airlines. Most airlines will charge an additional supplement for hold-baggage that is heavier than the allocated amount per passenger. Some budget airlines can charge large additional fees for any checked-in baggage.

Activity: Baggage allowances

Working in pairs, use the internet to identify the hand- and hold-luggage allowances for each of the airlines listed below. Make a note of any restrictions relating to size, weight and number of bags allowed. Also compare the charges for excess baggage.

- Ryanair
- British Airways
- Thomas Cook Airlines

BTEC Assessment activity 9.3 P5

Following on from assessment activity 9.2, the Elliott family have now booked their holiday to Cyprus based on the information you provided from holiday brochures. It is now your role to provide them with the essential information that will help their holiday planning. You need to advise them on:

- travel documentation
- insurance requirements
- travel health advice
- currency needed

- details of check-in times, restricted goods and baggage allowance
- amendment and cancellation policy.

In a role-play, you should carefully explain the information to the family and ensure they have understood the terms and conditions of the booking. You should use the holiday brochures you used in assessment activity 9.2 to help you. You should also answer any questions they have.

Grading tip

P5 Highlight the specific terms and conditions you need from the small-print section of the holiday brochure, or from a website print-out, to help you confirm the right details. You should also submit a comprehensive observation sheet completed by your tutor, which outlines how you met the criteria through your role-play.

I have been working as a Travel Advisor for just over a year now. I work in a high street travel agency and help customers to plan and book their holidays. My role is often very busy, particularly on Saturdays which is one of my busiest days.

My main duties are to sell a range of holiday products to our customers, including the standard package holiday, but also a range of optional extras including travel insurance, car hire and excursions.

Typical day

When the customer first comes into the shop, I try and make a note of all their details and needs so I can find holiday products that they will like. Some customers have no idea where they want to go, but have a fixed price, while others will have a good idea about the type of holiday they would like, but want advice on a particular resort or destination. A lot of customers think we just sell holidays so it's good to be able to offer them other products and services which they might need.

The best thing about the job

It's great to work in a team. Everyone in the office is really friendly and we often socialise outside work too. I love travelling and this job gives me some great discounts on holidays and free travel insurance too. As well as my basic salary, I also earn commission if I meet and exceed my sales targets.

As I work for a large chain of travel shops, there are lots of opportunities to try different roles and move up the organisation. I'm looking forward to working in the Foreign Currency Exchange Bureau soon and after I get more experience I would like to manage my very own branch.

Think about it!

1 Using the internet, research Travel Advisor positions for the main UK tour operators in a high street travel agency. Make a list of the starting salary and the additional benefits of the role.

2 Consider making a visit to your local travel agency and observe how Travel Advisors interact with the customers. What do you think are the key personal qualities that advisors should have?

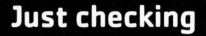

Just checking

1. What is the main ATOC-run UK website and telephone service used for planning rail journeys?
2. What is a 'low-cost scheduled' airline?
3. Identify two websites useful for planning a car journey.
4. Describe one advantage of using a paper-based timetable rather than the internet for planning a journey on public transport.
5. List three reasons an additional supplement may be added to the cost of a holiday package.
6. Explain the term 'allocation-on arrival'.
7. If a meal basis was described as 'FB' what would this mean?
8. List four items which are not permitted in hand-luggage on-board an aircraft.
9. Explain why travel insurance is needed even if a passenger is carrying a European Health Insurance Card.
10. What advice would you give to tourists travelling to a tropical country?

Assignment tips

- The two largest UK tour operators have websites with further information about holiday bookings, products and services available, terms and conditions and careers. Visit the Thomson and Thomas Cook websites. (To obtain a secure link to these websites, see the Hotlinks section on p.x.)

- Information on restricted and prohibited items on flights may often change. (To explore the latest information from the UK government from a secure website, see the Hotlinks section on p.x.)

- The internet might be a quick way to plan journeys and book holidays, but consider the disadvantages and limitations that the internet might have, particularly for different customer types such as retired people and those with specific needs.

10 E... tourism

Marketing is an essential activity for a modern travel and tourism organisation to compete in this highly competitive sector. This unit is designed to help you explore the principles of marketing and how organisations use them to communicate in order to attract and retain customers.

You will also explore how different organisations develop different products and services to meet the needs of different customers and how they communicate about these products to the customers.

You will need to develop your market research skills and learn how to design, carry out and evaluate market research material. You will need to understand how market research is needed in developing new products and services.

Finally, you will use your own creative talents to develop promotional materials for a suitable travel and tourism organisation to promote a product or service for a specific target market.

Learning outcomes

After completing this unit you should:

1 understand the principles of marketing in the travel and tourism sector

2 know how travel and tourism organisations provide a range of products and services to meet the needs of different types of customer

3 be able to design and use market research to meet specific objectives

4 be able to produce promotional material suitable for use in travel and tourism.

To achieve a **pass** grade the evidence must show that you are able to:	To achieve a **merit** grade the evidence must show that, in addition to the pass criteria, you are able to:	To achieve a **distinction** grade the evidence must show that, in addition to the pass and merit criteria, you are able to:
P1 explain the principles of marketing used by travel and tourism organisations to meet marketing objectives **Assessment activity 10.1, page 301**	**M1** review how the principles of marketing are used by selected travel and tourism organisations to meet marketing objectives **Assessment activity 10.1, page 301**	
P2 describe how the products and services of one travel and tourism organisation are provided to meet the needs of different types of customer **Assessment activity 10.1, page 301**		
P3 use secondary research to meet specific objectives **Assessment activity 10.2, page 308** **P4** design, use and evaluate primary market research in a travel and tourism context to meet specific objectives **Assessment activity 10.2, page 308**	**M2** explain the appropriateness of the primary market research in relation to the specific objectives **Assessment activity 10.2, page 308**	**D1** draw conclusions from the results of primary market research and make recommendations based on the conclusions **Assessment activity 10.2, page 308**
P5 produce a piece of promotional material to meet specific objectives in a travel and tourism context, justifying the choice and design **Assessment activity 10.3, page 316**	**M3** Show creativity and originality in the choice and design of a piece of promotional material, explaining how it meets objectives **Assessment activity 10.3, page 316**	**D2** critically assess how the promotional material attracts the target audience using AIDA, making recommendations for improvement **Assessment activity 10.3, page 316**

Ali, 16–year-old learner

I finished my BTEC First Diploma in Travel and Tourism last year. To start with, I found the language of the marketing unit a little confusing as there is a lot of jargon. When I got my head around this I really enjoyed the work.

In my college we did a lot of the work for the marketing unit when we were organising a study visit (for Unit 13). I did my secondary research when finding out what attractions were available in London and I also did research on who the attractions were aimed at, their location in London, cost of entry and how long we would be there.

For my primary research I did a survey using the information I found from my secondary research to help me decide where we should go. For my promotional material I put together a leaflet promoting the trip to London.

We ended up going to the London Dungeons and had a great time. My tutor got picked on by the actors at the dungeons and put in a torture chair. Then we caught a tube to Covent Garden for lunch. One of my friends had researched restaurants and prices and decided on the best choice.

I really enjoyed the unit in the end, as I could see where everything was going and how the marketing fitted into a project. This unit has given me so much more than I ever thought and I now have a good understanding of how marketing and promotion work.

Over to you

- Make a list of all the different types of promotion you can think of.

- Which type of promotion attracts your attention and why?

- Design a piece of promotional material of the type you find most attractive, promoting a local visitor attraction.

1 The principles of marketing in the travel and tourism sector

Set off

What is marketing?

In a group, think about what marketing means to you. Write all the ideas you come up with on a big piece of paper. Stick the paper on the classroom wall where you can look at it from time to time as you study this unit and see how many of your ideas are covered.

1.1 Principles of marketing in the travel and tourism sector

Definition of marketing

Marketing is a complex management tool, which the Concise Oxford Dictionary defines as 'The action or business of promoting and selling products and services'.

Marketing is totally focused on the customers' needs and could be easily described as providing:

- the right product
- at the right price
- in the right place
- with the right promotion
- at the right time.

As you can see, these are all directed at the customers' needs and wants.

The marketing mix

The **marketing mix** is sometimes known as the 4 Ps: Product, Place, Price and Promotion. The marketing mix makes up the full package that you are selling to the customer. If any one of these parts is not well developed, the product may be unsuccessful. After all, there is no point in offering the most suitable holiday in the world, at the lowest price possible, available just around the corner, if the customer does not know about it!

Key term

Marketing mix – the mix of product, place, price and promotion which is sold to the customer.

Product

The travel **product** or **service** that you are providing can change from customer to customer depending on their requirements. Different hotels or classes of airline seat will give a different experience and, in turn, a different product.

An organisation must understand its product, its features and benefits, and also its product's **unique selling point** (USP). In other words, how it is different from competitors' products. This could be something as simple as offering easier booking facilities. Products will require alteration, adaptation or even replacement in time as the customers' needs and tastes change.

Another important part of the product is the brand, that is the name of the product, or of the company producing or selling it, for example TUI, a large travel and tourism organisation, who are made up of brands such as Thomson, First Class Holidays and Late Rooms.com. Organisations spend a large amount of time and money developing brands. For some consumers, these brands symbolise status as well as the product itself.

Place

"Place" is about the distribution point of your product, not the holiday destination. It is the location where the customer goes to buy the product or service. For example, you would not just pop over to the Caribbean to buy your summer holiday; you would be more likely to book it through a local travel agent, over the internet, or on the telephone.

Price

Price refers to the amount that is charged for the product and includes discounts. Travel is a very price-sensitive marketplace, particularly with last-minute deals. Budget airlines compete on price for flights and some package holidays are sold almost solely on the price.

The lowest price you can charge for a product is the cost price – the price it costs to produce the product or service. The highest price you can charge is dictated by what the customer is willing to pay.

Promotion

Promotion is any activity that is designed to put across a positive image of the organisation or individual. In other words, any interaction with the public or media could be counted as a form of promotion. In fact, word of mouth (where people recommend a company) is one of the most influential forms of promotion.

Key terms

Product – the physical item a customer buys.

Service – the non-physical elements of the item a customer buys.

Unique selling point – how a product differs from competitors' products

Activity: Unique selling point

Consider the USP for each of the following brands:

- easyJet
- British Airways
- National Express
- Club 18-30
- Thomas Cook.

Look at their websites. Now compare what you thought with one of your friends. Do you both see the brands as the same?

Activity: Which market segment?

Go to your local travel agency and collect a holiday brochure. Pick a holiday from the brochure.

Look at the information and try and work out who the holiday is aimed at. How do you know which market segment it is aimed at? What has the organisation done to meet the needs of this market segment?

Example:

A Club 18-30 holiday is aimed at people aged 18-30, as the name suggests, and there are lots of organised fun activities targeted specifically at this age group, such as clubbing.

Key terms

Target marketing – creating products that are aimed (or targeted) at different groups of people.

Market segment – a group of customers with similar needs and wants

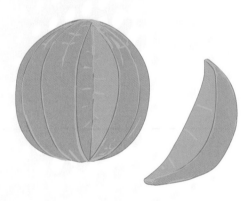

Figure 10.1 How is the travel market like an orange?

Target marketing

Not every product is going to appeal to everyone. If there was just one summer holiday that suited everyone, travel agents would only have to stock one summer holiday to sell. However, every customer has slightly different needs and expectations and these are addressed through **target marketing**. For example, the holiday requirements of a group of four 18-year-old males looking for their first holiday away from home without their parents, will be different from those of a couple who have just retired and are looking for a once-in-a-lifetime experience.

Market segmentation

A **market segment** is a group of customers with similar needs and wants. Imagine the travel market is like an orange and that the different groups are its segments. The more specific you make each segment, the smaller the segment becomes. For example, package family holidays form a large segment of the market, but you can break these down further to divide the market into smaller segments (e.g. package family holidays to Spain).

The market can also be split between business and leisure travel. Many travel agents and tour operators specialise in one area or the other; for example ETS Travel specialise in business travel, whereas Thomas Cook specialise in holidays. To obtain a secure link to ETS Travel and Thomas Cook, see the Hotlinks section on p.x.

Producing a unique travel and tourism product for each individual customer would make holidays too expensive for the average person, so, travel and tourism organisations create products that will appeal to large groups of people. Customers are grouped into segments and the organisation tailors their product around them. Common approaches to market segmentation include the following.

Demographic segmentation is where the market is divided according to a number of variables, such as age, gender, social class, income, lifestyle and race. Some of these will be discussed in the next section.

Socio-economic segmentation is more complex. It segments a market by salary or social class. Combining income and background is also a very useful method of segmentation. Socio-economic segmentation is about dividing people into groups with similar wants and needs.

Geographic segmentation divides the intended audience for a particular product according to where they live or work. There are regional and national variations when selling a product or service to a particular customer group; for example, in England hot chocolate is considered a calming night time drink, but in France it is a breakfast drink.

Segmentation by behaviour relates to how a person or family live their lives. This method is more complex and can be expensive to collect the data and analyse the results, but can give more information about the expectations and needs of the customers.

1.2 Marketing objectives

Marketing objectives are developed from an organisation's mission statement (see Unit 2, page 44). The mission statement outlines the specific area that an organisation wishes to address and what it wants to achieve in that area. For example, a company's mission statement might be:

- to be the number one choice for long haul passengers

- to offer customers a unique, relaxing travel experience

- to offer customers a complete travel experience

- to ensure the continued development of staff

To achieve their mission statement, the organisation develops a number of objectives. Below are examples of the marketing objectives an organisation could have.

Raise awareness

It is important for consumers to be aware of your products and services so that when they are deciding to choose a holiday they will associate your organisation with that purchase. Virgin Atlantic Airways' 25th Anniversary advertisement is a good example of this sort of awareness raising. To obtain a secure link to this website, see the Hotlinks section on p.x.

Increase market share

Market share is important for organisations, as a larger market share represents a larger number of sales and, in turn, larger profits. For example, the Thomson "Welcome to my world" advertisement shown from the beginning of 2010 is designed to increase their market share of the summer sun package holiday market. To obtain a secure link this website, see the Hotlinks section on p.x.

Increase profits

Most travel and tourism organisations require profits to pay their shareholders and owners. At Thorpe Park (a large theme park in Surrey owned by Merlin Entertainment) there are advertisements encouraging customers to buy a Merlin season pass. This is to increase the customer spend on ticket sales and to encourage them to return more often. Customers are also encouraged to secondary spend on food, drink etc.

Challenge competitors

If a competitor opens a new branch close to your location, or begins a new advertising campaign, it is likely they are trying to attract your existing customers or those you are trying to attract. This may lead you to increase your own promotional activities to retain and attract customers.

Introduce new products

Customers need to be aware of new products on the market. Promotion is one method of informing a large number of customers about these new products. When the low-cost airlines started trading in the 1990s, easyJet, Ryanair and bmibaby all carried out poster campaigns explaining how cheap their tickets were.

Inform product development

Product developments need to be publicised, just as new products do. This is particularly important if an organisation would like current users to upgrade; for example, Warner Holidays advertise that their hotels are child-free for adults who want a quiet stay.

Target new customers

Marketing activities can help you focus on the customers that your product appeals to and help you communicate your product to them. In the summer and autumn of 2009, Visit Yorkshire sponsored television programmes nationwide trying to encourage a younger age group to visit the area. It is worth noting that tourism to the North East of England increased by 25% in the summer of 2009.

Think about it

When watching television, do you notice clusters of advertisements for similar products, or from different companies in the same field?

Retain existing customers

Customer needs and expectations develop over time and these changes need to be catered for. Many long-haul airlines have started to provide better sleeping conditions in business class cabins as they have identified a desire among business travellers for better sleeping arrangements.

Branding

The branding is the name, logo or image that is associated with your product. The brand is the image that the consumer identifies with. For example, the brands of clothes that you choose to wear reflect on the way you choose to be identified.

Case study: National Trust for ever, for everyone

"The National Trust is a charity and is completely independent of government.

We have over 3.6 million members and 55,000 volunteers. More than 14 million people visit our pay for entry properties, while an estimated 50 million visit our open air properties.

We protect and open to the public over 350 historic houses, gardens and ancient monuments.

But it doesn't stop there. We also look after forests, woods, fens, beaches, farmland, downs, moorland, islands, archaeological remains, castles, nature reserves, villages – for ever, for everyone."

Source: The National Trust

How does the National Trust communicate what they do through their logo and strapline?

2 Products and services for meeting the needs of different types of customers

2.1 Types of customer

The whole of the travel and tourism market is segmented into different groups so that products can be provided to meet these different groups' needs. As you've seen earlier, there are many different methods that you can use to segment a market.

By segment

Socio-economic groups

You can segment society according to employment status and income. The Office for National Statistics (ONS) has identified eight classifications, from higher management to never worked and long-term unemployed.

Although the groups are graded 1–8, it does not mean group 1 is better than group 8, just that they have a different employment. However, it is reasonable to say that groups 1 and 2 could have similar needs and wants.

Specific age groups

Another way of segmenting the market is by age. This is used in package holidays, with companies producing packages for different age groups. Saga Holidays, for example, specialise in holidays for the over-50s, whereas Club 18–30 produces a completely different type of holiday targeted at 18–30-year-olds. This segmentation works well for these products, but age is a very broad way of segmenting a market. After all, not all 18–30-year-olds are the same, or have similar needs.

Lifestyle and family circumstances

Segmenting by lifestyle and family circumstances examines how you live your life. Your personal needs will change as you go through the stages of the family life cycle. At each stage of the life cycle a person's income and responsibilities change and each change is significant because it will affect the individual's needs and therefore what product they will buy.

Table 10.1: Stages of life

Stage	Comments
Bachelor	Young and single with limited or no family responsibility
Newly married	Young and married with no children
Full nest 1	Family with youngest child under school age
Full nest 2	Family with youngest child of school age
Full nest 3	Children are still at home but are now working
Empty nest 1	One partner working and children have left home
Empty nest 2	Both partners are now retired
Solitary survivor 1	One partner left who is still working
Solitary survivor 2	One partner left who is retired

Lifestyle segmentation is slightly more complicated than segmenting by employment and income or age. Most organisations set their own segments and names for lifestyle division; for example 'the Baked Bean family' has a low household income and usually more than one child. Although this is a low spending-power segment, it is also a large segment, so various products are targeted towards it (e.g. holiday camps and package holidays). The segment is very price-sensitive, but also has child provision needs such as 'kids' clubs'.

Groups

Groups are considered separately as they tend to have a large number of customers, making it possible to produce a product tailored to their needs. Groups could include clubs, schools, colleges and other organisations. Kuoni (the tour operator) has a department that specialises in producing tailor-made trips for these groups, which includes organising sports tours, etc.

Ethnic groups

Although segmenting by ethnicity might seem a good idea, it can create some issues. People of the same ethnic group do not necessarily share the same needs and wants. However, there are organisations that segment their market on ethnic grounds. There are also some cultural-based holidays, which have more appeal to one ethnic group than another. For example, tours around 'Bollywood' locations in the UK have brought over 200,000 Indian tourists to the UK and Al Badr World Heritage Tours who organise holidays for practising Muslims.

Religious groups

There are a large number of organisations that provide holidays and travel arrangements for different faith groups, such as a pilgrimages, retreats for people to contemplate on their faith, or simply holidays that have provisions for a particular faith. For example, Richmond holidays provides family package holidays that also have provision for practising Christians.

By need

Families with children

Families travelling with children have their own specific needs depending on the age of the children and a number of travel and tourism organisations produce holiday products that are specifically targeted at this segment. Their provisions could include things such as baby listening services in hotels, play areas, kids' clubs (to keep children occupied and give their parents time to themselves), special menus for children, and discounts or free child places. This is a very competitive segment of the market and most major travel and tourism organisations offer a family friendly product.

Lone travellers

As the name suggests, these are people travelling on their own. Lone travellers may have concerns about their own security, as well as needing support with their planning and travel arrangements. A number of companies charge lone travellers a single supplement because a lot of holidays are priced based on two adults sharing a room. There are companies that specialise in singles holidays, such as Solos holidays.

Activity: Special considerations

Look at the Richmond holiday website and identify what special considerations they have made to suit their target market. To obtain a secure link to this website, see the Hotlinks section on p.x.

Key term

Special interests

A major growth area is special interest travel and tourism. As people are becoming more knowledgeable about holiday destinations, more people are deciding to have holidays that cater for a particular interest. This could be to follow a sports team, to participate in a particular activity or to develop or gain a new skill. There are, for example, a number of hotels and bed and breakfast hotels throughout the UK that specialise in accommodation for bikers, with secure parking for motorbikes, drying rooms and easy access to main routes.

2.2 Travel and tourism products

Travel and tourism is a huge sector with a wide range of different products. Unlike some industries, travel and tourism products tend to be services and experiences rather than tangible (physical) goods. For example, if you were going to buy a car, you would look at the car, give it a test drive and make a decision whether you were going to buy it – the car is a tangible product. However, if you are going to buy a holiday or a plane ticket, you can not try it first before making the purchasing decision.

Package holidays

A **package holiday** is a holiday that has at least three different elements put together. Two of these elements will be transport to and from the destination and accommodation while on holiday. The third element is usually made up of either the transfer from the airport to the hotel or excursions while on the holiday.

A package holiday could be as simple as a weekend coach trip around the Cotswolds or as complicated as a two-week, fly-drive holiday across the USA.

Package holidays are created by tour operators. This is done in advance and then information about the package holiday is sent to travel agencies. When the customer goes into a travel agency the agent has a number of different packages that they can sell to the customer. It is similar to buying a computer package with everything you need, rather than buying each part and assembling your own computer.

The advantage to the customer is that they only need to buy one product for their holiday rather than having to organise each component, or part, separately.

Cruising

Cruising is a unique type of holiday as accommodation, transport and, to some extent, the attraction itself are all rolled into one. Cruising holidays can be purchased either from a travel agent or from the cruise line directly. The range of cruises is huge, from short trips in the Mediterranean, to round-the-world trips. Traditionally, cruising has been seen as targeted at the elderly market, but cruise companies such as easyCruise and Royal Caribbean Cruises are now targeting a younger demographic.

Tourist attractions

Attractions draw people to a particular area. There is a huge range of different attractions, from natural features such as the seaside or beautiful scenery, to man-made attractions such as theme parks or heritage sites. Britain's main attraction to foreign visitors is the country's history and heritage.

Accommodation

Accommodation refers to where you stay on holiday. The range of different types of accommodation is wide, depending on your needs and how much you wish to spend. A tourist could stay in a suite in a five-star London hotel and spend hundreds of pounds a night. Alternatively, a youth hostel, or bed and breakfast accommodation, could cost under £20 a night. The type of accommodation is dictated by where you are travelling to, your budget and your needs.

Transport

There are three main ways to get to your destination:

Air
This includes airlines and helicopters, both chartered and scheduled. Chartered flights are booked for a specific trip whereas scheduled flights run according to a timetable.

Land
This includes a huge range of travel options, including trains, hire cars, coaches, buses, taxis, motorbike hire, cycle hire and even rickshaws. In the context of travel and tourism products, land transport does not include your own transport, such as a car, but only transport that you have hired or booked a ticket to travel on.

Sea, lakes and waterways
Transport by sea, lakes and waterways includes a wide range of boats, including cruise ships, ferries and catamarans.

Waterways transport can include travel via rivers, lakes and canals. Lake transport is limited in the UK, but is more popular in countries such as Italy and the USA. The UK has a large network of canals, because this was the country's transport infrastructure before the growth of the railways and the road network.

The type of transport used to go on holiday depends on the needs of the individual. Some people want to reach their destination as quickly as possible while others view the travelling as a part of the holiday. This is particularly so with walking, canal holidays and cycling tours.

Did you know?

The Visit Heart of England website claims that Birmingham has more canals than Venice. To obtain a secure link to the Visit Heart of England website, see the Hotlinks section on p.x.

2.3 Services

Travel and tourism products are a combination of physical products and a number of services. The services are no less, or more, important than the physical product: the level of service will influence the customer's overall holiday experience just as much as the location of the holiday.

Customer services

Most travel and tourism holidays have a number of customer services that are designed to meet the needs of customers; for example, hotels offer room service so that guests can have their meals in their hotel room. This service is particularly popular with business people who are staying in a hotel on their own, as it means that they do not have to sit alone in the hotel restaurant.

Other hotel services offered could include shoe cleaning, alarm calls, baby listening services, or spa treatments.

Additional services

Many travel and tourism organisations offer additional services, designed to make the experience more personalised for the customer. One example is pre-allocated seating. A number of train operating companies offer pre-allocated seating on their longer journeys so that customers' concerns of over-crowding are alleviated.

Most airports have a VIP (Very Important People) lounge. This is so that first class and VIP passengers can wait for their flights in private.

Other examples could include provision of transfers from home to the airport, or other extras such as flowers and champagne in the hotel room.

Services to meet specific needs

Not all customers have the same needs, so travel and tourism organisations have developed specific services to meet the needs of individuals. These could include special dietary needs: for example, flights to Israel will provide kosher food for Jewish people.

Disabled customers may also require additional services to support them. Remember that it is against the law to charge for extra services for disabled customers, as these services would be considered a reasonable adjustment under the Disability Discrimination Act.

BTEC Assessment activity 10.1   P1 P2 M1

1 Explain the principles of marketing used by travel and tourism organisations to meet marketing objectives.

Produce a report or presentation using visual aids or PowerPoint.

Your explanation must include: the marketing mix, target marketing and market segmentation. The explanation may be in general terms, but this must be supported by examples from the travel and tourism sector. In explaining the marketing principles, you should refer to all the marketing objectives given, although this can be in general terms, and should include the following:

- raising awareness
- increasing market share
- increasing profits
- challenging competitors
- informing product development
- introducing new products
- targeting new customers
- retaining current customers
- branding. **P1**

2 In a report, describe the products and services of one travel and tourism organisation.

Your description should relate to how different products and services are targeted to meet the needs of different types of customer. You could include details of how the organisation has modified it products and services to meet the needs of different types of customer. You need to check with your tutor that the organisation you have chosen gives you the opportunity to look at the full range of customer types. **P2**

3 Review how the principles of marketing are used by travel and tourism organisations to meet specific marketing objectives, such as increasing sales or raising awareness. You must say why certain principles are adopted in order to meet the objectives of specific organisations. You must use examples to illustrate your point, but your answer should not just be a list of examples. **M1**

Grading tips

P1 Use examples to support your answers when describing the objectives.

P2 Look at a travel and tourism organisation that offers a range of different products, such as an airline with different classes for passengers, a travel agency or a tour operator.

M1 Consider each of the marketing objectives individually, and use an example to explain how the principles of marketing have been applied in each case.

PLTS

Researching the principles of marketing, will help to develop your skills as an **independent enquirer**. When you complete the assessments for the unit to a deadline, you will develop skills as a **self-manager**.

3 Designing and using market research to meet specific objectives

3.1 Market research objectives

One of the main functions of market research is to find out what customers' needs are. Market research can also be used for the following purposes.

To identify customers

To develop a product or service for customers, you need to group customers together in market segments and develop products to suit each market segment. To do this, you would use one of the segmentation methods discussed earlier in this section.

To identify customer needs

Market research can be used to identify customers needs and requirements so that each product can be tailored to the needs of a specific market segment. For example the smaller the market segment, the more specifically you can address your customers' needs.

To inform product development

Products must continually develop in order to meet changing customer needs. Market research is used to identify these changing needs, and the results of this research are used to develop the product or service.

To measure customer satisfaction

Many companies spend a lot of time and money on gauging customer satisfaction. Traditionally, in the UK, people are not good at complaining about services and products. Although this sounds like a good thing, it may cause problems: if customers simply avoid using your service or product again, rather than telling you what was wrong with it, you will never find out what you need to change. This situation, however, is changing and customers are now more likely to complain.

Target new and existing products to customers

Market research is used to help organisations identify different customer types, as well as their needs and wants. Research is used not only to develop products to suit their needs but can also be the best way of communicating with them. The research can be done by using an existing customer database, or by running competitions or surveys to gather customer contact information.

Unless an organisation knows what the customer's wants or needs are, it cannot develop products and services to address those needs. Without research an organisation can only guess at what the customer wants. The more information an organisation has about its market, the better it will be able to segment the market, develop products, etc.

3.2 Types of market research

There are two main types of research:

- primary research
- secondary research.

Primary research

Primary research is a type of research being carried out for the first time and is purposely designed to meet an organisation's needs. There are four main methods of conducting primary research:

- questionnaires
- focus groups
- observation
- surveys.

Questionnaires

Questionnaires are commonly used in customer service to obtain customer feedback. The important thing to remember when designing a questionnaire is that it should be objective and should not cause any bias.

Questionnaires may be designed to obtain information that is factual and which can be turned into numbers, or statistics. For example, 20 people were asked to give a yes or no answer to the following question: "Was your flight on time?" Fourteen people answered yes, six answered no.

You might want an answer that gives a range of opinion, for example, "On a scale of 1–10, how did you rate the service (10 being good, 1 being bad)?" This type of data is called **quantitative data**. It is useful for identifying trends but does not go into the customers' personal opinions or feelings in depth.

This quantitative data is not just compared question by question; every individual answer is also looked at as a whole. For example, from a survey of 1000 people, the organisation is interested not only in the number of people who gave a specific answer, but also in those people's age, gender, income bracket, etc. By combining the answers to the different questions on a questionnaire, you can develop a more detailed insight: you will find out how popular a product is, and you will also discover the profile of those customers who are likely to be interested in buying the product. This detailed profile can then be used to make the product more specific to the customers' needs and to develop promotions that target these consumers.

Think about it

Go to a car hire, or other travel site, and look for a questionnaire. What type of questions do they ask? Do they want qualitative or quantitative data?

Key term

Quantitative data – data concerning values and amounts that can be used for statistical analysis.

When designing a questionnaire:

- only ask one thing at a time.
- do not ask the customer to speculate.
- do not ask personal questions.
- have a logical progression in the questions you ask.
- only ask as much as you need: long questionnaires are less likely to be answered.
- do not use jargon, as not everyone will understand it.
- do not ask leading questions and try and avoid bias.
- consider how you are going to analyse your data when designing the questionnaire.

Key term

Qualitative data – data that concerns opinions, feelings and emotions. Although it may give deep insight into the consumers' feelings, it cannot be statistically analysed.

Advantages of questionnaires

Questionnaires are a good method of obtaining customer feedback. The data is easy to manipulate and is used to work out trends. They are relatively cheap to use, after the initial time invested in developing the questionnaire and the printing costs, and customers can see that the organisation is interested in their opinion.

Disadvantages of questionnaires

Questionnaires tend to give polarised viewpoints. In other words, people tend only to fill in questionnaires if they had a particularly good or bad experience. Unless the data is rigorously collected and acted on, it tends to become less useful. Data collected can only be quantitative: it does not usually give details of customers' feelings, or information about how customers would like to see the product or service developed or improved.

Observations

Observing customers is a good method of research for monitoring how customers use a facility and how they interact with a product. For example, the managers of an international airport might observe how passengers move around the check-in area. They might wish to understand how space is used, in order to decide where facilities would be most useful, or to speed up customer flow around the area, etc.

For example, local councils in the UK pay observers to count the vehicle usage of roads. The reasons for this can be varied and may include new road developments, the introduction of traffic calming systems or the installation of speed cameras.

Advantages of observation

The main advantage is that you are not interacting with the customer; you are watching how they behave naturally rather than asking what they think. It is worth noting that a person's actual behaviour may be different from how they think they have behaved.

Disadvantages of observation

You are only monitoring the customer's behaviour. You do not have any insight into why this behaviour is happening.

Focus groups

A focus group brings together a small group of product users. It can be used to test products or gain detailed opinions and information about feelings. This is known as **qualitative data**. It cannot be used to show trends, but shows consumers' perception of products and their feelings about different products.

Tour operators may use focus groups when considering developing new package holidays, especially if the product is targeted at a particular type of customer.

Advantages of focus groups

Focus groups offer a detailed insight into what the customer feels about the product and service. This is the only method of primary research that really gives an understanding of customer perceptions of a product/service.

Disadvantages of focus groups

As the data is qualitative, the focus group has to be small enough to allow you to manage all the data. However, a small sample group might result in a misleading or non-representative sample (one where the people in the focus group do not truly reflect the market). Focus groups can be quite expensive to run and organise, in terms of both time and money.

Surveys

A survey is a targeted way of collecting data. To find out about general trends or 'average' opinions, an organisation could question everyone in the market. However, this would be too expensive and time-consuming, so smaller samples are used to save time and money; remember, it is important to choose samples that represent your market.

On your local high street, you may see researchers stopping people to ask them questions. You might notice that they do not stop everyone, but select people to ask. This is because they are only looking for a particular type of person for the sample.

Surveys can be carried out in three different ways:

- telephone survey
- postal survey
- person-to-person survey.

Sampling

In most situations it is not possible, or not viable, to ask everyone in a market or market segment for their opinion. You need to choose a sample that represents the market or market segment.

There are a number of ways of sampling; we will look at a few of the most common methods.

Random sampling

This is where you question people at random. This is the simplest survey method, but you have to be very careful when choosing people to talk to. You are more likely to speak to people you would like to talk to, or people who appear more approachable.

Nth sampling

This is where you question every nth person that passes you: for example, you may speak to every 3rd person who enters the shopping centre.

Remember

When observing:

- produce a chart to record your findings before you start observing.
- consider the time and place you are observing from.
- if you are observing customers using a service, consider looking at different times during the day.
- it may be difficult to work out what is really happening: do not make assumptions.

Remember

Focus groups

- Choose your focus group carefully. Do you want it to represent your current users or potential customers?
- Have structured questions to ask so that you can ask everyone the same questions.
- Do not let one person dominate the focus group or influence others.
- Have specific objectives in mind of what you want to find out.
- Try not to influence the focus group. If you are particularly involved in a product or service are you the right person to run the focus group?

Stratified sampling

In this method of sampling, you will question a specific number of people from each stratum. For example, you might ask 20 people of each of the following age groups: 0-18; 18-29; 30-39; 40-49; 50-65; over 65.

Bias sampling

This is where you design your sample with a specific bias, because this reflects the market segment. For example, imagine you are collecting data on customers for cruising holidays: people over the age of 40 are more likely to go on cruising holidays than people under 40, so it would be reasonable to reflect this in your sample.

Cluster sampling

In this sampling method, you choose a cluster of a segment to speak to, to represent that segment of the market. For example, you may choose to question everyone in a class at school to represent that year, or, in a postal survey, you may pick one street in a town to represent that type of housing or area.

Secondary research

Secondary research is research that has already been carried out for another reason: re-use of the data that has been collected will be the second use of the information. This is sometimes known as desk research, as this is where the research takes place. Secondary research could be information that an organisation has collected (such as sales figures or customer comment forms) or it could be information from outside the organisation.

You need to consider the following when using secondary data:

- How old is the data? People's opinions change over time, as do trends and fashions.
- What was the data collected for in the first place?
- How valid are the results?
- What method was used to collect the data?
- How big was the sample?
- Is the information reliable?
- Is the data relevant?

Secondary research sources

Trade journals

Trade journals are industrial magazines, published regularly, that will contain articles about developments and changes within the sector or industry. Examples include *Travel Trade Gazette* for the travel industries, the *Caterer* for the accommodation and food and beverage industries and *Tourism Today* for the tourism industry.

Government statistics

The Office for National Statistics (ONS) is a government department that is tasked with collecting statistical information on behalf of the government. This information is available either by post or through their website. You will find the travel trend report particularly useful as this will give statistics on passenger numbers etc. for **inbound**, **outbound** and **domestic tourism**. To obtain a secure link to the ONS website, see the Hotlinks section on p.x.

Publications

A number of organisations are in the business of gathering information on behalf of other organisations, either in response to direct requests or in general. This information can then be purchased from them. Such companies include Gallup and Pannell Kerr Foster (PKF).

Professional associations

There are a number of professional associations and organisations across the travel and tourism sector. These associations tend to be interested in a specific area of the sector, for example ABTA – The Travel Association is interested in the travel agency industry and IATA (International Air Transport Association) is interested in air transport.

These associations will collect information and statistics on issues within their area of specific interest. This data and information will be available to members of the association.

3.3 Evaluating market research

Summarising findings

When evaluating the sucess of your chosen research method, you will be checking to see if the objectives that you have set have been met. If the answer is yes, then you have been successful in choosing the right method. If the answer is no, then you need to think about using other research methods.

After you have collected all the data that you feel you need, you should summarise what you have found out. The data will then be analysed to produce useful information. Market research will not tell you what you need to do, but it will give you information from which you can make a more informed decision.

Information that is quantitative in nature will lend itself to being presented using graphs, charts and diagrams. Qualitative data cannot be easily analysed, but does contain details of people's feelings and experiences.

Both types of research are required to get an overall picture of potential customer opinion.

Key terms

Inbound tourism – refers to people travelling to the UK from abroad.

Outbound tourism – refers to people travelling from the UK to abroad.

Domestic tourism – refers to people who are not travelling outside the country they live.

BTEC Assessment activity 10.2 (P3) (P4) (M2) (D1)

1 You must access and use some secondary research to meet specific objectives. Discuss the objectives with your tutor. An example could include finding out visitor motivations and profiles for a specific attraction. Some examples of secondary research could include:

- Research into tourism in your local region, e.g. visitor numbers and profiles.

- Research into a specific visitor attraction. If you are studying *Unit 13: Organising a travel and tourism study visit* this could be used here. The evidence you present must show that you have interpreted your secondary data and used it for a specific purpose.

Your secondary research (P3) can be linked to your primary research (P4) for question 2. (P3)

2 You must select, design and use a suitable type of primary research to meet specific objectives in a travel and tourism context.

- Design a piece of primary research
- Carry out the research
- Summarise your findings.

You may use any of the primary research methods discussed in the chapter. The context should be discussed with your tutor, and could include:

- Research into where the group wants to go for Unit 13.

- Research for your work placement/work-related project/work experience for Unit 12.

- Research about where students at your school or college are going on summer holiday.

- Research into any of the marketing objectives discussed earlier in the chapter.

You will need to summarise and draw conclusions from the findings of your research. You can present this task either as a piece of written work or as an oral presentation. It is recommended that you use graphs, charts and diagrams for your findings. (P4)

3 Explain the appropriateness of the market research carried out for the objective of the research. You should say why you chose the primary research method you did and assess the advantages and disadvantages of this method. You also need to draw conclusions on the success or otherwise of your research and the method you selected.

This task could be presented either in writing or as a presentation. (M2)

4 Draw conclusions from the primary research findings and use them to make recommendations.

Produce a written report or a presentation. Your recommendations should be appropriate for the organisation or the context in which it is set. For example:

- If you are researching where to go on a study visit (for Unit 13) your recommendations may include destinations, the duration of the visit, the method of transport to use, what to do when you get there, whether to have a presentation or workshop session whilst on the visit, etc.

- If you carried out a work placement at a travel agency (for Unit 12) you might have researched the popularity of different types of holidays in the local area. Your recommendations could include what products the organisation should promote, what new products they should sell, and even additional services the travel agency should offer. (D1)

Grading tips

- (P3) Review the Office for National Statistics website.

- (P4) When designing your research material review, remember sections earlier in the chapter.

- (M2) You need to describe why you chose to use a particular primary research method and how you carried out your research.

- (D1) Your recommendations must be supported by the results of your research.

PLTS

Analysing and evaluating information, judging its relevance and value will help you to develop your skills as an **independent enquirer.**

Functional skills

Preparing a report or presentation will help you develop your **ICT** skills.

4 Promotional material for use in travel and tourism

Promotional methods vary as much as companies do, from the common to the bizarre. This section looks at the most commonly used techniques and media.

Promotion is an important part of the product delivery system. After all, if customers do not know what an organisation is offering, how can they purchase its goods and services?

4.1 Objectives

There are many different reasons why an organisation may decide to run a promotional campaign. Some of the most common objectives are detailed below.

To raise awareness

Not all promotional methods will encourage a customer to buy a product; however, they will make the customer aware of the product or service. For example, a television advert will not necessarily urge you to go out and buy a product, but it will make you aware that the product is available on the market and maybe put the idea of buying the product into your head.

To increase market share

Some markets are what we call 'saturated', meaning that there are no new customers available. For organisations operating in a **saturated market**, the only customers available are those of their competitors: there are no new customers. In this situation, market share is most important. This is the percentage of total users of a given type of product that will use your product instead of the competing products.

Consider the traditional family summer sun holiday. This could be considered a saturated market. The product is not particularly new or different from the competitors' offerings. There are a large number of consumers and many organisations offering products to this market segment.

To increase profits

Commercial organisations are in business to make a profit for their owners and shareholders. Advertising to increase sales and in turn increase profits is a logical objective; while increasing profits is not the only objective of promotion, it is likely to be the general aim of most advertising campaigns.

Remember

Promotion is how an organisation communicates with consumers.

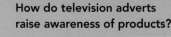

How do television adverts raise awareness of products?

Key term

Saturated market – where all potential customers are already using your or a competitor's product.

To challenge competitors

Organisations offering similar products will be competing for customers. If your competition spends a lot of time, effort and money promoting their product, this could have a direct effect on your organisation's success.

This is particularly so in a saturated market (see market share above), so if your competitors are advertising heavily, it is common practice for you to do the same, to protect your market share.

To introduce new products

When an organisation introduces a new product to the marketplace, it is vital that customers are told about it. The same also applies to changes to a product or service.

Examples could include the launch of a new aircraft, as was the case when Singapore Airlines brought the Airbus A380 into service, or the launch of a new holiday destination or type of special interest holiday.

To target new customers

Promotions can be used to target new customers. These could be new customers from a segment of the market you already service or they could be an entirely new target market. Promotion to new customers needs to include the benefits of the product or a unique selling point of the product. For example, First Choice taught over 7000 children to swim in 2008, as well as offering kids' clubs. (*Source: Firstchoice.co.uk*)

Retain existing customers

Just because a customer has used your product or service before does not guarantee that they will use your product or service again in the future.

Existing customers need to feel valued by a company. Promotion to existing customers helps to reinforce the impression that their previous purchase was a good thing and that they should continue to use the company's product or service.

In travel, since you tend to record customer details such as address and telephone number etc., direct marketing is a good way of communicating with your existing customers.

How did First Choice target new customers with recent advertising?

4.2 Promotional materials

Choice of promotional technique

The choice of promotional materials will be affected by a number of factors:

- What is your budget (how much can you spend)?
- Who is the target market (who are you trying to promote to)?

- What methods have worked successfully in the past and what has not worked so well?

- What time frame do you have to develop the promotional materials?

- Where is your target market located (local, national or international)?

You need to consider which methods and materials will give you most impact on the target market for your money. Advertising on YouTube could be very effective if targeted at a younger age group (teenagers or twenty-somethings) but would be less effective if targeting the 'grey pound' (the over 50s market).

Radio advertisement

This is a mass-market form of advertising. The obvious issue is that there are no pictures or printed words with eye-catching layouts on the radio, so the whole message needs to be put across in sound.

Advantages of radio commercials
Radio is the most popular entertainment medium, with the average person spending more hours each day listening to the radio than watching television. Radio commercials are cheaper to produce and to air than TV advertisements. Radio stations tend to be more regionalised, so small- or medium-sized organisations can afford to promote on this medium to their own local market.

Disadvantages of radio commercials
Unlike on television, where you now have special interest television channels, most radio stations tend to be based around a specific type of music. However, musical taste can be linked with socio-economic groups; for example, groups 1 and 2 are more likely to listen to classical music than groups 7 or 8.

As with television, there is no hard copy of the information. This means that the message has to be very clear or the advertisement has to be repeated regularly.

Magazine advertisement

Magazine advertisements are another popular way of promoting travel products. One of the most popular types of magazine used to promote holidays is Sunday newspaper supplements. With a magazine advertisement, you pay to have your message put into the magazine.

You pay for the size of the advertisement ranging from 1/64 or 1/32 of a page all the way up to a two-page spread. The larger the advert, the more it will cost you. Also, you will pay more for an advertisement in a more popular magazine (a magazine with a larger circulation).

Advantages of magazine advertisement

If you target your advertisement at readers of a particular publication, this makes it possible to tailor the product to specific interest groups. This is very useful when selling special interest holidays. If you wanted to promote a special interest holiday for people involved in quilting and needlework, a magazine specialising in quilting would be a good place to advertise.

Compared with other forms of advertising, for example television and radio, magazine advertising is a relatively cheap method of promotion. You have control over what is placed in the advertisement and the reader will have a hard copy of the information (unlike television and radio advertisements).

Disadvantages of a magazine advertisement

There can be a lot of advertisements close together in a magazine, so yours could be overlooked by the customer; also, offers can easily be compared. Printed advertisements are easy to ignore and difficult to make eye-catching.

Window or in-store display

Window displays are designed to encourage customers walking past the outlet to walk into the outlet, or to get the consumer to consider the outlet when it comes to buying that type of product. There has to be an element of the display that will grab customers' attention. This can be done through colour, pictures, wording or pricing. A lot of travel agencies will advertise last-minute deals in the shop window using cards.

In-store displays are slightly different as they will not encourage a customer to walk into an outlet. However, they could help a customer to consider different options and products once they're inside the outlet. They can also be used to promote additional services that are on offer; for example, travel agencies may have in-store displays that promote the availability of travel insurance, foreign exchange or money-wiring services.

Web page

Increasingly, people are booking and researching their holidays on-line. To be competitive it is almost essential to have an internet presence. This is usually through a web page. There are a number of key issues you need to consider when planning a web page.

How easy is it to navigate the web page?

It is essential that the customer finds it easy to navigate around the website. How effective are the links? How easy is it to make a payment? Is it easy to find the product the customer wants? The internet is a very competitive market place and if an organisation's website is not user friendly, the consumer will simply move on to a site that is more accessible.

Placement in search engine results

When you search for information on a **search engine**, where in the results does your organisation come? This is important, because with the huge amount of competition on the internet, the customer is unlikely to look at a second or third page of results: unless your organisation's website is in the first few results, it may not be found.

It is worth remembering that the internet is a selling channel, not just a communication method. This is particularly true in the low-cost scheduled airline industry where companies such as easyJet and Ryanair only take bookings online.

Competition

Competitions are another method used to promote a product. They help increase product awareness and give the organisation a way to communicate with potential customers. They are also a good way of collecting information about customers, such as contact details; this information can be used in future for sending out direct mail.

Direct mail

Most organisations keep a database of current and previous customers and enquiries. This can be used to send out information about products to those customers. For example, a theatre preparing to put on a particular drama can use its database to send out information to customers who have expressed an interest in that type of production in the past.

Direct mail is most effective if it is addressed and directed to a person by name rather than to 'Dear customer'. As a computer is used to generate the mail shot, it is the design of the letter that is most important, so that each customer feels it is a personal invitation, rather than just another circular communication.

Press release

A press release is when an organisation provides the press (newspapers) with information about itself or its products. A press release is usually written in the form of a newspaper story. It must contain a release date (date after which it can be used) and a contact name and details in case journalists require more information.

Advantages of press releases

Most people will read a newspaper story and are more likely to believe it than an advertisement. It is a cheap method of promotion as the only cost is the time taken to write the article.

> ## Key term
>
> **Search engine** – a website used to search the internet to find websites that may contain information relevant to the user. Current popular search engines include Google, Bing and Ask.

Case Study: Surfers Against Sewage

Below is a press release issued by Surfers Against Sewage (SAS), released on 22/12/09.

Surfers Against Sewage Send Rubbish Christmas Presents

Today Surfers Against Sewage (SAS) campaigners have sent identifiable marine litter back to the manufacturer wrapped in Christmas wrapping paper as part of the award winning Return To Offender campaign. These rubbish presents were found on beaches around the UK.

The Return To Offender campaign acknowledges that these manufacturers didn't drop the litter on beaches themselves, but urges manufacturers to improve their anti-littering message, reduce their packaging, invest in low impact packaging and support grass roots anti-litter campaigns.

Our beaches are the perfect and extremely popular environment for a family walk over the Christmas period. A beach walk, or even a surf, offers a great excuse to get out of the house and work off some of the Christmas time over-indulgence we so often enjoy. On all of our beaches we can find marine litter. The majority of marine litter is plastic and the 2008

Beachwatch survey suggest that there is 1 piece of marine litter every 40 cms of beach. The plethora of plastics and other litter on our beaches is not only an eyesore, but also a persistent and long-lasting danger to surfers, beach users, recreational water sports enthusiasts, and the wildlife and habitats all around the UK's coastline.

SAS Campaign Manager, Andy Cummins says: "Ho ho how many pieces of marine litter can be found on our beaches? Countless. We can all help send a Christmas Return To Offender message to these companies whose products litter our beaches and urge them to reduce their impact on our beaches. These polluters deserve a rubbish present this Christmas."

To obtain a secure link to the Surfers against Sewage website, see the Hotlinks section on p.x.

Source: Surfers Against Sewage

1 Do you think that the SAS approach will influence the behaviour of companies?

2 Why not check out the Surfers Against Sewage website and see their successes over the last 20 years.

Disadvantages of press releases

Newspapers have no obligation to use the story. The story can be changed or edited by the newspaper.

Using AIDA

The AIDA approach is used as a method of designing advertising so that people will take notice and remember it:

Attention   Interest   Desire   Action

A is for Attention

Unless you can attract people's attention, your advertising campaign is unlikely to be successful. Various methods can be used to attract people's attention, such as colour, fonts and print style, pictures and drawings, and humour.

I is for Interest

After you have attracted someone's attention, you need to keep them interested in your product or service. The most common way to gain a customer's interest is to develop their interest in a product slowly, rather than bombarding them with facts. Fun can be used as a way of keeping people interested. Adverts with a simple ongoing story line encourage people to watch them just to see what happens next.

D is for Desire

After a promotion has created attention and interest, you will need to create desire in the customer to visit or purchase the attraction or product. The three main ways that desire is created in travel and tourism are as follows:

1. By making the customer feel that they are already there.

2. By personalising the information so that the customer feels that they are the ones the product or service was created for.

3. By showing the customer the benefits of the product.

A is for Action

When you have persuaded a customer to buy a product or service, you need them to take action. Promotional material needs to enable the customer to buy the product, so the following information is often provided, to encourage a customer to take action:

* telephone number

* location map

* website

* email address

* address

* fax number.

If your promotional material suggests that there is a limited time frame or number of places/products, this could also encourage the customer to take action.

All-inclusive holiday
to St Lucia

Flights from:

London Gatwick or Birmingham airport

Dates available between

June and September 2011

Book early for a discount!

How do offers appeal to customers?

BTEC Assessment activity 10.3

P5 M3 D2

This follows on from assessment activity 10.2.

1 Produce a piece of promotional material to meet specific objectives in a travel and tourism context, justifying the choice and design. The piece of promotional material can use any of the different methods/media discussed in this unit. It may be a one-off piece such as a poster or a series of promotions (for example a special offer).

The promotional material should show some links to the objectives of a marketing campaign and to the target group, but may not fit the target market entirely. You must justify the choice and design of the promotional material.

You need to check with your tutor the appropriateness of your choice. **P5**

Examples could include:

- a poster promoting a package holiday to families with young children

- a leaflet which explains the benefits of buying your travel insurance from the travel agency.

2 To achieve **M3** you will need to show that that you have been creative and original in your choice of technique and design and explain how your promotional material meets your objectives. Do not worry if you are not that artistic as long as you represent your ideas in an articulate way.

3 You need to analyse your design and assess it using the AIDA principle. Assess how it attracts attention, creates interest, stimulates desire for the product or service and leads the customer to action.

You must suggest how your design of promotional material might be improved. This could be done by comparing it with other examples of promotional materials. Your analysis can be either a written report or a presentation.

If you are delivering a presentation at your work placement, you will need to make sure you have a witness statement; if your presentation is in class, you will need an observation sheet by your tutor. If you use PowerPoint or visual aids, these should be submitted to support your work. **D2**

Grading tips

P5 State your target market and the objectives of this piece of promotional material.

M3 Keep referring back to the marketing objectives that the piece of material was designed to achieve.

D2 Consider the AIDA principle one component at a time. How does your promotion fit the principle?

PLTS

When you generate ideas for your piece of promotional material to meet specific objectives in a travel and tourism context, you will develop skills as a **creative thinker**.

Functional skills

When you produce written documentation you will gain skills in **English** – writing and **ICT** – use ICT systems.

I work as a resort representative for one of the UK's largest tour operators. Last year I was in a family resort based in Alcudia, Majorca and this year I'm in Es Cana in Ibiza. Although I grew up in England my father is from Seville so I learned to speak both Spanish and English at home and this job gives me a chance to use both languages. My main duties include meeting customers when they arrive and throughout the holiday, arranging excursions and car hire, and resolving any problems.

Typical day

I get up early to check the local weather (in preparation for a talk in the afternoon) and eat some breakfast. I need to be at the hotel at 8am to check that all the customers leaving are packed ready for the coach to airport leaving at 9am.

The rest of my morning is spent making sure everything is ready for the new group of customers. I have to check the information board is up-to-date with all the latest information on trips and excursions. Then there is a meeting with the hotel reception to check that all the new customers coming in have a room allocated to them.

At noon the new customers arrive and the next couple of hours are spent settling the new customers into the hotel and solving any issues. I then get a few hours break to prepare for the welcome meeting.

In the evening I give a welcome speech to customers, explaining the resort, our excursions and selling car and scooter hire. I then sort out the paperwork and tickets for everything I've sold.

Think about it!

1   What products and services does Pedro sell to customer?
2   What promotional methods does Pedro use to communicate with customers?

Just checking

1 What is the definition of marketing?
2 What are the 4 Ps that make up the marketing mix?
3 What is a unique selling point (USP)?
4 Why do we segment markets?
5 Give four ways you could segment a market.
6 List six different marketing objectives.
7 Define 'tangible' and 'intangible'.
8 What are primary research and secondary research?
9 List four types of primary research.
10 What's difference between quantitative data and qualitative data?
11 When would a company use a focus group?
12 List five different advertising media.
13 What does AIDA stand for?

Assignment tips

- This unit is about applying the principles of marketing in real world scenarios. So keep your eyes open. Notice the advertisements on television, on-line or even on buses. Work out what the objective of the promotion is, who it is targeted at, what the brand represents, and whether (and how) it follows the AIDA principle.

- Remember, the customer wants to know the benefits of the product and service, so you need to refer to these in your promotional material. For example, you should promote a relaxing weekend break (the benefit being to relax) rather than a hotel room for two nights.

- Collect examples of print, or on-line, promotional materials that you feel are good illustrations of the various marketing principles and explain why you collected them; you could write your reasons on the back of each piece of material. These examples will help with the first assessment activity.

- Do not get worried by some of the jargon in marketing. As long as you understand the principles, you can learn the jargon in time. You might want to keep a list of definitions to refer back to.

- Keep in mind the target market which will affect what you say, where you say it and how. To communicate with teenagers, advertising on the internet, games consoles and mobile phones might be appropriate. Targeting the over 65s market could be done inside buses as all retired people get free bus passes.

11 Preparing for employment in travel and tourism

The aim of this unit is to prepare you for employment in the travel and tourism sector. In the first part of the unit you will look at the wide range of jobs across the different industries in the sector. You will also research the roles, entry requirements, duties, skills and qualities required for specific jobs before exploring the possible career pathways.

In the second part of the unit you will learn how to prepare for, and take part in, the recruitment and selection processes within the sector. This will include learning how to write CVs, supporting letters and speculative letters, completing application forms and participating in different types of interviews.

There are many more applicants than there are positions in travel and tourism so it is essential that you are prepared before applying. This unit will help you with the process of finding a job in this sector after your studies. It will also be useful if you are trying to get a part-time job during your studies. Many of the skills are transferable across a wide range of other sectors such as retail, hospitality, leisure and general commerce.

Learning outcomes

After completing this unit you should:

1 know about career opportunities in the travel and tourism sector

2 be able to undergo a job application process for the travel and tourism sector.

Assessment and grading criteria

This table shows you what you must do in order to achieve a pass, merit or distinction grade, and where you can find activities in this book to help you.

To achieve a **pass** grade the evidence must show that you are able to:	To achieve a **merit** grade the evidence must show that, in addition to the pass criteria, you are able to:	To achieve a **distinction** grade the evidence must show that, in addition to the pass and merit criteria, you are able to:
P1 identify career opportunities across the travel and tourism sector **Assessment activity 11.1, page 330** **P2** describe entry requirements, progression routes, duties and responsibilities for two jobs in the travel and tourism sector **Assessment activity 11.1, page 330**	**M1** for two selected job roles compare opportunities for further progression **Assessment activity 11.1, page 330**	
P3 complete documentation as part of the job application process **Assessment activity 11.2, page 336** **P4** prepare for interview **Assessment activity 11.2, page 336** **P5** use interview skills as part of the job application process **Assessment activity 11.2, page 336**	**M2** explain how a CV, application form and interview could contribute to gaining employment **Assessment activity 11.2, page 336**	**D1** demonstrate good practice and consistently project a positive image throughout all stages of the job application process **Assessment activity 11.2, page 336**

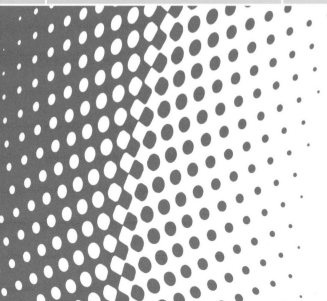

ow you will be as
ill be a

Tania, 15–year–old learner

I currently work as a customer service representative for one of the leading tour operators in the country. The part of the company I work for specialises in holidays for the youth markets.

When I was studying for my BTEC First Diploma in Travel and Tourism I was not sure what I wanted to do. I knew I wanted a job where I could work with people, but I did not really know what options there were for me.

The preparation for employment unit I did, really helped me understand what options were out there. When I did finally find a job I wanted, I found the skills I had learned about selection and applying for jobs must have helped, as I was successful and have been working here now for two years.

If I can give you one piece of advice, follow your dreams. I followed mine, I love my job and the people I work with and I have met some amazing people.

Best luck with your course!

Over to you

- Produce a list of questions you would ask if you were to interview someone working in the travel and tourism sector about what they like about their job.

1 Career opportunities in the travel and tourism sector

What do you want to be?

1 Make a list of all the jobs you can think of in the travel and tourism sector.

2 Produce a table of the terms and conditions you want from a job, for example "I like to work abroad", and things you do not want from a job, for example "I could not stand working in an office all day".

3 Using the list and table you have produced, try and identify which jobs on the list have the terms and conditions that you would like.

Do any of these jobs appeal to you?

1.1 Travel and tourism organisations

The UK travel and tourism sector is a huge sector of the UK economy. This huge sector requires a large number of staff across a range of different travel and tourism component industries, with wide-ranging skills and qualities. *Unit 12: Developing employability skills for travel and tourism* details the skills and qualities that are required within a range of different jobs.

Before looking at specific industries in the travel and tourism sector, it is worth bearing in mind most large organisations will have a range of support departments. These departments tend to be based at a head office and will cover marketing, human resources, purchasing, ICT, finance, product development and security. These will not be highlighted industry by industry to save repetition.

Travel agents

Travel agents sell travel products to the public and businesses. These products range from transportation, such as flights and train tickets, to accommodation bookings. They also sell secondary products such as foreign currency and travel insurance.

Each travel agent tends to employ 10, or fewer, members of staff. An agency manager will be responsible for the running of the outlet and they may be assisted by a deputy or an assistant manager. There may be a number of travel consultants, some of whom may be employed as senior travel consultants (a title showing their extra experience or qualifications). They may also employ one or two trainees or apprentices, learning how to be a travel consultant. Some agencies also sell foreign currency and will employ a cashier to work in the Bureau de Change.

Tour operators (head office)

Tour operators, such as Thomson or Kuoni, organise tours and package holidays which they distribute in a number of different ways, for example call centres, web-sites or travel agents.

Tour operators range in size from small companies employing just a few people to large international companies employing thousands. There are many job opportunities working for tour operators across a range of functional areas, such as:

- brochure production
- contracting
- customer service
- training
- resort operations (head office)
- reservations and ticketing.

In recent years disaster recovery and health and safety have become increasingly important for tour operators as they are responsible for their customers' safety. This has been highlighted during recent natural disasters such as Hurricane Katrina (see Case study, Unit 3, page 95).

Tour operators (overseas)

Tour operators employ staff overseas to look after their customers whilst they are on holiday. The size of the overseas team will depend on the number of customers on holiday in the area. The overseas team may consist of:

- **Area manager** – responsible for a number of resorts in a region.
- **Resort manager** – responsible for a single resort.
- **Head/senior representative or resort manager** – responsible for managing the team of representatives in the resort.
- **Holiday representatives** – responsible for looking after the customers in the resort.
- **Administrator** – responsible for the paperwork.
- **Transfer representative** – responsible for transferring customers from airports to hotels (and back).
- **Airport supervisors** – responsible for the transfer representatives and looking after clients in the airport.
- **Entertainers** – responsible for the entertainment of the customers.
- **Young person/children's representative** – responsible for looking after the children on holiday and run kid clubs.
- **Tour guide** – responsible for guiding customers on trips and excursions.

> ### Key term
>
> Head office – The base from which an organisation is run. Functions include human resources, marketing, accounts, IT, customer service and general management and there are a range of roles at operative, managerial and director levels.

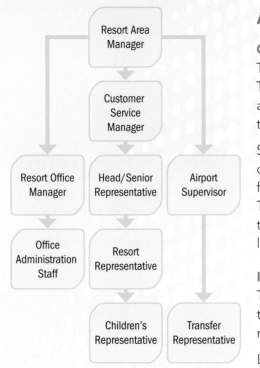

Figure 11.1: A basic resort organisational structure

Activity: Visitor attractions

Use the internet to find a visitor attraction. It can be anything ranging from a local to a national visitor attraction, such as a zoo, a theme park or a stately home. You might find the following organisations useful to research:

- The National Trust
- English Heritage
- VisitBritain
- Visit Wales
- VisitEngland
- discovernorthernireland

After choosing a visitor attraction, make a list of all the different people you think the attraction employs. Check your list by using the internet, visiting the attraction or emailing the attraction.

Airlines

On the ground (land side)

There are a range of different jobs depending on the airline and its size. These include, check-in staff, customer service staff, aircraft dispatcher, associated managers and maybe even a director of operations for the terminal/airport.

Some airlines employ companies, called ground handlers, to carry out the ground side of their operation. This is particularly common for smaller airline and airlines that have another airport as their base. The ground handling companies will employ a range of people at the airport, including customer service, information assistants and luggage handlers.

In the air (air side)

The flight crew fly the aircraft and depending on the type of aircraft there could be a pilot, co-pilot (first officer), flight engineer and navigator.

Looking after the safety of the clients there would be the cabin crew, senior cabin crew, cabin manager and purser.

Airports

Airlines are not the only employer at airports. For example, there are also roles for cleaners and security staff (not to be mistaken for police or customs and excise officers).

Accommodation providers

There are a huge range of accommodation providers from campsites to 5-star hotels. Each organisation will structure itself and its job roles to suit its needs. In this section we will look at the structure of a large hotel as most other providers are based on this structure.

Visitor attractions

There is a huge range of visitor attractions in the UK, ranging from national parks and natural attractions, to heritage attractions such as castles and stately homes, to purpose-built leisure attractions, such as theme parks. There is a wide and varied range of job roles and skills required, for example tour guides, who show customers around the attractions, who need to be highly skilled in customer service, as well as having a detailed knowledge of the attraction.

Most visitor attractions have gift shops and tea rooms which require retail staff, and food and beverage service staff. There are also positions in customer service, such as a crew member at a theme park, ticketing staff or security. Some visitor attractions also have an education officer who is responsible for arrangements during school trips. For example, they might give presentations and produce information packs to help learners in their studies.

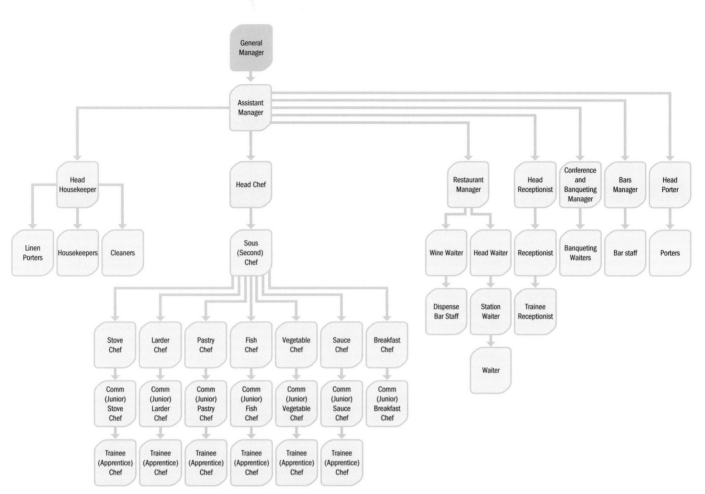

Figure 11.2: The basic structure of a large hotel

Some natural attractions have conservation staff, gardeners, ground keepers, etc. You may even find entertainers and actors in some attractions.

Other passenger transport operators

The main forms of transport (if we exclude airlines) are trains, coaches and buses, ferries and cruise ships.

Trains

Train operating companies employ a range of staff. At the railway station there will be customer service staff, ticketing staff or information centres where customers can get advice on tickets. Larger stations also have a dedicated station manager while, smaller stations may share a station manager.

Coaches and buses

Coaches and buses can be chartered, booked for a specific trip or, in the case of National Express, Megabus and Greyhound, scheduled to a timetable.

They will employ dispatchers at major coach stations who are responsible for checking customer tickets as well as dispatching the

How do visitor attractions appeal to tourists?

buses. Tickets are sold online, by telephone or through travel agents. Customer service staff work online or in call centres to sell the tickets.

Ferries and cruise ships
Ferries and cruise ships have a range of staff responsible for sailing the ship. There are also staff who look after the customers on and off the ship. Many cruise ships employ destination services staff who deal with shore excursions. There is also the entertainment team.

Case study: Jemma's career progression

Jemma started an apprenticeship with Thomas Cook as a Travel Consultant when she left school at 16. After two years she had completed her apprenticeship and was promoted to a Travel Consultant. After a few more years experience, and studying at night school for her diploma in management, Jemma applied for and was successful with an application for the post of Senior Travel Consultant at Going Places.

Although Jemma loved her new job and really like helping people organise their holidays she was starting to think that she could do with a new challenge. Jemma met up with a friend who had also been on the apprenticeship with Thomas Cook.

Jemma found out he was now working as cabin crew on an airline. He explained how he had worked in a travel agency and, using all the skills he had learned, applied for a job with the airline who employed him as cabin crew and put him through further training.

1 Give an example from the case study of internal progression.
2 Give an example from the case study of having to apply externally for a job to get career progression.
3 Give an example from the case study of someone moving their career path from one industry to another within the travel and tourism sector.

1.2 Entry requirements

Skills required

Each job role requires a different set of skills. These are referred to as the 'entry requirements.' Here are a few of the major skills commonly required in the sector.

Customer service skills – customers are the most important people in the sector. They spend money on products and services and in the end pay the wages! In this increasingly competitive sector good customer service is what separates a successful company from its competitors. In *Unit 2: Understanding customer service in travel and tourism* you looked at these skills in detail.

Presentation skills – being able to present accurate and up-to-date information is vital in travel and tourism. This could be as a holiday representative giving a welcome meeting or as a tour guide.

Teamwork – most job roles in travel and tourism are undertaken in teams. A group of people can achieve more than the same number of individuals working on their own.

Activity: Summer holiday

Consider the number of people involved in just one person's summer holiday abroad. Make a list of all the staff you can think of involved in this one product.

Person specification

A **person specification** is written by the organisation looking to employ a new member of staff. This document lists the skills, personal qualities, qualifications and experience required for the job role. This is usually divided into 'desirable' and 'essential skills'. The personal specification will be used to short list applications and also during the interview.

You will need to compare yourself against the personal specification before applying for any job.

Personal qualities

Certain job roles require particular personal qualities. These can be worked on and developed. They used to be known as personal standards.

Reliability – will you be where you say you will be and do what you say you will do? This quality is vital for teamwork as people have to be able to trust you.

Personal presentation – in any service sector industry people's first impressions are important. People will draw conclusions on your ability from how you look. How you present yourself at work will also influence colleague's belief in your commitment to the job. This could affect you when you are applying for a job or a promotion.

Commitment – you need to be committed to what you do, to the people you work with and the task you are doing. Will you still give 110% when you are tired at the end of your shift on a Friday evening?

Flexibility – the travel and tourism sector is fast moving and there are constant changes. Over the last 30 years job roles within the travel and tourism sector have changed dramatically and are still constantly evolving.

To be successful in this sector you need to be flexible you will need to constantly retrain and re-skill.

Key term

Person specification – the skills required for, and desired, from applicants for a job.

Activity: Presentation

"How can I trust someone to book my holiday, if he cannot even blank his own blank?"

In groups consider the above statement, by replacing the blanks with other words, for example iron and shirt, to make a list of other presentation issues. Use your list to make a poster to help you make sure you have good personal presentation

Case study: Changes

Over the last 30 years the day-to-day activities of a travel agent have changed dramatically. Even something relatively straightforward such as booking a holiday has changed significantly. For example, when booking a holiday the travel agent used to have to write the booking on paper forms, telephone through to the tour operator to check availability on that tour, before finally booking the tour on the phone. All records were kept manually and were mostly handwritten on standard forms. The bills would be calculated by the travel agent and kept with all the paperwork for that booking. All communication with customers tended to be either by telephone, or by letter which would have to be typed.

Today, a travel agent can check your holiday on-line with the tour operator, as well as booking it, with a press of a button. All your details are stored in a database and payment can be taken electronically.

How do you think travel consultants will work in 30 years from now?

BTEC's own resources

Qualifications

Qualifications are a formal recognition of achievements. They can be split between vocational and academic types of qualifications.

Vocational qualifications are specific to an industry or sector. They can be studied at school or college, or they can be taught in the workplace or by an outside educational provider. Examples include BTEC, Diploma, NVQ (National Vocational Qualification), SVQ (Scottish Vocational Qualifications) in Scotland.

Some of these vocational qualifications teach transferable skills which can be used in many different jobs, whereas other skills are specific to a particular role.

Academic qualifications are mainly studied at school, college or university. The subject knowledge covered tends to be less practical and applied and the qualifications do not often lead to a specific job. This does not mean that they have no value in the workplace, as they show your level of ability, but the skills developed may not be used specifically. Examples of academic qualifications include GCSEs, 'A' levels and degrees.

Experience required

A lot of jobs will require you to have experience, either in the specific role or of the skills required. This is because employers expect people with the appropriate experience will have the ability to do the job, for example major airlines often ask for two years' experience in customer service. Experience can be gained in any customer service role, such as a part-time job in a supermarket.

1.3 Job roles

Job descriptions

Job descriptions include the job title, location of the job, hours, pay scale, duties and responsibilities. As with the person specification you will need to compare yourself against this when applying for a job role.

Duties and responsibilities

Every job role will have its own specific duties and responsibilities. These will be identified by the company as part of the recruitment process. Every organisation will have a number of duties (functions) that need to be completed so that the organisation will function.

To put these duties in context, below is a review of the skills required in two specific job roles within the travel and tourism industry.

Cabin crew
You may think that cabin crew are just there to serve customers food and drink and look after them on the flight, but this is not their primary

Key terms

Vocational qualifications – these qualifications involve learning and skills specific to an industry, sector or job role.

Academic qualifications – qualifications involving learning about a specific subject rather than a job or industry.

Job description – the job that the company requires the employee to do.

role. The cabin crew are responsible for the health and safety of the customers when they are on the flight.

This will involve a number of different skill sets:

- Administration skills are required to ensure that the right people are on the flight in the first place. The cabin crew also need to keep records of complaints and incidents.

- An understanding of health and safety is required. Specific skills regarding the evacuation of an aircraft, fire fighting and first aid are also required.

- Customer service skills are also vital as you will be dealing with a range of customers, including reluctant flyers.

- Food and beverage service skills, as well as food handling skills, will be required for most airlines. This includes food hygiene knowledge and associated health and safety.

- Team working is also vital, as to carry out all the duties required on a flight a team that works efficiently and effectively is needed.

- Cash handling skills are needed for some airlines for the sale of food and drinks on the flight as well as Duty Free. This could include taking payment in multiple currencies.

Travel consultant (retail travel agency)

A travel consultant gives customers advice and help in choosing their travel arrangements. To be able to carry out this job role a travel consultant needs a number of skills:

- A good understanding of travel geography is very important. As you get experience in the industry your travel geography will dramatically improve.

- Administration skills are needed to make sure that the customer gets what they have booked.

- Good customer service skills are required as well as good selling skills.

- Numerical skills may be required to work out the cost of holidays, insurance, etc.

- Good communication skills will be required to communicate with customers, tour operators, transport providers, hotels and visitor attractions.

1.4 Career progression

During your career in travel and tourism you will constantly be developing and growing your knowledge and your experience, both through work and through training and development.

You are unlikely to have just one job, but rather a number of different jobs as you develop your abilities.

Within most sectors of the industry there is a traditional career path leading from an operative role to a supervisory role to a management role.

Why is customer service so important?

Assessment activity 11.1

P1 P2 M1

You have been asked by the local tourist board to help them produce a fact file for school and college leavers to help them decide on careers in the travel and tourism sector in your region.

1 Produce a list of job roles from a minimum of five different types of travel and tourism sector organisations. **P1**

2 From your list in question 1 select two jobs that interest you the most and that you could aspire towards. You need to check with your tutor that the jobs you have chosen will give you enough scope to achieve M1 in question 3. For each job describe:

- the entry requirements including the skills, qualities, qualifications and experience needed.

- progression routes for the two jobs including at least two further career steps.

- describe the duties and responsibilities for the two jobs you chose to look at in question 2. This could be done by producing a job description for each of the two jobs. **P2**

3 Compare opportunities for further progression for the two jobs. Explain clearly how staff from those jobs can progress into higher positions within the same type of organisation or other travel and tourism sector organisations.

You also need to consider and explain the similarities and differences of the two roles and pathways. **M1**

Grading tips

P1 Try using local travel and tourism organisations and visit them.

P2 For each job make sure you include entry requirements including skills, qualities,

qualifications and experience and two more career steps – why not try using them as subheadings?

M1 Ensure that you provide detailed explanations. Use charts for support.

PLTS

Exploring potential career opportunities will develop your skills as an **independent enquirer**.

Functional skills

You will develop your **English** skills both in reading (comparing, selecting, reading and understanding texts to gather information, ideas, arguments and opinions) and writing (extended writing pieces, communicating information, ideas and opinions, effectively and persuasively).

2 The job application process in the travel and tourism sector

2.1 Documents

When applying for a job you are usually asked to apply in writing.

Curriculum Vitae

Curriculum Vitae (CV), which is Latin for list of life, is a brief account of a person's education, qualifications and previous occupations, typically sent with a job application.

It is worth remembering that when you send a CV this is all the company will know about you. This is your opportunity to sell yourself and show why you are the best candidate for the job.

Personal details

Firstly you should start with personal details so that the organisation knows who is applying for the job and how to contact them. You should include the following:

- **name**
- **address**
- **telephone number**
- **email address.**

You do not have to include your racial background, age, date of birth, religion or marriage status on a CV, as legally these factors cannot determine who an employer hires.

Personal statement

A personal statement gives you the opportunity to tell the company about yourself. Remember to tailor the education and employment history sections to best support your application.

Academic qualifications

You should list the educational establishments, their addresses, when you attended and the qualification that you achieved. Start with the most recent achievements and work backwards.

Vocational qualifications

As stated earlier in this chapter, these are the qualifications you achieved at work or in school/college about a specific job role or about a sector of the industry.

These could include first aid certificates, or attendance at specific training courses such as Sage (an accountant software package) or Galileo (a central reservation system), as well as the BTEC First Diploma you are studying at the moment.

Membership of professional bodies

Within the travel and tourism sector there are a number of professional bodies you might be a member of and you should highlight your membership here.

Key term

Professional bodies – these are organisations which aim to further a profession, raise public interest in the profession and oversee the interests of people working in the profession.

Employment history

This is a list of the jobs you have had, with the dates you were employed, details of the employer including their address and the main duties of the job. Remember to check the job description for the job you are applying for and highlight the skills you have developed that match. You should list your jobs starting with the most recent and work backwards in time.

Notable achievements

If you have achieved something notable, you should mention it on your CV. This could include gaining the Duke of Edinburgh Award, being selected to play a sport for your county, raising money in a charity event such as the Great North Run, etc.

Hobbies and interests

You need to highlight what you do in your free time. You need to show that you have hobbies and interests that cover a range of skills including teamwork, intellectual pursuits and social interests.

Application forms

Nearly all companies produce a standardised application form. It can be an easier way to compare one candidate against another. When applying for a job, practise filling in an application form before completing the copy you are sending in. Get someone to check your spelling and grammar. You may need to paste text into Microsoft Word to spell check, as the form may not have this facility. Applicants who submit forms with misspellings may not even be considered for the job! Try to complete every box.

Letters

Because we tend to communicate through email and SMS (text) we do not get a lot of practice in writing a letter. If you send in an application, or CV, you must include a covering letter (either in hard copy or as a Word attachment to your email) explaining why you are applying for the job. You can use this as an opportunity to sell yourself. Figure 11.3 shows the generally accepted layout you should follow.

Appropriate content and format

Letters are a formal method of communication. There are certain rules to follow when writing a letter.

Use of technology

Word processing helps you to produce a standard letter and edit it for different jobs. You must keep a copy of the letter and you can then re-read it before the interview, so that you can remember what you said about yourself.

Speculative letters

Not all jobs are advertised and in some cases organisations may not even realise they need someone until the last minute. If there is a specific company, or type of organisation, you would like to work for it is a good idea to send in a speculative letter with a copy of your CV.

Your speculative letter should include what you would like to do and you should ask them to keep your CV on file in case a post does become vacant.

Letters of acceptance or decline

When you have been successful in the recruitment process and you been offered a job you need to write a formal letter of acceptance or decline. You should layout your letter in a formal structure, as you did with your application letter, and state your acceptance or decline of the post, and reconfirm your start date and time.

2.2 Interview/selection methods

During the interview and selection process an organisation will choose which candidates are most appropriate for the job. The organisation usually calls candidates in for an interview to get to know them a little better and to allow the candidates to find out more about the job role and the company.

Telephone pre-selection

Some jobs are very competitive with large numbers of applications for each post. Due to the costs involved it is not always possible to interview every appropriate candidate. A telephone interview is a cheap and viable way of selecting appropriate applicants to interview.

Individual interviews

In an individual interview candidates will be seen one at a time. The interviewers will have a list of questions that they will ask each candidate.

Group interviews

The purpose of a group interview is to allow the interviewer to see how the candidates interact with each other. This type of interview is very popular within the travel and tourism sector because customer service and teamwork are such important skills. There may be tasks to complete and these can include:

- individual numeracy
- literacy and travel tests
- group problem solving activities
- group discussions
- individual pre-set presentations
- on-the-day group presentations.

These activities are to give you an opportunity to show how you work with other people and how you perform in work-related tasks.

Abdul Khan
2 Evergreen Road
Middlesbrough
North Yorkshire
TS1 4ND

Human Resource Manager
Flyway Holidays
43 High Street
Darlington
Durham
DL1 4FR
6th June 2010

Application for post of Trainee Travel Consultant Ref 100034

Dear Sir/Madam,

Please find attached a copy of my application for the post of Trainee Travel Consultant with your company which I saw advertised on your website.

I finished my BTEC First Diploma in Travel and Tourism at my local college and during my studies realised that working as a Travel Consultant is the career path I would like to follow. I am interested in the role as I enjoy working with people and the challenge of meeting customer needs.

I am an honest, conscientious, hardworking and flexible individual who works well as part of a team but am also able to work well on my own initiative. I completed a work placement in your Middlesbrough branch under the supervision of Tracey, your Agency Manager whilst studying for my BTEC. I am very willing to undertake any training and development courses you feel would benefit me.

Thank you for taking the time to read my letter and I look forward to hearing from you.

Yours faithfully

Adbul Khan

Figure 11.3: The layout and content of an application letter is important

Why is it important to dress appropriately for an interview?

2.3 Preparation for interview

If you are successfully called for an interview you need to make sure you are prepared for it.

Company knowledge

You will need to find out about the company you are going to work for. You can look the company up on-line and find out what they sell or what they organise, where they are based and something about their history.

Finding out about a company and its history will give you some insight into how they work and what their aims are. This will help you decide if you would like to work for that organisation.

Knowledge of the job

In preparation for an interview you will need to find out what the job entails and what will be expected of you on a daily basis. The job description will tell you what the basic duties and responsibilities are, but you can find out further information on the internet, from career advisors and the Connexions service. This will show your level of interest in the job. If you know someone who has current or past experience, working in a similar role, ask them about their job.

Dress code

A lot of travel and tourism organisations have rules about how you should dress, be it a uniform or a code of dress. Make sure that you follow a similar code when dressing for an interview.

Personal appearance

Be careful with your personal appearance. Do not wear too much make-up or jewellery. A lot of companies are not impressed with visible tattoos or body piercings such as eyebrow bars. Do not chew gum and if you smoke make sure you do not smell of cigarettes before the interview.

2.4 Interview skills

Body language

For the interview use an open, positive body language (see page 156). Smile and maintain eye contact with the person speaking without staring. Try to be relaxed without being too informal, for example do not slouch in your chair. Think about your non-verbal communication, for example show you are listening and you are interested.

Social skills

You need to demonstrate that you have good social skills:

- remember to say please and thank you
- ask permission to sit or wait till you are asked
- address people formally
- let people speak and don't talk over them.

Due to the length of some interviews, the interview may include meals and coffee breaks.

Personal skills

You may be asked within the interview to demonstrate your personal skills. Make sure that you are prepared for this. For example, a person applying for a job as a holiday representative may be asked to give a presentation on a particular topic or object.

Peer interaction

How you interact with others during the interview process will highlight your team working ability and your ability to fit into the organisation. The organisation will be looking for team skills, such as listening to another person's point of view before putting forward their own ideas, taking a lead when appropriate but not being bossy and encouraging those members of the team who are not participating.

Active listening

You need to show the interviewers that you are listening and to do this you need to maintain eye contact, nod your head appropriately, smile and look interested.

Responding to questions

When responding to questions take your time. If you are not sure about how to respond, ask for clarification. Try to expand on your answers without waffling or going off the subject. Remember you are selling yourself so a one-word answer will not give the interviewer a lot to judge you by.

Asking questions

When you are preparing for the interview remember to include some questions to ask. If you do need to ask about pay try not to make this your first question, as it could look as though money is all you are interested in. Consider asking questions about on-the-job training, development within the organisation and career progression.

Participation in activities

The company may ask you to take part in an activity. If they do, then you should participate. This could be something you need to prepare

Remember

- All the time you are at the company you are being observed and the way you react to others and your manners may well be taken into consideration.

- Remember that your questions may be covered in the interview. If they are do not ask them again as this shows you were not really listening.

before the interview such as a presentation on a specific topic, a discussion or some other form of group task. Do not try to dominate the situation, rather try and make sure that everyone is involved and ask others in the group what they think.

All the skills we have looked at as being important in an interview can be learnt and developed over time, so before you have that important job interview have a practice, ask your friends, family, teacher/tutor or Connexions office to help you.

BTEC Assessment activity 11.2

You have almost finished your BTEC Travel and Tourism course and you are beginning to think about applying for a job.

1   Find a job that you are interested in and either complete a real application form and a CV along with a speculative letter, or write a letter to accompany your application form. Each document should be completed in an appropriate format using technology.

Question 1 will enable you to achieve **P3**.

2   You have been shortlisted for the job. It is time to prepare for the interview. In preparation for the interview you need to carry out research into the company and the job role for which you applied.

Question 2 will enable you to achieve **P4**.

3   Participate in group, individual and telephone interview simulations. Your tutor should arrange these.

4   The day of the interview is here. Use your interview skills throughout the interview process. Evidence can be in the form of observation reports from your tutor. Supporting evidence can include

video or audio recordings together with your list of questions and answers, peer evaluations, self-evaluations and witness statements from others participating in the interview process, for example the interviewers, external observers.

Questions 3 and 4 will enable you to achieve **P5**.

5   The interview is over and it is time to reflect on how the process of applying for the job went. Explain how your CV, application form and performance during the interview could contribute to you gaining employment. Refer to good practice in pre-selection activities as well as the interview processes.

Question 4 will enable you to achieve **M2**.

6   Put together a portfolio of evidence including observation reports, witness statements, peer-assessment, preparatory notes, visual aids used, and audio and video recordings. Your tutor will take everything into consideration when assessing you for D1.

Question 6 will enable you to achieve **D1**.

Grading tips

M2 You need to reflect on your learning. Consider what you did well and why did it go well. Both in the application as well as before and after the interview

D1 Ensure you demonstrate good practice and consistently project a positive image throughout all the stages of the job application processes

PLTS

When you are preparing for an interview, you will develop skills as a **reflective learner** and **self-manager**.

When you participate in an interview, you will develop skills as an **effective participator**.

I work as cabin crew for a leading airline in the UK. I tend to work on long haul flights to the USA although I do get to travel to other places from time to time. I started work here after leaving college and I love my job and the variety of people I get to meet.

My main duty is to look after the health, safety and security of passengers in the airplane. I am also responsible for making sure all the customers have a good experience with us.

My typical day

My day starts at different times depending on the flight I am scheduled to be on. At the start of my shift I go to the crew room for a pre-flight briefing which includes safety information and we discuss as a team any special needs. We need to be well-organised so we can work together seamlessly as a team.

When we arrive at the aircraft we do safety checks in the cabin. Then we board passengers, make sure they are all seated and check that their hand-luggage is stored properly. Before take off we show the safety video and demonstration and check the seats are upright and seat belts are fastened.

During the flight we look after customers. We serve drinks, snacks and meals. We also offer duty free. Before landing we hand out landing cards if appropriate, stow everything away and again check the seats are upright and seat belts fastened.

After the passengers have disembarked we check that everything is turned off and stowed correctly. We have a post-flight de-briefing in the crew room before going home or to a hotel if it is a stop over.

Think about it!

1 What is Jasmin's main duty?
2 What skills do you think Jasmin needs to do her job?

1 Name three different jobs roles that involve working overseas for a tour operator.
2 Name three different job roles in the transport industry.
3 What is a career path?
4 What are skills?
5 Why is teamwork important?
6 Why is flexibility important in the travel and tourism sector?
7 Name two different qualification types.
8 List five duties of a member of cabin crew.
9 What skills would be useful if you were a travel consultant in a travel agency?
10 What is CV an abbreviation for?
11 Why should you include your hobbies and interest in your CV?
12 Write a speculative application letter to a company you want to work for. How did you make yourself stand out?
13 Make a list of all the things you would need to prepare before you attended a job interview.

Assignment tips

Applications
- If you have a lot of qualifications and not much work experience put your education first. Put them the other way around if you have a lot of work experience and fewer qualifications.
- Photocopy paper-based forms before posting, and print out on-line forms before sending them.

Face to face Interviews
- If you do not know what to do with your hands hold them together behind your back or in front of you. Be careful not to fidget, it will probably be nerves, but could look like a lack of interest
- When you are working, you will be representing the company, so research the company.
- If you not sure what to wear dress up in a smart business manner: suits; smart plain shirt or blouse; trousers or a mid-length or longer skirt. Remember it not a fashion-show – it is a job interview.

Telephone interviews
- Turn off any background noise or go somewhere quiet to answer the call.
- Make sure you do not have a silly answerphone message on your mobile.
- Make notes of what you say.
- Take your time to think.
- Practise your best customer service skills on the phone – smile, it will come across in your voice.

12 Developing employability skills for travel and tourism

Organisations in the travel and tourism sector rely on their staff to perform effectively everyday. This includes front line staff to give the level of service the customers expect and back office staff to support the front line staff in the service delivery. Therefore all roles are crucial to an organisation's success. Underperforming in the workplace can seriously affect the reputation of an organisation.

This unit will show you the importance of employability skills by identifying skills and qualities in the context of jobs in the travel and tourism sector.

In this unit you will have the opportunity to identify, plan for and carry out a practical work-related project to meet set objectives and proposed outcomes in relation to skill development. You will monitor and review your skills throughout the project and identify and action any further development and experience required for entry into employment within the travel and tourism sector.

Learning outcomes

After completing this unit you should:

1. know the skills and qualities needed to work in the travel and tourism sector

2. be able to plan and carry out a work-related project in order to develop employability skills

3. be able to monitor and review skills development in a work-related project.

Assessment and grading criteria

This table shows you what you must do in order to achieve a pass, merit or distinction grade, and where you can find activities in this book to help you.

To achieve a **pass** grade the evidence must show that you are able to:	To achieve a **merit** grade the evidence must show that, in addition to the pass criteria, you are able to:	To achieve a **distinction** grade the evidence must show that, in addition to the pass and merit criteria, you are able to:
P1 describe the skills and qualities needed to work in the travel and tourism sector **Assessment activity 12.1, page 348**	**M1** produce a comprehensive review of skills and personal qualities and a realistic and measurable plan for personal development **Assessment activity 12.1, page 348**	
P2 review own skills and personal qualities **Assessment activity 12.1, page 348**		
P3 produce a plan for personal development based on identified needs **Assessment activity 12.1, page 348**		
P4 Plan and undertake a work-related project to develop employability skills **Assessment activity 12.2, page 358**	**M2** complete a work-related project which demonstrates the ability to monitor and review skill development, own development plan and proposed outcomes **Assessment activity 12.2, page 358**	**D1** Evaluate and provide evidence of development of skills, taking in account performance on a work-related project and recognising further development needs **Assessment activity 12.2, page 358**
P5 Monitor and review skills development, reporting on the project in an appropriate format **Assessment activity 12.2, page 358**		

Shane, 16–year–old–learner

To be honest I was a little worried about this unit. I thought I had no skills. After all, I only just finished school! But when I did my skill review I soon found out I had a lot more skills than I thought. I work on Saturday in the local shop – my tutor pointed out all the things I did at work such as customer service, cash handling, stock control etc.

When it came to the skills project I felt overwhelmed. I knew I wanted to practise and develop my customer service skills. One of the girls in my class has a little sister who goes to an after-school club for disabled kids. As a class we agreed that raising money for the club was a good idea. The college has a fête every year so we thought we should run a stall there. We had three stalls. I was in charge of the face painting. The boys in the class got a set of stocks and sponges and after writing letters to all the managers in the college managed to get some to take their turn in the stocks. The queue when the principal was in the stocks was huge! In the end we raised over £200 for the club, as well as having a great laugh.

I had a chance to learn some new skills and develop the ones I already had, particularly handling money. I was in charge of the takings, cashing up and banking the money. At work I handle money but I never cash up my till. I even got the cheque from college for the money we raised and I was one of the three people that went to the charity to hand them it. I felt so proud of my class.

Over to you

* What skills do you think are important for staff work in the travel and tourism sector?

* Why do you think the skills you have chosen are important?

1 Skills and qualities needed to work in the travel and tourism sector

Set off

Skills and qualities

In groups of three or four go to one of the websites for Fish4Jobs, Workthing, Reed or Monster and print out a copy of a job advert for a job in the travel and tourism sector.

Once you have selected a job make a list of the skills and qualities you need for the role. Some of them will be mentioned in the advertisement, while others you may have to think a little harder about. Produce a poster to display in the classroom with the skills and qualities you need for the job you looked at, making your poster look as interesting as possible.

To obtain a secure link to these websites, see the Hotlinks section on p.x.

Travel and Tourism Sector

Tour operators
Retail travel agents
Hotels

Visitor attractions
Airports
Airlines

Different industries in the travel and tourism sector

1.1 The travel and tourism sector

The travel and tourism sector is a hugely important to the UK and world economies. The World Travel and Tourism Council (WTTC) reports that the travel and tourism sector is one of the world largest sectors of industries, employing approximately 220 million people and generating over 9.4 per cent of the world's gross domestic product (GDP) (see Unit 1 for definition of GDP).

Due to the diverse nature of organisations in the travel and tourism sector there is a need for a range of different skills from employees across the sector. The table below gives some examples of key skills and qualities required in travel and tourism organisations.

Industry	Description	Skills
Retail travel agents	Retail travel agents sell package holidays and other travel products such as holiday insurance, foreign currency, etc, to their customers.	As travel agents sell to the public they need: • good customer service and interpersonal skills • organisational skills • ICT skills • numeracy • written and verbal communication skills.

Industry	Description	Skills
Hotels	The hotel industry provides food, beverages and accommodation to its customers.	Since the hotel industry provides hospitality to customers, hotel staff need: • good customer service skills • good communication skills • experience of computer booking systems • experience of point of sale computer systems • ICT skills • flexible proactive approach to customers.
Tour operators	Tour operators take the products of other industries in the travel and tourism sector, e.g. hotel rooms, transportation from airlines and trips to visitor attractions and package them together to produce tours and package holidays. Tour operators also look after the customers while they are on holiday. Tour operators tend to sell their products through travel agencies, but increasingly are going direct to their customers through the internet and call centres.	This industry relies on a number of different skills including: • ICT skills • negotiation skills • customer service skills • organisational skills • teamwork.
Aviation	Aviation is a complex industry, covering all aspects of the operations of aircraft and airports.	As airport staff sell to the public they need: • Good time keeping • good teamwork and customer service skills • ICT skills.
Airlines	Airlines transport customers to other destinations. This includes not only staff working in the air, but also the ground staff working specifically for the airline in the airport.	Cabin crew need a number of different skills including: • good verbal communication • good personal presentation • good problem solving • good teamwork • the ability to speak another language (this not essential, but is a big advantage).
Visitor attractions	Visitor attractions include theme parks, museums, historical sites, heritage sites, wildlife parks etc. There are a wide range of roles including hospitality staff, curators, zoo keepers, ticket sales staff to name but a few.	People working at visitor attractions need: • good communication skills • customer service skills • good personal presentation • good teamwork skills.

1.2 Skills

The term **skill** can be defined as "the ability to do something well". With practice and experience you can develop skills to a better standard.

Customer service

In Units 2 and 5 you looked at customer service, but here we will consider customer service as a specific skill. Customer service is the ability to support a customer with the expected level of service for them to be able to purchase and use a product or service.

Key term

Skill – the ability to do something well.

Customer service is not a stand-alone skill. There are a number of other skills you will need to be able to provide good customer service, including problem solving, written and verbal communication, etc.

Written and verbal communication

Being able to communicate effectively, both verbally and in writing, is an important skill within the travel and tourism sector. It is needed in a number of different situations, including selling products and services to customers, handling complaints, communicating with colleagues, etc.

Presentation skills

There are a number of techniques you can develop to help you present information including:

* the production of visual aids, such as posters or PowerPoint presentations
* projecting your voice
* timing
* pace of speaking
* the structure of your presentation and inclusion of the correct information.

Teamwork

Most job roles in the travel and tourism sector require staff to work together with colleagues as a team. For example, during a flight the cabin crew team have a large number of different tasks to complete. Working out of a small galley, they need to provide meals and drinks for all the passengers, as well as offering duty free, carrying out safety checks and demonstrations, and organising immigration documents as needed. Without good teamwork it would be quite impossible to carry out all these tasks in such a restrictive environment in the timeframe of the flight.

Problem solving

Every day at work you will come across problems that need to be solved. Some problems may be simple things that go wrong from time to time, for example a flight being delayed due to bad weather. Others may be major problems with systems and procedures, such as the problems British Airways encountered with losing customers' luggage when they opened Terminal 5 at Heathrow in March 2008.

You will be able to solve some problems yourself, but sometimes you may need to have support from a more experienced or senior member of staff. Being able to solve problems is a vital part of success in business.

Why do cabin crew have to work together as a team to be able to complete all their duties during the flight?

Activity: Technical glitches

The opening of Heathrow Airport's Terminal 5 was hit by a number of technical glitches. Look up what happened on the internet and list the causes of the problems. How were these resolved?

Remember, for a lot of problems there may be a number of different solutions. You will need to consider the effect of each solution and decide which would be the most appropriate.

Interpersonal skills

Interpersonal skills are about how you communicate with another person. This includes verbal and non-verbal communication. Verbal communication includes not just the words you say, but also your tone of voice, pitch and pace. Non-verbal communication includes facial expressions and body language.

Numeracy

Numeracy is your ability to work with numbers. This is an important skill to have when working in the travel and tourism sector. Numeracy skills are needed when dealing with bills, money, costs and exchange rates, but also in checking the numbers of customers, booking trips and events, ordering supplies, etc.

Using ICT

Information Communication Technology (ICT) skills are vital. Bookings and reservations are recorded on computers through central reservation systems (CRS), destinations are researched on-line and customers may communicate by email. Organisations train staff in using their specific systems and software, but a general understanding and ability with ICT is desirable, if not essential, for a wide range of jobs within the sector. Increasingly, employees need to be able to use data bases and spreadsheets and be efficient word processors, as well as be confident with a range of industry software, such as CRS and global distribution systems.

Languages

The ability to speak another language is increasingly important in the sector. For some job roles, such as a holiday representative, the ability to speak the native language in the country you are working in will make your job a lot easier and communication with local people a lot more effective.

1.3 Qualities

Unlike skills that can be learned, qualities are values that you have. You can work on developing qualities with the help of managers, teachers and mentors and you can practise and develop these qualities. Some qualities you have already practised and developed over time in school, for example timekeeping, working to deadlines, reliability, personal presentation, commitment and flexibility.

Proactivity

Do you plan to find ways of preventing issues and problems before they happen? A proactive manager will put systems and processes in place to prevent the problems from happening in the first place, giving them more time to focus on other issues within the business.

Ownership of tasks

Increasingly companies are looking for staff who will take responsibility for themselves and their work. Will you take ownership of a task? By accepting 'This is my job and my responsibility' and completing a task that you are responsible for on time, you will gain greater job satisfaction and a deeper sense of achievement.

Personal organisation

Personal organisation is also an important quality within this sector. As transport is organised according to a timetable, the staffs' timekeeping it vital to make sure that services run to time.

Compromise

Can you come to a compromise? Do you adjust to suit others or is your way the only way? The ability to adapt and compromise is essential to being able to work with others as part of a team.

Empathy

Can you put yourself in someone else's shoes? Trying to understand how someone else is feeling is vital for teamwork as well as for dealing with customers, both in selling and dealing with issues and complaints.

For more information on qualities, see *Unit 11 Preparing for employment in travel and tourism*, p.327.

1.4 Skills development plan

After discussing and considering these skills you will need to produce a skills development plan. This is a proactive approach, but can be difficult in practice and some people find it makes them feel uncomfortable. You need to be honest with yourself; don't underestimate or overestimate your ability.

Reviewing your skills and qualities

To review your skills and qualities you need to carry out a personal audit. You need to consider what your skills and qualities are. You might find the table opposite a useful tool.

For each of the following skills and qualities grade yourself from 1 (very strong) to 5 (very weak).

Why did Cristiano Ronaldo need to spend years practising and refining his skills?

Skills	1	2	3	4	5
Customer service					
Written communication					
Verbal communication					
Presentation skills					
Teamwork					
Problem solving					
Interpersonal					
Numeracy					
Using ICT					
Languages					
Qualities	1	2	3	4	5
Reliability					
Personal presentation					
Commitment					
Flexibility					
Proactivity					
Ownership of tasks					
Personal organisation					
Compromise					
Empathy					

Identifying skill development needs

Now that you have identified the skills and qualities you have, you are in a position to identify the skills and qualities you need to work on. To do this you will first need to identify the job role you would like to work towards.

If you apply for a job the company will send you a job description and a personal specification. From this information you should be able to identify the skills and qualities that are required for a specific job.

Preparing a development plan

Next you need to think about how you can achieve your goals. Some skills you may develop through qualifications, some through work experience or charity work, etc. It is worth remembering that a lot of these workplace skills are transferable, meaning that skills learned in one job can be transferred to another job.

Assessment activity 12.1

(P1) (P2) (P3) (M1)

1 You have started a new job working for VisitEngland. Your supervisor has asked you to produce a career guide handbook for travel tourism students. Focus on skills and qualities needed in the travel and tourism sector. Describe five skills and five qualities and explain how each relates to one or two specific jobs within the travel and tourism sector. (P1)

2 Demonstrate how to do a personal skill review for the career handbook. Produce a personal skills and qualities review. This could be in the form of a diagram, chart or table. (P2)

3. Using the review, identify the skills that you need todevelop. Your development plan can be general or for a specific job. If you studied Unit 11 this could be one of the jobs you research in this unit. (P3) (M1)

Grading tip (M1)

Ensure that your review is comprehensive and each identified skill has realistic and measurable objectives.

PLTS

When you review your own skills and personal qualities and plan for personal development based on identified needs, you will develop skills as a **reflective learner**.

Functional skills

You will use your **English** skills in reading to gather information and form opinions.

2 Plan and carry out a work–related project in order to develop employability skills

To help you develop your employability skills you are required to plan and carry out a work-related project.

2.1 Project

The project needs to be completed in groups, but what you plan can be any appropriate work-related project. You need to speak to your tutor to agree your project. Below are a few ideas you might consider.

Market research

Market research could be based on the needs for your local area, a local business or even the local council. For example, a visitor attraction may want to find out about the types of customer who visit their attraction. They may want to know how customers have heard about the attraction

Why is cleaning up after the event all part of the project?

or how far they have travelled to get there, or perhaps they need some demographic information about the customer, such as age, gender, income? For more information on market research travel and tourism see *Unit 10: Exploring marketing in travel and tourism*.

Event

You might decide to put on an event. This could be an entertainment event such as a musical event or an organised trip to a place or attraction.

Planning the event could involve sourcing a venue, organising entertainment, food and drink, etc. You would also need to consider the promotion of the event and all that entails, including producing promotional materials and selling tickets. Finally, you also need to consider staffing the event itself as well as cleaning up afterwards.

Play scheme

A play scheme could be organised over a half-term or on a weekend. This would be a particularly good idea if, in the future, you want to work with children as a children's representative. You need to consider things such as what to do for the scheme, who would you be aiming it at, what you plan to do, the cost involved, health and safety, etc.

Voluntary project

You could support a current voluntary project or run a one-off charity event, for example you may want to run a car wash or a stall at a local fête to raise funds for a local charity.

2.2 Planning a project

Identifying and setting key objectives related to travel and tourism skill areas

When you plan a project use SMART to help you set your objectives:

* Specific – make sure that the objective(s) is specific and everyone agrees on what is meant

* Measurable – you need to be able to measure your results

* Achievable – you need to have a target that you can achieve; however, the objective should be challenging, as if it is too easy there is little motivation and little satisfaction in achieving the objective

* Realistic – have realistic goals

* Timed – you need to have a timeframe so that you know when the objective needs to be achieved by.

For most people a number of small objectives with short timeframes are easier to stay focused on than one objective with a long timeframe.

> **Key term**
>
> **Objective** – An aim of what you want to achieve when doing a task.

Consider what individual and group objectives you would need to set for the following travel and tourism skill areas.

Customer service – What level of customer service will you be offering? How will you assess the customer service you have given?

Marketing – How are you targeting your customers? How are you going to promote your project to this target market? How will your material be produced? Where will the material be used?

Organisation practices – What needs to be done to complete the project? Who is to take responsibility for each task or area? How will the team communicate and report successes and failures? How often do you have meetings and how are they recorded? How are decisions made?

Teamwork – How will your team work together? Who will be set what responsibilities? How do you support each other if help is needed?

Acquiring new skills and techniques – What skills and techniques are you planning to acquire? How do you plan to gain them? How do you plan to assess your ability in these new skills and techniques?

Meeting needs of own skill development plan

Everyone in your team will have their own skill development needs. It will be very easy during your project to assign tasks to people who have ability in a particular area, for example a member of your group may have experience in customer service, but for this project, which is about developing and acquiring new skills, you need to assign responsibilities based on what skills people need to develop according to individual development plans.

Timescale considerations

All projects need to have a timescale. This is for two reasons. Firstly, so that the tasks are completed promptly and, secondly, because one task can be dependent on the completion of an earlier task, for example an aircraft cannot take off until it has been refuelled.

Without a timeframe the project will be delayed and resources and people will be wasted as they wait to be able to do their part.

Resources implications

All projects will have some resource implications and these need to be considered in the planning phase of the project. Before you start the project you need to be able to identify what resources you have available to you. These resources may be in the form of equipment or a budget.

Proposed outcomes

Every objective should be supporting the overall aim of the project. However, as this project is also about developing individually skills you need to consider the needs of every member of your team and their personal skill development plan.

2.3 Skill development within the project

This section will look at some of the key skills needed and how you might develop them through your project.

Personal skills

Practical

During your project you will be involved in a number of practical activities, from running an event, carrying out market research or being involved in a voluntary project. You need to consider what practical skills you are using and keep a record of how you used them.

Timekeeping

As mentioned under personal organisation, timekeeping is vital in a project as others will be dependent on you keeping to a schedule. Objectives should have a timeframe, though to complete an objective you may need to break down the timeframe into individual goals for separate parts of a task.

Motivation

In industry employees are motivated through bonuses, benefits and targets, as well as by the general ethos of the organisation. However, during your project you need to be self-motivated and motivate other members of the team.

Creativity

Creativity is an important skill as without creativity there would be no new products or services and no new ideas. However, creativity itself also needs to be focused on the objective of the project.

You should keep records of what you created during the project. You may have designed a questionnaire for market research, or designed promotional materials to sell your event or promote your voluntary project.

Technical

Technical skills are skills that involve interacting with systems and procedures. This could include learning to use new computer software such as a central reservation system (CRS) or a new piece of equipment. You may plan to develop your technical skills. For example, if you use a video camera to produce evidence of your project this could be considered development of a technical skill.

Other skills

Teamwork
Teamwork is the skill of being able to work and achieve objectives with other members of a team and maintaining your working relationship so that you can work together again on another project.

Listening
Listening skills are discussed in the *Unit 5: Developing customer service skills in travel and tourism*, page 158. Remember, listening skills are not only about hearing the words that someone says, but also understanding the emotion of the words, reading the body language and also encouraging the person to talk.

Problem solving
During any project, problems will occur; some we can plan for (proactively) others will come out of the blue. Problem solving is not about finding the first solution. It is about finding the best solution to solve the problem and also making sure that we prevent the problem from occurring again in the future.

Communication
In your Functional Skills classes you will be working on developing your communication skills for the workplace. This is a good practical opportunity to practice your skill development.

Communication skills can be divided between verbal and written skills. Writing skills include spelling, grammar and punctuation, and standard layouts and conventions.

Interpersonal
Interpersonal skills are skills that involve interacting with others. These include your listening and communication skills, your ability to compromise and empathy. It is possible to record your interaction with others and reflect on how you would change that interaction to get a better result if you were in that position again in the future.

2.4 Undertaking the project

During the project there are a number of skills and tasks that you need to keep doing to make sure that you achieve your objectives.

Prioritising

During the project different tasks will take priority at different times. The skill is to make sure that the tasks that need to be done are done in a timely fashion. This means you need to prioritise some tasks at the expense of others in the short-term. This does not mean that you miss tasks out, but rather that you focus on the most important one at any particular time. When the tasks that are a priority are completed you need to focus on the next important task.

> **Remember**
> The priority you give to a task should be based not just on its own importance, but also on the impact it has on the ability of other team members to complete their tasks.

Action planning

Action planning, as the name suggests is a plan of the action you are going to take to complete the project. It also includes who in the team will be responsible for each action, and the timeframe in which each action has to be completed. Your action plan may also include the equipment needed to carry out a task so that you can make sure that the action is taken.

Managing tasks

Every task needs to be managed. This is to make sure that it is completed to the standard that is required. Within your team you might decide that each task is assessed by the team, or a specific individual in the team, to make sure that it is completed to the highest standard. For more complex tasks you will need to manage them step-by-step.

Researching

Without proper research businesses are only guessing. Research allows them to make more informed decisions. The better the research the more accurate the data, which in turn gives a business more accurate information to base decisions on.

Asking questions

We use questions to find out information. When asking questions try not to ask too personal a question as people are unlikely to answer you, for example "How much do you earn?" or "How old are you?" are questions most people would be reluctant to answer.

If you do need to find out this information try giving the customer options within different ranges, for example "How old are you? Please indicate from the following age ranges: 0-10, 10-17, 18-30, 31-40, 41-50, 51-65, over 65".

Also try to keep your questions short and to the point. Do not use jargon as some people may not understand it.

Keeping records

You need to keep records of everything you do in the project. This is so you can record evidence for this qualification and also so that you can remember what was done and how you felt. This will support you when you carry out an evaluation of your skill development.

Observation

Observation can also be used as a form of evaluation. Observation is used a lot when considering how customers use a facility and how they move around a place, for example watching customers using an airport

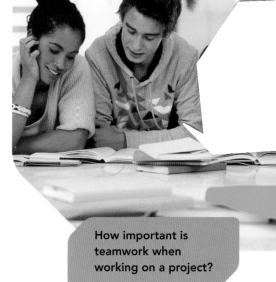

How important is teamwork when working on a project?

Remember

Always record any information or answers you are given. Don't think you will remember it!

Think about it

You may think that keeping a record is boring, or not really needed, but when it comes to evaluating your skill development can you really remember how you felt all those weeks ago when you started the project or what was said when two of the team had a disagreement?

will help you identify where there are bottlenecks in the customer flow around the airport.

Observations can be used as part of your evidence for your project. Tutors or other adults involved in the project may complete an observation evaluation on you, for example monitoring you on your work placement.

Reviewing progress

Sometimes when working in a team on a project, you can get too close to what you are doing. You need to take a step back and review your progress. You will need to revisit your objectives and your skill development plan. A good way to do this is to have a regular team meeting. You may consider it a good idea to have a 10-minute reflective time at the end of each working session to consider the skills you used and how you developed them.

This helps you re-focus on what you and your team are doing and where in your plan you are. It also means that if a problem occurs you can adapt to suit the changing situation.

Activity: Illness

You are planning a travel and tourism career fair. At the beginning of your team meeting a member of your team who was responsible for designing the promotional materials for the fair phones in sick and says they may not be in until after the fair. Suggest three possible solutions to the problem.

3 Monitor and review skills development in a work related project

3.1 Monitor

During the project you need to monitor and review your progress. This is so that you can make sure that you are achieving the goals set out in your skills development plan.

There are a number of different ways of monitoring and assessing your progress.

Keeping a log

A log will be an invaluable tool in monitoring your progress with your development plan. Comment on the new skills you have learnt, existing skills you have developed and where you need to do more work. Consider also how your project is progressing and which skills have helped this process.

Think about how your project team are working together. Has there been any issue, or problem, in the team? Have there been any changes to your team's plans? If so, why?

Progression against objectives

You must record your progression towards your development plan clearly. You might decide to keep a chart of your objectives and mark each skill off as it's developed. It is important that you have a reminder of your targets.

Methods for recording development

There are a number of different methods you can use to record your skill development within the project. Some lend themselves to different situations.

Interviews

An interview with your tutor, or members of your project team, can be used as supporting evidence of your skill development. The interviews should be arranged in advance. Make sure you have thought about your questions beforehand and that you collect the information that you need. Once you have decided how you are going to record the information you are told, make the interviewee aware of this beforehand.

Witness testimony

A witness testimony is a statement from someone in front of whom you have demonstrated a specific skill. It can be used to support other forms of evidence. For this project it likely to be from a tutor or perhaps an organisation if your project involves them.

Video and audio

Video and audio recordings are a good way of demonstrating your skills in action and can be used as evidence. Recordings are a particularly good way of documenting things as they happen.

How can a video recording help you on a project?

Key terms

Formative review – a review carried out during the project

Summative review – a review which takes place at the end of a project

Review

You can assess your progress in developing your skills through review. The two main types of review used are formative and summative.

A **formative review** is a review carried out during the project. As discussed earlier you will need to carry out reviews during projects to make sure you are on track and achieving your skill development targets.

A **summative review** takes place at the end of the project. This is to assess your skill development in the project overall. This is also the point where you make recommendations for your own skill development in future.

Strengths and weaknesses

In your review you need to consider your strengths and weaknesses. You will need to record the areas of your skill development in which you have made a lot of progress and those that you still need to work on.

With practice you will master them in the end. Everyone has skills that they need to develop further and we continue to learn all the way through our careers.

Skills achieved against the development plan

The reason for carrying out this project was to develop your personal skills. In your review you will need to revisit your development plan and evaluate your progress.

Review against objectives

Your review should also cover what you have achieved against your project objectives. Have they been achieved? Were there any difficulties in achieving these objectives and if so why? Did you have to review and change objectives and if so why?

Remember the objectives are your stepping stones to successful skill development.

Areas requiring further development and experience

Before you complete your review, you need to consider whether you developed the skills you wanted to. Do you feel confident in these new skills? Or do you need further development and experience?

By the end of the project it is unlikely that you will feel entirely comfortable with all the new skills you have learned and practised in the project. Produce a list of the skills you feel you would still like to improve or any new skills that you would like to develop.

3.3 Report on project

Now that the project is completed and assessed you need to report your findings to your tutor. Below are three of the main methods you might like to use.

* **Presentation** – produce a formal presentation using posters, charts or PowerPoint to support you. Make sure you use headings to help you cover all the things you need.

* **Display** – a display may be another method you choose to communicate your skill development project to your tutor. Think about the layout and the steps in your project. You could include photos and even a video in your display.

* **Report** – the last method you may decide to use is to produce a report. A report is a written document that systematically goes through the stages of the skill development project, as well as your review.

Whichever method you choose make sure you cover the whole of the project, including what your objectives and personal skill development plan was. Conclude with your assessment of the success, or otherwise, for your skill development plan.

Assessment activity 12.2

(P4) (P5) (M2) (D1)

1 Participate in a work-related project to develop your skills and further your experience. The choice of project needs to be agreed with your teacher/tutor. It may be work experience or participating in a group project or event.

The work-related project must give you opportunity to work towards your skill development needs. The evidence that you need to produce for this outcome includes:

- List of key objectives for skill development
- Proposed outcomes and how each will meet your skill development needs
- Timescale for the project
- Resources that you require for the project.

You must demonstrate that you have undertaken a work-related project and provide evidence that you have been able to:

- prioritise
- research
- action plan
- ask questions.
- manage tasks

Witness statements should be used to support this and must be written by an appropriate person. This could be, for example, your tutor or a mentor/manager on a work placement. Check with your tutor about who you should ask **P4**.

2 Produce a review of your skill development against your objectives. You need to produce evidence of your skill development within the project. This could include a log or other recording methods to demonstrate your progression against objectives.

Witness statements from employers or your tutor demonstrating your development of skills during the project can also be included. If you have undertaken work experience, feedback from the work placement should be used as evidence of skill development.

You must also report on the project. The report needs to focus on your skill development during the project. The report can be a presentation, display or a written report – check with your tutor. **P5** **M2** **D1**

Grading tips

M2 You need to demonstrate that you have taken full advantage of the opportunities available throughout the project and monitored and reviewed your own skill development.

Feedback from supervisor/teacher/tutor should be predominantly favourable, although there may be some objectives set which were not fully met.

D1 Ensure you evaluate the extent to which you have developed skills through the work-

related project. You need to have met the objectives, the proposed outcomes of your personal development plan and the travel and tourism sector requirements for entry to employment. This needs to be supported with a detailed witness statement from teacher/tutor or employer to confirm evidence of development of skills. Further development needs to be recognised and recorded

PLTS

When you monitor and review skills development, reporting on the project in appropriate format, you will gain skills as a **reflective learner**.

Functional skills

Using the internet to carry out research will help you develop your **ICT** skills in finding and selecting information.

WorkSpace Stephen Davies

General manager

I work as the general manager of a 4-star country house hotel. It dates back to the 16th century and was an old coaching inn, where the stage coaches used to change horses and the passengers stopped for a break.

My main responsibilities are to ensure the continued financial success of the hotel and that we meet high standards of customer service. I am responsible for overseeing everything in the hotel.

My typical day

My day starts at 8.30 am when I get to work after dropping my son off at school. Firstly I check with the head receptionist and restaurant manager if there have been any problems overnight or at breakfast. I then deal with any outstanding unresolved issues.

I check my mail, email and morning reports before my morning meeting with the heads of departments. This is usually followed by coffee with the head chef and restaurant manager to check arrangements for any events happening on the weekend, for example a wedding.

I then have a lunch meeting. This could be with a tour operator to finalise room bookings for next year, for example.

Most afternoons I meet with the head housekeeper to discuss things like the performance of the new linen supplier or a planned room refurbishment. Then I do the daily paperwork for head office and other admin tasks. Sometimes the restaurant manager will ask if I can help out with a coach party at afternoon tea.

Before going home I check with reception, restaurant and bar managers to see if there are any issues and hand over to the duty manager.

Think about it!

1 What skills and personal qualities do you think Stephen needs in his role?

2 Stephen is involved in the planning of a number of different events in the hotel. Write a list of things he might have to plan.

3 Who are the different heads of department that report to Stephen?

Just checking

1 What is a skill?

2 What is a quality?

3 Why are written communication skills important in the travel and tourism industry?

4 List five workplace skills.

5 List five personal qualities.

6 What does proactive mean?

7 Give four examples of a work-based project you could do to develop your skills and qualities.

8 What is an objective?

9 What does SMART stand for in reference to objectives?

10 Give four methods you can use to record your skill development during your project.

Assignment tips

Personal skills review

- Use the list on page 351 to assess your skills. Or ask someone you trust, such as a relative or friend.

- Consider experience as well as qualifications. Playing a team sport will develop your teamworking skills.

During the skills development project

- When planning your project make sure that you have set SMART objectives.

- When the timeframe of an objective comes to an end make sure that you evaluate the objective.

- Keep records. Keep minutes of meetings, a log, or an objective list. Record not just what happened and who did what, but also how things made you feel and what skills you have developed and learned.

- Be honest, this is a learning experience and not everything will go right. This is true in the workplace and in your project and you will only learn from your mistakes if you admit that they happened.

- 'The more you put in the more you get out'. Planning a trip to the local bowling alley may be fun, but planning a 'prom' for you school or college will give you more scope to learn and a lot more satisfaction at the end.

- Play to people's strengths. If there's a good artist in your team, why not get them to do the creative artwork for your advertisement.

- Remember you are a team. It is hard to trust someone but in doing so you are developing better working relationships.

13 Organising and tourism study visit

A study visit is a great way to bring all the different elements of the travel and tourism sector together in one experience and to learn more about the sector outside of the classroom. In this unit, you will help to plan and take part in a study visit. The visit may be a day trip or an overnight stay, either in the UK or overseas. You will explore different possible destinations, venues for your visit and what you want to achieve from it, recording your aims and objectives.

You will need to think about a variety of different considerations and constraints that will affect the success of the visit. Health and safety is a key part of any educational visit and you will explore the risks involved, how these risks can be reduced or removed and the process of risk assessment.

After the visit has taken place, you will reflect and evaluate how successful the visit has been, using different methods to gather feedback from your tutors and other learners. You will use this information to make recommendations on how the visit could be even better next time.

Learning outcomes

After completing this unit you should:

1   be able to develop a proposal for a travel and tourism study visit

2   understand the process of risk assessment

3   be able to contribute to a successful travel and tourism study visit

4   be able to review and evaluate the success of the study visit.

To achieve a **pass** grade the evidence must show that you are able to:	To achieve a **merit** grade the evidence must show that, in addition to the pass criteria, you are able to:	To achieve a **distinction** grade the evidence must show that, in addition to the pass and merit criteria, you are able to:
P1 propose a study visit stating aims and objectives and taking into account constraints and considerations **Assessment activity 13.1, page 368**	**M1** explain how the proposed study visit will meet the aims and objectives, taking into account constraints and considerations **Assessment activity 13.1, page 368**	**D1** evaluate the success of the study visit in meeting the aims and objectives, using analysis of the feedback and making recommendations for future visits **Assessment activity 13.4, page 378**
P2 discuss the reasons for, and the process, of risk assessment identifying potential hazards and risks for the proposed study visit **Assessment activity 13.2, page 372**	**M2** explain how hazards and risks identified will be minimised **Assessment activity 13.2, page 372**	
P3 make a positive contribution during planning, prior to and whilst on the study visit **Assessment activity 13.3, page 375**	**M3** analyse own contribution and the results of the feedback to judge the success of the visit **Assessment activity 13.4, page 378**	
P4 select and prepare different methods of gathering feedback to evaluate the success of the study visit **Assessment activity 13.4, page 378**		

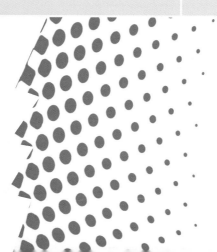

Magda, 15-year-old learner

This unit has been really fun, but also lots of hard work. As a group we decided to visit a museum in the morning and a zoo in the afternoon. I hadn't really thought about all the different factors that go into organising a study visit before, but there are lots – travel, venues, dates, times, risk assessment etc. I created a proposal document for the visit, which included all the different information that we needed to think about.

For the visit, we organised talks to be given at both venues and everyone in the class brought a question to ask the presenters.

To help us evaluate the visit we designed a questionnaire for everyone involved to complete. We then analysed the results and created graphs and bar charts which made it easy to see the overall results. I also interviewed the members of staff who came along to find out if they thought the day was a success.

The best part of this unit for me was completing my study log. I made a note of every task that I completed during the planning stages and on the visit day itself. When it came to completing my evaluation report, my log made it really easy to look back on all the different tasks involved.

Over to you

- What areas of this unit might you find the most challenging?

- Which section of the unit are you most looking forward to?

- What preparation can you do in readiness for the unit assessment(s)?

1 Proposal for a travel and tourism study visit

Why organise a study visit?

On your own, make a list of all the different reasons why you think it would be useful to go on a study visit linked to your travel and tourism course. Now compare this list with a partner. Have you both got the same results? Add anything new to your list.

Now work as a small group and compare all your answers. Make a list of any other responses that you hadn't thought of. Finally, look at your whole list and choose your top three most important reasons for planning and taking part in a study visit.

Key term

Study visit – is an excursion that has specific learning goals. The visit can be a day trip or residential (a longer experience that includes one or more overnight stays). It can be in the UK, overseas or a mixture of the two.

1.1 Aims and objectives

One of the first tasks to complete before planning any study visit is to explore the learning goals of the excursion. The learning goals are the educational purpose of the visit, such as finding out about a certain topic, destination, person or event. These goals can be broken down into more specific aims and objectives.

The aims are *what* the organisers hope participants will achieve from the study visit. The objectives identify *how* these aims will be met. Study visits may have more than one aim and will have various different objectives.

A study visit may provide useful links to many of your other BTEC units. Many travel and tourism organisations offer visits and talks relating to marketing, customer care and developing employability skills.

Activity: What's your objective?

An example of one aim for a study visit might be to *"provide opportunities for participants to work together as an effective team"*. How might a study visit provide opportunities for those participating in the visit to work together as a team? Make a list of three objectives for the study visit to meet this aim.

A study visit may have a variety of different aims and objectives, depending on those participating, how long the visit is for and the activities to be undertaken. The aims and objectives for your study visit may include:

- **Educational** – providing an opportunity to research or develop knowledge, understanding and skills linked to an educational programme or course.

- **Personal development** – developing key personal skills such as independence, social skills, confidence and being more responsible.

- **Interaction with others** – working as a team, for example, and dealing with a range of different people.

- **Outcome** – producing a specific outcome, such as a piece of coursework or a specific experience.

It is useful to discuss and decide on the aims and objectives of your study visit at the start of the planning process. This will then help you to make the best decisions about where to go and what to do on your visit in order to meet your objectives. While the general aims of your visit may be quite broad, it is often useful to make sure your objectives are SMART:

Specific – it is evident what aims have to be achieved.

Measurable – there will be evidence as to whether the aims have been achieved.

Achievable – is it possible that the aims can be done?

Realistic – having realistic goals.

Timed – set a time limit to achieve your aims.

By setting clear and SMART objectives, you will find it easier to evaluate how successful your study visit has been by examining how well each of your aims and objectives has been met, or not. For further details on SMART objectives see *Unit 12: Developing employability skills for travel and tourism*, pages 349–350.

Activity: How SMART are you?

Working in pairs, look at the three objectives below and discuss with a partner if they could be more SMART. Try and rewrite the objectives so they are 'SMARTer'.

One-day study visit to Liverpool

Aim: To give learners an opportunity to develop their key personal skills.

Objective 1: Participants will work in a team.

Objective 2: Participants will give a presentation.

Objective 3: Participants will lead a tour.

Case study: Museum of Science and Industry (MOSI)

The Manchester Museum of Science and Industry (MOSI) provides a range of activities for school, college and university learners arranging study visits to MOSI to meet specific educational objectives.

Located on the site of the world's oldest surviving passenger railway station, MOSI has a range of 12 galleries and collections in five different buildings, which tell the story of Manchester's scientific and industrial past, present and future. There are lots of learning opportunities linked to many different curriculum subjects including travel and tourism, art and design, history and science.

The museum has an Education Department and offers talks on a variety of subjects including museum organisation and funding, the marketing mix, market research and customer care. The museum also provides useful information for those planning a study visit, including help with risk assessment.

For more information, visit the MOSI website. To obtain a secure link to this website, see the Hotlinks section on p.x.

Which other travel and tourism organisations in your local area welcome study visits and provide links to educational objectives?

What are the advantages of participating in educational study visits?

1.2 Constraints and considerations

Once you have decided on the aims and objectives of the study visit, there will be a large number of other factors that you will need to consider. These will include:

- **What is the type of study visit and duration?** – You will need to decide if the visit will be a day trip or residential one with overnight accommodation. Will the visit be in the UK or overseas?

- **Which destination and how far?** – Some destinations will offer different activities and attractions. If your visit is just for the day, how long do you want to spend travelling?

- **How will you get there?** – Different methods of transport have their own advantages and disadvantages. Which method of transport will best meet the needs of your group? *Unit 1*, page 28–33, provides some useful information to consider when selecting the method of transport most suitable for your study visit.

- **What about the weather?** – If your visit involves a lot of time outdoors, what happens if it rains? If you are going overseas, the weather might be quite different from the UK. Does this matter?

- **Is it safe?** – Health, safety and security are the most important factors when planning any study visit. Are the risks involved with your visit acceptable?

- **What about the study?** – A study visit should have learning goals. Does your visit provide opportunities for learning, educational visits or talks?

As well as these considerations, there are also other factors which may limit or constrain the options for your study visit. Financial, legal and risk constraints are all important factors that need to be considered before deciding on your final visit plans.

Remember

A study visit may provide useful links to *Unit 6: UK tourism destinations* and *Unit 10: Exploring marketing in travel and tourism*.

Financial constraints

Study visits cost money; there's the transport, staffing costs, entry to visitor attractions and activities, food and drink, not to mention accommodation and any unplanned or emergency costs that may apply for residential visits. Who is going to pay for these costs?

Most study visits have a budget to meet these costs. The budget may be funded by contributions from each individual learner. The school, or college, may make a contribution to the budget and sometimes grants may also be available from other funding sources.

The study visit budget may well restrict which destination is chosen, the length of the visit, which activities are chosen and whether a day trip, or a residential visit, is selected.

Functional skills

- Using the internet to carry out research will help you develop your ICT skills in finding and selecting information.
- Calculating costs will help you to improve your functional skills in mathematics.

Activity: Money matters

There is no point in planning an expensive overseas residential study visit if the budget is not large enough to meet these costs. In small groups, carry out some internet research to find the basic costs for one of the study visit options below. Make a note of all the figures you find and calculate the possible total cost for the trip. Compare the figure with the groups researching the other visit options.

Each visit is for 15 learners and three members of staff departing from Sheffield.

- A day trip by coach to visit the Weston Park Museum and the Magna Science Adventure Centre.
- A UK residential visit to the Peak District, travelling by public transport and staying in a youth hostel overnight.
- A three night overseas residential to Bruges, travelling by overnight ferry from Hull.

Legal and risk constraints

There are particular laws relating to groups of learners on educational study visits. Tutors, and other staff, have a legal duty to care for all the learners in the visit party and certain procedures and guidelines must be followed. It may not always be possible for tutors to meet all the necessary legal and health and safety guidelines for longer, overseas and residential visits or the risk of these visits may be seen as too high.

Some visits, with a higher risk of accident or injury, may also not be possible, such as those involving outdoor activities and sports, visits around water, visits to farms and factories and visits to remote or potentially dangerous areas.

1.3 Visit proposal

Once the aims and objectives have been identified and all the various considerations and constraints have been fully explored, a study visit proposal can be created which shows how the aims and objectives of the visit will be met.

Key term

Itinerary – a detailed list of all the transport arrangements and activities for a visit, in time order. The itinerary will include details of the departure location and time of departure, arrival times at key points, details of any activities and venues to be visited, plus any accommodation details for a residential visit. An itinerary is usually provided to all participants before departure.

The proposal should include details of:

- the visit destination
- types of transport used to travel to, from and around the destination and chosen venue(s)
- arrival and departure points
- distances involved
- details of the costs
- key times
- links to learning goals, such as study talks and tours, and curriculum opportunities
- an **itinerary** for the visit.

Creating a proposal for a study visit is a useful process to ensure that all the necessary constraints and considerations have been taken into account and that the visit is able to go ahead. A proposal may be a written document, but it could also be presented verbally.

BTEC Assessment activity 13.1   **P1** **M1**

You have been asked to plan a possible study visit for your class. You should select a destination, choose activities suitable for an educational visit, research transport options and take into consideration a range of factors and constraints which will affect your planned visit. You should complete a written 'visit information pack' which includes the following details:

- aims and objectives of the visit
- destination
- means and range of transport available
- arrival and departure points
- distances
- costs
- times
- curriculum opportunities
- itinerary.

You should then continue to explain how the proposed study visit will meet your aims and objectives, taking into account the constraints and considerations you have identified. **P1** **M1**

Grading tips

- You may want to add relevant pictures and images to illustrate your information pack.
- **P1** Your information pack should clearly explain how your study visit will meet the aims

and objectives that you have set and take into account any constraints and considerations.

- **M1** Remember to explain how you have taken account of the necessary constraints and considerations.

Think about it

At this point, you might also consider how you might evaluate if the study visit has been a success or not. What methods will you use to help you complete this evaluation and get the opinions of all participants?

Functional skills

Writing an information booklet will help you develop your English skills in communicating information and ideas effectively.

PLTS

Proposing a study visit, stating aims and objectives and taking into account, constraints and considerations, will help you develop skills as a **creative thinker**.

2 The process of risk assessment

In order to make a judgement about whether a particular study visit is possible, there needs to be consideration of all the possible **hazards** that the group may face, what the **risk** of harm is and if these hazards can be removed and the risks reduced. This process is known as risk assessment.

2.1 Reasons for risk assessment

Carrying out a risk assessment before taking part in a study visit is a legal requirement and must be done by law. Your tutor, or another member of staff, will carry out an official risk assessment before your study visit. You may be asked to help with this process.

The process of risk assessment will help to identify all the potential hazards involved with your visit. There may be ways to reduce the risk of these hazards causing harm and the risk assessment process will record these. Carrying out a risk assessment helps to identify what actions must be taken to remove these risks, or reduce them to an acceptable level and who is responsible for taking these actions. It could be you, your tutor, the transport company or staff at the visitor attraction.

2.2 Process of risk assessment

There are three main steps when carrying out a risk assessment for a study visit:

1 Identification of all the possible hazards on the visit
Hazards can include:

- travelling to and from a specific destination by your chosen method of transport

- travelling around your chosen location which may involve walking and crossing roads

- hazards relating to specific activities or venues, such as outdoor pursuits and sports, busy public venues, rural or isolated areas, areas with machinery, animals, chemicals, kitchens and workshops.

2 Consideration of the risk of harm from the hazard
The hazards identified in step 1 may cause harm which could include minor injuries such as cuts and bruises, electrical shock, scalds and burns, more serious injuries or even death. Learners, staff, volunteers, helpers and members of the public may all be at risk of harm from the hazards identified. The risk assessment process may categorise these risks as low, medium or high.

3 Measures to remove or reduce the risk
There may be opportunities to put in place various actions that would reduce, or remove, the risks from the identified hazards. The third step

Key terms

Hazard – anything that can cause harm, such as loose wires, hot liquid, moving traffic, deep water, etc.

Risk – the chance that somebody could be harmed by the hazard. The risk may be rated as low, medium or high.

Think about it

What do you think the consequences might be of not completing a risk assessment for a study visit?

of the risk assessment process is to identify what controls or actions can be put in place and who is responsible for these actions. Examples of actions that could be taken to reduce or remove risks involved with a study visit might include:

- **Create a Code of Conduct** – This may be a set of rules, or guidelines, that all members of the visit party agree to follow. The code would set out the levels of expected behaviour and conduct whilst on the study visit, and could include rules about smoking, personal appearance, clothing and unsupervised free time. If everybody follows the code, the chance of things going wrong can be minimised.

- **Provide written and verbal advice** – This may include instructions about what to do in an emergency, safety and first aid procedures, contact details of supervisors and staff, meeting points, fire evacuation procedures and areas to avoid. A pre-visit briefing may be given by the **party leader** to make sure all participants understand the instructions and advice provided.

- **Carry out a pre-visit check of the venues to be visited** – It is sometimes useful to assess all the venues on the study visit before taking the full group. This will help with the visit planning process and to identify any hazards or problem areas that may arise.

- **Use of reliable and trustworthy organisations** – Organising a study visit is a responsible job. Using transport, accommodation and other travel and tourism organisations that are reliable and have a good reputation can help to minimise any risks, for example selecting a coach company that has reliable and clean vehicles, fitted with seat belts.

- **Create a checklist of any specific needs in the group** – There may be many people with specific needs in a large study visit party, for example people with allergies, those on medication, people with a disability, limited mobility or a learning difficulty. It may help to reduce the risks if the specific needs of these participants are clearly understood by all supervisors on the visit.

- **Check the student-staff ratios** – Making sure that there are sufficient members of staff to supervise the number of students on the visit is another way to reduce the risk. There may be more staff needed to supervise younger children, those with specific needs and those visits involving 'high-risk' activities, such as outdoor pursuits. Education authorities often publish guidelines of their recommended student-staff ratios for educational visits.

Key term

Party leader – the member of staff with ultimate responsibility for the study visit and the participants. They should be an experienced member of staff who has been trained in risk assessment.

Activity: Staff–student ratios

Working in pairs carry out some research to find the advice on student-staff ratios provided by your local education authority. You may find the internet useful or talk to any visit organisers in your school or college. Make a note of your findings and discuss as a group.

Recording the risk assessment findings

It is often useful to record the findings of a risk assessment, making a note of the hazards identified, the risks involved and how these risks can be reduced or removed, including what actions need to be taken and by whom.

This action checklist can then be reviewed to make sure all the necessary controls have been put in place to ensure the health, safety and welfare of all participants in the study visit.

Event or visit: _____ Date: _____ Venue: _____ Organiser/Leader: _____

Identify hazard e.g machinery, vehicles, travel, activities	**What** could go wrong?	**Who** is likely to be injured from these items?	**What** is the current **risk of harm?** Low/medium/high	**What** measures can you take to **reduce** or **remove** the risk of harm?	**Who** is going to take action and when?

Risk assessment completed by: _____ Date: _____ Review date: _____

Figure 13.1: A typical risk assessment form. What are the advantages of recording the details of a risk assessment in this way?

In this assignment you need to show your understanding of the risk assessment process. For the visit you planned in assessment activity 13.1, you should now consider all the hazards and risks involved with participating in that visit.

1 Take part in a class discussion about the reasons for risk assessment and the range of hazards and risks you have identified for your study visit. **P2**

2 Write a brief report which follows the three steps of risk assessment. You should identify:

- the hazards
- the level of risk
- the actions taken to reduce the risks.

You should explain how the hazards and risks identified will be minimised by the control actions you have suggested. **M2**

Grading Tip

- **P2** Make sure you consider a range of potential hazards and different methods of reducing or removing the risks, such as the student-staff ratio

- **M2** You should ensure that you explain how the control measures you have identified in your report will help to minimise the risks to those participating in the visit

PLTS

Discussing their reasons for and of process assessment, identifying potential hazards and risks for the proposed study visit, will help you to develop skills as a **independent enquirer**.

3 A successful travel and tourism study visit

In order to be successful in the assessment of this unit, you need to be able to make a positive contribution both in the planning of the visit and during your participation in the visit. To record your contributions, you may find it useful to keep a study visit logbook. Use this logbook to record all your roles, responsibilities and duties that you have completed in the planning stages and throughout the visit. The logbook will help you to evaluate the success of the visit.

You may find the following headings useful for your logbook:

- date
- actions
- tutor comments.

- task/contribution
- problems

Date	Task/ contribution	Actions	Any problems?	Tutor comments

Figure 13.2: Logbook for recording contributions throughout the organisation process

3.1 Planning the visit

There are many tasks involved with planning a successful study visit and your tutor may give you a particular role to help with the planning process. Tasks can include:

- devising a group code of conduct

- producing study visit information for participants, such as the itinerary and information about the destination and venue

- finance and administration duties, such as making the booking, collecting money and essential visit documentation.

Activity: Follow the code

Creating a code of conduct for the study visit can be an effective way of setting the levels of expected acceptable behaviour. In small groups, discuss what you feel is acceptable and unacceptable behaviour for your study visit. Draw up a list of ten rules that you feel should apply to the visit to reduce the risks for everyone.

3.2 Responsibilities prior to the visit

Once all the details have been agreed and the study visit date gets closer, there are many more tasks to be completed. All participants will need to complete and submit the necessary personal documentation. This will vary depending on, for example, whether the study visit is a day trip or a UK or overseas residential. Required documentation could include:

- **Consent form** – This form is required, by law, to confirm that the parents/guardians/carers of those learners under 18 have given permission to participate in the visit.

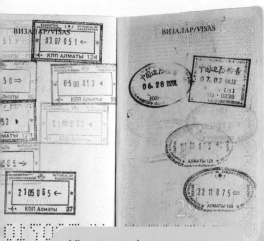

Visa stamps in a passport – different visas are available for single or multiple entries to a country.

Key term

Visa – an authorisation, or endorsement, that is often stamped into your passport before you travel to selected countries. The visa shows that you have permission to enter that country for a specific purpose. Different visas are available depending on the reason for your visit, for example just to visit as a tourist or to work.

Lunch time – what arrangements will you have for meals during your study visit?

- **Medical information form** – This is a record of the necessary medical and health details for each participant. It will often include details of any allergies, medication requirements and vaccinations information. The medical form may also authorise supervising staff to issue plasters and pain-killers to those participants requiring minor first aid.

- **Emergency contact details** – The day and night time contact details for each participant in the event of an emergency are essential. Home and mobile telephone numbers should be provided for parents/guardians/carers of anyone travelling on the visit.

- **Passports and visas** – If the study visit is an overseas trip, all participants will need a valid passport in order to travel. Certain destinations also require travellers to hold a **visa**.

You may also be involved with preparing and providing study visit information for the other participants on the trip. This information may form part of an information factsheet or booklet. Useful information to have before the visit may include:

- **What clothing to wear** – This may include a 'kit list' if the visit is to include taking part in sports or outdoor activities.

- **Weather information** – Information on the expected weather and average temperatures will help participants to pack and prepare for the visit.

- **Food and drink advice** – It is useful to know what arrangements have been made for eating and drinking throughout the visit. Are meals provided or do participants need to bring a packed lunch, or money, to buy meals and snacks?

3.3 During the visit

When the time has arrived to take part in the study visit itself, you and all the other participants will have a joint responsibility for yourselves, and each other, to make a positive contribution and to behave in an appropriate manner, in line with the code of conduct.

Responsibilities to yourself

While on the visit, you have a responsibility to make sure that your behaviour is appropriate at all times and that you don't put yourself in any unnecessary danger of harm. This will mean following the advice and information provided before the visit, listening to instructions from staff and visit supervisors, and following the agreed code of conduct.

The visit itinerary may involve some unsupervised free time and it will be your responsibility to ensure you manage your time effectively, to meet deadlines and arrive at meeting points on time. Being late may cause serious delays to your visit party.

Responsibility and consideration to others

You also have a responsibility to consider the needs of other people on the visit, including your peers, your tutors and supervisors, and other guests and passengers, including members of the public, any speakers, and staff, at venues you are visiting, and transport providers.

You may be visiting destinations with different cultures and traditions and it is important that you show due respect and consideration for these cultures and follow any guidelines that are necessary.

Figure 13.3: All participants should make a positive contribution to the visit and demonstrate appropriate behaviour

 Assessment activity 13.3 (P3)

You should now complete your logbook to record all of your contributions during the planning stages and during the visit itself. It should identify how you have made a positive contribution to the planning of the visit and on the visit itself.

Your contributions might, for example, include researching different aspects of the visit, creating the code of conduct and producing a visit information guide.

Grading tips (P3)

- Remember to date each of your logbook entries to show your contribution during the whole process.

- If you have worked with others on a particular task, make sure you identify your own contribution .

- You might want to use labels to identify at what point your contribution was made, for example in the planning stages, prior to the visit or during the visit itself.

PLTS

Making a positive contribution to the planning of the visit and by participating, will develop your skills as a **team worker**.

4 Review and evaluate the success of the study visit

4.1 Success criteria

An important part of any travel and tourism study visit is to reflect and evaluate if the visit has been a success. In order to do this, it may be helpful to consider a range of success criteria. These could include:

- **Aims and objectives of the visit** – Were these met as planned? Would you change any of the aims and objectives next time?

- **Budget and finance** – Did the visit run within the given budget or were there unexpected costs that had to be paid?

- **Itinerary and timings** – Did everything go to plan? Were there any unexpected delays or problems?

- **Travel** – Were the travel arrangements successful? Did the travel methods and providers chosen meet the needs of the group?

- **Accommodation** – if your visit involved an overnight stay, was the accommodation chosen suitable? Was the standard and location of the accommodation appropriate for your group's needs?

- **Suitability of the destination and venues visited** – Were these appropriate for the age, ability and size of your group? Did the venues provide appropriate learning opportunities linked to your course? Did any organised talks and tours meet the group's requirements?

4.2 Evaluation

Having considered a range of criteria on which to judge the success of the visit, you should then gather the thoughts, opinions and reflections of all those involved. These will include your own thoughts and opinions, those of the other student participants (your peers), your tutors and other members of supervising staff. You might also gather feedback from any other people involved with the planning and running of your visit, for example the coach driver or the speaker at the venue visited.

To gather this feedback, you may choose to use a variety of evaluation tools or methods, such as:

- **Your own observations** – what you saw and witnessed yourself by participating in the study visit. You might have taken photographs or recorded your thoughts in your logbook throughout the planning stages and whilst on the visit.

- **Interviews with participants** – you might ask your tutor, or peers, a series of questions to find out if they thought the visit was a success and what could be improved next time.

- **Questionnaires** – you might design a **questionnaire** to give to all the visit participants to find out their views of the study visit. You could analyse the results of the questionnaire and use a PC to create tables and graphs to show your results.

Key term

Questionnaire – a form designed to gain information relating to a series of set questions or statements. Questions might be 'closed' and require a set answer, such as "yes" or "no", "good" or "bad", or 'open', where people are able to express their views and opinions as they want to.

Name: _____

Role: _____

Study Visit _____   Date _____

Circle the answers which apply (1 = excellent; 5 = poor) or tick the appropriate box.

1) Did the study visit meet your aims and expectations?

    1   2   3   4   5

2) How satisfied were you with the choice of visit destination?

    1   2   3   4   5

3) How would you rate the transport used?

    Reliability   1   2   3   4   5

    Comfort   1   2   3   4   5

    Facilities   1   2   3   4   5

4) How would you rate the relevance of the educational talk?

    ☐ Not relevant to me

    ☐ Quite relevant

    ☐ Very relevant

5) Considering the costs involved with the visit, did you feel the trip was:

    ☐ Excellent value

    ☐ Satisfactory value

    ☐ Poor value

6) How would you rate the duration of the visit?

    ☐ Too short

    ☐ Just right

    ☐ Too long

7) Do you think the visit was an overall success? ☐ Yes ☐ No
Please explain your answer:

8) If you were to make one recommendation to improve the visit in the future, what would this be?

Figure 13.4: Post-visit questionnaire – a useful way to gain feedback from visit participants

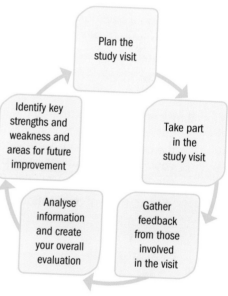

Figure 13.5: The study visit process

Plan the study visit

Take part in the study visit

Gather feedback from those involved in the visit

Analyse information and create your overall evaluation

Identify key strengths and weakness and areas for future improvement

By using a variety of different evaluation methods, you will be able to gather the views and opinions of as many people as possible involved in the study visit. This will give you lots of valuable information in order for you to complete an evaluation of the study visit, identify your own personal strengths and weaknesses, your areas for improvement, what was successful about the visit and what could be changed in the future.

The lessons learned from this evaluation process can be used to make sure that future study visits are even more successful and that you continue to develop your own personal skills in the future.

Assessment activity 13.4 (P4) (M3) (D1)

For this activity you should select and prepare at least two different methods for gathering feedback in order to help you evaluate the success of the study visit.

1 Design a questionnaire to be used following your study visit, to gather feedback from your peers.

2 Create a list of six interview questions to ask your study visit tutors regarding the success of the visit.

Questions 1 and 2 will enable you to achieve **P4**.

3 When you have gathered the information following your study visit, you should analyse the questionnaire and interview data, along with your own contributions and opinions to judge the success of the visit. You need to consider:

- suitability of destination

- travel
- timings
- venues
- budget
- personal expenditure
- meeting aims and objectives
- any other key success factors.

Question 3 will enable you to achieve **M3**.

4 You should then make realistic and justified recommendations for future visits based on the organisation of the entire study visit.

Question 4 will enable you to achieve **D1**.

Grading tips

- **P4** Make sure that you prepare and use two different feedback methods to help you evaluate the visit.

- **M3** How effective were your own contributions to the planning and running of the study visit? Use these reflections and the results of your feedback to help you evaluate the success of the visit overall.

- **D1** Make sure you consider all the factors involved with organising your study visit in your final evaluation, including your visit proposal, the aims and objectives, the risk assessment process, your own contributions and the contributions of others, and your methods of gathering feedback.

PLTS

Analysing your contribution and the results of the feedback to judge the success of the visit, will help you to develop skills as a **reflective learner**.

Functional skills

Using the computer to produce graphs and tables will help to develop your **ICT** skills in developing, presenting and communicating information.

Becky Knight
Museum Education Officer

I work in a large museum funded by the government and by various charity grants. We offer a range of attractions and facilities to all our visitors who include families, groups and overseas visitors.

As the Museum's Education Officer it is my job to organise a range of activities and events that will appeal to visiting school and college groups. This means looking at the courses that learners study and making links to what we offer here at the museum. This can mean organising tours and talks to groups, creating educational worksheets and helping teachers and tutors to plan their visit, including information on health and safety and risk assessments.

Typical day

December, February and May are very busy months for me as a lot of the schools and colleges arrange trips at this time. I arrive at the office around 9 a.m. and check my telephone messages and emails.

I then organise the learning materials I have prepared for the groups arriving and check my presentation slides and equipment. I will often give three or four talks to education groups on a busy day.

When the groups arrive I go out to greet them and deliver an initial briefing about the standard of behaviour we expect at the museum, particularly as we have other visitors who will want a quiet and relaxing visit.

After I have given my talks and tours of the museum I ask the tutors to complete an evaluation form about how much they enjoyed the day and what we could improve to make their visit better in the future.

Think about it!

1 What talks, tours and resources would be useful for your study visit?

2 Is it important to choose study visit venues that offer the services of an Education Officer? Explain your response.

Just checking

1 What is the different between the aims and the objectives of a study visit?

2 What does SMART stand for?

3 List three possible personal development objectives.

4 Explain two reasons for completing a risk assessment.

5 What is the difference between a hazard and a risk?

6 How might the level of risk be graded in a risk assessment?

7 Identify five control measures that could be used to reduce the risk of harm on a study visit.

8 Describe what a code of conduct is.

9 As well as a responsibility to yourself, list three other people you should also be considerate of on your study visit.

10 What are the two main types of question that are found in a questionnaire? Explain the difference between the two types and give an example of each one.

edexcel :::

Assignment tips

- When thinking about your study visit, it might be useful to talk to other learners who have organised their own visit before. Ask to have a look at their visit evaluations to see if you can learn any lessons from their experiences.

- If you have a local visitor attraction with an Education Officer, why not try to arrange a meeting with them to gain their advice about organising a study visit.

- For more information on risk assessment for study visits, the Government has produced a good practice guide, *Health and Safety of Pupils on Education Visits*, available from teachernet. To obtain a secure link to this website, see the Hotlinks section on p.x.

Glossary

A

Academic qualifications – qualifications involving learning about a specific subject rather than a job or industry

Air Travel Organisers' Licensing (ATOL) scheme – a financial protection scheme managed by the Civil Aviation Authority. All holiday companies in the UK selling flights and holiday packages that include a flight are required by law to hold a licence called an Air Travel Organiser's Licence (ATOL). ATOL protects travellers from losing their money or being stranded abroad by providing a fund to protect customers.

Allocated-on-arrival – a term used by tour operators where customers are given details of their accommodation, and sometimes holiday resort, only on arrival in the holiday destination. These deals are then often offered at a discount to customers and allows tour operators to be more flexible and to maximise their bookings.

Ancillary organisations – organisations that support travel and tourism. They offer tourists and travellers additional products and services that complement their main, or primary, product for example customers buying a package holiday may also require additional products and services, such as travel insurance and car hire, which are offered from ancillary organisations.

Après-ski – (literally 'after ski-ing') – means any of the entertainment or relaxing activities available in ski resorts. These could be tobogganing by torchlight, a sleigh ride or bowling while drinking schnapps (fruit brandy).

B

Body language – bodily movement, or posture, which transmits a message to the observer

Bonded – all tour operators and travel organisers must protect their customers by being bonded. This means if they go out of business before you travel, you should get your money back, or, if you are already abroad, you will be able to complete your holiday and return home without further payment should a firm fail.

Budget – how much money the customers have available to spend

C

Carbon footprint – according to the UK Carbon Trust, a carbon footprint is the total greenhouse gas emissions caused directly and indirectly by an individual, organisation, event or product

Carbon-offsetting – even one flight can produce lots of carbon dioxide, which can be harmful to the environment. Many travellers are now looking at ways to reduce this negative effect by contributing to schemes which have a positive effect on the environment and reduce carbon emissions, such as using renewable energy sources, tree planting and providing education about climate change. 'Reduce My Footprint' (to obtain a secure link to the website, see the Hotlinks section on p.x.) is a carbon reduction programme set up by ABTA (The Travel Association) with the Association of Independent Tour Operators (AITO).

Carrying capacity – the number of persons that a vehicle, such as an aircraft, can carry per journey

Chain of distribution – a chain of distribution shows how travel and tourism products are provided to the customer. The traditional chain of distribution shows how the principles of a package holiday – transport and accommodation – are 'packaged' by the tour operator and sold to the customer through a travel agent.

Closed questions – questions which can be answered with a single word or short phrase

CO_2 emissions – it is widely accepted that the main greenhouse gas responsible for recent climate change is carbon dioxide (CO_2). This has been released in huge quantities by our modern way of life, including our use of cars, train, coaches and planes. Large increases in man-made CO_2 are thought to contribute to the greenhouse effect on the planet and to have led to global warming and climate change. (To obtain a secure link to a website, see the Hotlinks section on p.x.).

Computer Reservation System (CRS) – a computerised system used to store and retrieve data and carry out transactions related to air travel

Concierge – a concierge is a member of staff in a hotel or apartment complex who assists guests with storage of their luggage, booking of tours and tickets, for a theatre show for example, and providing general information and advice about the local area. The concierge is often located in the reception area.

Customer – somebody who receives customer service from a service deliverer. A customer may be a person, but may be an organisation. An internal customer comes from another part of the same organisation as the provider.

Customer charter – a statement of standards and/or procedures that a business agrees will govern the relationship between itself and its customers. A charter can establish standards of service delivery, provision of information to customers, consultation processes, and complaint or dispute resolution mechanisms.

Cyclones – these occur mainly in the south-western Pacific Ocean and the Indian Ocean

D

Deforestation – this refers to the cutting, clearing, and removal of rainforest for the purpose of creating land for agriculture, cattle ranching, mines and gas or oil extraction

Demographic – this refers to segments of human populations broken down by age, sex, income etc.

Deregulation – the removal of government rules and regulations that may prevent an industry from expanding

Disposable income – the amount of money which an individual has available to spend on non-essential items, after meeting all essential bills

Domestic tourism – refers to people who are not travelling outside the country they live

Domestic visitors – visitors from within the same country

Dynamic package – mainly completed on-line, dynamic packaging is a term used to describe the process of tourists selecting different holiday components to create their own tailored holiday package. Unlike a traditional package holiday, the tourist has more control in selecting the different components that meet their specific needs and budgets.

Dynamic packaging – when the customer arranges the different elements of a package holiday, including flights and accommodation, independently

E

Economy – is the wealth and resources of a country or region, especially in terms of production and consumption of goods and services

Epidemic – is when a disease is transmitted amongst humans at a rate that is significantly higher than the expected rate

Expats – this is shortened term for expatriates or people who have moved to live in a different country

F

Formative review – a review carried out during the project

G

Gateway airports – so called because they are gateways to other areas. You can land there and then transfer to aircraft travelling to different destinations in a country.

Gross Domestic Product (GDP) – this can be thought of as the value of a country's economy. It measures the value of all goods and services over a specific time period (usually one year). Domestic and inbound tourism contribute to the UK's GDP but not all outbound tourism does as some of the money spent by outbound tourists will be in another country. The UK currently has the sixth biggest GDP in the world.

H

Hand- and hold-luggage – hand-luggage are items that are allowed in the cabin of the aircraft with the passenger. This is usually limited to one small bag containing personal items required throughout the flight. Hold-baggage is checked-in luggage and is stored in the hold of the aircraft. Specific conditions apply to the maximum size and weight of hold-baggage, often with specific variations for each airline.

Hazard – anything that can cause harm, such as loose wires, hot liquid, moving traffic, deep water, etc.

Head office – The base from which an organisation is run. Functions include human resources, marketing, accounts, IT, customer service and general management and there are a range of roles at operative, managerial and director levels.

Hurricanes – these occur mainly in the North Atlantic Ocean, especially the Caribbean and the Gulf of Mexico and the north-eastern Pacific Ocean

I

Inbound tourism – refers to people travelling to the UK from abroad

Inbound visitors – visitors from another country

Independents – small, private businesses that have one or a small number of travel agencies, often found in small towns. They are able to offer specialist advice and have a large number of repeat customers.

Infrastructure – the physical services and facilities, such as transport networks and communication systems, needed by a community to function

International Date Line – the internationally agreed place where the calendar dates change. The calendar date in the area to the east of the International Date Line is one day earlier than the date in the area to the west of the line

Itinerary – a detailed list of all the transport arrangements and activities for a visit, in time order. The itinerary will include details of the departure location and time of departure, arrival times at key points, details of any activities and venues to be visited, plus any accommodation details for a residential visit. An itinerary is usually provided to all participants before departure.

J

Job description – the job that the company requires the employee to do

L

Leading questions – questions worded so as to gain particular information, or a particular answer

Limited companies – there are two types of limited company: a private limited company (Ltd.) or a public limited company (PLC). Ownership of a limited company is divided into equal parts known as shares.

Shareholders have bought one or more shares in the company. A public limited company is still a private sector organisation but can sell its shares on the Stock Market to any member of the public, while a private limited company cannot.

Lines of longitude – the imaginary lines that circle the curvature of the Earth, running north and south and converging at the north and south Poles. Try and imagine them like the segments of a peeled orange. They are 15° apart and you will usually be able to see them marked on a globe.

Local time – is the term given to the official time in a particular location

Long-haul – an imprecise term meaning flights longer than three to four hours

M

Market segment – a group of customers with similar needs and wants

Market share – the share of the total sales of brands, or products, for organisations competing in the same market. It is usually expressed in percentage terms.

Marketing mix – the mix of product, place, price and promotion which is sold to the customer

Mass market – the majority group of consumers for a specific product

Mission statement – a concise statement about an organisation's purpose. Mission statements vary but usually contain information about products, services, beliefs and values.

Monopolies and Mergers Commission – an independent public body, established in 1948, which conducts inquiries into mergers, markets and regulation of the major industries in the UK.

Multiples – travel agencies which have a large chain of branches, often found on the high street in most large towns and cities, for example Thomas Cook and Thomson Holidays. Due to their size, they can often provide a range of different products and services at discounted rates.

N

Niche market – narrowly defined group of customers; a small but profitable section of the market.

O

Objective – an aim of what you want to achieve when doing a task.

Open questions – questions worded so that they will probably produce long answers

Outbound tourism – refers to people travelling from the UK to abroad

P

Package holiday – a single-product holiday created by tour operators that includes transport to and from a destination and accommodation.

Party leader – the member of staff with ultimate responsibility for the study visit and the participants. They should be an experienced member of staff who has been trained in risk assessment.

Passenger assistance – the term used by transport providers for the additional services offered to passengers with specific and additional needs, often relating to those with a disability or limited mobility. Transport providers may provide a member of staff to accompany travellers at stations and airports from arrival until they are safely on board.

Person specification – the skills required for and desired from applicants for a job.

Phonetic alphabet – code words for identifying letters in voice communication

Privatised – where the state sells assets previously in the public sector to the private sector in order to raise money

Procedures – these are a series of steps taken to accomplish a result, for example the driver's procedure for accommodating a passenger in a wheelchair on a coach might use the processes of (i) opening the door, (ii) lowering the floor, (iii) assisting the passenger in wheelchair to the wheelchair position on the coach, (iv) securing safety belts to the wheelchair.

Processes – tasks and activities needed to accomplish a specific goal

Product – the physical item a customer buys

Professional bodies – these are organisations which aim to further a profession, raise public interest in the profession and oversee the interests of people working in the profession.

Q

Qualitative data – data that concerns opinions, feelings and emotions. Although it may give deep insight into the consumers' feelings, it cannot be statistically analysed.

Quantitative data – data concerning values and amounts that can be used for statistical analysis

Questionnaire – a form designed to gain information relating to a series of set questions or statements. Questions might be 'closed' and require a set answer, such as "yes" or "no", "good" or "bad", or 'open', where people are able to express their views and opinions as they want to.

R

Recession – slowdown in economic activity measured over a significant period of time

Regeneration – the improvement or development of derelict land for residential or commercial purposes

Risk – the chance that somebody could be harmed by the hazard. The risk may be rated as low, medium or high.

Roaming – when you travel your mobile phone keeps working while you are roaming. You can make and receive mobile phone calls, write text messages (SMS) and access the internet on some phones even while abroad. The foreign network operator charges your home operator and this additional cost is passed on to you. When roaming in Europe, there are now regulations which limit the charges that operators can charge. To obtain a secure link to the European Union website, where more information can be accessed, see the Hotlinks section on p.x.

S

Saturated market – where all potential customers are already using your or a competitor's product

Search engine – a website used to search the internet to find websites that may contain information relevant to the user. Current popular search engines include Google, Bing and Ask.

Segmentation – this is the grouping of people who have common characteristics, for example a basic segmentation of travellers could be by reason for travel and consist of four segments: business travellers, leisure travellers, those visiting friends and relatives and those travelling for other reasons. These in turn could be segmented further, for example by age.

Service – the non-physical elements of the item a customer buys

Short-haul – an imprecise term meaning flights shorter than three to four hours

Skill – the ability to do something well

Study visit – is an excursion that has specific learning goals. The visit can be a day trip or residential (a longer experience that includes one or more overnight stays). It can be in the UK, overseas or a mixture of the two.

Summative review – a review which takes place at the end of a project

Supplement – an additional charge on the standard price of a holiday booking which takes into account any additional upgrades or extras. A supplement may also be applied to cover any fees lost on the price of a standard booking, such as a single person travelling alone staying in a room for two people.

T

Target marketing – creating products that are aimed (or targeted) at different groups of people, called market segments.

The Data Protection Act – protects customers' personal data with regard to processing and safe storage of their information.

The Health and Safety at Work Act – ensures that environments are safe and free from hazards for employers, employees and customers.

Third world – this is the term given to the less developed and developing countries in Latin America, Asia and Africa

Tour operator – an organisation that puts together different components of a holiday which could include accommodation, transport, excursions and transfers. Tour operators have contracts with hoteliers, airlines and ground transport providers, and package these components together to sell to the customer either directly or through a travel agent. Tour operators produce brochures to distribute their holiday and short-break packages.

Tourism-related employment – refers to employment in industries which largely depend on tourism. The Office for National Statistics (ONS) identifies tourism-related employment as including jobs in the following industries: accommodation; restaurants; bars, public houses and night clubs; activities of travel agencies, tour operators and tourist information centres; libraries, archives, museums and other cultural activities; sporting and other recreational activities.

Typhoons – these occur mainly in the north-western Pacific Ocean.

U

Unique selling point – how a product differs from competitors' products

V

Visa – an authorisation, or endorsement, that is often stamped into your passport before you travel to selected countries. The visa shows that you have permission to enter that country for a specific purpose. Different visas are available depending on the reason for your visit, for example just to visit as a tourist or to work.

Vocational qualifications – qualifications involving learning and skills specific to an industry, sector or job role

W

World Heritage Site – UNESCO (United Nations Educational, Scientific and Cultural Organisation) designates sites of natural and cultural importance. There are over 890 World Heritage Sites, including 27 in the UK. Examples include Hadrian's Wall, Durham Castle, Tower of London, Kew Gardens, Giant's Causeway and the City of Bath.

Index

Figures and tables are indicated by *italic* page numbers, key terms by **bold** numbers